NOW IN THEATERS EVERYWHERE

NOW IN THEATERS EVERYWHERE

A Celebration of a
Certain Kind of Blockbuster

KENNETH TURAN

Public Affairs
New York

Published in the United States by PublicAffairs™,
a member of the Perseus Books Group.

PublicAffairs books are available at special discounts for bulk purchases
in the U.S. by corporations, institutions, and other organizations.
For more information, please contact the Special Markets Department at the
Perseus Books Group, 11 Cambridge Center, Cambridge, MA 02142, call
(617) 252-5298, or e-mail special.markets@perseusbooks.com.

Designed by Trish Wilkinson
Set in 11.5 point Goudy by the Perseus Books Group

Library of Congress Cataloging-in-Publication Data

Turan, Kenneth.
    Now in theaters everywhere : a celebration of a certain kind of
blockbuster / Kenneth Turan. — 1st ed.
        p.   cm.
    Includes index.
    ISBN-13: 978-1-58648-395-1 (hardcover : alk. paper)
    ISBN-10: 1-58648-395-1 (hardcover : alk. paper) 1. Motion pictures—
Reviews. I. Title.
PN1995.T789 2006
791.43'75—dc22   2006026146

First Edition

10 9 8 7 6 5 4 3 2 1

To my wife and my daughters,
women of wonder, every one

CONTENTS

Part Four ANIMATION

INTRODUCTION

I didn't know it at the time, but the idea for this book began taking shape in my mind during the closing night of the Cannes film festival a few years back. Not because of the motion picture that won, but because of the one that didn't.

The year was 2003 and that film was Clint Eastwood's masterly *Mystic River*. I was too familiar with the ways of festival juries to think it would win the Palme d'Or top prize, but I was fairly sure that in a country that had been decades ahead of the curve in appreciating Eastwood's talent, some recognition would be forthcoming. I was wrong.

Despite the participation of Americans Steven Soderbergh and Meg Ryan, the jury, chaired by French director Patrice Chereau, totally shut *Mystic River* out. Not even the festival equivalent of a good-conduct medal came its way. The Palme d'Or ended up going to an antidramatic non-Hollywood film with impeccable artistic credentials: Gus Van Sant's *Elephant*.

I had been similarly wrong six years earlier, when I was convinced that the Cannes jury at least had to toss a chewed-over bone to Curtis Hanson's exceptional *L.A. Confidential*. It turned out they did not. The Palme d'Or that year ended up being split between a pair of recondite, commercially doomed items, Shohei Imamura's *The Eel* and Abbas Kiarostami's *A Taste of Cherry*.

You didn't need to be Philip Marlowe or Sam Spade to see a pattern developing, to see a determination to dismiss cinema contaminated by the stink of Hollywood. Films produced in the maw of the studio system, runs this line of thinking, couldn't possibly be worthwhile; and even if they were, they surely didn't require the kind of help or recognition a major film festival award can provide. Which is where those juries were wrong.

The problem with a point of view that treats *Elephant* like a precious flower and, unable to tell the difference between *Mystic River* and *Pearl Harbor,* assigns them both to the outer reaches of philistine hell is that it displays a dangerous obliviousness to the realities of the movie business, a confusion about what is endangered and what is not. Although critics and juries supporting films such as *Elephant* are the equivalent of politicians coming out for motherhood and the flag, it's not clear how much help these movies actually need.

The little-discussed truth is that the art film is one of the least introuble segments of the movie universe, as much an imaginary invalid as a patient in desperate want of assistance. I love high-quality smaller films to the point of devoting my last book, *Never Coming to a Theater Near You,* to them. But though it sounds counterintuitive, their being terribly difficult for most moviegoers to see doesn't mean that they're in great danger of not being made.

Rather, the combined impact of the ease and affordability of digital filmmaking, the existence of government subsidies in many countries, the eager involvement of cable channels such as HBO and Showtime, the ability of creative producers to string together multiple—and even multinational—sources of financing, and the passion of directors to make themselves heard means that the art film may be healthier today than it's ever been.

We also have to realize that the Hollywood side of the movie business has changed in our lifetime. In the pretelevision era, when adults had fewer entertainment options, it was a given that the studios made numerous films with them in mind, a way of being that continued at least through the 1960s, 1970s and early 1980s.

Now, with corporate owners demanding predictable profits from films that cost the earth to make and to advertise—close to $100 million for the average Hollywood motion picture at last count—the studios have understandably narrowed their focus to the kinds of un-demanding entertainments favored by the twenty-five-and-under au-dience that dominates theatrical attendance.

Because adult viewers are notoriously fussy, and younger audiences don't always care enough, there may be nothing harder to get made in today's movie business than intelligent entertainments that can divert thoughtful adults but also require the stars—and the deep pockets—of a major filmmaking entity.

Studios, of course, do turn these out from time to time, but the process is rarely easy. For though it is common Hollywood knowledge that even bad films can be arduous to make, the extra effort and de-termination needed to insure quality and acuity in a big-budget film is formidable.

In recognition of that, I've chosen to start *Now in Theaters Every-where* with an extended reported piece on the making of the enor-mously influential *Blade Runner*, a film that endured paradigmatic difficulties going from novel to screen in the form director Ridley Scott intended. Tellingly enough, the changes made to enhance *Blade Runner*'s commerciality led to its initial lack of success with its intended audience, a weakness that revisions and the passage of time have rectified.

Because these films need to surmount obstacles, they require our unstinting support and recognition if we want them to continue. *Now in Theaters Everywhere* is intended as a celebration of this dwindling cinematic species, once so omnipresent, that, like the carrier pigeon or the Atlantic cod, it was beyond imagining that it could be in danger of disappearing.

Although it may not be really fashionable to do so, these films need to be celebrated. First of all, as the ones included in this book demon-strate, the best of the lot are tremendously entertaining. But more than that, if we abandon mainstream studio films that reach out skill-fully and thoughtfully to a mass audience, we will be abandoning a key part of our artistic heritage, of film's legacy, of its gift to us.

Sitting in crowded theaters along with people from all walks of life and watching films intelligently and successfully pitched to the widest possible audience is one of the quintessential movie experiences, one of the reasons we go in the first place. We won't miss these films until they're gone, and, like the once mighty cod, they are closer to disappearing than people are willing to admit.

BEHIND THE SCENES:
BLADE RUNNER

Elegant cars gliding through a decaying infrastructure, the dispossessed huddling in the shadow of bright skyscrapers, the sensation of a dystopian, multiethnic civilization that has managed simultaneously to advance and to regress—these are scenes of modern urban decline, and if they make you think of a movie, and chances are they will, it can have only one name: *Blade Runner*.

Few, if any, motion pictures have the gift of predicting the future as well as crystallizing an indelible image of it, but that is the key to *Blade Runner*'s accomplishments. One of the most enduringly popular science fiction films, it revived the career of a celebrated writer, helped launch a literary movement and set a standard for the artistic use of special effects that many people feel has never been equaled. But until 1992, a decade after its original release, Ridley Scott's director's cut of this moody, brilliant film had never been seen in anything like the form intended by the people who created it.

Yet, if this movie seems like a simplistic tale of good triumphing over evil, be aware that absolutely nothing about *Blade Runner* is as simple as it first seems. For this was a film that was awful to make, even by normal Hollywood standards of trauma, and agonizing to restructure, and it was rediscovered by a total fluke. The people who worked on it called it *Blood Runner*, a sardonic tribute to the amount of personal grief and broken relationships it caused, and they recall it with horror and awe.

Production designer Lawrence G. Paull remembers it as "a dream and a nightmare all at once." Art director David L. Snyder, whose

1

personal life was one of those that broke under the strain, remembers that, psychologically, Ridley "beat the hell" out of him and that "beatings were in order all the time." But he now looks on that time as the most intoxicating of his career, calling it "keeping up with the genius, like working with Orson Welles." Although star Harrison Ford considers *Blade Runner* his worst movie experience, costar Sean Young calls it "still my favorite film." Director Scott finds himself "progressively amazed" as interest in the film "gets bigger and bigger and bigger." Yet it took veteran producer Michael Deeley, whose previous picture was the Oscar-winning *The Deer Hunter*, ten years to find the enthusiasm to produce another theatrical film.

More than anything else, *Blade Runner's* saga is, as the best Hollywood stories invariably are, a microcosm for the industry because it starkly underlines how irredeemably deep the classic split between aesthetics and commerce is, and also how painfully inevitable. As with an etching by Escher, the final decision on who the villains are here, or whether there are any villains at all, depends on your point of view.

The man who benefited most, albeit posthumously, from *Blade Runner* was the man who started it all. When he died at the age of fifty-three in March, 1982, not four months before the film's premiere, he was, according to his agent, Russell Galen, looking forward to that event "like a kid on Christmas Eve."

Philip K. Dick was one of the architects of modern science fiction. A passionate, emotionally unstable visionary, the author of dozens of books and hundreds of short stories, he was, according to critic John Clute, "the first writer of genre science fiction to become an important literary figure." As Richard Bernstein noted in a front-page *New York Times Book Review* piece (an august location the writer never expected to inhabit while he was alive), Dick articulated "our deepest fears and most persistent fantasies about technology and its potential to destroy us."

These themes come out vividly in his 1968 novel, *Do Androids Dream of Electric Sheep?* The main character, Rick Deckard, a futuristic bounty hunter in an unhappy marriage, is offered the job of hunting down half a dozen Nexus 6 androids, or "andys": synthetic human beings with four-year life spans who've escaped from Mars and are trying to pass as authentic humans on a bleak planet Earth.

Deckard agrees to the task because he wants the money to buy the environmentally plundered future's ultimate status symbol, a live animal—specifically, a sheep. He meets Tyrell, the maker of the Nexus 6 robots, as well as his nominal niece, Rachal, who, Deckard discovers, is an android. He has a brief affair with Rachal, terminates the six "andys" and, after much philosophical speculation about how androids and humans differ and ruminations about a futuristic religion called Mercerism, Deckard returns to a somehow strengthened relationship with his wife.

When Hampton Fancher, an actor turned screenwriter in search of a project, called on Dick in his Santa Ana apartment in 1975, he wasn't concerned about the writer's place in literature. He didn't care that *Androids* had been optioned three times before or that Dick thought Victoria Principal would make a perfect Rachal.

"Phil was crazy, wonderful; he'd stop and look at his hands for five minutes straight, like he was getting messages from Mars," remembers Fancher, a striking man with a casually bohemian air. "But he didn't like me. He kept insulting me, acting like I was Hollywood, some emissary from people with cigars." No deal resulted, but five years later, when Brian Kelly, an actor friend of Fancher's, was looking for a property to produce, Fancher, "just to put him off, knowing he'd be going up a blind alley," sent him off to Phil Dick. But the two got on; Kelly got an option on *Androids*, and Fancher eventually became screenwriter.

Fancher's drafts (he ultimately did eight) eliminated both Mercerism and the wife, upgraded Rachal to girlfriend and placed the *Androids* story in the dark, fatalistic world of film noir. "I wrote it for Robert Mitchum," he says, "a wiped-out guy with scars and hangovers who got up and did his job. But there was no love in his life. He was missing part of himself, and he found it through contact with this woman. He found his heart by falling in love with the Tin Man."

These drafts concluded with Deckard's taking Rachal out of the city, letting her see nature for the first time and then, because she has only a few days to live, shooting her in the snow.

While Fancher was writing, Kelly brought the project to the attention of the more experienced Michael Deeley, who in addition to *The Deer Hunter* had overseen dozens of films, including Sam Peckinpah's *The Convoy,* and had run successful companies such as British Lion and Thorn EMI. Deeley, a polished Briton, liked the novel; he saw it as "a thriller and a romance, like the Nazi commandant falling in love with the Jewish girl who's supposed to be his victim."

Deeley immediately thought of Ridley Scott, a filmmaker he'd known for some years. But Scott, a successful director of commercials whose only released film was the little-seen *The Duellists,* was in post-production with something called *Alien* and was not ready to commit to another science fiction project. So the script, the name of which kept changing from *Android* to *Animal* to *Mechanismo* to *Dangerous Days,* made the well-traveled Hollywood rounds.

Director Robert Mulligan, best known for the sweetly sentimental *To Kill a Mockingbird,* briefly became involved. "The romantic element was a lot softer then," says Deeley by way of explaining what now seems like a curious choice. Mulligan never got beyond preliminary discussions, but by then, Scott, who had become an A-list director through the success of *Alien,* decided he was interested after all. In April 1980, Filmways Pictures announced a $13 million budget for an as-yet-untitled tale of "technological terror."

Scott liked Fancher's dark take on the script. In fact, both men found their collaboration energizing. "For a writer it was awesome, really inspiring, a creative fun house," remembers Fancher. "And Scott had a way of speaking in shorthand. 'What's out the window?' he said one day. I told him I didn't know. 'Well, think about it,' he said," a brief dialogue that led eventually to the elaborately imagined future world that would become the film's trademark.

It was Fancher who uncovered the name *Blade Runner,* taken from the title of an obscure work by William Burroughs. During Fancher's tenure, Dustin Hoffman was seriously considered for the role of Deckard. But Hoffman pulled out, and Fancher, after all those drafts, was replaced. "Ridley and I had had disagreements, but I thought I'd won the arguments," he says with bemused irony. "I was so naïve, I didn't know that writers did what they're told."

David Peoples, the second writer on the project, had a background in the documentary field and had cowritten the moving Oscar-nominated study of J. Robert Oppenheimer, *The Day After Trinity*. But though they'd never been produced, he'd written seven or eight dark, futuristic spec scripts (and went on to write Clint Eastwood's *Unforgiven*) that had come to the attention of director Tony Scott, Ridley's brother.

Though excited by the opportunity, Peoples remembers being "totally bummed out" when he read Fancher's last draft: "This is brilliant; there is nothing I can do to make it better," he told Ridley Scott. But Scott, not for the last time, persevered. "He's very demanding," says Peoples. "He has something in mind and he goes after it."

Scott had Peoples, in the writer's words, "move away from Deckard in a lot of jeopardy to a plot involving clues, like *Chinatown*." Peoples also worked on the humanity of Deckard's adversaries, and, in fact, with the help of his daughter, who told him about the biological term "to replicate," he came up with the androids' new name: replicants. The change was necessary because Scott thought the sturdy science fiction term "android" was a cliché and he half seriously decreed that anybody who used it on the set would get his head broken with a baseball bat.

Just as Peoples was starting to work, he was informed that "a bit of a hiccup" had developed. After having invested more than $2 million in the project, Filmways had abruptly pulled out. This set off a frantic scramble to secure financing and distribution for the project, then slated to cost in the neighborhood of $20 million.

"For two weeks, Larry Paull and I did presentations to every studio in town," remembers Snyder. "Ridley and Michael Deeley kept making the point that they weren't trying to do *Star Wars*, they were trying something else, and the distributors kept saying, 'You should be so lucky as to do *Star Wars*.'"

Finally, a complex, three-cornered deal was announced early in 1981. Though the Ladd Co. would release the film (through Warner Bros.), their financial stake would be fixed. According to Deeley, the Ladd Co. put in $8.5 million, and the foreign rights were sold to Hong Kong film mogul Run Run Shaw for another $8.5 million. To cover the rest, Deeley sent the script over to the three partners at Tandem Productions—Norman Lear, Jerry Perenchio and Bud Yorkin—to see whether they were interested in the video and other ancillary rights.

"Jerry was a player; he'd been an agent and a boxing promoter, and he had excellent timing in buying and selling," remembers Deeley. Yorkin had directed such features as *Divorce, American Style* and *Come Blow Your Horn*. Lear passed on the project, but Perenchio and Yorkin were interested. The pair decided, in Yorkin's words, "Let's take a flyer."

Though they differ on the amount of money initially involved (Yorkin says it was $1.5 million, Deeley $4 million), both men agree on two points. First, without those dollars, however many there were, *Blade Runner* would never have been made. And Perenchio and Yorkin, in industry parlance, took the place of a completion bond company: If *Blade Runner* went over budget, they agreed to pay whatever it took to finish the picture. And that agreement gave them, not the Ladd Co. or Warner Bros., or even Ridley Scott, effective final cut of the movie.

Next, the casting fell into place. Harrison Ford, star of *Star Wars* and the as-yet-unreleased *Raiders of the Lost Ark*, was signed as Deckard. Sean Young, a twenty-year-old actress blessed with what cinematographer Jordan Cronenweth described as "wonderful, light, creamy, highly reflective skin," had exactly the look Scott wanted; she was signed as Rachal. The international star Rutger Hauer became Roy Batty, the leader of the "replicant" band Deckard was to track down.

Shooting was to begin on March 9, 1981, and was scheduled to last for fifteen weeks. In the beginning, all was sweetness and light. That first day, Yorkin sent Deeley a note: "I know that we are embarking upon a project that you have worked a long time on and that is going to be everything you have dreamed of."

That Ridley Scott did not work in a way anyone on the crew had ever experienced became obvious the very first day of shooting. The elaborate set for the Tyrell Corp. office, complete with nearly 6,000 square feet of polished black marble and six enormous columns, was to be used first. "It was a very pristine set. Everyone was standing around in their socks," Paull remembers, "and Ridley walked in, took a look at the middle columns and said, 'Let's turn them upside down,'" a decision that meant a major delay.

"Ridley literally changed everything. I can't think of one set we went into and shot the way we found it," Snyder says. "It was brutal." Adds Paull: "Working with him was the first time in my career as a designer that the paint was still wet as the cameras were rolling."

Scott, who was trained at London's prestigious Royal College of Art, had extensive experience as a set designer, and he had directed thousands of commercials (including Chanel's haunting "Share the Fantasy" spots). Even then, he had gained a reputation for possessing what production executive Katherine Haber describes as "an eye that was totally and utterly brilliant."

"Most directors are hyphenates," explains Snyder. "They can be actor-directors or editor-directors. Because Ridley was an art director-director, he spent the majority of his time with the art department." In fact, when Snyder was introduced as the film's art director, Scott, in a hint of things to come, shot a look at the man and said simply, "Too bad for you, chap."

Someone who'd rather sketch than write, Scott was tireless in pursuit of ideas for the film's look. The alternative comic book, *Heavy Metal*, was a major inspiration, and Paull and Scott screened everything from *Metropolis* to *Eraserhead* to *Citizen Kane* and *The Blues Brothers* (the latter inspired *Blade Runner*'s flaring gas fires).

As he had on *Alien*, where he'd worked with artist H. R. Giger, the director decided to bring in a conceptual illustrator to, as he put it in advertising terminology, "spitball with." The man chosen was Syd Mead, an industrial designer with a futuristic bent who had created visuals for such companies as the Ford Motor Co. and U.S. Steel.

Originally hired merely to design the film's cars, Mead put backgrounds in his sketches that intrigued Scott, and soon Mead, the director, Paull and Snyder were involved in conceptualizing the future.

Though Dick's novel was set in 1992, the script had updated things to 2020 (finally changed to 2019 so that it didn't sound so much like perfect vision). Scott, who'd been attracted to the film because of a chance to design a city-oriented future, knew he wanted to avoid "the diagonal zipper and silver-hair syndrome" à la *Logan's Run*. Based on his experiences with urban excess in New York and the Orient, *Blade Runner* was going to be the present, only much more so; "Hong Kong on a bad day," Scott says, a massive, teeming, on-the-verge-of-collapse city that the director at one point was going to call San Angeles.

"This was not a science fiction film so much as a period piece," Paull explains. "But it would be forty years from now, not forty years ago." The key design concept came to be called "retrofitting," the idea being that once cities seriously start to break down, no one would bother to start new construction from scratch. Rather, such essentials as electrical and ventilation systems would simply be added to the exteriors of older buildings, giving them a clunky, somehow menacing look. Progress and decay would exist hand-in-hand, and the city's major buildings, such as the massive, Mayan-inspired pyramid that houses the Tyrell Corp., would tower miles above the squalor below.

Though Mead and the director were involved in conceptualizing the future, the task of actually building it fell to Paull and Snyder. "Our job was not just design or dreaming," recalls Snyder, "it was to stand something up for principal photography." Which meant, among other tasks, renting some of the neon signs from the recently completed *One from the Heart* and salvaging spare parts from an air force base in Tucson. "Syd would do these illustrations, but you had to do it, you had to finesse it if things didn't work," Paull adds. "That was the tough, tough part."

The New York street, on the back lot of what was then the Burbank Studios, had been built for Warner Bros. in 1929. Once populated by Humphrey Bogart and James Cagney, it became the arena for Scott's painstaking artistry. Someone who sees a film as "a seven-hundred-layer cake," Scott is, in producer Deeley's apt phrase, "a pointillist, creating things out of masses of tiny dots, like Seurat."

Almost immediately, Scott began the time-consuming, gradual piling of precise detail upon precise detail. The never-to-be-seen magazines on the barely glimpsed newsstands had futuristic headlines such as "Guard Dogs You Never Feed." Hundreds of highball glasses were examined before just one was selected as a minor prop. Screenwriter David Peoples remembers sinking into a chair in Deckard's apartment and realizing with a jolt that "this was not like a movie set, this was like somebody's apartment, like somebody lived there. It was stunning that way."

Because much of the film was shot at night (partly for the look, partly to save the expense of hiding the Burbank hills), a twenty-four-hour art department had to be maintained. "Ridley and I would walk the street every morning at dawn," Paull recalls with something like a shudder.

"He'd say, 'Larry, why don't we take this and do that with it.' Then he'd leave with a twinkle in his eye, and I'd pull together fifteen or twenty guys so that by the time he walked on the set that night, it would be done."

With so much attention paid to the visuals, it was inevitable that the actors would be given shorter shrift. Edward James Olmos, who played a policeman, welcomed the opportunity to be left on his own to create a street language for his character, and Rutger Hauer was happy to be allowed to improve some of his dialogue, a privilege that resulted in his wonderful closing line about memories and their being "lost in time, like tears in the rain." But M. Emmet Walsh, who also played a policeman, complained to Snyder: "By the time you guys get finished lighting, we're lucky if we have time for three takes." Ford was, by several accounts, frustrated to be dealing with a director who was, as one observer put it, "happier to be sitting on a crane looking through the camera than talking to him."

Invariably, though, dealing with Scott was hardest on *Blade Runner*'s crew. "His view of what was finished work was different than everyone else's," Deeley explains. "If there was something not right in the top right-hand corner, the crew would say, 'No one's looking up there.' But Ridley was looking up there." Says Snyder, "When you didn't get it with Ridley, you were gone." The original physical effects people were fired just before principal photography commenced; the original set decorator was dismissed because Scott didn't like the look of some crucial department-store windows. "To get the detail I wanted to get," Scott said in a interview after shooting, "you do become a relatively unpopular fellow."

What brought all this pressure to a head, compounded by the threat of a directors' strike, was an impolitic interview Scott gave to the *Manchester Guardian*. "He said how much more he enjoyed working with English crews; they all called him 'Guv'nor,' and did what he wanted," remembers Katherine Haber. "A copy of the story was left in Ridley's trailer, and by the next morning 150 copies had been Xeroxed and distributed." Almost immediately, the crew declared a T-shirt war.

Though everyone involved remembers the shirts slightly differently, the likeliest scenario seems to be that the challenge "Yes Guv'nor My Ass" adorned the front, and the sentiment "Will Rogers Never Met Ridley Scott" appeared on the back. To retaliate, and to open lines of communication, the British members of the production team—Scott, Deeley and Haber—came back with shirts that insisted, "Xenophobia Sucks."

Over at Entertainment Effects Group, the special-effects house then run by Douglas Trumbull (who'd become a legend through his work on *2001: A Space Odyssey*) and Richard Yuricich, Scott's perfectionism was also taking its toll. "He drove the effects people crazy. At the end they were ready to lynch him," reports Don Shey, editor of *Cinefex* magazine, who devoted an entire issue to the effects created by Trumbull, Yuricich and David Dryer. "Not only did he beat them to death, it didn't bother him to take a shot that cost a quarter of a million dollars and say, cavalierly, 'It didn't work as well as I thought it would. I'm cutting it.'"

Though *Blade Runner*'s special effects are dazzling, they are hardly, Trumbull says, a result of an extraordinary expenditure of money. "It was the lowest budget we had ever seen, less than a third of that allocated for *Star Wars* or *Close Encounters*," he says. "We had no money to invent new gizmos, so we took a very conservative approach," doing things such as reusing the mold for the spaceship from *Close Encounters* as the landing dock on the roof of *Blade Runner*'s police station.

The effects were memorable for two reasons. One was the unusually close coordination between the effects and the live-action photography, what Trumbull calls "one of the most seamless linkups ever," ensuring a unified look for the entire production. The other was simply Scott's eye. "It's almost trite to say these days, but Ridley Scott had a vision, and *Blade Runner* is probably the first and only science fiction art film," Shey says.

Scott refused to be rushed. Haber recalls that "he'd fiddle and diddle until it was perfect." But Scott defends his actions to this day. "In a way, directors ought to get tunnel vision when they're doing a film, or they shouldn't be doing the job."

Hardly that philosophical about the situation were Bud Yorkin and Jerry Perenchio, the men who had contracted to pay whatever it took to finish the film. Deeley describes what he considered "panic from the front office, from Bud Yorkin, who somehow felt as a filmmaker himself that there should be a way to restrain the costs." He adds, "But he was a meat-and-potatoes, 'a-picture-is-a-picture' guy, not on the same creative wavelength as Ridley."

Yorkin, a silver-haired man with an air of melancholy, sees it differently. "Jerry and I didn't go into this naively. We knew it would be a very difficult shoot, and we left ourselves a pad of $1.5 million to $2 million," he says. But as the amount of money the pair had to put into the picture rose to something like $5 million, the frustration level escalated.

"We're not a studio, but unfortunately we were placed in the position of 'the heavy' that a studio would take," Yorkin says, still irritated. "We were two guys taking it out of our own pockets or going to the bank and borrowing it ourselves. Going on the set and watching someone take five hours longer to set up a shot, seeing a lot of money go out of your pocket, that kind of thing one doesn't need unless you have a very good heart."

The time is early 1982, the cities Denver and Dallas, and the feeling is one of happiness and anticipation as movie fans open their newspapers and see advertisements announcing the sneak preview of a science fiction epic starring Harrison Ford. The mood inside the theaters is cheerful and expectant because both of Ford's previous films have conditioned audiences to expect a lighthearted, action-oriented romp. But when the lights go down, something entirely different appears.

According to one source, the preview cards filled out after both screenings told the same story: "This was a film that made demands on an audience that wasn't expecting a movie that made demands on them, an audience somewhat befuddled by the film and very disappointed by the ending." It wasn't so much that people actively disliked *Blade Runner*, they were simply unprepared for it. Another crisis had arrived.

Though one participant emphasizes that, overall, "the cards were good, but not through the roof," Yorkin saw it differently. "After so much talk, so much anticipation about the film, the cards were very disappointing. We all were in a state of shock." It was at this point that changes in the film's structure were decreed. And though Yorkin says the changes made to the film were a group decision involving the Ladd Co., Warner Bros., Perenchio and the filmmakers, Fancher is not alone when he says angrily, "Perenchio and Yorkin came in and shoved people around. They brought in the money that was missing at the end, but they took more than their pound of flesh."

First, an extensive voice-over was added to help people relate to Harrison Ford's character and make following the plot easier. According to Haber, after a draft by novelist-screenwriter Darryl Ponicsan was discarded, a television veteran named Roland Kibbee got the job. As finally written, the voice-over met with universal scorn from the filmmakers, mostly for what Scott characterized as its "Irving the Explainer" quality. "You're looking at a red door, and it's telling you it's a red door," says film editor Terry Rawlings. "It was ludicrous." It sounded so tinny and ersatz that, in a curious bit of film folklore, many members of the team believe to this day that Harrison Ford, consciously or not, did an uninspired reading of it in the hopes it wouldn't be used. And when the writers, Fancher and Peoples, now friends, saw it together, each was so afraid the other had written it that both refrained from negative comments until months later.

The film's ending was equally troublesome. Scott had wanted the film to end on a nicely enigmatic line—"It's a shame she won't last forever; but then again, no one does"—to be spoken as an elevator door closes in front of a fleeing Deckard and Rachal. Scott had also decided he wanted to leave the viewer with a hint that Deckard himself was a replicant. So he had Deckard notice a small origami unicorn on the floor, a unicorn that would hark back to a unicorn dream that he had had earlier in the film; he would then realize that his very thoughts were programmed. None of the Ladd Co. executives was impressed, and neither was Yorkin. "You try and explain to some executive what thoughts are," growls Rawlings. "They don't have any."

"Is he or isn't he a replicant? You can't cheat an audience that way. It's another confusing moment," Yorkin says. And so the unicorn dream was never used, and a new, more positive ending line—revealing that Rachal was a replicant without a termination date—was written. To indicate the joy the happy couple had in store for them, scenes of glorious nature were to be shot and added on, but attempts to get proper footage in Utah were foiled by bad weather. Instead, contact was made with Stanley Kubrick and, remembers Rawlings, they ended up with outtakes from *The Shining:* "Helicopter shots of mountain roads, the pieces that are in all the *Blade Runner* prints you see everywhere."

Though he was far from happy with the changes, especially the loss of his beloved unicorn scene, Scott, surprisingly, did not kick up a major fuss. "It was the first time I'd experienced the heavy-duty preview process," Scott recalls, "and I was so daunted by the negative or puzzled reaction, I didn't fight it. I thought, 'My God, maybe I've gone too far. Maybe I ought to clarify it.' I got sucked into the process of thinking, 'Let's explain it all.'"

With the voice-over and new ending, *Blade Runner* tested better, and the Ladd Co. planned to open it on June 25, the company's "lucky day" when both *Star Wars* and *Alien* had debuted. True, another science fiction film, a little picture from Universal, was opening a month earlier; but, says Deeley with a wan smile, "we all thought that *E.T.* would be out of business in a few weeks, that people would be sick of that sentimental rubbish and be looking for something a little harder-edged. It didn't quite work out that way."

Although *Blade Runner* opened strongly, the critics did not embrace it; and they took special offense at that voice-over ("Should Be Seen Not Heard" read one headline). *E.T.* went on to become the highest-grossing film of all time, earning more than $300 million, but *Blade Runner* returned only $14.8 million in rentals. Viewers were reluctant to embrace the film's dark genius, and so it gradually disappeared. "It was painful to see it happen," Rutger Hauer says. "A film that unique pulled out of theaters." Even *Blade Runner*'s legendary visuals could not stand up against the elfin, feel-good lure of its strongest competitor: The film lost the visual effects Oscar to *E.T.*

When a film dies in Hollywood, no one expects it to come back to life, and the people around *Blade Runner* were resigned to its demise. Michael Deeley felt "so depressed" that he doesn't think he ever saw it, "never sat through it until the end." Having successfully fought a bitter battle with Warner Bros. and the Ladd Co. to release Dick's original novel instead of a quickie novelization as the official tie-in book, agent Russell Galen felt "that was the end of that."

But this plot had still more twists. *Blade Runner*'s availability on video kept it alive in the eyes of the always-loyal science fiction crowd, and gradually the film's visual qualities and the uncanniness with which it had appeared to see the future began to outweigh its narrative flaws.

Scott says he saw the interest rise: "And I thought, 'My God, we must have misfired somewhere; a lot of people like this movie.'" And not just in this country. In Japan, where the film had always been successful, "I was treated like a king," art director Snyder reports. "The fans would be too in awe to even look at you."

The film's look began to show up in art direction and design: Terry Gilliam's *Brazil* and the stage design for the Rolling Stones' "Steel Wheels" tour were influenced by *Blade Runner*. And when laser discs appeared on the market, *Blade Runner* was one of the films that everyone just had to get. It became the top-selling disc for Voyager, the leading laser disc distributor, immediately upon its release in 1989, never losing the number one spot.

Blade Runner's influence has been literary as well. Many people who saw the film ended up reading the novel, making it Dick's top seller and, according to Galen, sparking the Phillip K. Dick renaissance of the 1980s. Dick's *We Can Remember It for You Wholesale* became the basis of Arnold Schwarzenegger's *Total Recall*; and *Blade Runner*, along with *Road Warrior* and *Escape to New York*, is considered a key progenitor of the latest wrinkle in written science fiction, the darkly futuristic cyberpunk movement.

Yet, if anyone thought about Scott's original cut of *Blade Runner* while all this was going on (and some people did), the accepted wisdom was that it no longer existed. That's what Michael Arick thought when he took over as Warner Bros. director of asset management in 1989, a position that put him in charge of recovering and restoring material on the studio's films. Then, in October of that year, there occurred the first of a series of fluky events that would rearrange fate. "I was in the vault at Todd-AO's screening room, looking for footage from *Gypsy*, when I stumbled on a 70-millimeter print of *Blade Runner*," Arick remembers. "What had probably happened was that no one had remembered to have it picked up after a screening. In order to save it from collectors, I hid it on the lot."

Several months later, the management at the Cineplex Odeon Fairfax theater was in the midst of a classic-film festival featuring 70-millimeter prints. Having heard through the print grapevine that a 70-millimeter version of *Blade Runner* had been spotted, the Fairfax asked for it from Warner Bros. Arick, a supporter of revival theaters, agreed. But neither the Fairfax nor Arick (who had never screened the print in its entirety) knew what they had on their hands.

All this changed dramatically one morning in May. "Anyone who gets up for a 10:00 A.M. Sunday screening of *Blade Runner* really knows the film," Arick says, "and everyone knew immediately what they were watching. The audience was very rapt from the beginning; the atmosphere was incredible." The print, almost devoid of the voice-over and lacking the tacked-on ending, was closer to Scott's original version than anyone ever thought they'd see again.

Though there was an immediate stir in the film-buff community, Warner Bros. wasn't sure what to do with this new-old version. Scott came over to see it and told Arick that it was in fact not his final cut: The unicorn scene that he had come to love was still missing, and the music over the climactic fight scene was not the work of film composer Vangelis but temporary music lifted from Jerry Goldsmith's score for *Planet of the Apes*. The two talked about the possibility of adding the unicorn footage, technically known as a "trim," which was languishing in a film-storage facility in London.

What happened instead was that Arick and Warner Bros. parted company (although he continued to advise Scott), and the studio contacted Gary Meyer, executive vice president of the Landmark theater chain, which had earlier expressed interest in *Blade Runner*, and asked whether he still wanted to show it. Meyer was enthusiastic; fifteen theaters nationwide were booked, including the Nuart in West Los Angeles, and without knowing it wasn't quite true, Warner Bros. created a campaign advertising "The Original Director's Version of the Movie That Was Light Years Ahead of Its Time."

Scott was not pleased: "As I understand it, [Scott] said, 'This is not my version,' which left Warner Bros. in a real dilemma," reports Meyer. "My intuition is that the studio, which might want to hire him in the future, didn't want to alienate him over some two-week repertory booking." So a compromise was reached. The newly discovered version of *Blade Runner* would play in the Nuart and at the Castro in San Francisco, but nowhere else.

With little publicity, *Blade Runner* opened at the Nuart in the fall of 1991, and attendance went through the roof. The first week set a house record, and the second week bettered the first. When Hampton Fancher, whose screenplay had started it all, tried to get in, he even showed his passport at the box office to prove who he was. But there was absolutely no room at the inn.

The same pattern of success repeated at the Castro, where its more than $94,000 box-office take in one week made it the top-grossing theater in the country. Encouraged by this, and by lucrative showings of the old voice-over version of *Blade Runner* in Houston and Washington, D.C., Warner Bros. agreed to pay for the technicians and editing rooms so that Scott could put the film back just the way he wanted it and okayed a 1992 rerelease in 150 cities. Which is why, on a weak telephone connection from London, there was quiet satisfaction in the director's voice when he said, "I finally got my unicorn scene. Ten years later, but I got it."

The tale of *Blade Runner* turns out to be a curious one. No one went bankrupt, no one's life was ruined beyond repair, no one never worked in this town again. But the experience illuminated the oldest of Hollywood battles, the one about how much tribute must be paid to art in a multimillion-dollar business where money is always the bottom line. Movie executives have always tried to change films, often destroying any artistic merit on the screen in the process—and in the end, ironically, the mutilated films don't make any more money than the original versions would have made. So the dispute remains contentious—even though everyone agrees that *Blade Runner* was so ahead of its time that it wouldn't have been a major hit even if not a frame had been altered.

Still, this was for almost all involved the project of projects, the one that no one has forgotten and that everyone sighs the deepest of sighs over. "Everything on *Blade Runner* was a little bigger, a little better," says Rutger Hauer wistfully. "You can only be a genius so many times in your life."

Part One
ACTION/THRILLER

Introduction

There's something exhilarating about a skillful action movie, and it's encouraging that this is one genre Hollywood hasn't forgotten how to make. Though these films are often dismissed as mere genre exercises, the expertise they display—and the tension they create—are a source of continual pleasure. It's difficult to see one of these crisp, efficient vehicles without wishing the studios were up to releasing pictures of this type every week, just like the old days. The films included here are at least a beginning.

One of the reasons the genre has stayed so alive is that it covers a lot of bases. We have seen remakes of *Ocean's Eleven* and *The Manchurian Candidate*; reimaginings of foreign-language films, including *Insomnia*; films based on the works of John Grisham and Tom Clancy; sequels such as *MI-2* and the *Terminator* group; and wild and original works, on the order of *Three Kings* and *Mr. and Mrs. Smith*.

The action/thriller has also been fertile ground for directors from overseas, among them Wolfgang Petersen and John Woo, as well as for Americans such as Michael Mann and Doug Liman, both of whom have two films apiece here, as does Tony Scott, a Brit. Director James Cameron once said to me in an interview that though ideas of beauty, comedy, even romance, may differ around the world, one man hitting another plays the same way everywhere, and that may be the reason for the action/thriller's international success.

But the actors more than the directors define this genre; they can be counted on to guaruntee a satisfying experience. Names such as Clint Eastwood, Brad Pitt, Edward Norton, George Clooney and Al Pacino appear twice each; Tom Cruise, Harrison Ford, Tommy Lee Jones, and Gene Hackman three times; but one versatile and reliable performer, an Academy Award winner into the bargain, beats even those totals: Denzel Washington, who has five starring roles: *Crimson Tide*, *Inside Man*, *The Manchurian Candidate*, *State of Siege* and *Training Day*. If you want one action/thriller name to take to the bank, his would be the one.

Absolute Power
1997

Absolute Power's opening close-up of a painting by El Greco, an impeccable old master, is dead-on appropriate. For the pleasures of this sleek and satisfying entertainment come from the position of its director and star, Clint Eastwood, as the last old master in Hollywood, just as reliable in his sphere as Rembrandt and Rubens were in theirs.

A twisty tale of coincidence and deceit that might be subtitled *What the Burglar Saw*, *Absolute Power* marks Eastwood's fortieth starring role and nineteenth film as a director. What he's gained over the years is an exact knowledge of his own skills, an impeccable sense of what he can and cannot do in front of a camera.

In fact, *Absolute Power*, written by veteran William Goldman (from a novel by David Baldacci) and having each of its eight key roles knowingly cast, is a tribute to that increasingly rare commodity, Hollywood professionalism. Yes, this film's plot doesn't make a whole lot of sense, but there is so much pleasure involved in seeing how beautifully old-fashioned movie machinery can be made to work that it seems churlish to object.

As befits Eastwood's increasing age and status, *Absolute Power* is hardly *Dirty Harry* territory. It's more of a civilized entertainment, almost a drawing room thriller, unhurried and genteel but enlivened with suspense and surprising bursts of sly, even biting, humor.

And Eastwood's Luther Whitney is not an officer of the law but rather a master cat burglar, a blue-collar version of the tuxedoed brigand Cary Grant played in *To Catch a Thief*, able to disarm the most complicated security systems without breaking a sweat. Whitney lives alone in Washington, D.C., has no friends and few acquaintances and spends his days meticulously copying art at the National Gallery.

That same attention to detail pays off when it comes to working nights. *Absolute Power* opens with an extended burglary sequence, shot as calmly and fluidly as the man operates, shadowing Whitney as he breaks into a richly appointed mansion and proceeds to loot a vault room hidden behind a one-way mirror next to the master bedroom.

But the building, which is supposed to be empty, suddenly isn't. Into the bedroom comes an inebriated Christy Sullivan (Melora Hardin), the woman of the house, and an even more drunk man who, we know from a shot of the wedding pictures, is not her husband. Trapped behind that mirror in the vault room, Whitney sees things he shouldn't, witnesses a shocking series of events that place his life in peril.

A master of disguise and disappearance, Whitney soon finds himself in the radar of a gang of high-profile individuals, including the president of the United States (Gene Hackman), his brittle chief of staff (Judy Davis), a pair of crack Secret Service agents (Scott Glenn and Dennis Haysbert) and one of the wealthiest and most powerful men in the free world (E. G. Marshall).

This crew couldn't be tougher (or more seamlessly acted), and a lesser man would run like hell, which is what Whitney starts to do. But ducking out has rarely been in style for Eastwood's characters, and, soon enough, Whitney's fury over the hypocrisy of official Washington keeps him hanging around and in harm's way.

It also puts Whitney into contact with Seth Frank (Ed Harris), a shrewd and sensible detective who is investigating what happened in that fancy bedroom. One of the best scenes in Goldman's screenplay is the verbal fencing the first time these two meet; Whitney's various cracks about being old and in the way are especially well done.

Whitney appears to have no family, but in fact he does have a grown daughter named Kate (Laura Linney), still resentful about being "the only kid during show-and-tell who got to talk about visiting day." Now a prosecuting attorney, Kate wants desperately to have as little to do with her father as possible, but circumstances inevitably draw her in and make her central to the film's action.

Starting with cinematographer Jack N. Green and including production designer Henry Bumstead, composer Lennie Niehaus and editor Joel Cox, most of *Absolute Power*'s key creative personnel have been with Eastwood for years, and the smoothness of their collaboration shows. Adding to the family nature of things, the producer-director has cast two of his daughters, Alison Eastwood (as an art student) and Kimber Eastwood (as a White House guide) in small but visible roles.

What it finally comes down to, however, is the skill and presence of the man who hired them all, an actor who has aged spectacularly well and knows how to make his advancing years work for him on the screen. However woebegone the state of current Hollywood may be, without Clint Eastwood's ability to elevate such improbable trifles as *Absolute Power*, the movie business would be a sadder place still.

Eastwood remembered Linney when it came to casting his Oscar-winning Mystic River.

Air Force One
1997

No, Harrison Ford isn't the president, not even a candidate for the job, but given the chance, who wouldn't vote for him in a Beltway minute? A hero with a human face, Ford projects both rectitude and concern while playing engaging pragmatists who do the right thing no matter what. Wouldn't that be a switch on Pennsylvania Avenue?

Air Force One, directed by Wolfgang Petersen and starring Ford as President James Marshall, is not going to make anybody think twice about that vote. With the actor confidently in his element as the chief executive coping with the hijacking of "the world's most secure aircraft," this is a display of Ford at his best that holds us in a tight bear hug of tension from beginning to end.

Like Petersen's 1993 film, the Clint Eastwood-John Malkovich *In the Line of Fire*, *Air Force One* is at once vigorous and old-fashioned, a piece of expertly crafted entertainment that gets the job done with skill and panache. The director and his production team exhibit the same kind of crisp professionalism as does the U.S. commando unit that opens the picture by kidnapping General Alexander Radek, the rogue leader of Kazakhstan whose evil policies have, yes, put the entire free world at risk.

In Moscow three weeks later to celebrate that capture with Russian leaders, President Marshall departs from his prepared text to say (what a guy) he doesn't deserve to be congratulated. Having avoided appropriate action in the past, he vows never again to allow political self-interest to deter the United States from doing what it should when confronted by terrorists. Aides such as his chief of staff (Paul Guilfoyle) later snivel about consulting our allies first, but Marshall shuts them up with a brisk line: "It's the right thing to do and you know it."

Back on the plane home, the president is looking forward to relaxing with his wife Grace (Wendy Crewson) and their twelve-year-old daughter Alice (*The Little Princess* star Liesel Matthews). The only excitement he's anticipating is watching a tape replay of the latest Notre Dame-Michigan football game. Feeling at ease on an aircraft built to survive the pulse of a nuclear attack is an easy habit to get into.

Unfortunately, no one said, "Hey, that's Gary Oldman; he's always up to no good," when Russian television newsman Ivan Korshunov claimed a seat in the equivalent of coach. In an unexpected blitzkrieg, Korshunov and his cohorts manage to take over Air Force One. They notify the White House, specifically the all-business vice president, Kathryn Bennett (Glenn Close), that they will execute one of their numerous hostages every half hour until their hero, that nasty General Radek, is released.

Fortunately for the honor of the profession, Korshunov is not really a television journalist but a diabolic Russian ultranationalist zealot with zero interest in "the infection you call freedom." *Air Force One* pivots (as did *In the Line of Fire*) around a battle of wills between its personifications of good and evil, and Oldman is all he should be as a sadistic madman who is not overburdened with respect for human life.

Oldman does indulge in a few of his trademark temper tantrums (they must be in his contract), but he is mostly under control and does a convincing job of humanizing a man who says, "I would turn my back on God himself for Mother Russia." He knows everybody's weak spots and is not above responding to verbal attacks from the good guys with this savage retort: "You murdered 100,000 Iraqis to save a nickel on a gallon of gas."

Korshunov's opponent in the cat-and-mouse game that develops on the plane is not, of course, some desk-bound, lethargic politician. This president just happens to be a battle-hardened Vietnam veteran and Medal of Honor winner, and Ford has all the physicality necessary to make Marshall's ability to handle himself in a brawl completely plausible.

What keeps Ford well ahead of the pack as an action hero, however, is his ability to convey not only emotional intensity but also moral qualms, even worry. Placed in situations where his beliefs have a good chance of putting innocent people, including his own family, in terrible danger, President Marshall's convincing looks of anguish add more to this film's effectiveness than its inevitably explosive special effects.

Screenwriter Andrew W. Marlowe, whose first produced script this is, does more than come up with sharp lines for Korshunov. Though there is back and forth with the White House, most of *Air Force One* is a kind of locked-room mystery, a drama in which everything of interest has to happen in a confined environment, and Marlowe's script has the knack of coming up with surprising twists and multiple sources of tension.

Getting the most out of that script is the gift of Petersen and his team, including a world-class cinematographer (Michael Ballhaus) and a crack editor (Richard Francis-Bruce, responsible for *Seven*, *The Rock*, *Dead Calm* and *Mad Max Beyond Thunderdome*).

Together with Jerry Goldsmith's militaristic score and the across-the-board skill of the film's actors, this gang makes *Air Force One* tenser than it has any right to be. Petersen is a master tactician, adept (witness the remarkable *Das Boot*) at moving people around tight spaces and finding the best spot for the camera.

It was in *Das Boot* and its story of World War II German submariners that Petersen first showed the gift for tying action to psychology that is much in evidence here. Given that, it's nice to see him casting Jurgen Prochnow, exceptional as that film's U-boat captain, in the wordless but critical part of General Radek. As an affectionate tip of the hat to a marvelous shared past, it's especially welcome and appropriate.

The Bourne Identity
2002

Imagine awakening one morning and finding yourself suddenly blessed not only with nerves of steel and fluency in several languages but also the action reflexes of Bruce Lee, the driving skills of Michael Schumacher and the climbing ability of Spider-Man.

There are, however, a number of catches:

You wake up, two bullets in your back, not in your own bed, but in an Italian fishing boat in the Mediterranean after having been pulled from the stormy water; everyone in Europe who wears a uniform, and numerous people who do not, are seriously trying to capture and/or kill you; and, oh yes, you are suffering complete amnesia and have no idea who you are, how those enviable skills came to be yours or why any of this is happening to you.

That's the premise of The Bourne Identity, a tiptop espionage thriller starring Matt Damon that takes this crackerjack premise and runs with it. Based loosely on the 1980 novel by Robert Ludlum that was filmed for television in 1988 with Richard Chamberlain in the lead, this is an entertainment that really entertains because any number of interesting and unexpected choices were made, starting with the selection of Doug Liman as the director.

One of the bright lights of independent filmmaking, Liman was an unusual pick to do the kind of major-studio secret agent movie that usually ends up as stodgy and arteriosclerotic as Spy Game.

Liman is so jazzed at the opportunity to bring his outsider sensibility to mainstream material that he's been able to treat the story as if it were spanking new. He has successfully fused elements of both his previous features, the charming character-driven *Swingers* and the overreaching but still vivid *Go*, onto this production.

The Bourne Identity gets its initial impetus from a well-constructed screenplay by Tony Gilroy and William Blake Herron that takes the film's fairly straightforward plot and keeps it nicely streamlined and surprising enough to be involving. (Though the film had well-publicized script problems, they are not visible in the finished product.)

The man who wakes up on the boat (Damon) has but one clue to who he is: a mechanism, implanted in his hip, that displays a Swiss bank account number. He travels to Zurich to check it out and discovers not only an American passport that tells him he's Jason Bourne, but also a veritable UN's worth of papers in other names from other countries. Plus a whole lot of money. And a gun.

Bourne is still in the dark about the details of his identity, but the film—through glimpses of two distraught spymasters, Ted Conklin (Chris Cooper) and Ward Abbott (Brian Cox), at CIA headquarters—has already let us in on the secret. Bourne is a top Company assassin, part of a hush-hush project called Treadstone, but his lack of success in his last job has so compromised this super-clandestine world that Conklin feels compelled to insist, "I want Bourne in a body bag by sundown."

With no idea why everyone is chasing him, Bourne makes an accidental connection with Marie Kreutz (Franka Potente, the Lola of *Run Lola Run*), a beautiful young vagabond driving a tiny red Austin Mini Cooper who—for a tidy sum—agrees to take him to Paris. There, circumstances conspire to keep them together as Bourne attempts to survive the nonstop attempts on his life as well as piece together exactly what that life consists of.

In Liman's hands, this potentially overly familiar scenario takes on unexpected sparkle. For one thing, the director, occasionally serving as his own camera operator (and working with cinematographer Oliver Wood and editor Saar Klein), is so good at the mechanics of action that they don't feel like mechanics. Laced with great shock moments, *Bourne* draws us confidently into its orbit as it moves along smartly on its own steam.

Equally essential is the way Liman and his actors have used intense but low-key line readings to infuse a sense of reality onto these proceedings, to make this a character-driven story about young people we might know caught in a situation we can barely imagine.

With Cooper, Cox and Julia Stiles as the CIA folks and Clive Owen as a rival assassin, *Bourne* is notably well-cast in its subsidiary roles, but especially successful is the pairing of Damon as an earnest would-be teddy bear who can't understand why he's a killing machine and Potente as the woman who's attracted to him against her better judgment.

Though interpersonal relationships in espionage films often can't move beyond the emotional opaqueness of James Bond, the interplay here is surprisingly human. Bourne and Marie have a rapport that's tentative and tender; they are hesitant with each other because they're inescapably lost and confused. It's a small touch but a vital one, and it underlines why *The Bourne Identity* commands our attention and respect.

Clear and Present Danger
1994

Clear and Present Danger reaffirms, if reaffirmation is necessary, Harrison Ford's position as the most reliable action star around.

With those other big-ticket, big-muscle performers (you know who they are), it's not known until it's too late whether they've made a feast or a fiasco. Ford, by contrast, in searching for an emotional connection, even in the brawniest of projects, has become as earnestly dependable as the characters he plays.

In fact, since *The Empire Strikes Back* in 1980, the actor has been the equivalent of a *Good Housekeeping* seal for the adventure genre, his presence guaranteeing an enviable level of professionalism, excitement and involvement in the thrillers, from *Witness* to *The Fugitive*, that he has appeared in.

Clear and Present Danger is the third Tom Clancy novel about CIA analyst Jack Ryan to be adapted to the screen, and the second time Ford, director Phillip Noyce, cinematographer Donald M. McAlpine and other key members of the cast and crew have been involved, and the practice has been good for everyone. This is easily the best and most tightly wound of the Clancy films, notable for the intricacy of its plot and the nuances its actors bring to characterization.

Initial credit for this must go to *Danger's* jerry-built but effective script. Three writers with very different approaches—Clancy-adaptation veteran Donald Stewart, character-sensitive Steven Zaillian and action aficionado John Milius—share screen credit, and against all expectation the intelligent result is much closer to synergy than to chaos.

If *Danger* does have a problem, it is that it starts too slowly. Partially this is a situation endemic to sequels because all the familiar subsidiary faces, here including Anne Archer as Ryan's wife, Cathy, and James Earl Jones as his boss, Admiral James Greer, have to be laboriously reintroduced to a perhaps forgetful audience.

The plot, too, begins tentatively with a pair of almost simultaneous actions. Ryan is unexpectedly thrust into a more active role in the intelligence bureaucracy, and his new responsibilities include testifying before Congress and even briefing the president. And the first situation he has to deal with is the murder at sea of a lifelong friend and political supporter of the chief executive.

When Ryan traces the murders to the infamous Cali Colombia drug cartel, President Edward Bennett (Donald Moffat) is incensed. "Drugs pouring into the country and the drug dealers think we're powerless," he fumes to National Security Adviser James Cutter (Harris Yulin). Isn't it likely, he goes on, that the cartel represents "a clear and present danger to the national security of the United

States," a situation that allows for the commitment of American military power?

The expected thing for *Danger* to do at this point is to break down into a United States versus the drug lords scenario, but what happens is subtler. There turns out to be not one Colombian adversary but several, not necessarily on good terms with each other. And far from a monolithic American presence, there are various power centers, each having different perspectives and antithetical agendas.

What results is a pleasantly complex story line in which these numerous strands, both in Washington and Colombia, twist and turn as they combine and recombine in unexpected ways. This classic wheels-within-wheels situation makes each succeeding scene in the film just a little bit tenser than the one that came before.

Keeping this complexity involving and fast-moving is director Noyce, assisted by the adroit cross-cutting of the editor, Neil Travis, who also handles the rapid shifting of scenes between numerous South American locations (all apparently photographed in Mexico). The action-set pieces are crackerjack as well, especially a complex ambush filmed on a two-football-fields-long set, nicknamed "The Kill Zone," that required eight weeks of preparation.

What is rarer than good action is plausible dialogue and acting, and this is *Danger*'s key strength. Especially convincing, and especially timely, is the film's depiction of how covert operations go down in Washington, of how ambitious men operate in a world of suggestion and innuendo and of how an ambiguous "the course of action I'd suggest is a course of action I can't suggest" can set all sorts of mayhem into motion.

Not only have the key subsidiary characters of *Danger* been written in a subtle way but the parts have been cast with unusually capable actors. In this country, Donald Moffat makes a most convincing president, alternately affable and arrogant, and Henry Czerny and Harris Yulin are equally good as White House apparatchiks.

In Colombia, Willem Dafoe is an appropriately cool CIA field operative, and the Portuguese actor Joaquim de Almedia makes a clever and devious opponent. Even smaller roles, such as Ann Magnuson as an FBI secretary and the veteran actor Hope Lange as a suspicious senator, are perfectly carried out.

And once again, as in so many films in the past, Harrison Ford and his combination of intensity and integrity hold it all together. Capable of bringing to life and sympathy a character derided as "a damn Boy Scout" by his more cynical adversaries, Ford is an actor who believes his word to the audience is a bond guaranteeing the best he has to give. Would there were more like him around.

Ford remains a force on the screen, but his more recent projects have not lived up to his earlier standards.

The Client
1994

John Grisham's novels are like flypaper: insubstantial but entangling. Not noted for characterization or style, their shark-like sense of unstoppable narrative drive practically forces the reader to keep turning those pages. That is a nice talent to have in a nation that does much of its reading on airplanes.

Because the originals are so insubstantial, the film versions of Grisham's books are more porous than most adaptations: They are inclined to absorb the aesthetic coloration of the people who direct them. *The Firm* was better for the care Sydney Pollack took with acting and characterization, and now *The Client* comes to us with the mark of Joel Schumacher on it.

Though his name is not yet on the short list for the Life Achievement Award from the American Film Institute, Schumacher is in many ways a good match for Grisham material. The director of *Falling Down*, *Dying Young* and *Flatliners*, Schumacher is an unapologetically commercial filmmaker, and he is excited about the material in a way a more ethereal type wouldn't be.

The combination of Schumacher's on-the-nose eye for mass public appeal with Grisham's best-selling sensibility has produced a film that is probably truer to the spirit of the original novels than were its predecessors. Not particularly nuanced or fine-tuned, *The Client*, like its source material, is gimmicky and involving, a fast-moving comic-book version of a comic-book novel.

And though Schumacher has not been known as an actor's director, *The Client* is beefed up by a pair of satisfying star performances. Individually and in their scenes together, Susan Sarandon and Tommy Lee Jones are often more convincing than the film's story line, and the energy of their acting helps *The Client*'s plot over a variety of rough spots.

Initially, however, neither Sarandon nor Jones are anywhere in sight. Instead, on a hot Memphis afternoon, two boys, eleven-year-old Mark Sway (Brad Renfro) and his eight-year-old brother, Ricky (David Speck), go on the lam from their low-rent trailer-park home with a cigarette they've stolen from their working mother (a believable Mary-Louise Parker).

All kids have secret spots they favor, places they go to savor their triumphs, but on this particular day Mark and Ricky have their space in the woods invaded by a large, late-model car. Inside is a distraught Mafia lawyer from New Orleans named Romey Clifford (Walter Olkewicz). Romey is suicidal and inclined to talk too much; before long, he has told Mark things it could be worth his life to know.

And, not surprisingly, it doesn't take much time for interested parties both good and bad to focus in on little Mark. On the dark side, Barry "The Blade" Muldano (Anthony LaPaglia) and his cohorts would like to ensure the boy's silence, and ambitious, milk-drinking federal prosecutor Roy Foltrigg (Jones), called "Reverend" because he "knows Scripture better than the Lord," would scruple at nothing to get him to talk.

Mark is feisty to the point of obnoxiousness, but even he knows he's overmatched. And since this is one of those movies where emotionally troubled, bargain-basement lawyers just happen to be the equal of the best legal talent anywhere, Mark manages to stumble on just such a diamond-in-the-rough in Reggie Love.

As played by Sarandon (and helped by the dialogue in the Akiva Goldsman and Robert Getchell script), Reggie is the emotional center of *The Client*, a protective tornado who for personal and professional reasons wants to do the best for bratty Mark. Her interchanges with the Reverend Roy—as cool as she is hot, and expertly played by Jones—are the best *The Client* has to offer.

Though it never bores and creditably moves through all its paces, *The Client* on film plays like a series of predictable set-ups painted with too broad a brush. Yet such is the power of Grisham's narrative that even though much of what is seen isn't particularly convincing, it doesn't stop us from caring how it all turns out. Let other films worry about the fine points; *The Client* just wants to keep you turning the page.

Collateral
2004

Literally and metaphorically, *Collateral* peers deeply and persuasively into darkness. Skillfully directed by Michael Mann and featuring strong work by Jamie Foxx as a nightshift cabdriver and Tom Cruise as his all-night passenger, this sharp and exciting thriller examines not only the vast disconnected physical blackness that is Los Angeles at night but also the murkier aspects of its characters' souls.

Mann's first theatrical feature, *Thief* (1981), was a crime story, and though the director has gone on to work in a wide spectrum (*The Insider, Ali, The Last of the Mohicans*), he's retained an affinity for the genre. In films such as *Heat, Manhunter* and now *Collateral*, he's been especially good at depicting driven outsiders who are swallowed whole by their professions, case-hardened types on both sides of the law who take pride in what they do and demand to be respected for it.

Initially, Foxx's Max Durocher seems to be an exception to that rule. In a role that is a further departure from the high-energy comedy that started the actor's career, he convincingly plays a veteran Yellow Cab driver, twelve years behind the wheel with the glasses to prove it, a decent, almost diffident citizen who's not noticeably secure or self-confident.

Yet, as we see when Assistant U.S. Attorney Annie Farrell (Jada Pinkett Smith, elegant and empathetic) gets into his cab, Max does have a drive to excel at what he does. He doesn't back away from a contretemps with the confident Annie about the best way to get to downtown, and soon he's talking about his dream of starting Island Limo, a car service so relaxing you won't want the trip to end.

When Max drops Annie off at 6:00 P.M., his next fare is Vincent (Cruise), someone we've already glimpsed purposefully striding through the Los Angeles airport with a deliberate, unapologetic confidence. He tells Max he's in town to close a real estate deal, and he offers the cabby $700 to chauffeur him to five stops and get him to the airport in time for his early morning flight. Max is reluctant, but Vincent is a man who is used to getting his way.

What Vincent is also, Max very soon finds out, is an experienced, implacable contract killer, an unstoppable death machine given to saying such things as "I didn't kill him, I shot him. The bullets and the fall killed him." Even though events blow Vincent's cover, he is determined to keep going, likening the new situation to modern jazz: "It's off-melody, behind the notes, not what's expected, improvised— like tonight."

Vincent and Max will spend many hours together, and no one will be surprised to learn that the experience changes them both. Yet it is one of the virtues of Stuart Beattie's script that *Collateral* offers numerous unexpected moments as the intense time the two men share leads to the creation of a kind of connection neither one anticipates or even wants.

It's Max, whose anguished "I can't do this" is the understandable reaction to Vincent's postmurder demands, who has the most to cope with. But his exposure to Vincent's Gangster Way of Knowledge, his night of hit man therapy, if you will, finds Max increasingly capable of doing things he never imagined possible.

Similarly, the demands of the role call forth the most pleasantly nuanced performance of Foxx's career, improving even on the excellent work he did as Drew "Bundini" Brown in *Ali*. He is the film's audience surrogate, and imprisoned as he is in the small taxi space with Cruise for long stretches, his is the performance that draws us in and sustains us.

That said, however, neither Foxx's acting nor *Collateral* as a whole would be as successful as it is without Cruise's powerfully confident performance. The actor changed his hair color to silvery gray, changed his character's moral outlook to pitch black and made adroit use of his charisma and control to give us someone whose perfectionism has made him something of a star in his rarified profession.

Director Mann is a perfectionist as well, someone who knew exactly the kind of expensive but unusual suit ("made by the best tailor in Kowloon") he wanted Vincent to wear, and he didn't hesitate to use the name "Yellow Cab" on vehicles adorned with the Bell Cab colors because he didn't respond to the name "Bell."

Mann's passionate involvement in every area of filmmaking has paid off across the board. The director and his team have cast the film with uniformly fine actors, such as Mark Ruffalo in a key role as a suspicious police detective, Javier Bardem in a memorable cameo as a charismatic drug lord and Jason Statham in little more than a walk-on as an airport contact.

The director has also paid his usual meticulous attention to the soundtrack, playing the Groove Armada/Richie Havens "Hands of Time" over Annie Farrell's cab ride and Paul Oakenfold's pulsating "Ready Steady Go" over the film's action centerpiece, a spectacularly choreographed and edited (Jim Miller and Paul Rubell) example of virtuoso violence in a Korean nightclub that took nine days to shoot.

Production designer David Wasco and Mann have located *Collateral* in often unseen areas of Los Angeles, such as a nightclub in Pico

Rivera, and made the parts of the city we have seen look different. Cinematographers Dion Beebe and Paul Cameron have used a high-definition digital video camera called the Thomson Grass Valley Viper FilmStream for most of the shoot to give *Collateral* more clarity and color over a greater distance—we see downtown clearly from Pico-Union, for instance—than we've seen before.

As a result of Mann's craftsmanship and concern, *Collateral* moves with energy and purpose, a propulsive film with character on its mind and confident men and women on both sides of the camera. "It's what I do for a living," Cruise's Vincent likes to say when pressed. Making films like this is what Michael Mann does for his.

Crimson Tide
1995

Don't plan on getting much sleep after seeing *Crimson Tide*. It's not just that the tension, tangible enough to be eaten off a plate, is capable of squeezing out your every last breath. It's that a troubling moral dilemma has been placed at the heart of a crackling good piece of popular entertainment.

And if ever a picture crackled, *Crimson Tide* fits the description. Crisp as the creases in its naval officers' uniforms, this tale of seething conflicts aboard an American submarine on the eve of nuclear war is strictly by-the-numbers, but hardly ever are traditional elements executed with such panache.

Wedding a shrewd concept and a lean script to on-the-nose acting and direction, *Crimson Tide* is one of the rare times when filmmakers throw together a whole mess of commercial elements and everything works out for the best.

Though high-testosterone boy-toy films like *Crimson Tide* (especially those produced, as this one is, by Don Simpson and Jerry Bruckheimer) usually are oblivious to convincing writing and classy acting, this one is not; further, it is capped by taut performances from Denzel Washington and Gene Hackman and a brisk job of direction by Tony Scott.

Washington plays Lieutenant Commodore Ron Hunter, an impressively educated submarine officer first glimpsed wearing a silly hat at his daughter's birthday party. Those moments of frivolity, however, are fated not to last because soon a television news broadcast details a world in terrible crisis.

The rebellion in Chechnya has led to a civil war in Russia, and ultranationalist rebels led by one Vladimir Radchenko are attempting to capture nuclear-tipped ICBMs and threatening to use them on the United States if they succeed. "Is it as bad as it looks?" Hunter's pal Weps (Viggo Mortensen) asks. You know it is.

Hunter's assignment is with Captain Frank Ramsey, commander of the Trident submarine USS *Alabama* (hence the movie's name), modestly described as "the most lethal killing machine ever devised." Persuasively played by Hackman, Ramsey is one of those tougher than tough commanders that movies specialize in, in love only with the U.S. Navy and his dog, a No. 1 who believes that aboard ship "we're here to preserve democracy, not practice it."

The relationship between these two is the fissionable core of *Crimson Tide* and one of several places where the spare Michael Schiffer script, with well-publicized additions by the impressive trio of Quentin Tarantino, Robert Towne and Steve Zaillian ("These three guys could punch up *Hamlet*," Schiffer told the *New York Times*), makes its expertise felt.

Right from their initial meeting, the best kind of movie tension, a combination of distaste and respect, bubbles up between the captain and his executive officer. Ramsey, a seat-of-the-pants combat veteran, distrusts Hunter's book learning; the younger man, though irked at being continually needled, comes to understand that the captain really does care for his men.

Obviously energizing each other in a sweet display of complementary acting, Hackman and Washington, helped by expert supporting performances by Mortensen, the veteran actor George Dzundza and several others, bring their antagonism to life.

Aside from convincingly delineating character, *Crimson Tide*'s script gradually builds the tension from small incidents, such as a fire in the galley and the unwelcome attentions of a Russian Akula class submarine, until the ultimate in crises inevitably arrives.

That would be the news, transmitted via EAM, or Emergency Action Message, that those pesky rebels have captured both the ICBMs and their launch codes and are preparing to blast the free world. The *Alabama* is commanded to attack the Russian bases with its own nuclear arms before it's too late. Then, as if any more tension were needed, another EAM comes in that just might countermand that order to strike, but mechanical problems break off the transmission before the message is completed.

So the dilemma, which causes Ramsey and Hunter to lock horns for a final nail-biting confrontation, is this: Do you take the time to confirm the attack message and risk having the entire United States blown away during the delay, or do you fire without confirmation and perhaps start an unprovoked nuclear war?

Helping make all this chillingly plausible is the great sense of verisimilitude that *Crimson Tide* creates, both verbal and visual, including the convincing use of jargon ("zero bubble, commence hovering" is one of the more lyrical bits), as well as the story help of sub authority Richard P. Henrick and a combination of production design, art direction, lighting and cinematography that makes the inside of the *Alabama* look and feel compellingly real.

Tony Scott has always had the reputation of being a shooter, a director who can be counted on to make his footage look terrific, but with *Crimson Tide* he's added an expertness at moving plot along and a facility with his actors. As a result, none of his other films—including the mindless success *Top Gun*—has come close to what he has accomplished here.

Mortensen went on to save a different kind of world as Strider in The Lord of the Rings *trilogy.*

Deep Blue Sea
1999

Water is a liquid we rely on. It's right there when we're hot, when we're thirsty, when we want things to grow. But who speaks up for water's dark side, for its implacable force, the terrifying power of its raging torrents? *Deep Blue Sea* does, that's who.

A rousing adventure yarn that's paced to kill, *Deep Blue Sea* is an example of how expert action filmmaking and up-to-the-minute visual effects can transcend a workmanlike script and bring excitement to conventional genre material. There's little in this man-versus-shark story we haven't seen before, but we haven't seen it quite like this.

Deep Blue Sea is also a return to form for action director Renny Harlin. Considered one of Hollywood's top shooters after *Die Hard 2* and *Cliffhanger,* Harlin lost his way for a while in the great dismal swamps of *Cutthroat Island* and *The Long Kiss Goodnight.*

Here, helped by a trio of veteran editors (Frank J. Urioste, Derek G. Brechin, Dallas S. Puett), cinematographer Stephen Windon and top-of-the-line animatronic and computer-generated image people, Harlin has energetically pounced on this classic "Don't Mess with Mother Nature" premise.

In addition to reinvigorating Harlin, *Deep Blue Sea* also brings the shark back to a place of prominence in the menace hierarchy. Though this film doesn't approach the élan of the brilliant *Jaws,* that picture never did manage a completely workable shark. Here, the combination of animatronic and digitally created beasts, as well as footage of the real thing, gives us a twenty-five-foot mako and two smaller companions that are the epitome of destruction.

Yet, even though we see enough close-ups of nasty-looking teeth to enthrall a convention of orthodontists (no one has to tell these behemoths to open wide), it is the water as much as the shark that terrifies us. The nightmarish vision of liquid torrents roaring out of control in a confined space is every bit as scary, perhaps more so, than creatures that bite for a living.

That space is Aquatica's floating oceanic research station, an elaborate compound that's situated almost entirely below the surface. Here the all-business Dr. Susan McAlester (Saffron Burrows) heads up a team that includes hunky shark wrangler Carter Blake (Thomas Jane), comic-relief chef Preacher Dudley (LL Cool J), deep thinker Jim Whitlock (Stellan Skarsgard), a marine biologist (Jacqueline McKenzie) and an engineer (Michael Rapaport).

Working from the curious premise that sharks might produce a protein that would regenerate human brain cells and thus prevent Alzheimer's disease, Dr. McAlester and company have been breeding bigger and smarter sharks in the hopes of harvesting a potent version of that substance.

Some bad publicity leads money man Russell Franklin (Samuel L. Jackson) to consider pulling the plug on the project, but before he does, Dr. McAlester convinces him to take a flying visit to the facility to see the research for himself. Definitely not a good idea.

For what Franklin and the research team simultaneously discover is that these sharks, including a giant 8,000-pound beast with a brain the size of a V-8 engine, have gotten too darn big and too darn smart for anyone's good but their own. It's uh-oh time in a big way as the scientists realize the awful truth: "We've taken God's oldest killing machine and given it will and desire."

Deep Blue Sea's script (by Duncan Kennedy, Donna Powers & Wayne Powers) is not going to win any Writers Guild awards, but it's savvy enough to set the scene efficiently for the physical madness that follows and then get out of the way.

Yes, there are the expected moments, such as doors that are closed just in time and a fetching female who has to strip down to bikini underwear to save her life (don't ask), but the film does manage several twists that are surprising. And the casting of actors who for the most part are unknown to action audiences helps the scenario move closer to plausibility than films like this usually manage.

The thrills begin, classically, on a dark and stormy night, and once the mayhem commences, with raging waters, dangerous fires and out-of-control sharks attacking every human in sight, there is no rest for the weary. Harlin, orchestrating onscreen hysteria and menace as adroitly as he combines the work of the eight effects houses that contributed to the film's verisimilitude, is completely in his element when making sense out of the chaos. This is one action film that really knows how to move.

Enemy of the State
1998

Forget about Santa Claus coming to town. The National Security Agency is already here, and not only does it know whether you've been naughty or nice but it can also deliver some pretty nasty surprises if you get caught on its bad side.

That, at least, is the message of *Enemy of the State*, directed by Tony Scott and produced by Jerry Bruckheimer, a thriller about a man on the run from a super-powerful government agency. It's a paranoid's nightmare brought energetically to life, a solid and satisfying commercial venture that has more than enough pizzazz to overcome occasional lapses in moment-to-moment plausibility.

To do that, a film has to have convincing performers, and this one demonstrates why Will Smith is pretty much the hottest actor in Hollywood. As Robert Clayton Dean, the man unjustly placed at the top of the NSA's bad list, Smith adds dramatic skills to his comic gifts and his immense relaxed likeability and ends up as everyone's favorite Everyman, in a jam but determined to get out alive.

Just as good are the two actors who control Dean's fate. A convincing Jon Voight plays NSA zealot Thomas Brian Reynolds, the devil in a Brooks Brothers suit; and Gene Hackman, with his tough turn as a rogue surveillance wizard, helps make this film *The Conversation* on steroids.

More than that, casting director Victoria Thomas has dotted *Enemy of the State* with excellent performers in smaller supporting roles, including James Le Gros, Ian Hart, Gabriel Byrne, Tom Sizemore, Jason Robards and Lisa Bonet, who combine to make this probably the best-cast of Bruckheimer's efforts.

A man who didn't become the king of popcorn movies by worrying too much about real-world credibility, Bruckheimer has broken with form by commissioning a straight-ahead, non-tongue-in-cheek script that has a disturbing core. As written by David Marconi (with uncredited work by Henry Bean), *Enemy of the State* is, if anything, more convincing in its broad outlines than in its thriller specifics because it posits the existence of a surveillance-dominated society in which the collaboration of the government and the telecommunications industry makes the most complete invasions of privacy possible.

Director Scott has done some of his best work (*Crimson Tide*, *Beverly Hills Cop II*) for Bruckheimer, and, collaborating with cinematographer Dan Mindel, he does a compelling job of visualizing how satellites and computers could make this Truman-Show-for-real scenario happen. Practically an elder statesman compared to the technobrats Bruckheimer usually employs, Scott also pays attention to the acting and it pays off.

Smith's Dean is introduced as one of Washington's top labor lawyers, a suspenders-wearing Georgetown resident with the requisite strong-minded wife (Regina King) who has a great way with suspicious looks, and an adorable son.

Dean's current case involves a mobster (Sizemore) who's trying to muscle in on a labor union. As always when things get tough, Dean uses his old law school girlfriend Rachel Banks (Bonet) to make contact with Brill (Gene Hackman), a secretive private investigator who is capable of gathering the most hard-to-find information.

Simultaneous with this plot strand, bad guy Reynolds is getting a bead on a scientist named Daniel Zavitz (Jason Lee), who has possession of a tape the NSA official will do anything to keep from becoming public.

Though Dean is not aware of it when it happens, that tape ends up in his possession. What the lawyer does become aware of is that his life is turning into a nightmare overnight as Reynolds, the man who invented ruthless, conspires for his own nefarious reasons to ruin every aspect of Dean's life from his marriage to his credit cards to his career.

It's a measure of how audience-friendly an actor Smith is that he manages to keep viewers interested through the toughest part of movies like this—the long section when the audience knows exactly what's happening but the protagonist is without so much as a clue.

Helping to clue Dean in is Hackman's character, a convincingly angry and suspicious security expert who uncannily resembles the actor's Harry Caul persona in *The Conversation* more than twenty hard years down the road. (As a pleasant nod to that earlier film, a shot of Hackman as Caul is flashed briefly on the screen as part of Brill's out-of-date identity badge.)

People in *Enemy of the State* do a great deal of running around, with Dean for one getting briskly chased along hotel corridors, out windows and even down long tunnels wearing nothing but his underwear and a stolen bathrobe. All this activity serves to divert us from the film's periodic departures from plausibility. But with the whole world stacked against Smith's likable character, it seems only sporting to give his film that kind of a break.

Face/Off
1997

John Woo is known for a cinema of violent delirium so breathtaking it plays like visual poetry, and *Face/Off*, though his third film in Hollywood, is the first to expose mainstream audiences to the master at his most anarchically persuasive.

But, as those who've seen the director's idolized Hong Kong movies (*A Better Tomorrow*, *The Killer* and *Hard Boiled*) can testify, Woo is also known for the sincerely sentimental underpinnings of his work. Bonding between men links all his films, which classically feature an emotional connection between the hero and the villain that's the strongest one on the screen.

Which is why, though it was written by the team of Mike Werb & Michael Colleary before either one had seen the Hong Kong films, *Face/Off* is a kind of ultimate John Woo movie. Its tale of identity-switching takes the director's usual themes to their logical extreme and results in a delicious inside-out double-reverse movie that's as outrageous and over the top as anyone could want.

For *Face/Off*'s title refers not only to the inevitable confrontation between good and bad but to a literal switching of physical identities as well. It's a film that demands that its stars play two roles, one nestled inside the other like interlocking toy dolls, a task handled so persuasively by John Travolta and Nicolas Cage that they've inspired Woo to do his best work in years.

The director, who didn't seem to be quite hitting his stride with his first two American films, *Hard Target* and *Broken Arrow*, here offers a demonstration of action as it should be done. In its best moments, *Face/Off* practically mainlines fury, leaving audiences no time to think or even to breathe.

With an offbeat sense of humor, an eye for small visual touches and a weakness for white doves added to an intuitive grasp of the mechanics of large-scale pyrotechnics, Woo ensures that no one's eyes will be leaving the screen while he's spinning his apocalyptic web.

After a brief prologue set six years previously that establishes the reason for the enmity between Sean Archer (Travolta) and Castor Troy (Cage), *Face/Off* moves to the present, with Archer as the driven, humorless leader of the usual supersecret government antiterrorist team.

Archer's main target is, no surprise, Castor Troy and his sniveling sociopath brother Pollux (Alessandro Nivola). Castor, no bargain either, establishes himself early on as a showy and bombastic homicidal maniac, a terrorist-for-hire whose huge gold-dipped handguns decorated with custom-made dragon grips are the least flashy thing about him.

Castor and Pollux get defanged in *Face/Off*'s initial action sequence when they come out on the short end of a tussle with Archer, an unhappy man who has let his relationships with his wife Eve (Joan Allen) and his pouty teenage daughter Jamie (Dominique Swain) deteriorate in his manic quest to nail his nemesis. "It's over," he tells Eve after the battle, but we know better.

It turns out that no one but Castor, who's in one of those movie comas, and Pollux, who's in prison, know exactly where the pair have planted a poison gas bomb that will decimate Los Angeles in just a few days. The only way to save the city is for Archer to assume Castor's identity and worm the info out of the imprisoned Pollux.

We're not talking a fake driver's license here. Thanks to an experimental surgical procedure involving something called a "morphogenetic template," Archer, in a sequence that owes a lot to Georges Franju's indelible *Eyes Without a Face*, manages to disappear behind Castor's face and inside his body type. Everyone assures him it's reversible, but it's still awfully creepy.

Creepier still is what happens when, for no apparent reason, Castor wakes up and, because Archer's face and body are the only ones not spoken for, ends up grabbing them. So both men, each looking like his own worst enemy, try to complete the jobs they started when they looked like themselves.

Face/Off's script is not strong on dialogue or conventional plausibility, but its themes are sound, and one of its more intriguing ones is how flummoxed Archer and Castor are by having to live the lives of their hated opponents. Imprisonment and dissipation in no way agree with Archer, and Castor, despite sharing a bed with Archer's wife and leering at his daughter, finds married life is more complex and onerous than he had anticipated.

Cage and Travolta are equally successful with their double-barreled roles, and in fact both do better playing the self-loathing that comes with being a frustrated personality in an unwanted body. Travolta, when in the grip of Castor's persona, even gets to make some disparaging comments about his own chin. It's that kind of movie.

It's safe to say that Joan Allen, not usually found in films of this sort, will not get a third Oscar nomination for her work as Archer's sorely tried wife, but it's precisely her skill at making her character both grounded and believable that is essential in giving *Face/Off* what reality it does have.

Not surprisingly, it's John Woo, able to choreograph carnage to Olivia Newton-John singing "Somewhere Over the Rainbow," who is the real star of *Face/Off*. It's difficult to describe the jolt his films deliver when he's on, and he is on with a vengeance here.

The Firm
1993

When a book sells 7 million copies and is translated into twenty-nine languages, who can doubt that it is doing something right? So the inevitable film adaptation has to decide whether to play it perfectly safe or take risks with what is close to a sure thing.

The powers behind *The Firm* have avoided the dilemma by splitting the difference. They have carefully protected the core qualities of the John Grisham novel while radically rejiggering its plot line. The result is a top-drawer melodrama, a polished example of commercial moviemaking that manages to improve on the original while retaining its best-selling spirit.

Paramount Pictures, which purchased the movie rights to this story of lawyers on both sides of the law even before it was sold as a novel, clearly wanted the best for this project, and when Hollywood wants the best in mainstream directing, Sydney Pollack is always on the list.

He's had his share of misfires, but Pollack remains the total professional, an actors' director and one of the foremost practitioners of the kind of nicely calibrated work that is so smooth there is a danger of discounting the amount of skill that goes into it.

Casting was a similar gold-standard production. As hotshot attorney Mitch McDeere, heartthrob Tom Cruise was the obvious choice, and *The Firm* not only pairs him with Gene Hackman as legal mentor and Jeanne Tripplehorn as loving wife but also fills in the background with a strong and varied group of supporting actors.

The Firm's most intriguing credit, however, is the one for screenplay, divided as it is between a trio of exceptional writers who are as accomplished as any mob hit men: playwright David Rabe (*Streamers, Sticks and Bones*), four-time Oscar nominee Robert Towne (*Chinatown, Shampoo*) and longtime Pollack collaborator David Rayfiel, who also worked on the director's similarly themed *Three Days of the Condor*.

If the film's intention was simply to replay the novel, this much talent wouldn't be necessary. But what's been done here is similar to rebuilding an engine: The book's best-selling plot has been taken apart and put back together again in noticeably better shape. Subplots have been strengthened, characters have been switched around to make the jeopardy more emotionally involving and increased physical action has been added to the mix, all of which ratchets the excitement level up a number of notches.

The Firm's narrative focus, however, has been kept intact, and that involves the trials of lawyer McDeere. The film's opening sections quickly establish him as a top prospect at Harvard law, a loophole-loving tax lawyer whose days of waiting on tables and riding the bus home to patient spouse Abby are soon to end in a welter of big-money proposals from fancy firms.

But the offer McDeere ends up being unable to resist comes not from New York or Los Angeles but rather courtesy of a small, forty-one-lawyer outfit in Memphis named Bendini, Lambert & Locke. Not only do they propose to pay top dollar but they throw in a low-interest home loan and a new Mercedes, color to be determined later, as extra added incentives.

A visit to Memphis and lots of talk about how everybody in Bendini is one cheery family clinches things for McDeere. Though Abby is put off by the Stepford quality of some of the corporate wives and thinks maybe things are too good to be true, the ambitious Mitch, clearly too busy a young man to read many novels, is unworried by the surface perfection.

The first blemish on McDeere's dream comes when two members of the firm die violent and unexpected deaths. Then McDeere gets rousted by a pair of surly men who just might be government agents. Gradually, much against his will, McDeere comes to suspect that Bendini is not exactly the paradise it appears. But like the predicament of Harry Houdini, bound in chains and tossed overboard, McDeere's is one from which escape seems impossible, and every move he makes only serves to tighten his bonds.

Though Mitch McDeere can never quite escape from being more a cog in a thriller machine than a character, Tom Cruise goes a surprising distance toward making him believable. The actor's charisma has never been in question, but under Pollack's guidance his charm, though evident, has been so muted that when he's called on to be awkward and in jeopardy, it is convincing.

Even more impressive is the range and quality of performances *The Firm* has gotten from a wide range of supporting players. Included are Gene Hackman's major turn as McDeere's troubled associate, Wilford Brimley as the firm's ominous head of security, David Strathairn as McDeere's brother, Gary Busey and Holly Hunter as private investigator and loving secretary, Ed Harris and Stephen Hill as government operatives, even mogul Jerry Weintraub as the disreputable Sonny Capps and Karina Lombard in the small but critical role of a young woman on the beach.

When so much of the acting in a film is quietly effective, an extra nod must be given to the director. Sydney Pollack not only has taken the risk of letting his film run the two and a half hours needed to include relevant characterization but also has demonstrated how emotional shading and subtlety can be worked into big-ticket items. Contrary to so much of what we're used to seeing, *The Firm* proves that a presold blockbuster doesn't have to be the dumbest film on the block.

The Fugitive
1993

Dr. Richard Kimble never quits, never rests, barely even stops to catch his breath, and neither does the film that capitalizes on his dilemma. *The Fugitive* is a super-adrenalized stemwinder, a crisp and jolting melodrama that screws the tension so pitilessly tight it does everything but squeak.

Laced though it is with breakneck chases and eye-widening stunts, *The Fugitive* paradoxically succeeds because of qualities such as intelligence and wit not always associated with thrillers. Director Andrew Davis (working from a sharp script by *Die Hard's* Jeb Stuart and David Twohy) has done more than pack pounding energy into every sequence. He has paid attention to the credibility of all the film's characters, lesser mortals included, involving us even more completely in the action in the process.

And Davis has been fortunate in having as his leads two actors who could not have been better cast. The duel between Harrison Ford's agonizingly on-the-run Dr. Kimble and Tommy Lee Jones's fearsomely implacable Sam Gerard, a true Nemesis of mythological proportions, is a confrontation to remember.

Based on the 1960s television series of the same name (created by the film's coexecutive producer Roy Huggins), *The Fugitive* hews closely to its source's basic plot line, which in turn owed a lot to Victor Hugo's *Les Miserables*, a debt the movie repays by staging a chase in a storm drain that nicely echoes the novel's famous Paris sewers sequence.

In a move that is typical of its relentless pacing, *The Fugitive* gets going while most movies are still pulling on their boots. Intricately intercutting edgy black-and-white footage of the doctor's wife, Helen (Sela Ward), being brutally murdered in their Chicago apartment with color scenes that precede and follow the crime, the film neatly reveals the way things stand before the credits have fully rolled.

After spending the early part of the evening with his wife at a charity fund-raiser, Dr. Kimble, a prominent surgeon living a hell of a good life, is called to assist at an emergency operation. When he returns home, it is to a dying wife and a fierce battle with the one-armed assailant who has murdered her. But the killer has left no traces of his presence, Mrs. Kimble's skin is under the doctor's fingernails, and a fat insurance policy is under his name. The vise of circumstantial evidence inexorably tightens, and though the doctor croaks to the police, "You find this man," no one in authority believes the one-armed killer even exists.

Tried, convicted and sentenced to death, an understandably distraught Dr. Kimble is on his way to prison when a fracas erupts on the bus transporting him behind the walls. Then, in a sequence (overseen by crackerjack stunt coordinator Terry Leonard) guaranteed to leave audiences gasping, a massive seven-car freight train (yes, they used a real one) plows directly into the bus and creates more than enough chaos to allow Kimble to escape.

Smart, resourceful and determined to use his unexpected freedom to find his wife's killer, Kimble would appear to be a fair bet to make it all happen. But when the officer assigned to track him down turns out to be Deputy U.S. Marshal Sam Gerard, a lawman whose obsession with getting his man makes the Royal Canadian Mounted Police look like loafers, the whole situation changes.

Someone who last smiled when Grant took Richmond, Gerard is nerveless, ruthless, harder working then his bloodhounds and more cold-blooded than any killer. Jones, who has made a career of playing variants of this type, nails the role shut here, bringing a thrilling urgency and focus to Gerard and his way of continually barking out complex orders that is key to giving the movie its compelling, unforgiving pace.

Similarly Ford, who has been rugged and upstanding innumerable times, calls on his most distinctive trait, his vulnerability, to animate Dr. Kimble. Rare among action heroes, Ford is believable both in control and in trouble, someone audiences can simultaneously look up to and worry about. And with Jones's Gerard on his tail, it is no wonder the poor doctor looks so overwrought it seems he's going to have a coronary before he can manage to clear his name.

Jones has been in two of Davis's previous movies, the underappreciated *The Package* and *Under Siege* (starring Steven Seagal), but *The Fugitive* is the best of the lot and marks Davis's coming of age as a crackling good action director. He knows how to make the implausible plausible, an especially valuable talent when this film's far-from-clear explanation of what actually happened in Dr. Kimble's apartment finally unfolds.

Not, obviously, that Davis did it alone. Among the coconspirators are cinematographer Michael Chapman, who has given the film a rich, saturated look, and a crack team of editors (six are given screen credit) who've seen to it that no moment is ever dull. Most important of all, composer James Newton Howard has come up with a galvanizing score, reminiscent at times of the great Bernard Herrmann, that, like everything else in this nonstop film, wrings you out like a damp cloth and mercilessly hangs you out to dry.

Heat
1995

What's old has been made fine and new in *Heat*. Writer-director Michael Mann and a superlative cast have taken a classic heist movie rife with familiar genre elements and turned it into a sleek, accomplished piece of work, meticulously controlled and completely involving. The dark end of the street doesn't get much more inviting than this.

Though Mann is best known for directing *The Last of the Mohicans* and executive producing television's *Miami Vice*, moviegoers with a fondness for crime stories will remember *Thief*, his polished 1981 feature debut starring James Caan as a master safecracker and Tuesday Weld as the woman in his life.

With its poetically heightened dialogue and fascination with character and the mechanics of crime, *Heat* is a satisfying new venture into that same territory. No one sees as much epic existential heroism in the romantic fatalism of hard men and the women who try to love them as Mann does. Sometimes he even sees too much, and *Heat* (which at two hours and forty-five minutes wouldn't be harmed by a trim) does overreach at times. Yet its narrative pull, as unrelenting as a riptide, creates more than enough tension to compensate.

The story of the battle of wills between master criminal Neil Mc-Cauley (Robert De Niro) and LAPD detective Lieutenant Vincent Hanna (Al Pacino), *Heat* is an intensely masculine film, bent on mythologizing the lonely, driven men on both sides of the law and showing them to be as disciplined and directed as warrior monks.

Heat also makes explicit one of the themes implicit in films like these, that criminal and cop, hunted and hunter, have more in common than not. Obsessed and obsessive, dedicated to doing what they do best to the exclusion of anything else in their lives, the cool Mc-Cauley and the passionate Hanna are closer to each other than to their nominal partners in and out of crime.

Heat opens with one of the film's beautifully re-created criminal actions. McCauley and his regular crew of Chris (Val Kilmer) and Michael (Tom Sizemore) are joined by a new guy named Waingro (Kevin Gage) in a carefully planned attack on an armored car. Everything doesn't quite work out as intended, however, and detective Hanna gets to try on a new case for size.

Alhough Hanna is introduced making love to his wife, Justine (Diane Venora), don't be fooled. Justine is wife number three, and the marriage is not going well. Smart, ferocious and tireless, the detective barely has a life outside of pursuing those who break the law. Afraid that unburdening himself will make him lose his edge, Hanna is unwilling to share any of himself with anyone. "All I am," he admits, "is what I'm going after."

That's a sentiment Neil McCauley wouldn't have difficulty echoing. An ascetic criminal mastermind who lives in a furnitureless house by the Pacific, McCauley accurately describes his emotional state as "a needle starting at zero going the other way." At ease with all forms of violence but unwilling to raise his voice or say an unnecessary word,

McCauley lives by the strictest code: "Allow nothing in your life you can't walk out on in thirty seconds flat." Still, for all his caution and savvy, McCauley, with Hanna on his tail, ends up trying for that one last job no movie criminal can resist.

At the core of *Heat*'s success is the strength of its ensemble acting. By paring away nonessentials and clamping down on mannerisms and tricks, Mann has helped his actors to uncover and rediscover the core of their appeal, the innate qualities that made them stars in the first place. There is no one in the film, including Pacino, De Niro, Kilmer, Sizemore and a ravaged-looking Jon Voight, who does not give the kind of restrained yet powerful performance that ranks with the very best work of their careers.

And, surprising for a film that deals with outsized macho emotions, this concern for acting and characterization carries over into the opposite sex. Mann pays close attention to human moments, to what the script laconically calls "husband and wife stuff," and the gifted trio of Diane Verona, Ashley Judd and Amy Brenneman have more impact on this film than would ordinarily be so.

Heat does other things equally well. Its use of Los Angeles locations is excellent (as it was with Mann's earlier *Manhunter*) and its violence is for the most part carefully parceled out, potent without causing revulsion. Mann's dialogue can sound overwrought and self-consciously operatic, but it is more often muscular and to the point.

The notion of criminals as lonely, existential warriors is of course not new (Jean-Pierre Melville's *Le Samourai*, starring Alain Delon, did it especially well), but it's rarely done with as much dexterity and panache as Mann and company have provided.

In the Line of Fire
1993

Used to be that all a hero needed to operate was a weapon, a partner and a code of honor, with maybe a good woman thrown into the mix.

In these more uncertain times, however, a hero is hardly worth saluting unless a villain of stature stands mockingly in his path and matches him strength for strength.

And when the hero is played by Clint Eastwood, this requirement becomes even more critical. For Eastwood, no ordinary good guy, is a paradigm of virile qualities, a man who has been so invulnerable for so long he's become a one-of-a-kind icon whose movies are built around him with all the care of a necklace fabricated for the Hope diamond.

So with Eastwood starring as a veteran Secret Service agent in Wolfgang Petersen's crisply entertaining *In the Line of Fire*, the key question is who gets to play the implacable assassin sworn to drop the president in his tracks. The choice was John Malkovich, and it's difficult to think of a better one.

It's not just that Malkovich is an excellent actor with credits ranging from *Dangerous Liaisons* to *Of Mice and Men*. It's the kind of actor he is, an Obie-winning veteran of the prestigious Steppenwolf Theater Company who is at home on stages everywhere, including those of London's West End.

With a background so spiritually different from Eastwood's *Rawhide*/spaghetti-Western origins, Malkovich makes the best kind of villain for this piece by providing the kind of intrinsically adversarial presence that Raymond Massey, for instance, did for James Dean in *East of Eden*. And Malkovich's insinuating, carefully thought out delivery is in the same way an ideal foil for Eastwood's bluntly straightforward habits.

Eastwood's Frank Horrigan is not protecting anyone at first, he is working with partner Al D'Andrea (Dylan McDermott) on the service's anticounterfeiting detail and taking less guff than anyone in the federal government. One night, called on to investigate a suspicious lodger, he and Al discover enough disturbing evidence to make Frank sure they've stumbled onto an executioner's lair.

But not only has Frank recognized a potential killer, the killer has recognized Frank as well. For Horrigan is not just any Secret Service agent; he was John F. Kennedy's favorite, on the scene in Dallas and traumatized from that day to this (and for all we know in a support group with Kevin Costner's similarly disturbed *Bodyguard*) because he wasn't able to stop the bullet that found the president.

All this comes out in a series of phone calls that the assassin, who airily asks to be called Booth (as in John Wilkes) because that man "had flair, panache," makes to Frank out of sheer dark glee that this legendary agent is on his trail. "Going up against you raises the game to a much higher level," Booth says in his oily, menacing way. "Fate has brought us together. I can't get over the irony."

Booth's feeling of connection with Frank, his desire to admire him and taunt him simultaneously, is the strongest point in the film's script, which ends up giving many of its best lines to the predator. (It was written by Jeff McGuire on the suggestion of producer Jeff Apple, a Secret Service buff since he was a teenager whose continued fascination apparently led to extensive agency cooperation.)

More or less a genius of a hit man, master of weapons, phone trickery, disguise and no doubt much more, Booth is especially good at driving Frank crazy, messing with his head in all those needling phone calls. Hobbled by encroaching age, doubting superiors, pain-in-the-ass politicos who just don't get it, even a bad case of the flu, Frank manages to get himself reassigned to the presidential protection detail and perseveres. Still smarting over Dallas, he knows that Booth is going to make a try at this president and he wants to be there when it happens.

Given that everyone in the theater knows the same thing, to say that director Petersen completely involves us in the action is saying a great deal. Best known for the splendid *Das Boot*, Petersen brings many of the same qualities as Eastwood himself would to the project, including a lean, unadorned style, a concern with pace and an emphasis on keeping the audience intrigued. With his professionalism and his understanding of genre, Petersen is as good a match for Eastwood on one side of the camera as Malkovich is on the other.

As for Eastwood himself, his laconic mastery of screen acting has become such a given that *Line of Fire*'s script feels free to have some gentle fun with his durable persona by having Horrigan claim "a good glare can be just as effective as a gun." The film has also tried, with only partial success, to broaden Eastwood's appeal, to make him less Dirty Harry and more Jimmy Stewart by entangling him romantically with a feisty female agent played by Rene Russo, similarly matched with Mel Gibson in *Lethal Weapon III*. We are patient through it all because when the bullets finally fly, there is no one more than Eastwood we'd rather see pumping them out for our side.

Inside Man
2006

What's going down inside Manhattan Trust's Wall Street branch may or may not be the usual bank robbery, but *Inside Man*, the crime drama that details those nefarious doings, knows how to keep its distance from your standard heist movie.

Smartly plotted by newcomer Russell Gewirtz and smoothly directed by, of all people, Spike Lee, *Inside Man* is a deft and satisfying entertainment, an elegant, expertly acted puzzler that is just off-base and out of the ordinary enough to keep us consistently involved.

The broad outline of *Inside Man*, of course, couldn't be more familiar. We're talking perfect crime territory here, the classic cat-and-mouse encounter between criminal mastermind Dalton Russell (Clive Owen) and Detective Keith Frazier (Denzel Washington), the NYPD operative charged with outthinking the man with the master plan.

Screenwriter Gewirtz, though, is not interested in doing anything quite that formulaic. Though its eye is always on the final showdown, his script is especially good at doling out confounding information on a need-to-know basis, on providing a multitude of incidents to occupy our minds until all the pieces fall into place. This is one of the rare films Lee has directed without at minimum cowriting the script, and you can see why.

He has made his own versions of standard Hollywood films before, witness the classic biopic *Malcolm X*, also starring Washington, but its obvious that Lee is more at home with argumentative, provocative, socially relevant films than he is with this kind of genre material. Which turns out to be a good thing.

For though he is capable of crisply handling nuts-and-bolts action scenes such as the quartet of robbers securing the bank and taking dozens of hostages, that is never going to be enough to hold Lee's interest.

So the director found ways to be slightly off the mark, from the minor—starting the film with the beautifully disorienting rhythms of Bollywood superstar composer A. R. Rahman—to the major, including the decision to use both Washington and costar Jodie Foster in roles that depart a bit from what these actors usually do. And what else could the shot of Brooklyn's legendary Cyclone roller coaster under the opening credits be telling us except this is going to be quite the wild ride?

Lee has also been able to make political points around the film's edges, to be himself without sacrificing the project's plausibility in the process. A Sikh hostage complains of police mistreatment and of being called "an Arab." Two police officers have a racially charged conversation. A boy is chided for playing a particularly brutal and insensitive video game. And one of Inside Man's themes, the notion of systemic political corruption, surely found a receptive audience with the filmmaker.

Finally, like any nongenre director, Lee is interested in people, in what they look like and how they behave. It's an interest that exists outside of considerations of suspense, but when characters are made individual, it inevitably means that we worry more about them, which of course heightens tension.

One person who is cast exactly to type with excellent results is Owen, who opens the film by looking directly at the camera and saying, as only he can, "My name is Dalton Russell. Pay strict attention to what I say. I choose my words carefully and I never repeat myself."

What Russell, no paragon of modesty, proceeds to tell us is that he's planned the perfect bank robbery. The film immediately shows him and his team, all dressed identically in painters' coveralls, swiftly taking over the bank in question and telling the cowed hostages, "My friends and I are making a very large withdrawal. Anyone who gets in the way gets a bullet in the brain."

Charged with negotiating with the man is Washington's Detective Frazier and his partner Bill Mitchell (the always convincing Chitwetel Ejiofor). Frazier, however, is not the superstar cop you might be expecting. He is a veteran detective second grade with the slightest hint of a paunch who only got the assignment because the department's top guy is on vacation.

At first the situation develops like any other bank robbery, with Russell eventually demanding the usual fully-fueled jet ready to take him and his team out of town. But first the audience, and then Frazier, begin to sense through the actions of others that there are as yet unnamed factors in play.

The first hint of this comes when Arthur Case (Christopher Plummer), Manhattan Trust's chairman of the board, is informed of the robbery and says, "Oh, dear God." He next calls Madeline White (a picture-stealing performance by Foster), the ultimate ice-princess powerbroker in a city of powerbrokers, and asks for her services.

From that point on, *Inside Man*'s plot takes more twists and turns than the venerable Cyclone, and includes the interesting technique of periodically flashing forward to police interrogations of the hostages after the siege is over. Like everything else about this engrossing thriller, it's a tactic intended to keep the audience on its toes, and it does.

Insomnia
2002

"When does it get dark around here," Will Dormer asks the local cops in Nightmute, Alaska, the halibut fishing capital of the world, and they only smile. During the summer months this far north of the Arctic Circle, the only darkness, as the Shadow liked to say, lurks in the hearts of men, and there is plenty to go around.

A Los Angeles Police Department detective on loan to the Night-mute force to investigate a particularly disturbing homicide, Dormer (masterfully played by Al Pacino) will be disoriented by more than the midnight sun in *Insomnia*. As this taut and intelligent psychological thriller, a kind of white nights film noir, investigates moral ambiguity as well as bad behavior, it illuminates the risks even decent people run of losing their way in the dense thickets of crime.

As both his earlier films, the less-seen *Following* and the indie powerhouse *Memento*, demonstrated, director Christopher Nolan is a filmmaker at home with dislocation and dissociation. *Insomnia* shows an equally welcome gift, one for intelligent popular entertainment.

This is a skill Nolan shares with one of *Insomnia*'s executive producers, Steven Soderbergh, who recognized a kindred spirit in Nolan and supported him on the project. Having a director this thoughtful doing genre material results in considerably more texture than usual and gives us a film that understands how immorality can ooze into goodness like a drop of blood seeping into a white shirt.

Though smartly written by Hillary Seitz in a promising debut, *Insomnia*'s origins go back to an excellent 1997 Norwegian thriller of the same name directed and cowritten by Erik Skjoldbjaerg and starring Stellan Skarsgard in the Pacino role. Seitz's script sticks closely to the original, but Nolan has had no trouble using a variety of skills to make the material his own. Working with his *Memento* collaborators cinematographer Wally Pfister and editor Dody Dorn, and shooting largely in British Columbia, Nolan once again displays an unmistakable visual confidence and a feeling for bravura moments, notably a nerve-wracking chase across a slippery logjam floating down a frigid river.

As he showed with Guy Pearce in *Memento*, Nolan is also adept at working with actors, and the beneficiaries this time are not only Pacino but also costars Robin Williams and Hilary Swank, all of whom profit from the director's ability to elicit reined-in performances. No one benefits from this tight control more than the veteran Pacino, who owns the film from the first moment we see Detective Dormer: He's flying into Nightmute with his LAPD partner, Hap Eckhart

(Martin Donovan), and looking as drained and bloodless as the crime scene photos of murdered seventeen-year-old Kay Connell that he holds on his lap.

An actor who's been around and looks it (and who was playing cops as far back as 1973's *Serpico*), Pacino was a natural choice for one of those bleak veteran detectives who's next door to a legend in law-enforcement circles. Dormer may look tired, he may actually be tired, but he remains a watchful hawk, patiently waiting for the opportunity to strike.

Dormer and his partner are not really in Nightmute as a friendly gesture from a large city chief to a small one. They're in town in part for a respite from an Internal Affairs probe of their conduct back home. Dormer, especially, is worried and agitated that his reputation, his very life's work, will be destroyed by those he thinks "suck the marrow out of real cops."

If Dormer and company represent experience, Swank's Detective Ellie Burr is all innocence and enthusiasm as the youngest member of the Nightmute force, someone who actually studied Dormer's cases when she was at the academy. Swank's performance inevitably opens on a gee-whiz note, but it toughens and gains more heft as the case takes increasingly serious turns.

It doesn't take Dormer long to establish that Kay was murdered by someone who knew her well, someone who took enormous trouble and care to groom the corpse he'd savagely beaten to death. "This guy, he crossed a line," Dormer says, "and he didn't even blink." But despite this insight, Dormer finds the case uncommonly difficult. An unexpected crisis causes his situation to unravel, and the twenty-four-hour sun, which makes sleep impossible, starts to prey on his mind. More and more, Dormer feels trapped by the unceasing light, unable to escape from its punishing, insidious brightness.

Adding to his difficulties are a series of taunting late-night phone calls from a voice audiences will recognize as belonging to Robin Williams. The detective immediately focuses on his character, Walter Finch, as the main suspect. Finch, it turns out, is an especially clever man, eager to engage Dormer in elaborate mind games, trying to make him somehow complicit in a growing moral darkness that threatens to envelop the entire case.

For Williams, Walter Finch is one of several dark roles, including *Death to Smoochy* and *One Hour Photo*, and it is the most effective of the lot. It's also perhaps the most compelling of the actor's noncomic performances, noticeable for the way the character's unflappable calmness leads to greater and greater complexity.

It is also unusual to see Pacino this outwardly calm, but his restraint has a formidable power. This is an actor especially suited to playing a man who knows all the moves, who has no trouble allowing us to feel the weight of experience on his soul. By not going over the top, Pacino allows us to intuit the strength behind the anguished, haunted mask, reminding us why he was such a compelling actor in the first place.

Holding all this together without apparent effort is director Nolan, who revels in the intricate push-pull relationship between detective and suspect that is at *Insomnia*'s core. As *The Asphalt Jungle* famously considered crime merely a left-handed form of human endeavor, this film explores the nature of truth, how cops and criminals can appear to be two sides of the same coin, how difficult it can be to know what to reveal and when to reveal it. As Dormer says to Ellie, "People give themselves away in small lies, small mistakes. It's just human nature."

Moving on to still bigger budgets, director Nolan followed Insomnia *with the blockbuster* Batman Returns.

Kiss of Death
1995

The dark, twisty kingdom of film noir, a shadow world that leaks fatalism, pessimism and romantic despair, is the drug of choice for contemporary directors. Hardly a month passes without one filmmaker or another attempting a modern-day noir knockoff, so strong is the lure of this brooding bad-guy genre. But it takes a film as compelling as *Kiss of Death*, one of the most effective neo-noirs, to underline why so many of the others haven't been able to go the distance.

Most of the modern copies are content to mimic the surface moodiness of the classics, but *Kiss of Death* duplicates their emotional impact as well. Written by Richard Price, directed by Barbet Schroeder and starring *NYPD Blue*'s David Caruso in his first poststardom movie role, *Kiss* is not after dispassionate admiration. Its depiction of fallible characters whipsawed by pitiless antagonists on both sides of the law is wrenching to experience, and that is as it should be but hardly ever is.

As noir fans will know at once, *Kiss of Death* takes its title from a 1947 film remembered for showcasing Richard Widmark as the unbalanced Tommy Udo, a character whose idea of fun was pushing frail old ladies down flights of stairs. But rather than a conventional remake, screenwriter Price has come up with a new story suggested by the original's theme of a loner pressured to break the criminal code and turn against his own kind.

A successful novelist as well as an accomplished screenwriter, Price gives *Kiss of Death* all the noir essentials: an intricate plot that flows and eddies in unexpected places, dialogue that is juicy as well as wised-up and characters whose anguish is easy to connect with.

With brisk economy, *Kiss of Death* introduces its protagonists, Jimmy Kilmartin (Caruso) and his wife, Bev (Helen Hunt). Just the looks they exchange in their Queens apartment indicate how difficult it has been for them to remain in love, how grateful but skittish they are about having survived the rigors of alcoholism (for her) and a prison stretch for stealing cars (for him).

Later that night, with Bev out and Jimmy babysitting their daughter, there is hysterical knocking at the door. It is Jimmy's cousin and former cohort Ronnie (Michael Rapaport), and he is desperation itself. If he can't get one small final criminal favor from Jimmy, he's going to end up a dead man. Jimmy, out on parole, knows he should say no, we all know he should say no, but this isn't that kind of picture.

Inevitably, nothing is as easy as Ronnie says it will be, and much against his will Jimmy gets sucked into the dark heart of amorality where it's difficult to tell the criminals from the crusaders. Everyone wants something from him, from the ambitious district attorney Frank Zioli (Stanley Tucci) to a relentless cop (Samuel L. Jackson) to Little Junior (Nicolas Cage), a mesmerizing crown prince of crime. Jimmy's instinct is to refuse everyone, but no one is willing to leave it at that. When difficult decisions are forced on him, Jimmy desperately tries to balance what he believes in against the effects his actions will have on the family he values so much because it has been so hard to create and maintain.

Stories like this don't work unless the actors hit all the right notes, and in *Kiss of Death* they do. The very warm Hunt deftly establishes Bev's character, and Jackson brings his usual extra dimensions to the role of a wary, embittered cop. On the other side of the law, Rapaport, last seen as the confused neo-Nazi in *Higher Learning,* adds another to his list of idiosyncratic Iagos. And Cage, one of the few American actors who gets more interesting from film to film, comes close to kidnapping the picture as Little Junior, a pumped-up but asthmatic thug who, like King Kong, is a gorilla with a wistful air about him. Adroitly written and beautifully realized, Little Junior is a character whose words and actions defy prediction. Except that no one is likely to forget what happens when he's around.

Fine as Cage is, without an equal presence in the leading role, *Kiss of Death* would not satisfy. And Caruso turns out to have a classic film noir look about him. His face never loses its pose of cool, but there is a sadness around his eyes, a vulnerability modifying his surface toughness. As *NYPD Blue* proved, Caruso knows how to make you care, and that ability has survived intact on the big screen.

A fair share of the credit for all this must go to Barbet Schroeder, a director who has worked largely in France but sporadically in this country. Collaborating with veteran cinematographer Luciano Tovoli, Schroeder's experience and expertise are visible from the opening shot, a smooth crane movement revealing an enormous auto junkyard that immediately establishes a sense of place, a New York that only native New Yorkers ever see.

What Schroeder also brings to the mix is a welcome unobtrusiveness and sense of balance. This is the kind of film where the violence is parceled out in small but intense doses, and a key sexual event is signaled by nothing more than an open top button on a pair of jeans. Though his interest in the dark side has been evident at least as far back as the kinky *Maitresse*, except for Nicholas Kazan's Oscar-nominated effort on *Reversal of Fortune*, Schroeder's American films have until now suffered from below-par scripts. With a fine piece of work in his hands, the director has brought all his skill to bear on *Kiss of Death*, and it has made all the difference.

The Manchurian Candidate
2004

Pulp is powerful.

The strength of sensational material joined to excellent acting, superior filmmaking and uncanny political relevance has made *The Manchurian Candidate* into exceptionally intelligent entertainment and a high point of director Jonathan Demme's career.

The story of one man's struggle to confront an insidious conspiracy, *Candidate* gives a strong cast—Denzel Washington, Meryl Streep and Liev Schreiber in the performance of his career—plenty to chew on and asks nothing more than a willingness to go along for the ride.

The film's political relevance is uncanny because this *Candidate* is a remake. The 1962 original—directed by John Frankenheimer and written by George Axelrod from Richard Condon's novel—starred Frank Sinatra, Laurence Harvey and Angela Lansbury in one of the most unsettling films of the decade.

The new *Candidate* is smartly written by Daniel Pyne and Dean Georgaris, who worked from the original material. It has built on the first film's strengths and cut back on its weaknesses while delicately shifting some of the plot dynamics. The result is a political and psychological thriller that is richer in texture and nuance than its predecessor without sacrificing impact.

Candidate has made itself at home in the post–September 11 environment, trading up from the 1960s fear of the Communist menace to today's much more unnerving arena of terrorism alerts and unilateral invasions.

Though its characters and situations are fictitious, *Candidate*'s world is eerily similar to our own. It's a place where an imminent presidential election will turn on the way the current administration conducts itself militarily, where background news broadcasts talk of bombing raids and problematical electronic voting machines. Conspiracy theories that once might have seemed far-fetched seem all too plausible, and the reach and ambitions of Manchurian Global, a multinational corporation that makes out like a bandit (sound familiar?) on no-bid war contracts, can seem at least as frightening as the Chinese Communists of the bad old days.

One reason *Candidate* is so successful is that director Demme responds strongly to both the pulp and the political aspects of the project. His *Philadelphia*, and even *Beloved*, connected to real-world concerns (as do his Haitian documentaries, including *The Agronomist*), and *The Silence of the Lambs*, winner of multiple Oscars, says all that's necessary about the director's thriller gifts.

Using his usual crack production team of cinematographer Tak Fujimoto, production designer Kristi Zea and editors Carol Littleton and Craig McKay, Demme knows how to best unfold *Candidate*'s complex, multilayered plot, how to first unsettle us and then make things clear. And, unlike many directors who understand tension, he is also adept at the kind of subdued dramatic moments that raise this film considerably above the norm.

Because those moments are important to him, Demme has seen to it that the film was cast especially well—even apart from his three stars. He's put the strongest possible actor's actors, such as Jeffrey Wright and

Vera Farmiga, in smaller but critical parts. He's made excellent use of Jon Voight in his least-mannered performance in memory and given cameos to people from his past, one of them producer Roger Corman. He's even continued a Demme tradition by using (and identifying in the credits) a photograph of his old mentor, now deceased, producer Kenny Utt.

As far as his leads go, Demme has encouraged performances that we might not have expected. This is most true with Denzel Washington, cast as Major Ben Marco of the U.S. Army, introduced as a commanding figure exchanging fire with the enemy during Gulf War combat. It's a moment to savor, because this familiar Washington gradually—and scarily—recedes.

Candidate picks up in the present, with a subdued Marco giving a talk to a Washington-area Boy Scout troop about the Medal of Honor, describing how a sergeant under his command, Raymond Prentiss Shaw (Schreiber), won it in the engagement we've just seen. But it's not only Boy Scouts who've turned out for his talk; former Gulf War comrade Corporal Al Melvin (Wright, brilliant as always) is also waiting at the back of the room.

The corporal does not look well, not well at all. He has these dreams every night, terrible, soul-destroying dreams, that have caused him to twitch and shudder and fill up worn-out notebooks with strange writings and unsettling drawings. Has the major had dreams like that, Corporal Melvin wonders? No, the major firmly replies, he has not.

It turns out, however, that Major Marco is not as together as he seems. His apartment, far from being as tidy as his uniform, is a pack rat's cluttered warren, and he has, in fact, been having those same agonizing dreams. Melvin's appearance further disturbs the major's fragile equilibrium, and he heads to New York to find the former Sergeant Shaw and see whether he's anxious as well.

The well-connected Shaw has morphed into a two-term New York congressman who is better known for being the son of the powerful Senator Eleanor Prentiss Shaw (Streep). A riveting scene introduces the senator: She is persuading party leaders to give the vice presidential nomination for the upcoming election not to the liberal Senator Thomas Jordan (Voight) but to her Medal of Honor–winning son.

This is the role that earned Lansbury an Oscar nomination in the 1962 film, and Streep has her own compelling take on it. Her Senator Shaw starts over the top and a bit foolish, but that is almost a pose, a way to distract the world from just how smart and ruthless she can be. She teases her son, calling him "my plucky idealist" and "Mr. Grumpy," but she is proud of having separated him from the only woman (Farmiga) he's ever loved. And she can, in some of the film's most unsettling scenes, be terribly tender to the boy she's pinned all her hopes on. The heart of *Candidate*, however, is the relationship between Marco and Shaw, old war comrades who share an experience that changed them both and a secret neither fully understands.

Schreiber, a well-regarded actor with a wide range of credits, has never been as compelling; he brings poignancy and dignity to a frighteningly ambivalent character, someone who's simultaneously victim and villain. No one ever steals a movie from Washington, but Schreiber comes closer than anyone could have predicted.

As for Washington, he provides the narrative drive of *Candidate*, but under radically different circumstances than he's used to. His Major Marco, aided by an acquaintance named Rosie (*Beloved*'s fine Kimberly Elise), trudges around New York pulling at the loose threads of his dreams, trying to figure out what they mean, but without the competence and charisma that are usually the actor's trademarks. We sense the major's potential power, but it is often muted. The man himself is on the verge of a perpetual fog, not sure who is a friend, who is a threat, and he exudes a kind of helplessness that is as uncomfortable for audiences as it is for him. It was a risk for Washington to play the role this way, a clear departure not only from his previous parts but also from the way Frank Sinatra handled the original. But those chances taken make the result even more powerfully effective.

In a similar vein, *The Manchurian Candidate* disconcerts as much as it comforts. Traditionally the lure of these films is that once the smoke has cleared a moral balance is restored, the world on film makes reassuring sense even if the world outside does not. *Candidate* does this to a point, but because it's a film for our particularly difficult geopolitical times, it can go only so far. Its ambivalence gets into our heads, making us as troubled as the major, and it's a stronger, more significant film for having the nerve and the skill to do so.

The Mask of Zorro
1998

The Mask of Zorro does not stint on its Zs: There's an Old Zorro (Anthony Hopkins), a Young Zorro (Antonio Banderas), even a Ms. Zorro (Catherine Zeta-Jones). No wonder the villains can be heard to gasp in fear, "It isn't just one man, damn it, it's Zorro!"

Spanish California's very own masked avenger and righter of wrongs is someone with a past: More than fifty features, serials and a television series have been made about him worldwide, and everyone from Douglas Fairbanks and Tyrone Power to George Hamilton, Frank Langella and France's Alain Delon have carved that final initial on all available surfaces.

Reviving such a venerable franchise can be a tricky business, but *The Mask of Zorro* is not a corpse that came C.O.D. A lively, old-fashioned adventure yarn with just a twist of modern attitude, it's the kind of pleasant entertainment that allows the paying customers to have as much fun as the people on the screen.

Much of the attention for this new *Zorro* understandably focuses on the beautiful Zeta-Jones, a spirited and sensual British ingénue whose eyes flash as much as her sword. But she is matched by Hopkins, who brings his distinctive substance and dignity to the proceedings, as well as Banderas, whose casual charm is made for a movie like this.

The Mask of Zorro's unheralded mastermind appears to be director Martin Campbell. Best known for reviving the James Bond franchise with his work on *GoldenEye*, Campbell has an it's-so-old-it's-new knack for getting audiences excited about revered, not to say hoary with age, material. So it matters not that the dazzling swordplay, the stunt leaps, the tricks with horses, were not new when Fairbanks and friends employed them in the 1920s. Campbell throws himself and his cast into the proceedings with so much energy and movement that he carries us along with him.

If *The Mask of Zorro* is not cutting edge, it's also not a film to look to for plausibility. How can Zorro stride through the center of a hot, dusty plaza without a spot of dust on him, appearing for all the world as if he had just stepped out of a dry cleaners? How can he still have the strength of ten men and the agility of Baryshnikov after spending twenty years heavily shackled in a pitiless Spanish prison? You're just not supposed to ask.

The first close encounter with the masked man is in Old California in 1821. A defender of the downtrodden with a rock star's popularity, Zorro, the secret identity of Don Diego de la Vega (Hopkins), is the idol of two young boys and the sworn enemy of the area's snuff-taking Spanish governor Don Rafael Montero (Stuart Wilson), who will stop at nothing, nothing do you hear, to put him away.

After a particularly dashing adventure that photogenically ends with his horse rearing up in front of an enormous setting sun, Don Diego tells his wife and infant daughter that "today is Zorro's last ride." But instead of a quiet retirement, Don Diego endures a family tragedy and ends up imprisoned in all those chains. Twenty years later, the villainous Don Rafael returns to California with an even more nefarious plan, accompanied by Elena (Zeta-Jones), a striking young woman who thinks (though we know better) that she's the evil one's daughter.

Escaped from prison and looking like Ben Franklin with the benefits of a personal trainer, Don Diego is searching for someone to pass his skill and ideals on to. Alejandro Murieta (Banderas) was one of the worshipful young boys of twenty years past, but he lacks the patience for the Zen and the Art of Swordsmanship lessons the older man has in mind. All you have to know about the weapon, he insists, is that "the pointy end goes into the other man." Alejandro, to be sure, needs instruction in this area, as he does about romance, horsemanship and fine manners. And though he's initially overmatched by the film's fine pair of believable villains, Wilson's shrewd Don Rafael and his icy American enabler Captain Harrison Love (Matt Letscher), this man is nothing if not a fast learner.

Written by John Eskow, Ted Elliott & Terry Rossio, *The Mask of Zorro* builds self-deprecating humor into all these situations in a way that amusingly undercuts the heroism. With good chemistry between Banderas and Zeta-Jones, especially in their numerous comic/passionate moments, this is one film that knows what to take seriously and what to leave alone.

Though Zeta-Jones went on to a major career lightning did not strike this franchise twice: the 2005 sequel The Legend of Zorro *was not in this league.*

M:I-2
2000

Except for irredeemably artistic types such as Taiwan's Hou Hsaio Hsien or Iran's Abbas Kiarostami (though even they might have been tempted), star-producer Tom Cruise could have gotten any director in the world to do the sequel to his very successful *Mission: Impossible.* The man asked was John Woo, and the result, now cryptically titled *M:I-2,* lavishly displays the reasons for that choice.

Woo, who parlayed a legendary career as a Hong Kong actionmeister into domestic extravaganzas *Broken Arrow* and *Face/Off*, is a master of movement and chaos. Though they feature cascades of bullets and fists of fury, his films are more about the plasticity of the medium than the pedestrian concepts of blood and violence. A director without limits who respects neither the laws of physics nor those of probability has made some of the most delirious films imaginable.

Once Woo unleashes his bad self and ignites the proceedings here, once the glass shatters, the flames erupt, the gunshots ricochet and the doves fly, all is well with *M:I-2*. One of the film's drawbacks is that it takes a while until that feverish point is reached, but everyone tries hard and mostly successfully to keep us occupied until the killer moments arrive.

Cruise himself, obviously, is one of *M:I-2*'s strongest weapons. Looking a bit shaggier but still appropriately steely eyed in this new incarnation of special agent Ethan Hunt, Cruise is involved in a lot of running and jumping but very little standing still. He takes on stunts ranging from climbing a sheer cliff face in Utah to doing things with a motorcycle that would have intimidated Steve McQueen.

Also demanding attention is the film's Robert Towne plot, a basically simple tale told with so much artful misdirection and disinformation that it takes a bit of time to figure out. You may not understand what's happening from moment to moment, but with Woo setting the pace, you may not have the opportunity to care.

M:I-2 opens with scientist Vladimir Nekhorvich (Rade Sherbedgia) injecting himself with a mysterious substance and sending a Delphic message to agent Hunt that ultimately proves to be the key to the plot: "The search for a hero begins with something that every hero requires, a villain."

Speaking of bad guys, *M:I-2*'s is former agent Sean Ambrose, played by Dougray Scott, so ruthless he is capable of using a cigar cutter to remove the fingertip of one of his own men. Though fans of *Face/Off* may feel that Nicolas Cage's style of florid criminality was better suited to Woo's operatic sensibility, Ambrose's more controlled evil proves to be a good match for Cruise's coolly heroic Hunt.

The link between these two rivals is the oh-so-beautiful and spirited Nyah Nordhoff Hall, puckishly named after the men who wrote the *Mutiny on the Bounty* trilogy and played by Thandie Newton (*Jefferson in Paris*, *Beloved*). A master thief who looks good in designer clothes, Hall is recruited for the operation by Hunt at the insistence of his boss (an unbilled and not particularly energetic Anthony Hopkins), who neglects to say what her job will be.

Turns out that Hall is the former flame of the turncoat Ambrose, and the boss wants her to function as a seductive Trojan horse in the evil one's compound and find out exactly what nefarious plots are hatching behind those surveillance-proof walls. Hunt, who in the interim has fallen for Nyah himself, says that will be difficult. "This is not *Mission: Difficult*, this is *Mission: Impossible*," the top guy dryly notes.

Helping everybody do their jobs in *M:I-2* is a whole lot of gadgetry, so much computer and electronic gear that the film plays at times like a James Bond extravaganza without the smug 1960s overlay. Though agent Luther Stickell (Ving Rhames) returns from the last film, he spends so much time tediously sitting in front of the computer you start to wonder whether he's physically glued to the chair.

Even when *M:I-2* is at its exposition-heavy early stages, Woo's marvelous visual sense is always an asset. Working with cinematographer Jeffrey Kimball, Woo brings a showy flair to the most potentially pedestrian situations. Woo's films, and this one is no exception, are also characterized by an over-the-top emotionalism that amplifies all feelings to mythological status. The power of film to transform and exalt without benefit of rationality is almost a religion to Woo, and another reason why he was the natural go-to guy for this lucrative movie franchise.

The Missing
2003

What's missing, gone, vanished almost (but not quite) without a trace from *The Missing* is the Ron Howard most of America has come to know and love. The master sentimentalist has made a dark, menacing film, a sinewy and disturbing Western with some modern subtexts that goes where no Ron Howard film has gone before.

A change like that doesn't come without expert assistance, and Howard got it from his two stars, Tommy Lee Jones and Cate Blanchett. They play Samuel Jones and Maggie Gilkeson, a savagely estranged father and daughter who've not seen each other for decades but together have to face a life-or-death threat.

The combined intensity of these two performances obliterates objections and raises the stakes in what might otherwise have been a standard Western. It's powerful enough to create its own reality, and whenever *The Missing* threatens to go sentimental around the edges, the fused energy of their cold fury is simply too compelling to allow that to happen. No film will be going soft while they're in the neighborhood— no film would dare.

Jones has made a career out of these implacable roles, most notably in *The Fugitive*, and as he's aged into a face so lined it would scare Botox, he's lost none of his innate aura of menace and danger, the sense that he would as soon kill someone as look at him.

Which makes it all the more thrilling that Blanchett, as gifted an actress as is working today, is his match and more in barely controlled rage. Capable of rising to whatever challenges her screen appearances demand, Blanchett brings a deep and biting anger to her part. Each word she directs at Jones's character is a whip lash intended to cut to the bone, and cut it does.

Those words also come from an unlikely source, Ken Kaufman, whose previous credits include *Space Cowboys* and *Muppets from Space*. He's adapted *The Last Ride*, a novel by Thomas Eidson, that focuses on the kidnapping of Maggie's eldest daughter, Lilly (*Thirteen*'s Evan Rachel Wood), by a band of Apaches and white outlaws who intend to sell her in Mexico to the highest bidder.

There are lapses in *The Missing*, uncertain moments when Howard's touch is not as sure as that of Clint Eastwood, who considered directing the script. But, as it did with his earlier *Ransom*, the theme of child kidnapping seems to have touched a chord in the director and kept false notes to a minimum. It's as if all the black emotions missing from so much of Howard's work have finally found a home here.

Here is the New Mexico Territory, 1885, a place no less godforsaken because such modern inventions as the telegram have made an appearance. Working with talented cinematographer Salvatore Totino, who makes this part of the world look epic, unexpected and forbidding, Howard has visualized the West as an especially pitiless place where bad things routinely happen and to do something stupid is to risk having someone die.

No Western is complete without a bad man, and one of the things that makes *The Missing* both effective and particularly modern is the nature of its villain. He's nameless in the film, though Samuel Jones refers to him by the Spanish *brujo*, and the credits call him Pesh-Chidin, an Apache term that means the same thing: witch.

Today's audiences, aware of alternative forms of spirituality, are potentially receptive to the presence of a Native American shaman, a powerful sorcerer capable of clouding men's minds. Convincingly played by a heavily made up Eric Schweig, the scarred and creepy *brujo*, whose murderous handiwork makes everyone who sees it, audiences included, squirm, is a disturbing, distinctive bad guy who proves to be very much a match for the forces of good. But before any of this can happen, Samuel Jones has to come back into the life of his daughter, who has made a home on a small cattle ranch with her daughters and her ranch hand/boyfriend, played by Aaron Eckhart.

An outcast from the white world who's lived among the Apache for decades and speaks the Chiricahua dialect perfectly (the actor learned it, subtitles translate it), Samuel Jones wants to reconcile with the daughter he abandoned and make peace with the memory of the wife whose death the daughter thinks he caused. Maggie furiously wants nothing to do with him, and lets him know: "What you've done, you can't undo."

But then her daughter is kidnapped, people are killed in horrific ways (don't ask) and the cavalry (led by Val Kilmer) proves ineffective; now Maggie understands that as much as she detests her father, his knowledge of Apache ways makes him her best chance to get Lilly back.

Though this rescue-the-white-girl scenario inevitably echoes John Ford's classic *The Searchers*, it is more interested in the working out of family relationships, and that includes ten-year-old daughter Dot (well played by Jenna Boyd), a mini-termagant who is very much her mother's daughter. In fact, one of the pleasures of this film is to view father, daughter and granddaughter as a set matched in willfulness.

What stays with you most about *The Missing*, finally, is the quality of Blanchett's performance. With her rawboned, angular face that makes her look at home on the land, she experiences every one of the film's variety of emotions right up to the hilt, and the unnerving raw-ness of her feelings combined with the implacability of her resolve will put your heart right in your throat. You can't ask for any more from an actress than that.

Mr. & Mrs. Smith
2005

Marriages, even the happy ones, can sometimes feel like combat zones. But what if a marriage really was a combat zone, with the husband and wife literally trying to kill each other? And what if the spouses were really good at that sort of thing—professionally good?

This is the world of *Mr. & Mrs. Smith*, and if you think that premise sounds farfetched, especially for an action-based romantic comedy, you don't know the half of it. Plot contrivance and major league implausibility are the bread and butter of a film for which the motto might be "Look all you want but don't think too hard." Fortunately, when your stars are Brad Pitt and Angelina Jolie, looking—and listening—will keep you well satisfied.

Yes, this is the film that launched a tidal wave of tabloid coverage when gossips detected the germ of a relationship between the two stars. To see *Mr. & Mrs.* is to understand why everyone cared: It's hard to think of a more compellingly attractive onscreen couple. But Brad and Angelina are not just eye candy. Under Doug Liman's tutelage, they are having it both ways: enjoying themselves and each other while simultaneously having fun with their public images.

Working from a droll script Simon Kinberg wrote at film school as a master's thesis, director Liman does what he did before in *Swingers* and *The Bourne Identity*: bring a pleasantly offbeat and knowing sensibility to genre material.

It's not that *Mr. & Mrs.* doesn't have its problems. For a project that *Entertainment Weekly* reported went through more than a hundred screenplay drafts as well as assorted reshoots, it's not surprising that the film is noticeably slow getting started and could use some trims throughout. But in the end, star charisma and Liman's style win us over and we relax into a sophisticated diversion that is noticeably intended for adults.

Who else but adults would recognize the film's framing device, as John and Jane Smith are introduced facing the camera and reluctantly participating in a marriage therapy session. "We don't have to be here," John grumbles, but as we listen to their answers and observe their private life, it's clear they do.

The pair cute met five (or was it six?) years ago in Bogota, Colombia. Unknown to each other, both were highly skilled lone assassins who on this day were in less danger of being picked up by the police if they hooked up in the hotel bar. Each thinks the other has a square job and both assume that marriage to a civilian will provide convenient cover for their deadly activities.

Unlikely as this scenario is, the next notion we have to buy into is more illogical still: In all those years of marriage, neither one has so much as suspected what the other does for a living, or that huge caches of weaponry are secreted around the house. It would be an impossible concept to sell without the glamour of Pitt and Jolie, which is precisely why they got the jobs.

It takes about an hour for the inevitable to happen: In the middle of their marital crisis, not only do the Smiths discover the nature of their spouses' careers but they end up being assigned to kill each other by the competing organizations they work for. James Bond never had problems like this.

It is at this point that *Mr. & Mrs. Smith* begins to entertain us in earnest by juggling some droll simultaneous happenings, starting with the notion that a series of mishaps and misunderstandings makes it seem to each of the Smiths that the other is actually trying to kill him or her, triggering an understandably lethal reaction.

At the same time, the Smiths are bickering as only married people can, trying, in classic talk-it-out tropes, to save their relationship. Lines such as "Don't go to sleep angry" and "Where there is no trust, there can be no love" acquire an amusing resonance when played out against a backdrop of focused mayhem. As Mr. Smith explains to a third party just before threatening to dismember him: "The missus and I are working through some domestic issues." Aided by Liman, both Pitt and Jolie prove themselves adept at the kind of arch innuendo the script demands. And Liman himself, though he can't resist an excessive hyperaction finale, orchestrates several touches that generate smiles.

There's *Swingers* veteran Vince Vaughn as Mr. Smith's partner Eddie, who replies to a simple greeting with a shambling "Same old, same old; people need killing." There's the film's unexpected use of music—in one particularly adroit case pairing "Express Yourself" with a scene of hand-to-hand combat.

Most of all, what Liman does here is make fun seem like fun. It's a harder thing to accomplish than might be imagined.

Ocean's Eleven
2001

Ocean's Eleven is a champagne bubble of a movie, lively, effervescent and diverting. If it bursts earlier than we'd like—and it does—that takes nothing away from the considerable pleasure it provides along the way.

A suave caper movie that involves George Clooney and Brad Pitt in a scheme to walk away with all the money in Las Vegas, this *Ocean's Eleven* has taken its name, let's-rob-the-casinos concept and general air of insouciance from the dated and frankly tedious 1960 original that starred Frank Sinatra and his celebrated pals. Otherwise this *Ocean's* is very much its own film, with a specific air of hipster bemusement and a particular sense of style. It is also part of what is starting to be director Steven Soderbergh's personal quest to keep the phrase "intelligent popular entertainment" from becoming an oxymoron.

Starting with *Out of Sight* in 1998 and continuing with *Erin Brockovich* and *Traffic*, Soderbergh has revealed a magician's gift for reviving traditional genre materials by treating them with astuteness and respect. He's been especially potent when he has a good script to work with, and he has that here.

Sharply written by Ted Griffin, *Ocean's* does run out of energy before the close, but until then it does everything a caper film should. It's got a clever plot, amusing characters and a fine ear for entertaining, unforced banter. *Ocean's* not only has lines such as "I'm gonna drop you like third period French" and the classic "I owe you from the thing with the guy in the place," it also has the actors who know what to do with them.

Cool may be the hardest thing to portray effectively on the screen, but Clooney and Pitt, impeccably dressed in clothes that wouldn't have the nerve to wrinkle, own the franchise. Clooney plays ringleader Danny Ocean, a scoundrel whose unflappable reply to the standard why-were-you-in-prison question (a tart "I stole things") tells you all you need to know. Newly paroled, he immediately contacts best pal Rusty Ryan (Pitt), currently employed teaching Hollywood heartthrobs to play poker, and unveils a scam to end all scams.

The idea is to break into the vault of the Bellagio in Las Vegas, home to the receipts from three casinos owned by the smart and ruthless Terry Benedict (an on-the-money Andy Garcia). Given a hotel security system rivaling that of a nuclear weapons arsenal, the job would have to have a payoff worthy of its risks: $150 million to be split among the eleven crooks, cons and grifters needed to make it happen. (Sign of the times: In the 1960 film, the take was $11 million from five casinos.)

As in many action films with numbers in their titles (*The Seven Samurai*, *The Magnificent Seven*, *The Dirty Dozen*), one of the best parts of *Ocean's Eleven* is the gathering of the gang, the recruitment of the skilled operatives needed to do the job. Among the most fun to watch are:

- Reuben Tishkoff, the money man, once a major casino player and now, in Elliott Gould's irresistibly excessive performance, a Vegas version of Nero in exile;
- Linus Caldwell (a well-used Matt Damon), a second-generation grifter with the fastest hands in town;
- Saul Bloom (Carl Reiner in good form), a retired gonif who hasn't lost his touch for larcenous impersonation;
- Turk and Virgil Malloy, lunatic brothers who know a lot about cars and even more about arguing, well-played by the mix-and-match combination of Scott Caan and Casey Affleck;
- Yen (Shaobo Qin), a Chinese acrobat for whom agility is everything.

But just as it never goes exactly as planned in a major heist, so a few things about *Ocean's Eleven* are not quite right, most noticeably Julia Roberts in the inevitable cherchez la femme role as Tess Ocean, Danny's estranged wife and Terry Benedict's current girlfriend.

Though it may have made sense in the abstract, having Roberts play this character in a perpetual humorless funk, as happens here, is to badly misjudge what is needed. In truth, the most enjoyable thing about the actress's performance is her droll onscreen credit: "And introducing Julia Roberts as Tess." A good deal of Tess's screen time is in the postheist aftermath, which doesn't help the situation because this is already the film's weakest link. Though *Ocean's Eleven* starts strong, it ends anticlimactic and unresolved, like a runner completely out of energy when the finish line is in sight.

Still, a weak ending doesn't negate the fine work that has come before, and *Ocean's* is especially a success for Soderbergh. Shooting in the real Bellagio (producer Jerry Weintraub is nothing if not connected), the director, who doubled as his own cinematographer (though he didn't take a credit), keeps things visually interesting without being too showy. Working with a well-chosen cast, he shows an instinct for knowing his actors' strengths and how to bring them out. He's constructed an elaborate edifice designed strictly for pleasure. Just like Las Vegas itself.

Definitely not to be confused with its lackluster sequel, Ocean's Twelve.

Primal Fear
1996

Primal Fear makes fools of us and makes us like it. A tight courtroom melodrama that serves up twist after twist like so many baffling knuckle balls, this film handles its suspenseful material with skill and style.

Adapted from a best-selling William Diehl potboiler by Steve Shagan and Ann Biderman, *Primal Fear* follows top Chicago defense attorney Martin Vail through the case of his life, one with enough ups and downs to reduce Perry Mason to tears. Slick and well-crafted, this film builds up a terrific want-to-know even as it informs us that figuring out what's going to happen is not going to be logically possible.

Accomplishing this feat is director Gregory Hoblit, making his theatrical debut after an extensive career in television that included nine Emmys for his involvement in *Hill Street Blues, L.A. Law* and *NYPD Blue.* Lawyers' wiles and the workings of courtrooms are nothing new to him, and he adds a gift for crisp pacing and an attention to quality visible in things like Michael Chapman's cinematography and James Newton Howard's music.

That concern includes Hoblit's way with actors, which extends from offbeat use of familiar faces—John Mahoney, Alfre Woodard, Steven Bauer and Frances McDormand—to getting the kind of polished, spirited performance out of Laura Linney that will surprise those who know her only from her weak last film, *Congo.*

The best choice *Primal Fear* made was casting Richard Gere as Martin Vail, a former prosecutor who is now Chicago's premier defensive specialist, the kind of self-confident, not to say voracious "big-shot attorney" who likes to tell clients: "You've been saving up for a rainy day? It's raining."

Gere's memorable performances, from *An Officer and a Gentleman* through *Pretty Woman*, have always been in roles that saw him as, at least initially, cold, cocky and heartless. As the ruthless, hyperfocused Vail, a lawyer who practically glows with self-satisfaction and malevolent assurance, Gere is at his peak, the active core of Shagan and Biderman's intense scenario.

So it's typical of the man that while most of Chicago is horrified at the gruesome death of a particularly beloved archbishop, hacked to death via seventy-eight stab wounds, Vail sees it as a juicy career opportunity. "A lot of guys are going to want this one," he tells his staff of two (Andre Braugher, Maura Tierney). But we know who's going to get it.

Caught by police fleeing the scene in bloody clothes (and promptly dubbed "the Butcher Boy of St. Mike's" by an unruly press) is the unlikely Aaron Stampler. An awkward, soft-spoken stutterer from a tiny town in Kentucky, Aaron was an altar boy and a choir member who looked on the archbishop as a surrogate father. Prone to blackouts, moments when he "loses time," Aaron swears he's not guilty but can't account for how the gore got on his clothes. Aaron Stampler may sound like a familiar character, but a strong performance turns things around. Making his feature debut is Edward Norton, an actor with a remarkable amount of presence and a gift for tentativeness who turns Aaron into someone baffling and unique.

Aside from his client's goofy personality, Vail faces other courtroom problems. The judge on the case (Woodard) has no patience for his usual shenanigans, and prosecuting attorney Janet Venable (Linney) is both a former colleague and a disaffected former lover. She proves more than Vail's match before the jury, and the noticeable sparks their verbal jousting sets off is one of the film's pleasures.

Most of *Primal Fear* takes place while Stampler's trial is going on and Vail is scrambling to defend him. He searches for Aaron's friends, hires a psychiatrist (McDormand) to look him over and wonders whether a contretemps between the state's attorney (Mahoney) and another of his clients (Bauer) has any bearing on this case.

At first Vail takes his usual hands-off "I don't have to believe you, I don't care" attitude with Aaron Stampler. But gradually, he feels an unfamiliar sense of personal involvement, and that adds another, more human, dimension not only to his actions but to Gere's performance.

Primal Fear doesn't linger as it spins its many webs, which is doubtless the best policy with a film so intricately, and at times unbelievably, plotted. The story is always just a bit ahead of us, which is as it should be, and though it is hard to shake the feeling that the picture outsmarts itself with some of its final twists, what's come before is satisfying enough that it seems beside the point to mind.

Norton has gone on to a considerable career after this powerful debut.

The Score
2001

Nick Wells is Mr. Careful. He hasn't made it to the pinnacle of the safecracking world by being hot-headed or impulsive. The man is smooth, solid, the epitome of professionalism, and *The Score* does so well detailing what Nick hopes will be his last job because it's as prudent, methodical and frankly old school as its protagonist.

A top-drawer heist movie that ratchets up the tension inch by careful inch, *The Score* will remind you of the classic caper films of the past, and that is a good thing. Engrossing and diverting, it shows how simple success can seem if you pay attention to the right things.

That means first of all a more-than-respectable script, credited to four writers (story by Daniel E. Taylor and Kario Salem, script by Salem and Lem Dobbs and Scott Marshall Smith) who thankfully didn't get in each other's way. A high-stakes burglary is at the film's heart, but this is as much a character study as a thriller, so having a trio of exceptional actors, in effect representing three generations of performers, is a powerful plus.

Robert De Niro, the model of onscreen proficiency, plays the phlegmatic Nick, who is enmeshed with Max, his fey older fence, played by Marlon Brando, and Edward Norton's Jack Teller, the young and restless new thief on the block. These actors not only enlivened the script with occasional improvising, they also brought their own particular gifts and styles to the table and inevitably sparked to one another's presence as well.

To make this ensemble work at its best, a director was needed who wasn't afraid to be traditional, restrained, even old-fashioned. Surprisingly, that turned out to be Frank Oz, who started with the *Muppets* and whose career has been devoted to comedy ever since. Who would have guessed that lurking inside the man who lurked inside Yoda and Miss Piggy was a thriller director eager to get out?

The Score opens with De Niro's Nick on the job, breaking into a safe under conditions that show him to be completely composed even in the most stressful of situations. As he makes his way home through a carefully worked out escape route, we see the steeliness that we come to understand characterizes Nick and why he believes that, in his business, "talent means nothing; lasting takes discipline."

Home is Montreal, where Nick runs a successful jazz club as a cover (Mose Allison and Cassandra Wilson make cameo appearances) and maintains a no-strings "I'll see you when I see you" romantic relationship with a sophisticated flight attendant named Diane (Angela Bassett).

It's one of Nick's many rules never to do a job in the city where you live, but his resolve is tested when Max comes to him with the opportunity for one last multimillion-dollar score. Sitting inside the well-fortified, heavily guarded Montreal Customs House just happens to be one of France's national treasures, a rare royal scepter that will fetch a mighty ransom from an eager buyer. It is, says Max, the opportunity of a lifetime.

The showy, flamboyant Max, given to rakish hats and canes, is not the role of a lifetime—it's more in the nature of an amusing cameo—but it is still marvelous to see what Marlon Brando does with it. At this stage of the game, acting seems like something of a well-paid diversion for Brando, but even when, as here, he's taking it only partially seriously (which for him is a lot), he's awfully good at it. Once Brando gets in front of the camera, he can't not act, even if he doesn't feel like it. Even when he's doing nothing, he's doing something, and it's always fascinating to see what that something is.

The third member of this criminal triangle is Norton's Jack, the job's inside man, who pretends to be mentally impaired to get work as the Customs House's assistant janitor. Norton is a gifted young actor, and he's able to give Jack levels and colors he might not otherwise have, turning him into someone who is as earnest and needy of respect as he is cocky, insistent and almost charming.

Naturally, things being as they always are in the world of movie heists, nothing but nothing goes as anticipated for this trio. The plot's wrinkles get wrinkles, wheels spin inside wheels and a variety of ancillary characters (Jamie Harrold's computer nerd is especially memorable) get drawn into the mix.

You might sometimes wish that Oz's direction was a tiny bit jazzier, but in general he handles the material just right. The characters' motivations are plausible, the film's jazzy soundtrack is appropriate, and even the safecracking tools Nick uses are as complex as a heart surgeon's. "If somebody built it, somebody can unbuild it" is one of his maxims, and in the end, *The Score* leaves us wondering why so few people are willing to build films like this one anymore.

The Siege
1998

The Siege is a political thriller with more plausibility—and yes, more thrills—than most. It's a "what-if" movie on a stark subject, terrorist bombings in this country, that tries to serve the two masters of drama and reality and does it for longer than you might predict.

Though *The Siege* loses its way in its final sections, the extent of the film's success is considerable, and largely due to the fine performances of stars Denzel Washington and Annette Bening. It's a pleasure to have actors of this caliber working together on what in many ways is, political relevance aside, strictly cops-and-robbers material.

The Siege also benefits from being well-crafted. The work of director Edward Zwick and his team is crisply professional, and the film's script (credited to Lawrence Wright, Menno Meyjes & Zwick), is notable for its careful plotting and dialogue that avoids missteps for a good while.

Ratcheting up the tension is the unfortunate fact that a scenario involving a wave of terrorist bombings hitting New York City does not seem out of the question. To watch *The Siege* is to be aware to the point of discomfort that the film's fatal explosions could appear as soon as tomorrow morning's paper.

The terrorist organization in *The Siege* is an Arabic one, and though Arab American organizations expressed anger at this, the choice has a basis in fact and was clearly not a knee-jerk decision for a film that's more concerned than most to acknowledge the existence of nonterrorist Arabs and present them in a sympathetic light.

After a prologue introducing the fictitious Sheik Ahmed Ben Talal, thought to be behind the bombings of the U.S. base in Saudi Arabia, *The Siege* switches to Manhattan and the charismatic presence of Anthony "Hub" Hubbard, head of the FBI's antiterrorism task force in New York.

It's difficult to watch Washington giving his usual commanding performance in this, his third film with Zwick (after *Glory* and *Courage Under Fire*), and not harbor the fond wish that our government agents were as capable as this. So intent on his job he at one point doesn't notice that his nose is badly bleeding, Hubbard is adept at pushing his people to track down every lead.

A fake terrorist attack on a city bus introduces Hubbard to the mysterious Elise Kraft (Bening), a woman who is at the very least his match. A CIA agent who knows a great deal about Arab terrorism but is reluctant to share her information, the tough and world-weary Kraft seems ravaged by her experiences, determined not to trust and troubled by that determination.

These collaborators and combatants have numerous scenes together, and the way Bening and Washington handle the script's sharp repartee—toying with an undercurrent of sexual tension but sticking strictly to business—is a textbook case of how strong acting and empathetic direction can elevate all kinds of material.

Helping the mix is veteran Tony Shalhoub, an actor of Lebanese heritage best known for playing other nationalities (such as the uncompromising Italian chef in *Big Night*). Here he plays Hubbard's right hand, Frank Haddad, an Arab American FBI agent who finds his loyalties torn as the situation worsens.

The Siege is at its best when Hubbard's FBI team, with Kraft's uncertain cooperation, works frantically to track down the committed bombers who are working their will on the city. The film's script reveals its credible twists a little at a time, and Zwick, who wisely chooses to indicate carnage rather than actually show it, is expert at making the twists tense and nerve-wracking. The film does run into trouble, however, at its key plot turn regarding the willingness of the president to declare martial law (hence the film's poster art of heavily armed soldiers marching across the Brooklyn Bridge) and place the city under the control of by-the-book General William Devereaux (Bruce Willis).

It's not only that Willis, who's made a career out of playing tongue-in-cheek roles, is miscast and not credible in what ought to be a straight-ahead performance. The rationale for going to martial law feels like a contrivance (other countries with bombing problems haven't done it) and the script not only loses a level of plausibility, it comes on increasingly broad-brush and preachy as it gets closer to its conclusion.

But even at its most unbelievable, *The Siege* has the performances of Washington and Bening to fall back on, and a theme that understands that what's difficult is not choosing right from wrong but "choosing the wrong that's more right." It's the rare thriller that's this immediate and that asks audiences to consider, even fleetingly, the dangers we face as a society.

The World Trade Center bombings nearly three years later made this film eerily prescient and relevant.

Sneakers
1992

From its first words right through to its closing scene, *Sneakers* is programmed for playfulness. A confident caper movie with a most pleasant sense of humor, it goes about its business in such a good-spirited way that it manages to make its familiar *Mission: Impossible* plot seem as good as new.

Those first words ("A Turnip Cures Elvis," which turn out to be an anagram for Universal Pictures) are an early hint of *Sneakers*'s twisting plot, which has a lot to do with cryptography and codes. They're more telling, however, as a precursor of the film's witty, hang-loose tone. Even its title, which refers not to footwear but to a gang of five who literally sneak around looking for information, has the kind of clever, self-deprecating twist that is rarely seen but always welcome.

These light spirits are due both to the ensemble cast, headed by Robert Redford, Sidney Poitier and Dan Aykroyd, and to director Phil Alden Robinson, who cowrote the smart though convoluted script with producers Walter F. Parkes and Lawrence Lasker (who nurtured this project for more than a decade). Robinson, best known for the sleeper hit *Field of Dreams*, managed to get all his big names to relax and enjoy themselves. And when they have fun, it's easy for us to do likewise.

Redford plays Martin Bishop, the titular head of a San Francisco–based organization with a most unusual staff. Crease (Poitier) is a cranky twenty-two-year veteran of the CIA, Mother (Aykroyd) is a paranoid gadget freak who thinks the CIA caused an earthquake in

Nicaragua, Whistler (David Strathairn) is a blind man with an over-powering sense of hearing, and Carl (River Phoenix) is the new young computer whiz on the block.

Well-versed in the latest in technological gimmickry, handy with hidden microphones, surveillance devices and all manner of computer tricks, these renegade masters of derring-do hire themselves out to companies eager to see whether their security systems are really secure. They're paid to break in, in other words, so that nobody else can.

Unbeknown to his partners (but revealed in a title sequence flash-back), Bishop has something of a checkered past. Back in 1969, while he and best friend, Cosmo, were still in college, they engaged in a spate of illegal computer hacking, performing such puckish acts as having the Republican Party make a generous donation to the Black Panthers. The authorities are not amused, and when Cosmo gets caught and goes to prison, Bishop goes permanently on the lam.

Though all this is supposed to be hidden in the dark past, it turns out to be common knowledge to two bullying representatives of the supersecret National Security Agency who want the help of Bishop and his boys. It seems a brilliant cryptographer has created a (no kid-ding) little black box that is set to turn the world of protective gov-ernmental computer codes upside down, and the NSA wants Bishop's sneakers to lift it. Or else.

This "the secret that could change the world" stuff is reminiscent of thrillers without number (the Redford-starring *Three Days of the Condor* comes most obviously to mind), and, despite its labyrinthine twists, *Sneakers* quite frankly has nothing new to add in the plot de-velopment department.

But director Robinson proves surprisingly adept at creating tension at appropriate moments, and also makes good use of the script's clever cheerfulness to move us swiftly through some of its more convoluted turns. Finding the characters so likable, we are happy enough to fol-low them just about anywhere.

Though the key to *Sneakers*'s charm is that the actors (including a glowering Ben Kingsley and an appealing Mary McDonnell as Bishop's on-again, off-again girlfriend) make this kind of ensemble camaraderie look easy, it is in reality much harder to manage than it seems.

Leading the way is Redford, who hasn't let the fact that he's made a career out of this kind of role prevent him from being smoothly at his ease. Poitier's all-business CIA type is a nice foil to both Redford's casual blarney and Aykroyd's comic paranoia. And though Phoenix does what he can with an underwritten role, Strathairn (a John Sayles regular) makes easily the most entertaining impression as the sightless seer who knows all the answers.

It's often unclear exactly what specific talents each of these operatives actually brings to the organization, but it is the easy interaction among them that is *Sneakers*'s strongest point. This is a film that knows enough not to take itself too seriously, and watching the gang wryly adjusting to each other's quirks and foibles is diverting enough to quash any lingering cavils.

Strathairn went on to acclaim as the star of 2005's Good Night, and Good Luck, *but* Sneakers *turned out to be one of the last roles for the gifted Phoenix, who died in 1993 at age twenty-three.*

Speed
1994

Action directing is a put-up-or-shut-up game, a skill that can't be faked or finessed; even a ten-year-old can tell whether you've got it or not. And on the evidence of the invigorating *Speed*, Jan De Bont has definitely got it.

Though this story of a mad bomber versus the LAPD's stalwart SWAT team is De Bont's first film as a director, he has not exactly come out of nowhere. A cinematographer for more than thirty years, De Bont has worked frequently with his fellow Dutchman Paul Verhoeven, and has been behind the camera on such big-time action pictures as *Die Hard*, *The Hunt for Red October*, *Black Rain* and *Lethal Weapon 3*.

De Bont's newness does show in the pro forma nature of some of the characterizations as well as the film's uninspired dialogue and overall derivativeness. But *Speed* moves too fast for any of that to matter much, and where pure action is concerned, De Bont and his team have turned in a visually sophisticated piece of mayhem that makes the implausible plausible and keeps the thrills coming.

Making *Speed* involving is the premise of Graham Yost's script, which does a neat twist off the traditional action premise of coping with machines that are going too fast. Here the problem is not, as might be expected, restraining a runaway bus on a crowded freeway, but just the opposite: making sure it doesn't even come close to slowing down.

For the diabolical madman (a smooth Dennis Hopper) that no action film can exist without has rigged up a deadly explosive device that will detonate if the bus is allowed to go at less than fifty miles an hour. Quite a dilemma for leap-before-you-look hero Jack Traven (Keanu Reeves) and his SWAT team pals.

Centering action on one of Santa Monica's friendly Big Blue Buses and its load of drab citizens (plus Sandra Bullock as the inevitable attractive and available woman) is a proven way to make tension personal to an audience. And screenwriter Yost has helped things out by coming up with a surprising variety of problems that can bedevil an ungainly vehicle attempting to keep up speed.

Working with director of photography Andrzej Bartkowiak, editor John Wright and veteran stunt coordinator Gary Hymes, De Bont has taken great pains to make these crises exciting on the screen. For the bus sequences, for instance, he had ten identical vehicles on call, and routinely used from four to six cameras to film them, moving up to as many as a dozen when recording the most challenging stunts.

None of this work would have mattered, of course, if De Bont didn't also have an understanding of the mechanics of onscreen movement and a fine sense of the visual possibilities that action presents. Nothing *Speed* puts on the screen, from fiery explosions to mayhem on the freeway, hasn't been done many times before, but De Bont and company manage to make it feel fresh and exciting.

De Bont's talent is visible not only in the bus sequences but also in *Speed*'s nervy opening sequences involving a bomb in an elevator, shot in a specially constructed fully operational five-story shaft. It's here that we first meet the forceful Jack Traven, his slightly saner partner Harry Temple (Jeff Daniels) and Captain McMahon (Joe Morton), their no-nonsense superior.

With a brush-cut hairdo and an intense game face that is anything but Buddha-like, Reeves not only gives *Speed*'s strongest performance, his unexpected intensity is crucial in giving the film its drive. Playing Traven with an appropriate edge of take-charge surliness, Reeves is surprisingly believable as a barely human law enforcement machine that even his pals view as "deeply nuts."

Reeves's costars, however, haven't been given very much to work with in the way of dialogue or directorial help in building character. But if no one is going to leave theaters raving about acting and characterization, it will probably matter little. Tension and release is the name of *Speed*'s particular game, and not many films have played it so well.

Terminator 2: Judgment Day
1991

He has built it. And yes, without a doubt, they will come.

He is the gifted James Cameron, the consensus choice as the action director of his generation. What he's built is *Terminator 2: Judgment Day*. More elaborate than the original, but just as shrewdly put together, it cleverly combines the most successful elements of its predecessor with a number of new twists (would you believe a kinder, gentler Terminator?) to produce a *Twilight of the Gods* that takes no prisoners and leaves audiences desperate for mercy.

If you don't count *Piranha II* (and Cameron doesn't), the original 1984 *Terminator* was his first job as a director. It remains an exceptional debut, a lean, laconic action classic that benefited not only from the man's enviable skills as an orchestrator of mayhem but also

from the tale he came up with: a machine that looks like a human being is sent from the future to the present in order to kill one Sarah
Connor, a hapless waitress whose yet unborn son will, in a distant,
postnuclear holocaust time, lead the forces of humanity in a war
against (what else but) power-mad machines.

That assassin is the Terminator, a very tough nut whose modus
operandi is described as follows: "It can't be bargained with. It can't be
reasoned with. It doesn't feel remorse or pity or fear. And it absolutely
will not stop until you are dead." As played by Arnold Schwarzenegger, whose witty *Night of the Living Dead* delivery turned this into the
role of a lifetime, the Terminator became a major antihero, the monster from the id you couldn't help but admire.

Terminator 2 takes up a decade after the first one ends. Sarah Connor (Linda Hamilton, returning from the original) finds herself in a
state mental hospital for insisting that the Terminator was not a fig-
ment of her imagination. Her ten-year-old son, John, the future hope
of the world (newcomer Edward Furlong), is a whiny brat living in
the Valley and making life miserable for his foster parents. He thinks
his mom is, not to put too fine a point on it, a loser.

Though thwarted in the past, the evil machines of the future refuse
to wimp out. They send a new model Terminator, the T-1000 (Robert
Patrick), to finish the job and kill young John. Based on the same
computer-generated technology that Cameron first used in *The Abyss*
(remember the water magically turning into a face?) the T-1000 is a
remarkable piece of special effects sleight-of-hand, a mercury-like
creature able not only to change shapes at will but also to return to its
original form no matter what. Like an old Timex watch, it takes a
licking and keeps on ticking.

Sarah and John are not, however, without resources. A now-
outmoded but still canny T-800 model (Schwarzenegger) is reprogrammed to look kindly on humans and sent back to give them a
hand. Adding to the T-800's difficulties, however, young John suddenly develops a humanitarian streak and insists that his Terminator
not kill anyone when a good maiming will do just as nicely. Watching

Schwarzenegger's Terminator cope with these new ethical guidelines is one of this sequel's more delicious conceits.

Despite these new wrinkles, Terminator 2 does not so much start slowly (for Cameron likes to let you know whose film you're in as soon as possible) as derivatively. Some of the film's opening sequences, such as the way the T-800 goes about getting clothes and wheels, feel like more elaborate but not necessarily more involving versions of scenes from the first film. Even in action films, bigger is not necessarily better.

But Terminator 2, like its namesake, is nothing if not determined, and we are soon won over. For one thing, though Edward Furlong is more irritating as John Connor than he really needs to be, that is more than made up for by the other principals. Schwarzenegger, for one, reembraces this role like a long-lost relative—no one can say "It must be destroyed" quite the way he can—and Hamilton brings a level of physical intensity to her new model, pumped-up paranoid Sarah Connor that even devotees of the first film will find pleasantly surprising.

As for the script, Cameron and cowriter William Wisher have done more than make sure that Terminator 2 is well-stocked with the kind of wised-up, shoot-from-the-hip wit that characterized the first film. Sensing that a series of Terminator vs. Terminator chases would soon become boring no matter how excellent the effects, they sensibly opted to take the middle of the film down a different, more intriguing road, one involving a computer scientist (a very fine appearance by Joe Morton) who is investigating the relics of the first Terminator.

Most of all, what makes Terminator 2 come alive in a major way is Cameron's intuitive understanding of the mechanics and psychology of action films. It's not so much that his virtuoso stunts break an ungodly amount of glass (which they do) as that he packs an astounding ferocity into his sequences. And he manages to do it without turning our stomachs. This is one director who really knows how to direct.

Equally at home in small-scale skirmishes like one-on-one chases down narrow corridors and complex, bravura effects involving tottering helicopters, exploding buildings and as many as five different special effects houses, Cameron flamboyantly underlines, for those who may have forgotten, why the pure adrenaline rush of motion is something motion pictures can't live without for very long.

Terminator 3: Rise of the Machines
2003

"I am an obsolete design," Arnold Schwarzenegger's T-101 says with as much melancholy as a machine can muster, but hearing the line spoken in *Terminator 3* makes you wonder whether the actor had himself in mind as much as his character.

For as a fifty-five-year-old action hero whose most recent films include such inert efforts as *End of Days, The 6th Day* and *Collateral Damage*, Schwarzenegger might well be considering whether he's being similarly frozen out by a film industry that assumes his best fighting days are behind him.

But, like that resilient mechanism, Schwarzenegger still has enough moxie in him for at least one last hurrah before possibly heeding the siren song of public service. *Terminator 3: Rise of the Machines* and its story of the 101's battle to stay competitive with the newest model assassin, the sexy T-X (Kristanna Loken), fills that bill quite nicely.

An expertly paced and efficient sci-fi thrill machine, *T3* effectively marries impressive action sequences with persuasive storytelling and its star's uniquely appealing style of "No" drama—as in no reaction, no expression, no emotion of any kind.

Though *T3* would not have been made without Schwarzenegger's participation, it would not have succeeded without the ability of its lesser-known director, Jonathan Mostow. His name lacks the marquee value of that of James Cameron, who ably directed both predecessors, but Mostow's skillful work in his own previous features, *Breakdown* and *U-571*, made him a shrewd choice here.

In those films as well as this, Mostow shows a gift for doing action correctly by not dumbing things down and by emphasizing the underlying reality of even far-fetched situations. And, unlike directors who come to action from music videos and commercials, he understands the necessity of connecting mayhem to human storytelling.

In *T3*, Mostow has in effect made a big little movie, bringing the spareness and pacing of old-fashioned B-pictures to an elephantine $175 million project that has five producers and four executive producers. Unlike the original *Terminator* or the first *Matrix*, this film does not break any new ground stylistically or thematically, but it also doesn't have a big head and thus avoids falling victim to the pretension that hampered the *Matrix* sequels.

Also, again paralleling B-movies, Mostow and screenwriters John Brancato and Michael Ferris (working from a story credited to them and Tedi Sarafian) have given *T3* an unexpected level of darkness. An intriguing sense of malaise and dread hangs over this film, as though the creative team had thought through the implications of the original *Terminator* narrative and realized they are not necessarily happy ones.

If anyone in the audience doesn't know that story, *T3* smartly recaps it in the film's opening voice-over, in which twenty-something John Connor relates that mechanical killers from the future, terminators, have twice tried to murder him because he is fated to grow into a commander who will lead remnants of the human race to victory in a war with a deadly machine complex called Skynet.

Instead of being ecstatic at the prospect of all this glory, Connor, ever the reluctant champion, has opted to hide instead. Since he knows that something awful—the destruction of almost all humanity in a nuclear attack called Judgment Day—has to happen before he can become a hero, he "feels the weight of the future bearing down" on him.

One of the many shrewd moves *T3* has made is casting Nick Stahl, Marisa Tomei's lover in *In the Bedroom*, as Connor. Stahl is especially good at conveying the lost, haunted, fearful side of this young man. Connor should feel safe after defeating the machines in the previous film (when he was played by Edward Furlong), but he doesn't, instead choosing to live off the grid, without address or phone number, so the machines can't find him.

As Connor surmises, Judgment Day turns out not to have been stopped but merely postponed, and the machines have sent T-X to kill not only him but also his future lieutenants, who include—though neither he nor she is initially aware of it—old childhood friend Kate Brewster (Claire Danes).

Convincingly played (no small task) by Loken as the kind of glacial blond who would have given Alfred Hitchcock fits, T-X comes factory-equipped with quite a range of nifty powers. This forbidding Terminatrix/dominatrix can change shape at will and telepathically makes other machines, including cars and trucks, do her bidding.

T-101, officially a replica of *T2*'s cyborg, ought to be worried, and in fact might be if machines could fret. But as brought to artificial life by Schwarzenegger in the role he was born to play, this old-style Terminator, reprogrammed by the resistance to help Connor survive, is more stoic than the Stoics, and a lot more physical.

Though Schwarzenegger was a given, casting directors Randi Hiller and Sarah Halley Finn saw to it that the rest of the ensemble was equally appropriate. The empathetic Danes was a good choice for Kate, a thankless role that is especially hard to make palatable because, apparently not having seen either of the first two films, this woman spends half the movie in whiny hysteria because she has no idea what is going on. *T3* manages to find some time for humor, engaging in bits of business such as T-101's search for the perfect sunglasses. A film like this, however, lives and dies by its action and its stunts, and—as put together by Mostow, stunt coordinator Simon Crane and cinematographer Don Burgess—*T3* has at least one classic.

That impressive sequence comes relatively early on, as T-X commandeers an enormous 100-ton Champion crane and uses it and some police cars to chase down the good guys, with the T-101 hanging on and trying to gum up the works. Snappily edited by Neil Travis and Nicolas de Toth, the chase features a bravura slamming of the crane arm into a collapsing glass building that was shot by fourteen cameras because it wasn't going to happen again.

Impressive as all that is, *T3*'s greatest accomplishment may be the simple ability to make us worry about its characters, the way it allows us to feel that the people being chased are in actual danger. Not even $175 million ensures that that will happen. In fact, it sometimes ensures just the opposite.

Schwarzenegger found another role of a lifetime when he became governor of California. Thus pass the glories of the world.

Three Kings
1999

You could argue it's a pity the three-hunks-looking-heroic poster for *Three Kings* looks so conventional, because this Gulf War scam gone awry adventure extravaganza is anything but. You could say that, but you'd be wrong. Or would you?

Actually, the truth is that like many of the best efforts coming out of the big studios, the ambitious *Three Kings* is Hollywood with a twist; it demonstrates how far a film can stray from business as usual and still deliver old-fashioned satisfactions. Unexpected in its wicked humor, its empathy for the defeated and its political concerns, this is writer-director David O. Russell's nervy attempt to reinvent the war movie and a further step in the evolution of an audacious and entertaining filmmaker.

Just as Russell's first film, the modest, Oedipal-themed *Spanking the Monkey,* gave no hint of what he'd accomplish with the effervescent, hugely comic *Flirting with Disaster,* so *Disaster* doesn't really prepare us for the scope of *Kings.* Traditional in its conclusions, anything but along the way, this film gives its protagonists and its audience considerably more than anyone anticipated.

Three Kings begins as the 1991 U.S. war against Saddam Hussein's Iraq is ending. Its opening line of dialogue—a question by Army

Sergeant Troy Barlow (Mark Wahlberg), plaintively wondering, with an Iraqi soldier in his sights, "Are we shooting people or what?"—perfectly encapsulates the bizarre uncertainty of a military action that plays at first like an extended fraternity party with automatic weapons thrown into the mix.

It's Barlow, assisted by worshipful hillbilly high school dropout Private Conrad Vig (Spike Jonze), who discovers a key document hidden in the posterior of a captured soldier and thereafter known, via the film's scabrous sense of humor, as "the Iraqi ass map." On it are the directions to some of Saddam's secret bunkers, where all manner of spoils from the ill-starred invasion of Kuwait are likely hidden.

Also finding out about the map are God-fearing Staff Sergeant Chief Elgin (Ice Cube) and world-weary Special Forces Major Archie Gates (George Clooney), who thinks the document is the key to locating millions in gold bullion Saddam removed from Kuwait. "Bullion? You mean like those little cubes you make soup from?" Vig wonders. No, private, not like those.

Teaming up to raid the bunkers and get rich quick, these cynical, self-involved and opportunistic individuals initially come off as the usual amoral heroes for the modern age. As they head off in a Hum-Vee with Homer Simpson plastered on the front grill and explosive-filled footballs in the rear, they, and we, can be forgiven for thinking that this is going to be a tough-guy joy ride, a quintessentially macho adventure yarn.

But writer-director Russell (who spent eighteen months researching and writing the script, with story credited to John Ridley), has no intention of letting us off that easy. Yes, we're meant to enjoy the excitement, but not to the exclusion of knowing the cost, not to mention a whole lot of other things Russell has on his mind.

For the first thing that happens to the guys is a collision with the Iraqi civilian population and the gradual realization that internecine warfare is going on between those who naïvely heeded the U.S. call to rise up against Saddam and brutal government forces who are taking advantage of America's abrupt avoidance of all things Iraqi.

This chaotic war within a war, an irrational free-for-all where tankers filled with milk are treated as lethal weapons, is vividly captured by the high-energy, frenetic visual style used by Russell and cinematographer Newton Thomas Sigel. Brief, oddball sequences take us inside the human body to show exactly the kind of damage a bullet inflicts, and Sigel even utilizes three different film stocks to convey a variety of emotional states, including a grainy, disorienting use of Ektachrome, a film usually found in tourists' cameras.

Surviving from *Flirting with Disaster* is Russell's trademark sense of humor, his feeling for the absurdly comic in the most potentially horrifying situations. Who else would put a glimpse of the Rodney King beating on Iraqi television, or be able to fashion an unlikely running joke about whether it's Lexus or Infiniti that offers a convertible model.

Also intact is Russell's gift for eccentric characters, such as Private Vig, an excellent first acting job for video director Jonze. Minor players, among them Walter (Jamie Kennedy), a soldier who wears night-vision goggles during the day, and television newswoman Adriana Cruz (Christiane Amanpour look-alike Nora Dunn), are treated with as much care as audience surrogates Barlow and Elgin. Especially effective is Clooney, who perfectly conveys the combination of capability, authority and a touch of larceny the film insists on.

Russell is also someone who enjoys being provocative, a trait that comes out in the disquieting character of Iraqi Captain Sa'id (Said Taghmaoui), a sympathetic villain whose employment of torture as a means of political education is daring and effective.

Though the film's title nominally derives from the biblical three kings who followed the star to Bethlehem, it echoes, intentionally or not, the names of other pertinent films. There's *The Man Who Would Be King*, also about Westerners who thought they could get rich off native peoples, and John Ford's *Three Godfathers*, about tough guys who have a change of heart in the desert. Off-and-on cynical and sentimental, Russell's darkly comic tale shows how much can be done with familiar material when you're burning to do things differently and have the gifts to pull that off.

The more recent Iraqi War makes Three Kings *an especially provocative experience. Costar Jonze went on to direct* Being John Malkovich *and* Adaptation.

Training Day
2001

A great performance makes its own rules. It can allow a director to look better than he is, transform and heighten a script in ways even the writer may not have anticipated, add strength and balance to a costar's work. In these ways and more, Denzel Washington's exceptional acting elevates *Training Day* to a place it wouldn't otherwise occupy.

Washington is an actor who seems to be always pushing himself to go beyond where he's been before. And even the edge he displayed in *The Hurricane* isn't preparation for what he does with the slashing, streetwise abrasiveness of LAPD Detective Sergeant Alonzo Harris.

The head of his own undercover narcotics unit, Harris is a fearless, ostentatious law unto himself. Wearing gold chains and black leather and driving a customized 1978 Monte Carlo low rider that doubles as his office, Harris uses a piercing stare and charisma you can taste to intimidate everyone in his path, especially rookie cop Jake Hoyt (Ethan Hawke). It's a driving, galvanic piece of acting that Washington seems to relish at least in part because he's fully aware how much of a departure it is.

Equally surprising is how Washington's performance spurs on his key collaborators, who, at least on paper, do not look all that promising:

- Director Antoine Fuqua, a veteran maker of commercials and music videos with an eye for flash, didn't give any indication in previous features such as *The Replacement Killers* and *Bait*

that he'd recognize, let alone know what to do with, a fully
realized piece of acting.

- Costar Hawke has worked consistently since his career-making
performance in 1989's *Dead Poet's Society*, but much of what
he's done has had the indifferent impact of films such as *Great
Expectations*, *The Newton Boys* and *Snow Falling on Cedars*.
- Screenwriter David Ayer's previously produced work, the submarine drama *U-571* and the street racing *The Fast and the
Furious*, showed a gift for keeping things moving rather than
the creation of character-intensive dialogue.

Yet though you might not anticipate it, each of these had something
to bring to the table that raised the possibility of better work. Fuqua,
for instance, had the ability to create a Los Angeles street ambience
infused with an essential wall-to-wall uneasiness. It turned out that
Hawke, playing a stubborn idealist, could hold his own against Washington. Also, he could be believable as the in-over-his head audience
surrogate, a capable but inexperienced cop who could handle most
things but wasn't prepared for the detective sergeant. And Ayer, who
in part grew up in South-Central and was fascinated by the cop-
criminal dynamic, brought a real-world sense of how police can cross
the line that preceded the LAPD Rampart scandal by several years.

Washington, too, had something special to contribute aside from
his great talent. He could, and shrewdly does, play off the kind of decent characters he's always been associated with. So though it's apparent almost from the first moment that this is a policeman who
bends the law, we cut him slack because the good-guy voice we're familiar with from Washington's previous roles make his explanations
as plausible for us as they are for Jake Hoyt, who knows that Harris is
a productive, thirteen-year veteran whose efforts have led to 15,000
man-years in sentences.

Training Day (set entirely in a twenty-four-hour period) opens at
5:00 A.M. with Hoyt, married and a new father, up and looking worried.
He's asked for a tryout for Harris's unit because it's a path to promotion

and higher pay, but he's not sure what he's in for. All he knows is that he's got twenty-four hours, "today and only today" in Harris's words, to show his superior he's worth being on the team. He doesn't know it, but his world is about to be turned first inside-out and then upside-down.

From the first moment they meet in a small coffee shop, his superior's forceful irascibility all but leaves Hoyt gasping for breath. Harris stops his car in the middle of an intersection if he feels like it, rousts people just to keep in shape, plays with everyone's mind just for the fun of it. Even relaxing and visiting old friend Roger (Scott Glenn), a retired LAPD veteran, the man is always playing the angles.

Yet it's key to this role, and something Washington expertly conveys, that Harris absolutely believes himself to be one of the good guys and is intent on convincing his young charge to feel the same. "To protect the sheep," he tells him, "you got to catch a wolf. It takes a wolf to catch a wolf." Do you, the film in part asks, have to be this kind of a vigilante to survive as a cop in the city? Is Harris simply a different kind of good guy than the ones we are used to? Is he fooling himself, fooling us, or both?

As *Training Day* moves toward an answer, it's got some unexpected strengths, at least initially. Ayer has put together a twisty plot that shrewdly changes direction, one of the rare thrillers it's difficult to stay ahead of. And smaller roles such as Glenn as the ex-cop, Snoop Dogg as an unsavory street pusher and singer Macy Gray as a drug dealer's wife with an indescribable voice, are all smartly done.

Unfortunately, *Training Day* can't sustain its momentum all the way to the close. The film is noticeably violent and its enthusiastic demonizing of "the hood," its well-executed intention of making crime-ridden neighborhoods seem as ugly and as unpleasant as possible, gets a little wearing and leads to a savage and largely implausible ending. But even though *Training Day* doesn't resolve itself as well as it deserves and ends strictly cops-and-robbers style, it's given us some great acting and something to ponder. Not every cop show can lay claim to that.

Training Day *won Washington the "Best Actor" Oscar.*

Part Two
COMEDY

Introduction

Given how many comedies Hollywood makes, it's regrettable but not particularly surprising that there are not more of them in this section. Unless you add in animation, which is a strong enough genre to merit a grouping of its own, critically successful comedies are the rarest birds in the studio aviary.

That's not surprising because comedy is one of the genres—horror is another—where younger-than-twenty-five interest and willingness to spend are so strong that younger-than-twenty-five taste is catered to.

It is, of course, quite possible to make a film intended for that demographic that amuses all age groups, witness *American Pie*, *Clueless*, *School of Rock* and *Spy Kids*. But comedies that take place outside of high school and don't depend on lowest-common-denominator laughs are definitely to be cherished. As the saying goes, dying is easy, comedy is hard.

This section also shows that when gifted comic actors are at the top of their games they can make even the unlikeliest material wildly funny. Possibly more than any other genre, comedy couldn't exist without its performers. Without such actors as Jim Carrey, Hugh Grant, Eddie Murphy, Jack Black, Ben Stiller, Whoopi Goldberg, Cameron Diaz, Will Ferrell and Will Smith there'd be a whole lot less to laugh at than there already is.

American Pie
1999

American Pie is the darndest thing. Both warmhearted and foulmouthed, this unlooked-for hybrid of *South Park* and Andy Hardy uses its surface crudeness as sucker bait to entice teenage audiences into the tent to see a movie that is as sweet and sincere at heart as anything Mickey Rooney and Judy Garland ever experienced.

As a card-carrying contemporary youth comedy, *American Pie* does have its gross-out credentials in what you might call apple pie order. Front and center are jokes about voyeurism, diarrhea, premature ejaculation, the drinking of beer with a semen chaser and, in the film's signature moment, masturbation with one of those homemade pies.

It all sounds as vulgar as the ever-tolerant Motion Picture Association of America allows, but to see *American Pie* is to know that all this foolishness is only window-dressing for a film that, at its core, is surprisingly innocent and good-natured and that even finds the time to promote decent values. If America's teenagers have a biological need to sneak into crass R-rated movies, and apparently they do, this is the one parents not only can feel safest about but might even enjoy themselves.

American Pie is the feature debut for screenwriter Adam Herz, who apparently used his own not-that-distant school years at Michigan's East Grand Rapids High as inspiration. Paul and Chris Weitz, the director and coproducer, respectively, collaborated on the writing of both *Antz* and *Madeline*, and should the nuns in the latter film need a stretcher after exposure to some of the humor here, they'd find a lot to like as well.

For one thing, this has got to be one of the least mean-spirited of recent American comedies. Cast from top to bottom with extraordinarily likable young actors whom we instinctively want to be happy, *American Pie* also benefits from screenwriter Herz's clever plotting and his sense of what is due to each character, even the most hostile and profane.

More than that, *American Pie* is unusual in its ability to mix bodily functions humor with a sincere and unlooked-for sense of decency. Though its characters obsess endlessly about sex, even to the point of wondering whether Ariel in *Little Mermaid* would be an appropriate partner, the film finally comes down emphatically in favor of treating people with consideration and acting from the heart as the keys to happiness.

American Pie opens with the sounds of a woman moaning in sexual ecstasy in a teenager's room, but it's not a real woman, it's a scrambled broadcast on an adult channel, which is as close to actual sexual experience as Jim (Jason Biggs) and his friends have had, endless talk and fantasizing notwithstanding.

Kevin (Thomas Ian Nicholas) does have a steady girlfriend, the beautiful Vicky (Tara Reid), but they've yet to find the perfect moment to go all the way. Totally without female companionship are Chris "Oz" Ostreicher (*Election*'s marvelous Chris Klein), who devotes his life to lacrosse, and the dry, intellectual Finch (Eddie Kay Thomas), who enjoys using Latin to make jokes about the dog eating his homework.

Clustering around this core group are other archetypal high school characters. On the hip side are the crude party animal Stifler (Seann W. Scott), who calls his house "Stifler's Palace of Love," and the wise, sexually experienced Jessica (Natasha Lyonne of *Slums of Beverly Hills*). Further down the pecking order are braces-wearing Sherman (Chris Owens), a.k.a. "the Sherminator, a sophisticated sex robot sent back through time," and Michelle (a delightful Alyson Hannigan), a flute player who thinks of nothing but band, band, band.

Fearful of, God forbid, graduating high school as virgins, Jim, Kevin, Oz and Finch make the pact that drives *American Pie*'s plot: They will motivate and support one another so that, by prom night, exactly three weeks away, they will no longer be sexual novices. "We will become," Kevin proclaims in a mock-passionate speech, "masters of our sexual destiny."

This vow, not surprisingly, becomes the basis for numerous moments of embarrassment and mortification; if there is a wrong or awkward thing to be said or done, one of these guys will say or do it. The most intriguing scenarios involve Oz, who meets the beautiful Heather (Mena Suvari) when he expands his sensitive side and tries out for jazz chorus, and woebegone Jim, who endures a father (Eugene Levy) whose attempts to help are tone-deaf, and what he fears is an unattainable crush on a stunning Czech exchange student, Nadia (Shannon Elizabeth).

Though wincing at what its characters go through is the main source of *American Pie*'s laughs, the film manages to treat almost everyone with respect, even, for the most part, the women, which rarely happens in films like this. Naturally, everything comes down to a postprom party at Stifler's mom's (Jennifer Coolidge) lakeside vacation home, where the typically wacky plot turns culminate in the kind of unexpected good feelings that characterize this most surprising of teenage films.

Regrettably, none of this successful film's numerous sequels came close to American Pie's engaging tone.

As Good As It Gets
1997

Before computer-generated images, before blue screens and the optical printer, even before stop-motion animation, there existed the most special effect of all, the power of the written word. James L. Brooks is royalty in this nondigital domain, and in *As Good As It Gets*, his mastery of the nuances of language and emotion has turned the most unlikely material into the best and funniest of romantic comedies.

Calling this film's scenario unlikely is being kind. Even for a writer-director such as Brooks (a multiple Oscar winner for *Terms of Endearment* and nominee for *Broadcast News*) it's difficult to make a story line about a cute dog, a gay artist, an earthy waitress and an author who is certifiably mentally ill sound coherent, let alone appealing. Stars Jack Nicholson and Helen Hunt help, of course, but can they do enough?

In fact, it's a mark of how magically written, directed and acted *As Good As It Gets* is that we end up loving this film despite knowing how haphazard, scattershot and almost indefinable its charm is. Like its troubled characters, convinced to make the best of things despite being perennially on the edge, and at least a little bit crazy, *As Good* ultimately knows how to make moving, amusing, quintessentially human connections.

At home with mania and delighted to be pushing against conventional perceptions of the boundaries of humor and romance, Brooks and coscreenwriter Mark Andrus (working from Andrus's original story) have come up with very choice dialogue indeed. Ranging from killer oneliners (a crack about HMOs invariably brings down the house) to wise and evocative arias about love and relationships, these words bind us to their characters with the force of contract law.

Character is, once again, too mild a word for the personality of Jack Nicholson's Melvin Udall. Having written sixty-two top-selling romance novels, he may be a productive member of society, but he can stand no one in it and no one can stand him. Homophobic, racist, anti-Semitic and all-around misanthropic, Melvin is a sarcastic, sadistic terror whose idea of a good turn is tossing a neighbor's pesky insect dog down the garbage chute of their Manhattan apartment house.

That dog, given name Verdell, belongs to Simon Nye (Greg Kinnear), a gay artist who lives on the same floor as Melvin. Like everyone else, Simon is strafed by Melvin's acid tongue: "Do you like to be interrupted," the writer says with a snarl in one of his milder sallies, "when you're dancing around in your little garden?" Fortunately, Simon has an art dealer friend named Frank Sachs (Cuba Gooding Jr.) who is able to keep Melvin more or less in line.

Melvin is more than a true bastard, he's in thrall to an obsessive-compulsive disorder. Unwilling to be touched or to step on cracks in the sidewalk, addicted to bars of Neutrogena soap he throws away after just one use, insistent on bringing wrapped plastic utensils with him on trips to restaurants, Melvin is as much a prisoner of his routines as the Man in the Iron Mask.

The only person Melvin can tolerate turns out to be Carol Connelly (Hunt), a waitress at the neighborhood restaurant where he has his daily breakfast. Still living with her mother (Shirley Knight) in Brooklyn, Carol is unaffected and unafraid, but her life has its manias as well. She's furiously concerned about and overprotective of her seven-year-old son, Spencer (Jesse James), who suffers from pervasive allergies that unhinge his life.

To Melvin, Simon and Carol, three people who barely tolerate one another, crises come calling. An unexpected altercation puts Simon in the hospital, and someone has to be found to take care of Verdell. And Carol, increasingly distraught about her son's health, takes what may be a permanent leave of absence from her job. Both these situations put pressure on Melvin to do the unheard of and reconnect with the human race, and the unexpected repercussions of what he does do are the core of *As Good As It Gets*.

To see Nicholson, who frequently gives the appearance of coasting through his roles, working as hard as he does here is a wonderful thing. Discarding almost all his familiar mannerisms, the actor takes more care than usual with this role, maintaining the mastery of bravura humor and timing that leads to big laughs while allowing his character to be honest and vulnerable for the first time in years. As Melvin struggles, ever so tentatively and delicately, with the possibility of being a better person, we are grateful for the synergy between actor and director that allowed it to happen so truthfully.

As all-stops-out as Nicholson is, *As Good As It Gets* wouldn't succeed without its excellent costars, especially Hunt. Best known for her starring role in television's *Mad About You*, she has done excellent work in such underseen films as *The Waterdance* and *Kiss of Death*. There's a newly visible maturity and a feisty stability to her characterization of Carol that works beautifully with Nicholson's swooping highs and lows.

Though Gooding reaffirms the positive impression he made in *Jerry Maguire*, that Kinnear does everything the part calls for is a surprise after his *Sabrina* debut. Also unexpected is the presence of several other directors—Harold Ramis, Lawrence Kasdan and Todd Solondz—in cameo roles. Maybe it's them the closing credits are referring to with this line: "The actors used in this film were in no way mistreated."

Watching these people warily circle one another, trying to decide whether the chance to form closer attachments is worth the risk of pain, it's impossible not to be struck again and again by Brooks's nonpareil ability to create humor out of catastrophe. Though his obsessive characters invariably worry, as Melvin asks at one point, "What if this is as good as it gets?" it's good to know their creator, maybe even against his better judgment, believes in the existence of something more.

Hunt and Nicholson won Oscars for their performances.

Bandits
2001

"Is this a joke?" asks a disbelieving hostage.

"No, ma'am," comes the reply. "This is a bank robbery."

Turns out they're both right.

An amusing tale of larceny triumphant, *Bandits* is an entertainment with a rogue's imagination. The most surprising thing about this criminal history of the celebrated Sleepover Bandits, directed by Barry Levinson with his usual gift for the humanity in the human comedy, is that it manages to be surprising at all.

That's because Harley Peyton's droll script either makes references to or is reminiscent of so many movies—*It Happened One Night*, *Bonnie and Clyde*, *Jules and Jim*, *The Odd Couple*, *The Ransom of Red Chief* all come to mind—it's not difficult to figure out exactly where *Bandits* is going well before its casual, leisurely pace gets us there.

Yet this quirky heist comedy manages to hold our interest even through its slower, more self-indulgent moments not just because of the writing and directing but also because of the acting, which features familiar performers (Bruce Willis, Billy Bob Thornton, Cate Blanchett) in diverting variations of what they usually do.

It's Thornton who plays most against type as Terry Collins, a quite unlikely bank robber. A nervous, neurotic hypochondriac prone to all manner of fanciful ailments and allergies (including one to antique furniture), he's introduced complaining to best friend and fellow prisoner Joe Blake (Willis) that the warden has banned the sale of that underappreciated wonder drug, fresh garlic.

Impulsive, charismatic, a prime candidate for anger management classes, the violence-prone Blake is admittedly not much of a stretch for Willis. But something has induced him to take this character more seriously, to bring more focus to the part. That something might possibly be Blanchett as Kate Wheeler, the disaffected housewife who threatens to come between the boys. One of the most consistently convincing of actresses, Blanchett has chameleon-like abilities that can't help but raise a film's level by creating a challenge everyone has to rise to or look second rate.

Kate isn't in the picture when the boys make their spur-of-the-moment escape from a prison in Oregon. They hook up with Harvey J. Pollard (Troy Garity), Joe's pea-brained cousin, a would-be stunt-man whose name might be a tribute to actor Michael J. Pollard, who played the feeble sidekick in *Bonnie and Clyde*.

As they later tell Darren Head (Bobby Slayton), host of television's *Criminals at Large*, an *America's Most Wanted* clone, they decide the best way to rob banks is to spend the night before the heist with the manager and then accompany him or her into the establishment early the next morning.

Joe and Terry might have continued unencumbered on their bumbling, picaresque way, robbing banks down the Oregon coast and into California and putting away money for a "tuxedos-and-margaritas" resort they want to start in Mexico, had they not run into Kate.

A flame-haired trophy wife at the end of her tether, Kate is a walking nervous breakdown, a deeply unhappy woman who is completely unfazed by her new companions. "Desperate?" she says mockingly when they try to scare her by using that description about themselves. "You don't know the meaning of the word."

By turns wistful and feisty, Kate upsets the strange balance between Joe and Terry, to quite funny effect. A would-be singer fixated on Bonnie Tyler's version of "Total Eclipse of the Heart," she's a minx who has an unsettling effect on both men. Her ability to make her confusion as well as her choices believable is the key component in the success *Bandits* has, at least up to its rather pro forma conclusion.

Several other factors figure into the equation, starting with the film's visual variety (it was shot by Dante Spinotti) and the good use it makes of nearly sixty locations in Oregon and California.

Casting director Ellen Chenoweth has seen to it that the smallest roles employ the right kind of eccentric actors, and costume designer

Gloria Gresham has gotten a surprising amount of fun out of dressing everyone, putting special efforts into the series of increasingly ridiculous disguises the boys wear.

Director Levinson has kept his hand in everything, and it's given *Bandits* a sense of balance none of its characters can even aspire to, let alone achieve.

Bowfinger
1999

People bring out the best in Eddie Murphy: the more of them he plays on the screen, the funnier he becomes.

Murphy doesn't turn into an entire family in *Bowfinger* as he did in *The Nutty Professor*, but he is able, with the help of writer and costar Steve Martin, to create two completely different characters whose cumulative comic impact is delicious. It was Martin who came up with the idea for this likable farce, directed by Frank Oz, which deals with low-rent dreamers on the fringes of the movie business determined to make it big in Hollywood.

Martin has the right touch for Bobby Bowfinger, the alpha and omega of Bowfinger International Pictures, a company so threadbare that even schlockmeister Ed Wood would've looked down on it. But it's Murphy who has the showier and funnier part, or parts, and he makes the most of it, or them.

Murphy is first met as Kit Ramsey, a.k.a. "the hottest, sexiest action star in the world." But though the man has the requisite mansion, fancy cars and entourage, success has not brought him mental stability. Far from it.

Murphy takes special and biting glee in delivering Ramsey's delusional tirades—his fury at getting scripts that make extensive use of the letter "K" (they remind him of the KKK) and his disgust that white actors get all the good punch lines and black actors win Oscars only when they play slaves. It's no wonder that he seeks the help of MindHead (a clever spoof of Scientology-type organizations), where cool Terry Stricter (Terence Stamp) is in charge and believers walk around with triangles on their heads.

Ordinarily, Bobby Bowfinger would never cross Kit Ramsey's path. A producer-director so impoverished he shoplifts his wardrobe and can't pay a $5.43 phone bill, Bowfinger includes in his past credits the Glendale Tent Players' production of *Once Upon a Mattress* and a film called *The Yugo Story* (it's about the car, not the country). But dreams die hard, and Bowfinger's latest is a script called *Chubby Rain*.

Written by his accountant (Adam Alexi-Malle), *Chubby Rain's* story of aliens disguised as raindrops sounds like a winner to Bowfinger. When top executive Jerry Renfro (a Robert Downey Jr. cameo) tells him he might go for it with Kit Ramsey attached, Bowfinger tells his crack team of dimwits ("the most promising group of young professionals I've ever worked with") to get ready to go.

These include a star-struck ingenue from Ohio (Heather Graham), a handsome if limited actor (Kohl Sudduth), an overly dramatic leading lady (Christine Baranski) and a studio gofer-cameraman (Jamie Kennedy) who knows how to walk off the lot with any piece of equipment that's not tied down.

What the group doesn't include is Kit Ramsey, who, not surprisingly, wants nothing to do with *Chubby Rain*. Fueled by desperation and feeling his last chance slipping away, Bowfinger comes up with a lunatic idea: He'll follow Ramsey around town and secretly film him interacting with the cast members. "Kit doesn't want to see the camera," he tells his own gullible actors. "It breaks his concentration."

Murphy is especially funny in the scenes of panicky befuddlement that result when these strangers come up to him talking "some secret white language I can't decode." His confusion eventually leads to chaos, which is where Jiff, a look-alike for Ramsey that Bowfinger hires when his unknowing star proves temporarily unavailable, enters the picture.

As the innocent, glasses-and-braces-wearing Jiff, someone whose show business experience is limited to being "an active renter at Blockbuster" and who would consider a career running errands to be a major break, Murphy has even more fun than he does with Ramsey. And it's his zeal for creating such disparate comic characters that gives *Bowfinger* its particular zest.

For Murphy has the ability, not shared by all comics or even all actors, to become unmistakably different people with different voices and even different physical auras. Playing multiple characters seems to liberate a kind of manic energy in him, as it did in Peter Sellers, an energy that heats up Martin's cool, cerebral humor and helps it ignite.

Bowfinger has its share of down time, proves better at its set pieces than in the continuity between them, and also misses Murphy when he's not on the screen. But given how many people he plays, it's not long before someone shows up to make us laugh.

Bridget Jones's Diary
2001

"It's only a diary," Renee Zellweger's Bridget Jones innocently whines about the red-covered volume she confides her secrets to, but who in the world does she expect to believe her?

Starting as a London newspaper column by Helen Fielding and morphing into a novel and a sequel that have together sold 5 million copies and counting in thirty-two countries, *Bridget Jones's Diary* and its candid and witty tales of a thirtysomething's romantic woes became such a phenomenon that the *London Evening Standard* grandly announced that its protagonist "is no mere fictional character, she is the Spirit of the Age."

So when it came to turning this bona fide cultural sensation into a film, a lot of significant players were part of the mix. Top British actors Hugh Grant and Colin Firth (both of whom are mentioned in the book) are Zellweger's male costars, and two of that country's cleverest screenwriters, *Four Weddings and a Funeral* and *Notting Hill*'s Richard Curtis and *Pride and Prejudice* adapter Andrew Davies worked with Fielding on the script. Four heavyweight companies from three countries (Miramax, Universal, Studio Canal and Working Title) flash their logos on the screen before we even get a glimpse of an actor.

Instead of being suffocated under all this attention or suffering overly much from the liberties the film admittedly takes with her diary, Ms. Jones prospers. The dramatic feature debut for filmmaker Sharon Maguire (a documentary director and apparently the inspiration for Bridget's friend Shazzer), *Bridget Jones's Diary* is cheerful, cheeky entertainment, a clever confection that makes jokes about Salman Rushdie and literary critic F. R. Leavis and survives its excesses by smartly mixing knock-about farce with fairy-tale romance.

It could do none of this without a performer who is definitely not a Brit, the Texas-born Zellweger. An unlikely choice for the part (she had to learn what turns out to be a serviceable British accent from scratch and add a by-now-celebrated twenty pounds to play the pudgy Jones), the actress turns out to be the kind of ideal match that producers fantasize about.

Zellweger's strongest suit is her vulnerability, the empathy she unerringly creates by having her feelings play nakedly on her face. Taking on a character identified with and embraced by so many, the actress is very much who she is supposed to be on the screen.

Given that *Bridget Jones* is largely a comedy of embarrassment, it's critical that Zellweger is a hugely game performer, willing to look bad in intentionally unflattering costumes, as well as someone with a gift for being a plucky wreck. To watch her alone in her apartment, drunkenly singing along with Jamie O'Neal on "All By Myself," is to know everything worth knowing about this at-risk character.

Bridget may be her own worst enemy, a woman with a gift for self-sabotage who drinks too much, smiles too hard and puts her foot wrong at every opportunity, but she soldiers her way through with zest and spirit. Maybe she is "ever so slightly less elegant under pressure" than Grace Kelly, but her resilient good-heartedness never deserts her for long.

It is this essence of the character, rather than literary fidelity, that *Bridget Jones* is successfully focused on. Key central elements from the book do remain, but many things, critical details from the kind of sweater worn in a key scene to the kind of man Bridget's mother is attracted to, have been changed. The screenwriters have pared down the book but pumped-up selected elements, such as the rivalry between the two men in Bridget's life. They've also strengthened the book's charming parallels to *Pride and Prejudice*, down to having Firth, who played Mr. Darcy in the BBC version of the Jane Austen novel, expertly play the modern Mark Darcy here.

Introduced in "my thirty-second year of being single," publishing house publicity assistant Jones has a tart tongue and a vivid imagination. Locked in a perpetual battle with her weight, disgusted with "smug marrieds" and their know-it-all satisfaction, terrified of dying fat and alone only to be eaten by huge dogs, she begins a diary to keep a record of her life and get a handle on it. One of Bridget's first resolutions, however, turns out to be a tough one: "Will find nice, sensible boyfriend to go out with and won't continue to form romantic attachments to any of the following: alcoholics, workaholics, commitment-phobics, peeping Toms, megalomaniacs."

Human rights barrister Mark Darcy doesn't fall easily into the Mr. Right category. His dark good looks are hampered by an awful sweater provided by his parents and he's the favorite of her parents (the very funny Gemma Jones and Jim Broadbent), who are soon to have romantic problems of their own. He's also undeniably haughty and he's got an attractive and very lean legal partner (the reliable Embeth Davidtz) who wants to extend the relationship into other areas.

Bridget, if she is honest (and she is nothing but) knows she's much more attracted to her boss, Daniel Cleaver, "a bona fide sex god" who is also so much the office scoundrel he practically has a Mr. Wrong sign pasted on his back. Does this stop Bridget? Obviously not. As the irresistible Mr. Cleaver, Hugh Grant (who is skewered in the book for his Sunset Boulevard assignation) presents one of his best, most satisfying performances. Giving in to his dark side, he gets to play the worst possible version of the kinds of enticing men he's been previously cast as. With Grant in the part, there's never any doubt why Bridget finds it so difficult to disregard her better judgment and stay away.

Finally, however, it is Zellweger as Jones who almost wills this film to succeed. There are flat patches, and you can see the plot twists coming, but with this spirited a performance in the title role, it's hard to protest too much. Bridget Jones's search for inner poise may be doomed, but her film is anything but.

Clueless
1995

To hear almost-sixteen Cher Horowitz tell it, "I actually have a way normal life." True, her mom died during "routine liposuction," but she now lives happily with her fierce litigator father—"He gets paid $500 an hour to fight with people"—in great Beverly Hills style. "Isn't my house classic?" she enthuses. "Its columns date back to 1972."

Effervescent and supremely pleased with herself, Cher (delightfully played by Alicia Silverstone) is the comic centerpiece of *Clueless*, a wickedly funny high school farce from writer-director Amy Heckerling that, like its heroine, turns out to have more to it than anyone could anticipate.

Heckerling, of course, has been to high school before. In 1982, she directed Sean Penn and Phoebe Cates in the hip *Fast Times at Ridgemont High*. *Clueless* is as smart and amusing, and this time Heckerling has the advantage of a heroine even Jane Austen could love. In fact, she had a hand in creating her.

For though Paramount is not exactly basing its ad campaign around the fact, *Clueless* is a shrewd modern reworking of some of the themes and plot lines of Austen's beloved *Emma*, another story of a self-confident, socially prominent young woman who was surprised to find out how much she had to learn.

That connection points out the unexpected cleverness of *Clueless*, which may be about high school but depends on familiarity with Billie Holiday and *Hamlet* for its laughs. Put together with verve and style, *Clueless* is a sweet-natured satire about L.A.'s overpampered youth that gets more fun out of high school than most people had attending it.

Named, like her best friend Dionne (Stacey Dash), after "great singers of the past who now do infomercials," Cher is absolutely the most popular girl at Bronson Alcott (Beverly Hills High under another name). Convinced that "looking for a boyfriend in high school is as useless as searching for meaning in a Pauly Shore movie," Cher is also a self-assured virgin who blithely explains herself: "You see how picky I am about my shoes, and they only go on my feet."

Still, even for Cher, life does present problems. Like her serious former stepbrother Josh (Paul Rudd), a future environmental lawyer who wears Amnesty International T-shirts, listens to "complaint rock" and takes pleasure in observing the superficiality of Cher's life while helping her dad (Dan Hedaya) with some legal chores.

Even though it makes extensive use of voice-over, always a dicey choice, the *Clueless* script is a treat. And because Heckerling knows just where the jokes are, her direction is dead-on as well; every actor in the extensive cast understands and responds admirably to the material.

Responding best of all is Silverstone, who gives a performance as flawless as Cher's complexion. Cher can sound off-putting and manipulative, but Silverstone emphasizes her good-hearted guilelessness until we have no choice but to embrace her, maxed-out credit cards and all.

Dave
1993

Dave is the best kind of comedy, one whose jokes can't be given away. Though replete with amusing situations and clever lines, its strongest suit is the delicately pitched comic performances of its actors, most especially star Kevin Kline.

As *A Fish Called Wanda* (for which he won an Oscar) and his celebrated stage performance in *The Pirates of Penzance* demonstrated, Kline has a magnificent talent for farce. No one can slip out of a chair or take a fall quite as he does, and his way with the simplest facial expressions and the broadest physical gestures is unendingly funny. So to allow him, as *Dave* does, to fool around with two characters in the same film can't help but be pleasing.

It is the premise of this light-on-its-feet political satire (written by Gary Ross and directed by Ivan Reitman) that William Harrison Mitchell, the humorless president of the United States, has a double. That would be Dave Kovic, the hang-loose owner of a temporary employment agency who wears funny ties and isn't averse to riding a pig if the situation demands it.

Though President Mitchell is a ruthless policy wonk whose political philosophy seems to be "when I kill something, it always dies," he does have a weakness for philandering after hours. Which is why his Secret Service agent, Duane Stevensen (Ving Rhames), is always on the lookout for a chief executive look-alike, someone who can stand in for the president when he feels like slipping away.

Dave is naturally recruited, but events transpire to turn what everyone thinks will be a one-night stand into a longer engagement. "We want you to extend things a little," is how Bob Alexander, the president's icy chief of staff (Frank Langella), carefully puts it, and so the most ordinary of guys sees what it's like to be the majordomo of the free world.

Though its look-alikes in politics premise echoes everything from *The Prisoner of Zenda* to *The Prince and the Pauper*, *Dave*'s theme of an innocent confronting and mastering experience has more than a little in common with the Oscar-nominated screenplay for *Big*, which Ross cowrote with Ann Spielberg.

And though director Reitman (*Ghostbusters*, *Kindergarten Cop*, *Twins*) has not been known as the most subtle of filmmakers, the combination of his sure commercial sensibility and Ross's fastidious writing has resulted in a smoothly professional comedy that has an appealing air of low-key ridiculousness about it. Especially well-done are the scenes of Kline as Dave trying to get used to the perks of the White House, wondering nervously whether, for instance, he needs to dial "9" before making an outside call.

And since Ross is something of a political junkie, the film was not only able to get august Washington figures from Senator Alan Simpson to PBS's *The McLaughlin Group* to appear, it also came up with witty and appropriate things for them to say. One of *Dave's* sharper conceits is that far from going unnoticed, the difference in the post-Dave presidency is chewed over by Capitol Hill pundits to a gleefully ridiculous extent.

But aside from Oliver Stone (who makes a very funny conspiracy theorist appearance), the only person who is truly suspicious about the president's change in demeanor is his wife, Ellen (Sigourney Weaver). An outspoken social activist who barely speaks to her husband, she starts to wonder why he has become so warm and personable just as, in yet another twist, bachelor Dave starts to think that the first lady is an extremely attractive woman.

As a veteran of Reitman's *Ghostbusters*, Weaver knows just how to behave in these films, but she is pretty much overshadowed by the premier farceurs she is surrounded with. Besides Kline, Frank Langella has his power-mad power-behind-the-throne act down perfectly, Kevin Dunn is equally adept as a prevaricating press secretary, and Rhames seems much too funny to be the same actor who played Cinque in *Patty Hearst*. Best of all, though, is Charles Grodin as Dave's perplexed friend Murray Blum, an accountant whose stony double-takes are things of wonder.

Despite all these good things, *Dave* does sag a bit in the middle when it goes soft and teary a la *Mr. Smith Goes to Washington* about the swell virtues of good government. But this is just a momentary blemish on the face of what otherwise looks to be the most coolly refreshing of comedies, Washington-based or otherwise.

Elf
2003

Elf is an example of the good things that can happen when hipsters do it on the square. The fable of what transpires when a young man raised by elves goes back to investigate his human roots, it manages to be genuinely sweet and just a teensy bit wised up.

Directed by Jon Favreau from a script by David Berenbaum, *Elf* returns to the hip but warm-hearted spirit of *Swingers*, which Favreau wrote and starred in. It brings sophisticated glee and a sense of innocent fun to what could have been a moribund traditional family film.

Making this pay off without winking at the audience is a difficult task, and *Elf* doesn't always feel all of a piece. But in *Saturday Night Live* alumnus and star Will Ferrell, the film has a guide who steers it unerringly over the bumpy patches.

Ferrell is exactly right as Buddy, who as an infant at an orphanage found his way into Santa's bag and became the first human to penetrate into his remote North Pole workshop. Adopted by Papa Elf (an amusingly dry Bob Newhart), Buddy grows up convinced he's an elf himself, even though several factors point strongly in a different direction.

For one thing, Buddy, lacking a true elf's nimble fingers, might just be the worst toymaker in North Pole history, a self-described "cotton-headed ninny muggins." Papa Elf takes pity on him and lets him work on Santa's sleigh, which runs on Christmas spirit that's measured by the uncannily accurate Clausometer.

Then there's the matter of his size. At six foot three, Buddy is bigger than your normal elf, a whole lot bigger, a size difference that director Favreau, determined to keep things old-school, shows via the venerable technique of forced perspective rather than resort to modern computer generated imagery.

There is one area, however, where Buddy is an elf all the way, and that is in his bottomless good humor. Despite having to wear the typical elf costume of bright green suit and a conical hat over yellow tights and pointy shoes, Buddy radiates cheer as it's never been radiated before.

He's always ready with a hug, even for angry raccoons, and when he says, "I just like to smile, smile is my favorite," you know he's not just blowing smoke up Santa's chimney.

Since *Elf* is something of a one-joke movie, it's essential that Ferrell get this limitless innocence right—and he does. His Buddy, a cheerful combination of Stan Laurel and Tom Hanks in *Big*, is an endearing elf Candide, a true naïf who can't help but make the best of everything.

This kind of attitude is fine for the North Pole, where Edward Asner's Santa is the only person allowed to get cranky, but the challenge for Buddy and this film is to make it creditable in "a magical kingdom called New York City."

For, once he finds he's a human and learns that his mother is dead, that's where Buddy heads, determined to find the father who doesn't know he exists. "This is a golden opportunity," Papa Elf tells him, "to find out who you really are."

Not for nothing, however, does Buddy's father, Walter Hobbs (James Caan), have a prominent place on Santa's naughty list. The Simon Legree of the children's publishing world, he's too busy repossessing books from kindly nuns and shipping out stories without the final pages to pay attention to his wife, Emily (Mary Steenburgen), or his ten-year-old son, Michael (Daniel Tay). Clearly a big dose of Christmas spirit is in order.

Ditto for comely young Jovie (the always welcome Zooey Deschanel). She's not a real elf, but even though she plays one in Gimbel's toy department, she is a tad on the disaffected side and in need of the kind of infusion of good cheer only the genuine article can provide.

Naturally, New York being New York, not everyone is happy with Buddy's attitude, which, as *Elf* illustrates, can be unexpectedly trying. A dwarf children's book writer (*Station Agent*'s Peter Dinklage) is furious when Buddy mistakes him for an elf, and a department store Santa goes ballistic when Buddy, alive to the impersonation, hisses at him: "You sit on a throne of lies." *Elf*'s conscious employment of old-fashioned elements in the service of whimsical innocence extends to the use of the simplest kind of special effects to animate North Pole residents like a friendly narwhal and Leon the Talking Snowman.

That genial creature is voiced by Leon Redbone, who collaborates with Deschanel on a sparkling duet of "Baby, It's Cold Outside," the highlight of an eclectic soundtrack that includes Eartha Kitt's "Santa Baby," Ray Charles's "Santa Claus Is Comin' to Town" and Wayne Newton's "Jingle Bell Rock."

Even at a brisk ninety minutes, *Elf*'s single focus means it has to strain a bit to fill all its time, but director Favreau so wants this to succeed, and Ferrell plays Buddy with so much goofy conviction, that everything turns out for the best. As Papa Elf reminds Buddy: "Some people lose sight of what's important in life. All they need is a little Christmas spirit." Coming right up.

Get Shorty
1995

"The guy's a crook."
"So? This town he should fit right in."
—*Get Shorty* BY ELMORE LEONARD

The town, of course, is Hollywood, and the genial premise of Leonard's novel and the diverting film that's been made from it is that being a success in the movie business is a piece of cake for those schooled in more traditional criminal pursuits.

The crook in question is Chili Palmer, a smooth Miami loan shark and movie fan who finds himself in Los Angeles on mob business. Once he discovers that "I don't think the producer has to know too much," he sees no reason why he shouldn't be getting some of that action as well.

Wittily directed by *Addams Family* veteran Barry Sonnenfeld and adapted from Leonard's effortlessly savvy work by Scott Frank, *Get*

Shorty is light comedy in an amoral setting. The jokes are quick, with clever jibes alternating with double-crosses and the occasional murder, and the streamlined plot unrolls like a colorful ball of twine.

At the center of it all, an island of calm with every hair carefully razor cut, is Chili, a hard guy with a soft heart. John Travolta plays him as a Mafioso Cary Grant in a black leather coat, and the fit is perfect. Sexy, funny and completely charming, Travolta gives a splendid, old-fashioned star performance that pushes the picture to a level that would not have been possible without him.

Chili gets to Los Angeles via Las Vegas, where he went looking for a nervous Miami dry cleaner in hock to the mob who supposedly died in a plane crash. The dry cleaner, however, turns out to be alive enough to be spending his way through the $300,000 he scammed from the insurance company.

As a favor to a Vegas pal, Chili also pays a visit to a producer named Harry Zimm (Gene Hackman), who owes money to a casino. Though Harry's credits are of the *Slime Creature* variety, Chili has heard of them and, almost as a lark, pitches the dry cleaner story as a major motion picture. Harry is interested, but the B-picture scream queen (Rene Russo) in whose house Harry is crashing is not amused— though we can tell she finds Chili kind of cute.

The longer Chili stays in Los Angeles, the more complicated things become. Harry has his hands full with nasty Bo Catlett (Delroy Lindo), who runs drugs and a limo service and, yes, is also eager to move into producing. For his part, Chili has to deal with a surly Miami associate, Ray (Bones) Barboni (Dennis Farina). And everyone has to cope with Martin Weir (Danny DeVito), the hottest actor in Hollywood since his starring role in *Napoleon*, the man with the power to turn everyone's movie dreams into gold.

This is the briefest outline of a pleasantly complex criminal confection that Sonnenfeld and Frank keep moving at an amusing pace. Though the entire cast (including unbilled cameos by Bette Midler and Harvey Keitel) contributes, Travolta is the man who keeps this soufflé from collapsing. Watching him charm his way through contin-

ual difficulties, it's hard to believe that the movie business all but ignored him for years and that he himself turned down this dream assignment twice before *Pulp Fiction*'s Quentin Tarantino, the godfather
of the actor's current rebirth, convinced him to do it.

Elmore Leonard's novels and short stories have been made into numerous films, but *Get Shorty* comes the closest to re-creating his casual yet dazzling verbal style, characterized by sentences that surprise
you and dialogue that knows its way around. And the film also does a
good job with the book's gentle digs at the inane way the movie business tends to function. Unlike Chili, *Get Shorty* is not going to knock
anybody out, but in the category of amiable diversions it's awfully
tough to improve on.

Honeymoon in Vegas
1992

He'll always be the Other Bergman to some people, less glamorous
than Ingrid, less morose than Ingmar, more obscure than either one.
But no matter, because when it comes to modern screen comedy,
writer-director Andrew Bergman is, as *Honeymoon in Vegas* proves one
more time, nothing less than the emperor of the absurd, a man who is
funny in a way quite his own.

Beginning with his screenplay work on *Blazing Saddles* and *The In-
Laws* through *So Fine* and *The Freshman*, his first features as writer-
director, Bergman has polished a distinctive, giddily anarchic comedy
style that is as hard to define as it is easy to recognize.

Working so close to the edge of the envelope that you often don't
know whether to laugh or gasp, Bergman comes up with comic situations so extreme that his put-upon characters often have difficulty accepting just how lunatic their predicaments are.

Take the story of Jack Singer (Nicolas Cage). A regular guy with a
fairly regular job as a detective specializing in divorce work, he is very
much in love with Betsy Nolan (Sarah Jessica Parker), the sweetest of

second grade teachers, who feels likewise about him. A wedding might ordinarily be expected, except that Jack's take-no-prisoners mother (a crusty cameo by Anne Bancroft) has extracted a deathbed promise that he will never do the deed.

Finally, faced with the possibility of losing Betsy, Jack uncertainly decides to make the best of things. "Let's get on the plane," he says, breathing hard. "Go to Vegas. Do it." Which turns out to be his first mistake, and not just because the city is simultaneously hosting what looks to be the largest gathering of Elvis impersonators ever held in one place.

Rather it's because Vegas is the home of Tommy Korman (James Caan), a big-time gambler with a killer instinct. Mobster though he is, Tommy is also something of a romantic and still mourns his late wife, who spent too many hours around too many pools reading too many Sidney Sheldon novels before falling victim to the sun's deadly rays.

So when Tommy spies the still-unmarried Betsy, the image of his departed wife, across a crowded hotel lobby, it stands to reason that he will do anything to get her to marry him. And given that this is an Andrew Bergman movie, anything includes arranging a high-stakes poker game with an Asian Elvis imitator, a towel-chewing Jerry Tarkanian (not playing himself) and a glasses-heavy gambler know as Tommy Cataracts (a dyspeptic Seymour Cassell).

Suddenly, Jack is in such a fearsome hole that Tommy's suggestion that spending a chaste weekend with Betsy would be the only acceptable payback starts to make a kind of demented sense. What happens when Betsy gets this particular piece of news is when *Honeymoon in Vegas* really gets started, and a typically frenetic series of events (involving the state of Hawaii, a dentist named Sally Molars who doubles as a bookie and says things like "eight-to-five you need root canal," even more Elvis imitators and a full twenty of the songs the King made famous) zestily unwinds.

The more chaotic the farce, the more delicate the casting must be, and the three principals in *Honeymoon in Vegas* are just as they should be. Nicolas Cage, whose best work has always been in seriously over-the-top comic/romantic roles (*Moonstruck, Raising Arizona, Valley Girl*), once again displays the quintessential air of frenetic desperation, eyes widening more and more as his plight grows increasingly preposterous.

James Caan, whose Tommy Korman mimics *The Godfather*'s Sonny Corleone in the same way that Marlon Brando echoed the glowering Don in *The Freshman*, displays more than fine comic timing here. He makes the gambler sweeter and more human than comic performances usually are, and his touching fervor about marriage gently underscores Jack's continuing ambivalence. And as the object of both men's increasingly manic affections, Sarah Jessica Parker not only looks appropriately attractive but also brings an essential down-to-earth sanity to the role.

Among the major treats of any Andrew Bergman film are the subsidiary characters, and they are especially rich here. In addition to Sally Molars, we meet the musical-obsessed Chief Orman (Peter Boyle), an officious hogger of airline counter space (Ben Stein), a client of Jack's (Robert Costanza) who emotionally insists that his unlikely wife is having a torrid affair with Mike Tyson, and, of course, all those Elvises.

Though *Honeymoon in Vegas* has one of his most accessible premises, Andrew Bergman has never suited everyone's taste, and probably never will. He is something of a spritzer in the Mel Brooks mode, someone who spews out such a torrent of manic material that by definition not all of it is going to work. But in an age where screen comedy tends to fit snugly in a handful of preset synthetic molds, his all-natural craziness comes as a special treat. Especially if you like to laugh.

Both Cage and Sex and the City's *Parker went on to greater things, which makes their teaming here even more delicious.*

In Good Company
2004

In Good Company is all the things we've come not to expect anymore from a major studio comedy, including genial, generous-spirited and unmistakably entertaining.

It's not every day you see a comedy about the consequences of corporate takeovers, let alone one that finds time for a little romance and intergenerational conflicts. *In Good Company* does have a lot of balls in the air, but thanks to smart acting and expert writing and directing, it handles them pretty well.

Much of the credit should go to writer-director Paul Weitz in his initial solo outing. Weitz had collaborated with his brother Chris on the adaptation of Nick Hornby's *About a Boy* and on the first and most palatable of the *American Pie* productions.

As part of a team and by himself, Weitz's gentle touch presents a pleasing twist on conventional comic plotting. Adept at not forcing things, he gives this film the kind of seductive spirit that wants to surprise us into smiling, not bludgeon us into submission.

Though the cast, especially costars Dennis Quaid and Scarlett Johansson as father and daughter, are all in on the joke, the performance that is really essential to the film's success is the central one by Topher Grace. Best known as the star of television's *That '70s Show*, Grace has been under the radar on the larger screen despite effective performances in movies as different as *Traffic* and *Win a Date with Tad Hamilton!*

Here Grace has the chance to display one of the most persuasive comic touches around. There is a lightness to the actor that wears surprisingly well; he is able to be pleasant without being sappy and to gloat without being irritating. Careers have been built on considerably less.

When Grace's character, Carter Duryea, is introduced, he has a lot to gloat about. A hot young executive at the multinational giant Globecom and given to saying things to his bosses such as "I am going to be your ninja assassin," Carter has so impressed his superiors that he's been given a plum assignment heading advertising sales for Globecom's newest acquisition, *Sports America* magazine. That despite being all of twenty-six years old with no experience to speak of in that area.

It's a promotion that doesn't exactly sit well with the man who's had that job with *Sports America* (a *Sports Illustrated* clone) for quite some time and is now being demoted. That would be fifty-one-year-old Dan Foreman (gracefully played by Quaid), who's got so much going on in his private life he almost can't concentrate on this newest crisis.

For one thing, Dan's wife, Ann (Marg Helgenberger of television's *CSI*), has just become pregnant. For another, his oldest daughter, Alex (Johansson), has decided she wants to study creative writing at New York University, adding a hefty tuition payment to Dan's economic burden. Carter, it turns out, has personal problems of his own, so when Dan inadvertently invites his new boss home for dinner, he leaps at the chance.

There he meets Alex, or actually remeets her, for she mistook him for an intern on a chance cute-meet on an elevator in her dad's building. Soon Alex and Carter will be making doe eyes at each other while Carter and Dan try to forge a workable business relationship.

It's a situation not covered in Harvard Business School's curriculum. It takes a lot of plotting to make all these strands work together, but the acting (it's especially good to see Johansson bringing her ethereal qualities to a normal young woman her own age) and the writing and directing make it happen. *In Good Company* truly is the kind of company we'd all like to be in.

Jerry Maguire
1996

As a top agent at Sports Management International, Jerry Maguire has always wanted more. More clients, more money, a more desirable girlfriend, possibly even more phone calls than his daily average of 264. Then one day there is no more, and Jerry Maguire can't even guess what will happen next.

As a filmmaker, Cameron Crowe has always wanted a different kind of more. Starting with his script for *Fast Times at Ridgemont High*, he's been pushing for more character and less convention, smarter comedy and sharper relationships.

But Crowe's first quirky films as a director, *Say Anything* and *Singles*, left audiences convinced of his ability but dissatisfied with the results. Now, with *Jerry Maguire*, that promise is realized.

With the cooperation of Tom Cruise, being all he should be in the title role, *Jerry Maguire* shows how to use Hollywood stars and traditional romantic comedy forms to build something satisfying and personal. So much the opposite of high concept that attempts to boil it down to a sentence (or a coming attractions trailer) miss the point, this is a wholly unexpected film, as heady and surprising in its humor as in its emotional texture.

Utilizing an offbeat story arc that trusts us to be savvy, *Jerry Maguire* also finds the space to deal with what the worship of money and success is doing to cultural values and, almost incidentally, to offer a believable look at the pluses and stresses of interracial friendship. Not bad for what might be mistaken for a charming little romance.

Crowe's core idea, and one of his shrewdest, was to place all this where it fits best, namely, in the world of professional sports, where honesty and trust are suspect and the victory-at-all-costs ethos covers all manner of cutthroat sins.

Not only is Jerry Maguire of this world but catch-phrases such as "no one said winning was cheap" allow him to flourish in it. With his practiced grin and high-wattage confidence, Jerry's shark-in-a-suit persona is, initially at least, perfectly in line with the characters Cruise has played in the past—what *Top Gun*'s Maverick would look like with briefcase in hand.

Then, late at night in his millionth hotel room, something happens. Maguire has "a breakdown or a breakthrough" and writes a feverish manifesto titled "The Things We Think and Do Not Say: The Future of Our Business" that questions his firm's greedhead policies.

Naturally he's fired within a week by protege-nemesis Burt Sugar (a cruelly funny Jay Mohr). Making it worse, in a sequence of manic comic brio, Sugar works the telephone like a virtuoso, insisting that "it's not show friends, it's show business" and grabbing all of Maguire's clients.

Not quite all his clients, it turns out. Maguire still has an outside shot at retaining top NFL draft pick Frank Cushman (Jerry O'Connell). But the one athlete he has for sure is also the one client he might not have minded losing, Rod Tidwell (a brash success for *Boyz N the Hood*'s Cuba Gooding Jr.).

A wide receiver in the last year of his contract with the NFL's Arizona Cardinals, Tidwell makes up for a lack of height with a larger-than-average attitude. A nonstop talker dismissed by his team as a locker room malcontent, Tidwell decides that Maguire is the man to renegotiate his next contract into the eight-figure range he has no doubt he deserves.

Paralleling his lone client is the one person Maguire convinces to leave with him when he's drummed out of SMI. Accountant Dorothy Boyd (Renee Zellweger), a low-level drone he has barely noticed, and a single mother to boot, was so touched by that late-night mission statement that she quits and agrees to an uncertain position as Maguire's entire office staff.

The kicker for Jerry Maguire in his new stripped-down life is that, as all his ex-girlfriends testify, he cannot stand to be alone. "Great at friendship, bad at intimacy" is how he puts it, and watching the directions his enforced closeness with Dorothy Boyd and Rod Tidwell take him is this film's great pleasure.

The one-line "hotshot gets fired and faces consequences" outline of *Jerry Maguire* is nothing new, but the film itself is fresh and refreshing due to Crowe's outstanding script (he spent four years on it, counting well-spent time for research) and his ability as a director to bring everything to life on the screen.

Jerry Maguire's actors are key here, starting with Cruise, who shows a willingness to explore the darker implications of his usual persona. As loved by the camera as any actor of his generation, Cruise starts with the familiar but expands to show his character in extremis, the self-confident grin being pushed to the cracking point. It's his ability to play this both ways that keeps the question of whether Maguire can become a recognizable human being an open one all the way to the end.

Easily holding her own with Cruise is costar Zellweger. Sensual and offbeat, with great relaxed comic timing and the ability to glow without being glamorous, Zellweger's way with the interplay of feeling and humor makes her the film's emotional center.

Surrounding these two is a remarkable supporting cast, starting with the irresistible Jonathan Lipnicki, the only movie kid you'd really want in your own life, as Dorothy's son Ray. Also outstanding (in addition to those already mentioned) are Kelly Preston as Jerry's girlfriend, Bonnie Hunt as Dorothy's sister and Regina King as Rod's wife, all benefiting from Crowe's ability to write characters that are real and distinct, each alive in his or her own particular way.

The argument can be made that Crowe's four films form a chronological progression from *Ridgemont High*'s teen crises to *Jerry Maguire*'s more intractable grown-up situations. Yet it's this film's satisfying premise that even as adults we're all deserving of what the Bob Dylan song played over the final credits promises, a little "Shelter from the Storm." Even Jerry Maguire.

Jerry Maguire won a best supporting actor Oscar for Cuba Gooding Jr., and remains a high point in costars Cruise and Zellweger's careers.

The Mask
1994

Much of the early buzz about *The Mask* involved the wizardly computer-generated special effects that allow kick-sand-in-my-face bank clerk Stanley Ipkiss to turn into an off-kilter superhero whose India rubber body contorts like Spider-Man's and absorbs punishment like something out of Looney Tunes.

And, masterminded by the imps at Industrial Light & Magic, who ought to just wrap the visual effects Oscar and take it home, the tricks in *The Mask* are something to see. When the Mask's body recovers from being flattened like a tortilla and his eyes literally pop out at the sight of a beautiful woman, audience eyes are likely to roll as well.

Yet despite all this technology it is heartening to report that *The Mask*'s sine qua non, the factor it would be hardpressed to live without, is the actor who plays the cartoon and the alter ego Ipkiss, Jim Carrey.

Best known as the lucky man whose salary made a Roadrunner leap to millions per picture after the unexpected success of *Ace Ventura: Pet Detective*, Carrey is revealed here as a comic actor of charm and talent. Not only is he adept at physical humor, the kind of knockabout stuff that recalls the classic silent clowns, but Carrey also has a bright and likable screen presence, a lost-puppy quality that is surprisingly endearing.

And when he plays the Mask, wearing a supple and nonconfining latex facial apparatus designed by Greg Cannom, Carrey displays a manic side as well, doing riffs from old movies and dishy impersonations of everyone from Elvis to Clint Eastwood to Sally Field accepting her Oscar.

Amid all these amusing elements, it may not matter very much that *The Mask* runs out of energy faster than its star does. Though director Charles Russell knows how to keep things loose and playful, the movie doesn't aspire to be more than a gaudy showcase for Carrey's ability and ILM's magic, and anyone looking for something else is open to disappointment.

In line with this, Mike Werb's screenplay, based on a story by Michael Fallon and Mark Verdeiden and, before that, on a comic-book character, is less a sturdy narrative than an extended premise on which all these assorted antics can be hung like ornaments on a tree.

The pre-Mask Ipkiss lives and works in Edge City and wonders why nice guys finish last. A shy pushover and dupe whose primary emotional attachment is to his clever terrier Milo (one of the more entertaining of recent dog performances), Ipkiss just about stops breathing when sultry Tina Carlyle (Cameron Diaz) stops by his desk at the bank.

A headliner at the chic Coco Bongo Club, Tina is also the girlfriend of mobster Dorian Tyrel (Peter Greene), but Ipkiss can't get her out of his mind. And though the movie presents Tina as little more than the scantily clad physical embodiment of Roger Rabbit's wife Jessica, model Diaz, in her first screen role, has enough presence to help us see past the tinsel.

At a particularly morose point in his life, Ipkiss comes across a nondescript green wooden mask, which, he later learns, is probably of Scandinavian origin and carved to represent Loki, the Norse god of mischief, permanently banned from Valhalla for his pranks.

Not surprisingly, then, when Ipkiss puts the mask on, havoc breaks loose. Normally timid, he becomes an amoral livewire out of one of the Tex Avery cartoons he admires, a party animal with a face the color of key lime pie capable of robbing banks and whirling off like a pastel tornado.

That robbery aside, the Mask isn't really a bad guy, and his most memorable moments are song-and-dance riffs so antic that in interviews Carrey has taken to calling his character "Fred Astaire on acid." Whether passionately twirling with Tina in a canary-yellow ensemble, playing the maniac French boulevardier in beret and loud pants or turning a SWAT team into a conga line with his Cuban Pete impersonation, Carrey is a treat on his feet. Yes, it would be nice if all this pleasure were attached to a story even a trifle more inventive or involving, but, given everything, maybe that is too much to ask.

The film lost the visual effects Oscar to Forrest Gump, *but Carrey and Diaz remain delightful in this early effort.*

Meet the Parents
2000

Hollywood Boulevard, the outlandish 1976 Joe Dante-Allan Arkush satire on the movie business, featured a studio called Miracle Pictures whose motto was, not surprisingly, "If it's a good picture, it's a miracle." In that spirit, and in the best possible sense, *Meet the Parents* is something of a miracle.

This buoyant, giddy comedy of catastrophe is the most amusing mainstream live-action comedy since *There's Something About Mary*. But what's really striking about this story of a prospective son-in-law meeting the father-in-law from hell is the way it came into the world.

Most funny pictures these days, especially those that come from studios, have the easily identifiable imprint of one key creative force, whether it be the writer-director or the actor. This film, however, apparently got developed the old-fashioned way, with individual pieces coming together as they rarely do successfully anymore. A sharp producer named Nancy Tenenbaum acquired the rights to a short film (story credit going to Greg Glienna & Mary Ruth Clarke) and hired comedy writer Jim Herzfeld to turn it into a feature. Director Jay Roach liked an early draft, and once stars Robert De Niro and Ben Stiller were added on, a second writer, John Hamburg, was brought on to help fit the script to their verbal styles. It's the kind of studio-coordinated process that has ruined more films than it's helped, but here it worked, well, miraculously.

How *Meet the Parents* gets its laughs is equally traditional: an old-fashioned emphasis on shrewd casting, well-timed line readings and clever, on-target acting. Nicely complementing the light and genial but very sure touch Roach provides is an elaborate plot featuring visual and verbal gags that are worked out to a remarkable degree.

Even *Parents'* premise is time-honored and durable. Take an inevitably awkward situation—a young man eager to make a good impression on the couple he hopes will be his future in-laws—and ratchet the embarrassment factor up through the roof. The result is a series of insanely improbable but genuinely comic situations, a cacophonous forty-eight hours that only some especially devilish screenwriters could devise.

Stiller stars as Greg Focker, a deeply sincere male nurse, clean-cut but something of a worrier. Going out with schoolteacher Pam Byrnes

(Teri Polo) has made the past ten months in Chicago the happiest of his life, and he's nervously plotting and planning for just the right way to ask her to marry him.

Literally at the last moment, however, Greg accidentally discovers that the politic thing to do would be to ask Pam's father's permission before he asks Pam. An expert in rare flowers who lives in tony Oyster Bay, New York, Jack Byrnes is, his daughter assures Greg, "the sweetest man in the whole world." And since Pam's sister is about to be married, a trip to meet the parents seems the natural thing to do.

As soon as Jack opens the door and Greg sees a serial killer look-alike scowling suspiciously as only De Niro can scowl, the young man knows there's been a break in communication somewhere. A prickly human minefield who's so strong-willed that he took exactly one week to train his beloved Himalayan cat Jinx to use the toilet, Jack is clearly not the person Greg has been led to believe.

De Niro has ventured into comedy many times before, and not always with the happiest results. *Meet the Parents*, however, is a different story. With a part that allows him to draw on and spoof his previous sinister roles, it's the dead-on funniest the actor has ever been. Who else could make the benign concept of "a circle of trust" sound as comically threatening as he does here?

As the man who feels so threatened, Stiller is little short of ideal. Always a gifted comic actor, he's the engine of earnestness that drives the film, a Jew in a nest of WASPs (something mentioned in passing and then smartly used only as subtext) who simply can't catch a break. Greg's gift for saying and doing the wrong thing rises to the level of genius, and, as things go from bad to unimaginably worst, he's within his rights when he says, "I feel like this is not going well at all."

With Blythe Danner as Jack's happy-face wife and Owen Wilson formidably funny as Pam's obscenely wealthy ex-boyfriend, *Meet the Parents* is finely cast (by Ellen Chenoweth) and always outrageous in depicting Greg's misery and the unintentionally chaotic payback he delivers to his tormentors. Love never had more calamities to conquer, nor did it ever get more laughs in the process.

Men in Black
1997

Go ahead, admit what you've always suspected: A certain percentage of people met in daily life are so strange, so out-and-out weird, they have to be aliens from another universe. Now, at last, comes a major motion picture that dares to tell you it's all true.

Smart-alecky and offhandedly funny, *Men in Black* introduces us to the supersecret government agency, known as MiB for short, that makes those aliens toe the line. Starring the inspired pairing of Tommy Lee Jones and Will Smith, *Men in Black* is a genially twisted riff on the familiar alien invaders story, a lively summer entertainment that marries a deadpan sense of humor to the strangest creatures around.

Based on obscure comic-book material, *Men in Black* has maintained the energy and sass of the form while taking on, in Ed Solomon's screenplay, a hipster attitude that extends to the protagonists' ever-present black suits and ubiquitous Ray-Ban sunglasses. Barry Sonnenfeld is an excellent director for this point of view, and *Men in Black* is a blend of the strengths of his previous films, the knowing humor of *Get Shorty* and the visual razzmatazz of *The Addams Family*. And Sonnenfeld also oversaw the smooth blending of the different comic styles of the picture's two leads.

Jones, as his dead-on reading of the most memorable line in *The Fugitive* revealed, has a definite flair for gruff, acerbic humor. His Agent K is a no-nonsense government operative who suddenly shows up at a routine Border Patrol investigation of a suspicious truck near the Texas-Mexico line. One of its passengers, it turns out, has come from a lot farther away than Cuernevaca.

In the meantime, James Edwards (Smith), a New York City cop who exhibits a glib, engaging cockiness, is doing his best to chase down a suspicious person with the unnerving, practically extraterrestrial, ability to just about leap tall buildings in a single bound.

Though MiB boss Zed (Rip Torn) is worried about Edwards's insouciance, K admires his perseverance and is soon recruiting the cop to sever all human contact and join "the best of the best of the best" as Agent J. But not before a whole lot of explaining is done.

Unbeknownst to most people, the planet Earth has volunteered its services as a safe zone where political refugees from other galaxies can live in peace, "kind of like Casablanca without Nazis," in K's helpful phrase. Mostly they're law-abiding citizens, but MiB is around to hold the line when they turn rogue, which means using outlandish weaponry on some pretty weird individuals.

A good deal of the fun of Men in Black is joining Agent J as he gets acquainted with the variety of wacky aliens masquerading as humans that form K's beat. Created by four-time special-effects Oscar winner Rick Baker, with an assist from Industrial Light & Magic, these include beings that sprout new heads that look like weeds, intergalactic emperors tiny enough to live in hollowed-out skulls and much larger and more formidable beings.

Though its charm is in its attitude and premise (and Danny Elfman's rousing score), Men in Black does have a serviceable plot that kicks in when a rusty flying saucer crash-lands in a rural area. Out comes an unseen-for-now creature who promptly rips off (literally) the ill-fitting skin of a local resident named Edgar (Vincent D'Onofrio) and lurches around Manhattan looking for the Arquillian galaxy, one of the treasures of the universe. That search involves considerable mayhem, which is where the boys make contact with the city's deputy medical examiner, mistress of sang-froid Dr. Laura Weaver (Linda Fiorentino).

Men in Black has been set in New York at the suggestion of its director, a native son, and that sets up inventive use of such landmarks as the Guggenheim Museum, the old World's Fair grounds in Queens and the Battery Park vent room for the Holland Tunnel, as well as the expected jokes about what percentage of cabbies are not of this Earth.

Hard to ignore because it's partly unexpected is the film's slime factor. Men in Black has periodic moments of gross-out humor that will not be to everyone's taste, and when Edgar the invader finally reveals himself, he turns out to be more disturbing and off-putting than the film's genial tone would have you expect.

But mostly what you get with *Men in Black* is the opportunity to spend some high-quality time with the Kings of Cool in a world where inconvenient memories get erased and supermarket tabloids offer the most reliable alien tips. It's not the traditional world where only the bad guys wear black, but you already knew that, didn't you?

My Best Friend's Wedding
1997

The smile is back.

After a run of roles dour enough to do credit to Calvin Coolidge, Julia Roberts in *My Best Friend's Wedding* returns to the kind of smart romantic comedy she's especially good at: She plays a young woman who decides she's in love with a great pal only when he announces he's marrying someone else.

Fortunately for all parties, the director here is P. J. Hogan, an Australian whose lightly mocking but sympathetic tone made *Muriel's Wedding* a major success. Based on a script by Ron Bass, who's been known to let bathos get the best of him, this *Wedding* benefits from Hogan's subversive temperament, his skill at leeching out excess sentiment. The director's ability to approach formula material with a fresh eye keeps this film bright and lively even when it verges on wearing thin.

Hogan's tartness is on display as early as the gleeful opening credit sequence, when a bride and bridesmaids in full wedding regalia, picture-book pretty but with the devil in their eyes, drolly lip-sync their way through Ani DiFranco's version of the old standard "Wishin' and Hopin'." Business as usual this is not.

The same can be said for a winning Roberts, whose relaxed and confident performance is, along with superb supporting work from Rupert Everett, the film's cornerstone. But she is not a conventional romantic heroine, and her smiles come noticeably on her own terms.

As New York restaurant critic Julianne Potter, Jules to her friends, Roberts manages to play not only the film's older female character but also a sometimes bad girl, someone who uses her smile as a weapon calculated to distract and disarm opposition.

The opposition in this case includes the people she should be rooting hardest for, starting with sportswriter and ex-boyfriend turned best friend Michael O'Neal (Dermot Mulroney at his most handsome). For nine years these two have joked that if they didn't marry by age twenty-eight, they'd wed each other. But when Michael phones on a Wednesday night to announce that he's marrying someone else in Chicago on Sunday, Jules flies in, determined to use those four days to get him to change his mind and marry her.

Naturally, her main target is Michael's endearing intended, the well-scrubbed, barely-out-of-her-teens Kimmy Wallace, bright-eyed and beautiful and unspoiled by her wealthy family. It's an ultimate ingenue role, the kind Roberts herself might have taken in a previous incarnation, and Cameron Diaz, who seems to improve with every role, plays it perfectly.

Since time is short, Jules gets right to work, trying to sow dissension and undermine the relationship any way she can, especially as regards to whether Michael will stay in his "low-paying, zero respect" sportswriting job. Her confidant in this, and the film's sole voice of reason, is her gay editor, George Downes, superbly played by Everett (the impatient Prince of Wales in *The Madness of King George*), who has all the film's best lines. "I don't send you men anymore," he tells Jules. "You don't have the faintest idea what to do with them."

Helped by Hogan's sharp directing and expert acting all around, these shenanigans are amusing, but *Wedding* really gets into gear when George appears in Chicago to lend moral support. A desperate Jules introduces him to everyone as her fiancé, and the comic madness that results, culminating in a wild group sing-along of "I Say a Little Prayer" at an unsuspecting seafood restaurant, enables Everett to well and truly steal the picture from everyone concerned.

As if echoing the script's description of Jules's machinations as "a series of underhanded, despicable, not terribly imaginative things," *My Best Friend's Wedding* feels repetitive at times, but its star power and willingness to undercut convention come through at the end. With so many good things on its plate, it's no wonder this picture has what it takes to make Roberts finally smile.

Notting Hill
1999

"What am I doing with you?" Julia Roberts's Anna Scott—a.k.a. "Hollywood's biggest star by far"—says to Hugh Grant's William Thacker, the shambling and seemingly ordinary bookstore owner she is in the process of being smitten with. But if Anna doesn't know, everyone watching *Notting Hill* surely will.

For if all romance is a process of recognition, of noticing someone else who's noticing back, movie romance ups the ante. No matter who they're pretending to be on the screen, even if they're royalty and regular people (as were Audrey Hepburn and Gregory Peck in *Roman Holiday*, or even Carrie Fisher and Harrison Ford in *Star Wars*), it's the first law of cinema that stars recognize each other and find a way to be together, no matter what the circumstances.

A collateral descendant of *Four Weddings and a Funeral*, the film that made Grant an international star, *Notting Hill* is a smartly cast and consistently amusing romantic comedy. As with its predecessor, the key to this film's considerable charm is the script by Richard Curtis, his first solo credit (he collaborated on *Bean*) since *Four Weddings*.

The idea (and Curtis says it came from his fantasizing about turning up at dinner with friends with Madonna or Princess Diana) is that megastar Anna wanders by chance into William's travel bookstore in the happening Notting Hill section of London. He shyly recommends a book ("I think the man who wrote it has actually been to

Turkey"); she ignores him and buys another, and in that brief moment the scent of mutual attraction, faint but unmistakable, passes between them.

Naturally, there are problems, a whole caboose of them, ranging from his deranged Welsh roommate Spike (a zany Rhys Ifans) to a gap in their fame and status so considerable that neither one can believe at first what is happening to them.

Given how familiar and predictable this scenario is, it's much to Curtis's credit that he regularly surprises us with either a situation or a line of dialogue that creates contagious laughter. Like when William spills orange juice on Anna in a classic cute-meet situation and promises to have her quickly "back on the street again, but not in the prostitute sense."

Taking advantage of Anna's star-of-stars status, some of *Notting Hill*'s funniest situations deal with the movie business, as when Anna discusses the ins and outs of her contract's nudity clause or William helps her run her lines in a script that smoothly skewers *Armageddon* and its spawn.

Best of all is an extended sequence in which William, mistaken for "Britain's preeminent equestrian journalist" on assignment from *Hare and Hounds*, participates in a press junket for Anna's latest film and finds out firsthand (as if he didn't already know) just how inane those Q&A sessions can be.

Speaking of Hollywood, one obstacle *Notting Hill* has had to clear that *Four Weddings* wasn't burdened with is its status as a mixed marriage of character-intensive contemporary British comedy with mainstream studio moviemaking.

The Hollywood influence is apparent in the film's intrusive "get in the mood or else" Trevor Jones music and its use of sandwich board songs, including "How Can You Mend a Broken Heart" and "Ain't No Sunshine When She's Gone." And it shows up in the way *Notting Hill* occasionally gives in to more sentiment than the moment really demands.

But under the able direction of Roger Michell (whose version of *Persuasion* is the best of the Jane Austen adaptations), *Notting Hill* has the enviable ability to right itself before it gets too far gone, to follow a borderline saccharine moment with just the right biting line or tart scenario.

It also helps to have the right actors delivering those lines, and Grant especially has a delightful time with Curtis's arch dialogue. Convincing as a bumbling sophisticate, a hangdog Cary Grant, this Grant has such an expert way with words that it's no surprise that Anna is taken with him despite herself.

Though Grant wins us over immediately, Roberts has a tougher time. This is partly because, despite the actress's insistence that a picture about heroic nuns ministering to lepers in equatorial Africa couldn't be further from her life than this one, Notting Hill does seem within at least shouting distance of a self-portrait.

Finally, though, it is the connection—acknowledged or not—that Roberts makes with this material that makes her portrait surprisingly effective. To see her in moments of diva pique, to hear her forlorn tone of voice when she talks about how "every time your heart gets broken newspapers splash it around like it's entertainment," is to see the genuine vulnerability without which her character would be neither believable nor sympathetic.

Its modus vivendi with Hollywood may make Notting Hill creak around the edges, but the film's romantic core is impervious to problems. Roberts and Grant are the most glowing of stars here, the people who keep us alive in the darkness, and we want so much for their characters to be happy in their turn.

The Parent Trap
1998

The premise couldn't be less plausible, but who has ever cared?

Since it came out in 1961, *The Parent Trap* has been an embraceable fantasy, a sugarplum vision of a world where parents are perfect though apart, and children are the only ones with the sense and savvy to bring them together again.

Beloved though it is, the original *The Parent Trap* (starring Hayley Mills) shows its age more than fond memory admits. The filmmaking team of Nancy Meyers and Charles Shyer took on the task of doing it again, and irresistible entertainment it turns out to be.

Hewing so closely to the original structure that 1961 writer David Swift shares a screenplay credit, this new *Parent Trap* is right at home in an age when the line "It's scary the way no one stays together anymore" seems even more to the point than it did nearly four decades ago.

It's not only the offspring of broken homes who will be attracted to this film about children planning to trick their split folks into reuniting. Everyone's onscreen life is so completely perfect, each parent such an amalgam of shining beauty and caring virtue, that it's hard not to wish you were a long-lost family member, too.

Adding contemporary comedy to the tale (based on German writer Erich Kastner's *Das Doppelte Lottchen* or *The Double Lottie*) is the Meyers & Shyer team, whose past credits include *Private Benjamin*, *Irreconcilable Differences* and the remade *Father of the Bride*.

Shyer has been the directing half of the team in the past, but Meyers gets her chance this time, and she makes full use of the opportunity. *The Parent Trap* is a glossy, high-energy entertainment, always smooth and clever. Though the film could use shortening, it's been directed with an easy touch and has the considerable virtue of not pushing the sentiment harder than it needs to.

In this, in fact in all things, *The Parent Trap* can't be imagined without its young redheaded star, Lindsay Lohan. Her bright spirit and impish smile make for an immensely likable young person we take to our hearts almost at once. Lohan's the soul of this film as much as Hayley Mills was of the original, and, aided by a gift for accent and considerably improved technology, she is more adept than her predecessor at creating two distinct personalities for the unknowing twin sisters who meet at Camp Walden in Moose Lake, Maine.

Hallie Parker is a completely California girl down to her painted nails and her love for horses. She lives on an idyllic vineyard in the Napa Valley with her handsome and loving father Nick (Dennis

Quaid) and has developed quite an affinity for poker and fencing. Well-behaved Annie James knows a few things about poker and fencing, too, but otherwise she is Hallie's opposite, more Little Princess than Brat Pack. Annie lives in London with her beautiful and loving mother Elizabeth (Natasha Richardson), a designer of exclusive wedding gowns (Vera Wang's are the ones we see).

When Hallie and Annie discover each other at camp, they can't stand what they see, the shared sentiment being "That girl is without a doubt the lowest, most awful creature that ever walked the planet."

That shared enmity leads to a series of ghastly pranks that land both girls in the dreaded Isolation Cabin, where they discover: (A) that they share a taste for Oreos with peanut butter and (B) that they are identical twins separated at birth by photogenic and loving parents who somehow decided this was the sane thing to do.

Barely daunted, the twins come up with "a brilliant beyond brilliant idea." They will switch places so that each can meet the parent she's never known. When the time is right they'll reveal themselves and so force their mother and father to meet again to unswitch them.

Everything goes fine when Hallie arrives in London; but back at Napa, Annie discovers that handsome and loving Nick is being stalked by a calculating blond vamp named Meredith Blake (Elaine Hendrix), nicknamed "Miss I'll Just Have Half a Grapefruit," who is intent on marrying him for his money. A series of panicky transatlantic phone calls follows, and soon enough Nick and Elizabeth are heading for that fateful reunion.

Casting Quaid and Richardson as the parents is one of *The Parent Trap*'s shrewder moves. Though they've never played roles this dreamy before (who has?), these two are up to the task and display excellent chemistry. Because this is a contemporary movie, they've both got household help, and her butler Martin and his housekeeper-nanny Chessy are strongly played by Simon Kunz and Lisa Ann Walter. (In a nice touch, Joanna Barnes, who played the gold digger in 1961, is cast as Meredith's mother.)

The Parent Trap manages to have it both ways. It uses lines of dialogue from the original but puts Leonardo DiCaprio's photo where Ricky Nelson's used to be, and it also has its own set of unexpected comic moments, such as a camper with the chubbiest cheeks working away at the bugle. And having Lohan star as a girl whose happiness you can't help but share in doesn't hurt a bit.

Meyers went on to direct What Women Want *and* Something's Gotta Give *and Lohan went on to become a major teen star and paparazzi target.*

School of Rock
2003

You think you are strong, strong enough not to laugh at anything silly. You think you can resist Jack Black, no matter what he throws at you, but the first lesson *School of Rock* teaches is that you can't. He is that funny.

An amiable farce tailored specifically to the actor's generous dimensions, *Rock* takes a clever premise and Black's unflagging manic energy and comes up with a pleasing mainstream comedy that uses new people and attitudes to entertain in old-fashioned ways. Knowing that opposites attract, *School of Rock* poses a pair of sharp questions: What if a rowdy rock musician taught at a straitlaced private school? More to the point, what if Black's perpetually adolescent persona matched up against a roomful of young people who behaved like responsible adults? The result, which resembles *Mr. Holland's Opus* on mind-altering drugs, always makes you smile.

Mike White is the writer behind *School of Rock*. Since he lived next door to Black for three years, White has intimate knowledge of the actor's Energizer bunny rhythms, a style that led to his breakout role in *High Fidelity* and, later, parts in lesser films such as *Shallow Hal* and *Saving Silverman*.

Here Black, who fronts a band called Tenacious D in real life, plays a guitarist named Dewey Finn who doesn't let his questionable abilities and unlikely physique keep him from feeling like a god of rock 'n' roll.

No one has ever believed more in the music than Dewey. There's no holding him back, not when he tears his shirt off and reveals a not-ready-for-prime-time body, not when he dives into the crowd and lands with a thud on the floor.

If thinking so could make you a star, Dewey would be in the firmament for sure. His band mates, however, aren't entranced by his zeal and, intent on winning a local battle of the bands contest, they give Dewey the boot. Where he sees rock's last angry man, they see, not to put too fine a point on it, "a fat, washed-up loser."

Things are not much better on the home front, where Dewey has been freeloading for years off his nerdy substitute teacher pal Ned Schneebly (screenwriter White). But now Ned has a take-charge girlfriend (*Saturday Night Live*'s Sarah Silverman) who insists that Dewey pay up or leave.

Shaken to his slacker bones, Dewey intercepts a call intended for Ned, puts on a bow tie and a *Dead Poets Society* scarf and takes a job subbing at prestigious Horace Green Prep. It's a place where the students wear little uniforms and principal Rosalie Mullins (the reliable Joan Cusack) is highly suspicious of Dewey's teaching methods, which include a heavy emphasis on recess and lunch.

But one day Dewey hears his ten-year-old fifth-graders playing beautifully in the school orchestra and an idea is born: Why not turn them into a rock band good enough to enter that upcoming citywide battle? It could even be a school project, something that will "test your head and your mind and your brain, too."

Naturally, there are problems. The project must be kept secret from downer parents and principal Mullins. Jobs must be found for class members who can't play. Most daunting of all, this class of baby stockbrokers doesn't have a clue about the music, about the way, in Dewey's standard phrase, "one great rock show can save the world."

Dewey plows through these would-be difficulties with the zeal of the true believer he is. Not only does his energy power the film, but it's in the contrast between his wild and crazy exuberance and the timidity of students who believe they're not cool enough to be in a band that director Richard Linklater (taking a major studio sabbatical after such films as *Slacker* and *Dazed and Confused*) finds his humor.

Selected after the usual nationwide search for youngsters who knew how to make music, the kids in the class, even nonplaying ones like the officious Summer (Miranda Cosgrove) are especially good. It is a little unsettling to see a film whose motto is "We Don't Need No Education," but the fact that the kids are learning to feel good about themselves does seem to help. Even if a great rock show can't save the world, it can make for quite a funny movie.

Supporting player Silverman came into her own with the 2005 concert film, Sarah Silverman: Jesus Is Magic.

Sister Act
1992

Sister Act doesn't break new ground. Its plot isn't particularly original, its director is in no one's pantheon, and it doesn't feature actors doing anything you never imagined they could do. All it does is make you laugh.

And laugh.

And laugh some more.

Sister Act is a tribute to those often denigrated qualities, slickness and professionalism. Graced with a clever script, a cast that will make you smile until you ache, and a snappy sense of pace, *Sister Act* is the funniest by-the-numbers comedy in who knows how long, one of those rare occasions where everything almost magically falls into place.

The engine that drives *Sister Act* from start to finish is the irascible mistress of the double take, Whoopi Goldberg. Entertaining as she was in her Oscar-winning performance in *Ghost,* she is even stronger here in much more of a starring role, appearing in almost every situation and easily holding her own among some very adroit scene stealers.

Sister Act opens with a brief prelude in a parochial school. A mischievous teenager (Isis Carmen Jones, a dead ringer for the star) is asked by a stern nun to name the four apostles. "John, Paul, George and Ringo," comes the elfin reply, causing the exasperated sister to grit her teeth and ask, "Have you any idea what girls like you become?"

Just like that we cut to the most marginal of lounges in Reno, and a girl group knockoff captained by the selfsame Deloris Von Cartier (Goldberg). The songs are familiar Motown standards, the entertainment value uncertain, and the sparse audience of compulsive gamblers and hopeless insomniacs is understandably stingy with applause, but hey, nobody said show business was going to be easy.

Deloris has a personal as well as a professional interest in Reno: Her married boyfriend, Vince LaRocca (an amusing Harvey Keitel), is a player in the hierarchy of organized crime. Fed up with Vince's refusal to break with his wife and the feeble pace of her career, Deloris is about to quit both Reno and LaRocca when she accidentally witnesses a major crime.

Persuaded by tough cop Eddie Mulcahy (Bill Nunn) to testify for the prosecution, Deloris faces the dilemma of where to hide until the trial begins. It's Eddie who comes up with the solution: a small cloistered community of Carmelite sisters in San Francisco. The high-living Deloris is not exactly wild about the idea ("There's nothing but a lot of white women dressed as nuns," she complains, not unreasonably), but Eddie makes her see that it's truly the last place Vince and his cronies would think of looking.

The idea of criminal types hiding out in a house of God is at least as old as Edward G. Robinson's going on the lam in a monastery in the 1940s film *Brother Orchid,* and the humor inherent in women of the cloth is no doubt older still. But *Sister Act*'s playful script (credited to the pseudonymous Joseph Howard but largely written by Paul

Rudnik) is not only replete with wicked one-liners but manages the more difficult task of making this well-trod material seem fresh.

The heart of the film, the influence the convent has on Deloris, and vice versa, is conveyed with a maximum of manic good humor. Again and again, just when you're fearful that *Sister Act* will run out of steam, the script comes up with unexpected moments (the sisters do things in a biker bar, for instance, that would give even Eddie Murphy pause) and show-stopping situations that gleefully demand your attention.

As critical as good lines are, actors having the wherewithal to deliver them with brio are even more so, and it's here that *Sister Act* really stands out. Starting at the top of the order, Maggie Smith as the iron-fisted mother superior who is definitely not amused by Deloris is the ideal foil for Goldberg's limber performance. "God has brought you here," she says with exemplary hauteur. "Take the hint."

An outgoing sort, Deloris, or Sister Mary Clarence, as she's known in the trade, soon makes friends with the other nuns. And, like Smith's top gun, each is a classic type impeccably cast.

Kathy Najimy (of *The Kathy and Mo Show*) claims to have based her awesomely cheerful Sister Mary Patrick on *Entertainment Tonight*'s Mary Hart, but wherever it came from it could not be bettered. Wendy Makkena is earnestness itself as the sweet ingenue, Sister Mary Robert; and comedy veteran Mary Wickes, who's been in everything from *The Man Who Came to Dinner* to *I Love Lucy* in more than fifty years in the business, knows exactly how to play the tough-talking Sister Mary Lazarus, a convent veteran who longs crankily for the bad old days when nuns were nuns.

Whether it was in the monster hit *Dirty Dancing* or other films that didn't do quite so well, director Emile Ardolino never gave any indication that he could be so adept a director of comedy, so good (no doubt with the help of editor Richard Halsey) at keeping the pace lively and the spirits high. Still, ours is fortunately not to reason why, ours is merely to be grateful and enjoy a comedy that reminds you how good it feels simply to sit back and laugh out loud.

Spy Kids
2001

Anyone who's been a child on the verge of adolescence can empathize with twelve-year-old Carmen Cortez (Alexa Vega) when, awash in disbelief, she manages to gasp, "My parents can't be spies. They're not cool enough."

Cool or not, the mother and father of Carmen and her eight-year-old brother, Juni (Daryl Sabara), are definitely secret agents. In fact, the senior Cortezes, Gregorio (a self-deprecating Antonio Banderas) and Ingrid (Carla Gugino) were rivals at the peak of their profession when they married, retired and traded active espionage for parenthood or, in Ingrid's words, "exchanged one life of adventure for another."

This has all been kept secret, until now. For it is the notion of Robert Rodriguez's *Spy Kids* that these veteran espionage operatives, rusty after nine years as desk-bound consultants/parents, are captured on a crucial new mission and have to depend for their lives, not to mention the fate of the free world, on the abilities of their plucky but untrained offspring. This is a very engaging premise, and it's been made into a lively and imaginative winning family film with a playful sense of humor that's clever in the best kind of offhanded way.

The possessory credit has often been the subject of understandable debate, but there's little doubt that this is a case where the "a film by" line would have some meaning. Rodriguez not only wrote, directed and coproduced *Spy Kids*, he was also the editor and camera operator, shares credit as visual-effects supervisor, rerecording mixer and music composer, and he even reportedly flew to Chile so that he could personally shoot needed background footage. Does the man never sleep?

Though working like this is something of a Rodriguez trademark, the blood-and-guts nature of previous credits, from his debut *El Mariachi* through *Desperado, From Dusk till Dawn* and *The Faculty*, make him not the most obvious choice for a family venture.

But, if *Spy Kids* is any indicator, Rodriguez is also something of a big kid at heart, a fantasizer who thought up many of the film's genial collection of gizmos and gadgets, such as the Super Guppy underwater escape vehicle and Electroshock Gumballs. And, as the father of three kids, the filmmaker also has a good sense of the mechanics of sibling bickering that is put to use here.

Also, there are some similarities between this and Rodriguez's earlier films. *Spy Kids* has his trademark high spirits and gift for keeping things moving. And the filmmaker's celebrated ability to squeeze a dollar (*El Mariachi* was reportedly made for $7,000) has served him well in what looks like made-on-a-budget special effects, the bargain sensibility of which actually adds to the picture's old-fashioned charm.

One of the conceits of *Spy Kids* is that nemesis Fegan Floop (the versatile Alan Cumming), aided by his well-named assistant, Minion (Tony Shalhoub), divides his time between the No. 2–rated kids show *Floop's Fooglies* and making bad things for the evil Mr. Lisp (Robert Patrick).

These include a scary army of strong and sneaky robot children who can be made to look like the offspring of the world's leaders, and the much less successful—but much more amusing—Thumb-Thumbs, creatures that are about as effective as you'd imagine something with thumbs for arms, legs and a head would be.

Again, not making a big deal about it, *Spy Kids* layers in messages about the importance of family, belief in yourself and looking after your younger siblings. Also, without calling attention to itself, the film creates an all-Latino family of heroes, throws in music by Los Lobos and visual references to the great Spanish architect Antonio Gaudi.

Producer Elizabeth Avellan, who is married to Rodriguez, says one of the impetuses for *Spy Kids* was to have "a movie we can proudly show to our own children," and this the filmmakers have cheerfully done. If James Bond could inspire dozens of sequels, surely there ought to be at least one in the works for this intrepid gang.

Not one but two Spy Kids *sequels have appeared in theaters so far.*

There's Something About Mary
1998

The Farrelly brothers can't help it, they get these ideas, cheerfully crude and way over the line. Nothing delights this writing-directing team more than making audiences laugh hard at what conventional good taste says isn't even worth a smile. With *There's Something About Mary*, Peter and Bobby Farrelly have hit their own kind of jackpot.

An outrageous goofball farce, *There's Something About Mary* is a giddy symphony of rude and raucous low humor. Codirectors who shared the writing credit with Ed Decter & John L. Strauss, the Farrellys here show a gift not just for finding humor where others have feared to look but for presenting it in a way that is surprisingly close to irresistible.

The Farrellys first made a splash with *Dumb and Dumber* (starring Jim Carrey) and the bowling-themed *Kingpin*. With *Mary*'s story of a woman everyone falls in love with, they display a sharpened ability to make comic situations grow incrementally. Several of the picture's more out-there sequences, such as a desperate attempt to electroshock a dog back to life and a man's dreadful accident with a pants zipper, benefit from how laughs are structured to build on each other.

There's Something About Mary also displays the Farrellys' most paradoxical quality, their good-natured innocence amid all the bad taste. This enables them to blithely make light of a whole range of potentially offensive comic subjects—the gaffes of mentally challenged individuals, the pitfalls of masturbation, the travails of people on crutches—without giving major offense.

The Farrellys have a secret weapon, this time around, in its star, Cameron Diaz. A natural comic talent and a major asset in every film she's been in, Diaz is irreplaceable here. More than being completely believable as the delight of all eyes, her intrinsic, knockout wholesomeness puts a *Good Housekeeping* seal on the raunchy proceedings and keeps the film alive during those moments when it raggedly slows down to catch its breath.

Diaz's costars are just as well cast and just as funny, though both come to humor from different starting points. Although Ben Stiller has done drama, he's mostly known for his impeccable comedy work in 1996's *Flirting with Disaster* and his own *Reality Bites*. Matt Dillon has been thought of mostly for serious roles, but the growing list of comedies he's improved (*The Flamingo Kid*, *To Die For*, *In & Out*) reveal him to be surprisingly gifted at deadpan humor.

Working beautifully together, and backed up by comic sidekicks (Chris Elliott, Lin Shaye, Lee Evans and Jeffrey Tambor), this terrific ensemble throws itself into *There's Something About Mary*. No matter how far-fetched and preposterous the film's plot becomes, the cast's ability to treat ridiculous situations with complete seriousness creates a whole lot of laughter.

Mary starts with a flashback to a Rhode Island high school in 1985 and an astonishingly geeky Ted Stroehmann (Stiller), a loser with more metal on his teeth than the Iron Giant. Stepping in to save the mentally handicapped Warren (W. Earl Brown) from a bully, Ted gains stature in the eyes of Warren's gorgeous sister, Mary Jenson (Diaz), the school's blond princess. In the twinkling of an eye they are planning a senior prom together until an ill-timed errant zipper changes everything.

Cut to thirteen years later. Ted is a writer living in Providence (the Farrellys' hometown) and still pining for Mary. His best friend, Dom (Elliott), suggests he hire a private detective to track her down, and even suggests a coworker, Pat Healy (Dillon), who turns out to be a lowlife ladies' man with a thin mustache and a roving eye.

Pat agrees to search for Mary and, in fact, tracks her down in Miami, where she's nominally an orthopedic surgeon but mostly plays golf and looks in on brother Warren. Completely smitten, Pat lies to Ted about what he's discovered and moves to Florida. Using a technique Woody Allen's character employed in *Everyone Says I Love You*, but to much more comic effect, he eavesdrops on Mary, finds out her likes and dislikes, and attempts, against hellacious odds, to turn himself into Mr. Right.

Of course, Ted finds out what's happened and heads to Miami himself. His trip, though, is far from smooth, and, in a fine example of crossed-wires comedy, he ends up in prison facing some serious charges before he can continue his romantic quest.

Though *There's Something About Mary* relishes finding opportunities for humor where more prudent filmmakers see roadblocks of political correctness, the Farrellys don't neglect the chance for quick, throwaway moments of verbal and visual wit. And they make excellent use of singer-songwriter Jonathan Richman, who, along with drummer Tommy Larkins, provide a blank-faced musical Greek chorus that periodically comments with bleak irony on Ted's woeful plight.

Bursting with antic ideas and vulgar energy, *Mary* has enough enthusiasm left over to inspire a crazed sequence that runs alongside the closing credits, where the cast sings the rock standard "Build Me Up, Buttercup" while doing the kinds of manic things only the Farrellys could dream up. It isn't high-toned, but it will certainly make you laugh.

Part Three
DRAMA/ROMANCE

Introduction

What does it mean that the director whose name appears the most in this category is a man whose first big break was playing cattle-drive ramrod Rowdy Yates on the cowboy television series *Rawhide*.

Partly this is just the luck of the draw, of the inevitably arbitrary way films are categorized. But it is also a function of something more serious: Dramas are so hard to make in today's Hollywood that it takes someone with the clout of actor-director Clint Eastwood to succeed consistently in getting them through the system. And even he has had more trouble gaining approval than his international status would lead you to believe.

It is also a tribute to the difficulty of doing drama that so many of the films on this list have a romantic component. It's almost as if the studios can't bear to trust the audience with serious material without throwing in a love story to soften the potential bite.

Drama also has a connection to action/thriller; many of the same actors, such as Denzel Washington and Robert Redford, appear in both categories, as do directors Michael Mann and Spike Lee.

Especially strong here are filmed biographies, accounts of real lives ranging from the political (*Malcolm X, Michael Collins*) to the musical (*Ray, Selena, What's Love Got to Do with It*) to the indefinable (*The People vs. Larry Flynt*). Maybe you don't have to have a tragic/troubled life to have a film made about you, but it certainly doesn't hurt.

8 Mile
2002

How angry is Eminem, the brooding dark prince of perpetually aggrieved sensitivity? Let us count the ways.

Angry enough to sell 30 million albums, a record for rap. Angry enough to outrage guardians of public decency and allow every disaffected teenager in America to slipstream on his inextinguishable hostility. And angry enough to attract commercially savvy producer Brian Grazer and Curtis Hanson, one of the most adept and sophisticated of directors, to make 8 Mile, a major studio release based loosely on the first steps in the up-from-the-underclass journey Marshall Mathers took to become one of the rulers of rap.

But just as 8 Mile's story is book-ended by battles, one-on-one gladiatorial rap contests in which the audience picks a winner, so the film itself is a battle between God's angry man, this creature of insatiable rage and the boa constrictor Hollywood system, willing and able to swallow anything whole and make it fit a predigested mold. Even an artist whose justifiable boast is "I just say whatever I want to whoever I want whenever I want wherever I want however I want" could disappear without a trace.

Remarkably, however, that did not happen with 8 Mile, a fascinating, surprisingly entertaining stand-off that has adroitly managed to satisfy both of its constituencies, legitimately allowing all sides to claim victory.

Yes, with a script credited to The Mod Squad's Scott Silver, 8 Mile is very much an old-fashioned somebody-up-there-likes-me kind of story, replete with traditional plot devices (will the hero have to work on the night of the climactic battle?) that are decades old. This venerable structure in effect facilitates the mainstreaming of rap, enabling civilian audiences to feel the safety and security of familiarity that's simply not in the cards when listening to Eminem's earlier, more nasty and threatening work.

Yet, though you can see 8 Mile and not really know exactly why the man aroused passion pro and con across America, you certainly get a strong hint. Eminem has such intense presence that even in the film's somewhat denatured form, he and his music have undeniable power and integrity. In fact, Eminem's seething fury, impossible even to think of disguising, is not only the realest thing in the film but also the heart of its appeal. His hostility, savagery and disgust as well as his undeniable musical gifts come from too deep a place to be completely blanded out the way Elvis's talents notoriously were, and fans who come to ride this particular whirlwind will also not be disappointed.

Given the past history of rock-star movies, it was far from certain that this particular marriage of sensibilities would work. Two interlocking factors were key in enabling us to forget how formulaic 8 *Mile* is. One was Eminem's genuine presence and onscreen charisma; the other, director Hanson's filmmaking gifts, including an ability (witness Guy Pearce and Russell Crowe in *L.A. Confidential* and Michael Douglas in *Wonder Boys*) to get memorable performances from his lead actors.

With deep-set, out-from-under eyes and an eight-mile stare, Eminem is someone the camera likes from the moment he steps onscreen. With his tattoos covered by a hooded sweatshirt and his piercings on hiatus because of the film's 1995 setting, the actor has something of the quality of an updated James Dean (the director suggested he watch *East of Eden*, but apparently that never happened) and he carries the picture as if it were second nature.

Eminem plays Jimmy Smith Jr., a.k.a. Bunny Rabbit, an aspiring Detroit rapper with a genuine gift for language but an uncertainty about what to do with his life. When 8 *Mile* begins, he's carrying everything he owns in a black plastic trash bag and is about to move back in with his impecunious mother, Stephanie (Kim Basinger, who won an Oscar in Hanson's *L.A. Confidential*), and her loutish boyfriend, Greg (Michael Shannon).

Jimmy and his friends dream of rap stardom, and in fact two people insist that they are Bunny Rabbit's ticket out. One is his pal Future (Mekhi Phifer of *Clockers* and *O*), who wants Jimmy to persevere in the rap battles he hosts; the other is neighborhood entrepreneur Wink (Eugene Byrd), who insists, "I'm building my empire, and I'm taking you with me."

With a guy as good looking as Jimmy, a romantic entanglement is also inevitable. He runs into the attractive Alex (the talented Brittany Murphy), an aspiring model, at the car-bumper factory where he works. At the same facility, Jimmy has 8 *Mile*'s most curious scene, a rap battle in which he comes to the defense of a maligned gay fellow worker, a sequence that feels as if it had more to do with the star's well-publicized difficulties with the gay community than with furthering the film's plot.

Though Jimmy has run-ins with rival rappers, Eminem has such an overpowering presence that the only involving conflict his character has is with himself. Like Shakespeare's Prince Hal, he is royalty in mufti, wrestling with inner demons before feeling the confidence to declare himself the heir apparent, if not the king.

This is a classic story, and in Hanson 8 *Mile* has one of Hollywood's most accomplished classicists, a director whose films seem instinctively to make all the right moves. Hanson was also shrewd enough to build in a six-week rehearsal schedule to enable his star to feel comfortable with the moviemaking process.

Hanson also insisted that 8 *Mile* (named after a Detroit street that is a racial and economic dividing line) have the particular texture of the Motor City, Eminem's hometown. He shot the film on location and used Philip Messina, the production designer on *Traffic*, and cinematographer Rodrigo Prieto, who did the gritty *Amores Perros*, to ensure an authentic look.

Though some of 8 *Mile*'s realistic touches become wearing—there's more use of "dog," as in "Yo, dog," than at the annual meeting of the Westminster Kennel Club—the film is never more real than when Jimmy unloads his anger on someone close to him, a frequent occurrence. Eminem is an actor with a rare gift for rage, and movie careers, even big ones, have been built on less.

Despite that real promise, Eminem has yet to make another feature.

The Age of Innocence
1993

Imagine a society where any love at all is a love that dares not speak its name. Where proper form is everything, women are nothing, and emotions are so rigidly repressed that the unbuttoning of a glove can be a breathtakingly sensual moment. A world "balanced so precariously its harmony could be shattered by a whisper." And then imagine Martin Scorsese putting it all on film.

This was the problematic setup for *The Age of Innocence,* based on Edith Wharton's Pulitzer Prize–winning novel of New York society in the 1870s. Skeptics said that the visceral director who made *Taxi Driver, Raging Bull* and *Cape Fear,* the man who specialized in characters who had never suppressed an emotion in their lives, was not an ideal choice to take on one of the great romantic novels of the twentieth century, a love story of surpassing delicacy and almost agonizing restraint.

But just as the Wharton novel surprises by its velvet-gloved power, so Scorsese impresses by how masterfully he has come up to the challenge. His *Age of Innocence* (coscripted with Jay Cocks) is a beautifully done adaptation of the novel, polished, elegant and completely cinematic. It is also a bit distant, a film that doesn't wear its feelings on its sleeve, but given the effects it's after, that would be counterproductive.

Looked at from another point of view, the director's success here is hardly surprising. For a lesser-known Scorsese has always existed alongside the more celebrated one: the student of film history, the zealot for preservation, the champion of pictorial directors such as Michael Powell and Luchino Visconti, whose joint influence on this strikingly visual film is noticeable.

Aside from the expected potent support from cinematographer Michael Ballhaus and editor Thelma Schoonmaker, both Scorsese regulars, the director has the advantage here of a cast headlined by Daniel Day-Lewis, Michelle Pfeiffer and Winona Ryder, and chosen from top to bottom with exceptional shrewdness.

Day-Lewis plays Newland Archer, lawyer, dilettante and a pillar of proper society in 1870s Manhattan. Engaged to May Welland (Ryder), the most eligible as well as the most giggly young woman around, Newland takes the nature of the social order he is a part of more or less for granted until Ellen Olenska (Pfeiffer) enters his life.

Actually, reenters is more like it, for Newland and Ellen were child-hood friends. But Ellen's family moved to Europe, where she eventually married Count Olenska, an apparently dissolute type whose mistreat-ment has led Ellen to leave him behind and return to what she hopes will be the safety of the city she grew up in.

Ellen is also May Welland's cousin, and, as an unattached woman soon to be related by marriage, partly Newland's responsibility. So when he hears that malicious gossips, one being Larry Lefferts (Richard E. Grant), are beginning to target her, he chivalrously moves, much to May's satisfaction, to act protectively toward his old friend.

But Ellen, spirited, independent and unbound by convention, is a woman unlike any Newland has known. When, for instance, with typ-ical mock sophistication he archly tells her he loves his fiancée as much as one can, she replies with disturbing directness, "Do you think there's a limit?"

And, in fact, the more Newland sees Ellen, the more he starts to feel stifled by the society whose suppression of women he took for granted and the less he feels sure about his love for May. And when, as an attorney and Ellen's friend, he is called on by the family to talk Ellen out of her plans for a scandal-provoking divorce from the count, the intensity of his feelings gradually comes into sharper focus.

But no more than gradually, for one of the ways Scorsese and Cocks's script are faithful to the novel's nuances is by demonstrating how imperceptibly society's strictures and his own qualms turn New-land into "a prisoner in the center of an armed camp." Essential in setting and keeping this tone is the decision to have Joanne Wood-ward contribute a letter-perfect voice-over narration that catches Wharton's witheringly ironic sensibility.

And it is not just the verbal tone that has been preserved, but also the visual one. Like the old master he's become, Scorsese (helped by production designer Dante Ferretti and all kinds of experts from a Table Decoration Consultant to a Chef, 19th Century Meals) has re-created a bygone New York with special, almost tactile attention paid to such details as the way a cigar end was cut or how clothing was worn. For Newland Archer's world is a world of things, a place where creature comforts inhibit and suffocate life as much as ease it.

Scorsese and casting director Ellen Lewis have carefully selected actors who seem at ease in this world, ranging from Miriam Margolyes's amusing Mrs. Manson Mingott to Stuart Wilson's audacious Julius Beaufort. And the director has enlivened the telling with an overall cinematic elan and a range of effects, including a by-now trademark Steadicam sequence and the expressive use of the old-fashioned iris close.

Finally, however, the story of *The Age of Innocence* is the story of Newland, Ellen and May. Winona Ryder captures May's genteel self-satisfaction exquisitely; and Pfeiffer, though readers of the book will wish she was rather more mysterious, is especially effective in the film's most emotional scenes.

It is Day-Lewis, who couldn't be more different here than he was in *The Last of the Mohicans*, who appears to greatest effect. He is the ideal Newland, a young man whose sensitivity and poetic indecision are reflected in his bright, handsome face. Longing, loss and an almost indescribable poignancy cross that face as well, signposts of emotions that, both Wharton and Scorsese know, are all the more affecting for being inarticulate and unexpressed.

Beloved
1998

Directed by Jonathan Demme, *Beloved* is ungainly and hard to follow at times, like the proverbial giant not quite sure how to best use its strength. But that power exists, present and undeniable, and once this film gets its bearings, the unsentimental fierceness of its vision brushes obstacles and quibbles from its path.

Already a modern classic, *Beloved* the novel was awarded the Pulitzer Prize and was critical to author Toni Morrison's receiving the Nobel

Prize in literature. Set just before and just after the Civil War and telling the story of Sethe (Oprah Winfrey), the survivor of an unspeakable hell for whom "the future was a matter of keeping the past at bay," it deals as potently as only fiction can with the nightmare legacy of slavery and the deadly, terrifying weight of the past.

Yet as devastating as the book is, its use of a multilayered narrative, its complete acceptance of the supernatural and its exceptional way with language add up to a story that seems to be too large and too poetic to fit comfortably into a film of any length.

Beloved was director Demme's first feature since 1993's *Philadelphia* and only his second since 1991's Oscar-winning *The Silence of the Lambs*, and in some ways this film combines the social consciousness of the former with the facility for horror (and by extension the supernatural) of the latter. The work that has resulted, strange, troubling and powerfully imagined, is rough going at first, but the more time you spend with it the more the strength of the underlying material exerts its will.

The film's screenplay (credited to Akosua Busia, Richard LaGravenese and Adam Brooks) takes the sane way out, paring the book down to its essential events, most of which take place in 1873 in and around a small house on the outskirts of Cincinnati. What's been sacrificed is the book's extended look at life at Sweet Home, the ironically named Kentucky plantation where the horrors begin, though the flashbacks that are shown (shot by longtime Demme cinematographer Tak Fujimoto on special, deliberately grainy film stock) are critical to the film's impact.

All this, however, takes a while to unfold. Initially, almost from its opening *Poltergeist, the Early Years* sequence—a chaotic, demonic night when a tormented dog called Here Boy gets tossed around, mirrors break and two young brothers flee for their lives—*Beloved* comes across as a film that knows its source so well that it underestimates how confusing its events are to nonreaders.

The next scene reintroduces Sethe and her daughter Denver (Kimberly Elise) on a sunny day in 1873, eight years later. Coming up the road is a man Sethe hasn't seen in eighteen years, Paul D (Danny Glover), a friend from the prewar days at Sweet Home and an intimate of Halle, Sethe's husband and Denver's father, whom Sethe also hasn't seen since the day in 1855 she precipitously fled the plantation.

Invited into their house, Paul D is unnerved to find a room filled with undulating, vibrating red light. It is, Sethe tells him matter-of-factly, the sad but not evil ghost of her baby daughter, who died at the age of two. It's the same ghost that drove her two sons away eight years ago, the ghost that keeps neighbors from coming over and relieving the bleak isolation these women live in.

Paul D's presence does two things. It precipitates a physical struggle with Baby Ghost, as Denver calls it, who apparently leaves, though Denver does say, "I think the baby ain't gone, I think the baby got plans." And having Paul D around leads Sethe to relive, and us to see in flashback, the agonies of her final night at Sweet Home.

What happens at Sweet Home, the multiple tortures inflicted on Sethe by the white men who run things, are painful, deeply difficult to watch, even in the brief shards of flashback we're given, and aesthetically problematical. What we see onscreen, perhaps to protect our sensibilities, is shown in short, often frenzied bursts. When that frantic tone combines with the film's determination to give its actors accurate accents, past events end up rushing by in a blur. In fact, to read Morrison's novel after seeing the film is to say again and again, "So that's what that was all about."

Determined to bring some normalcy into Sethe and Denver's lives, Paul D takes them to a local carnival. When they return home, however, they find in their front yard a beautiful, almost catatonic young woman whom we've seen emerge fully clothed and soaking wet out of a nearby stream. Asked her name, the woman croaks a single word in the deepest of voices: Beloved.

Partly young woman, mostly child, Beloved can't or won't say where she came from and has to learn from scratch what it is to act her age. She slobbers, drools, snores, eats sweets with a vengeance, and, though Denver is eager for her companionship, it is Sethe that

Beloved is hungry for. Morrison's limpid prose notes that "rain water held on to pine needles for dear life and Beloved could not take her eyes off Sethe," who, in turn, felt that "the company of this sweet, if peculiar guest pleased her the way a zealot pleases his teacher."

With the appearance of Beloved, the film that's her namesake comes fully alive, and Thandie Newton's performance in the role is the largest part of the reason. Previously seen in *Flirting* and *Jefferson in Paris*, Newton hits the right unnerving notes with her work here. Pleading, screaming, importuning, her Beloved is a truly disconcerting, unfathomable presence that deeply troubles Paul D. It gives the film the critical sense of unease the book has, in effect freeing it to be itself.

Because her eerie, insinuating "Tell me" can't be resisted, Beloved's persistent questions slowly lead Sethe to recount even more of her past. We see how she escaped from Sweet Home, the circumstances of Denver's birth, and how she got to Ohio and the comforting presence of her mother-in-law, the unchurched preacher Baby Suggs (Beah Richards). Sethe also gets closer and closer to her own terrible secrets as well as the hard truths that are in the possession of Beloved and Paul D.

It was Winfrey's persistence as a producer that got *Beloved* made, and though her relative inexperience as an actress is visible, it turns out not to be a problem. Winfrey is convincing enough to make an impact with such lines as Sethe's "I will never run from another thing on this Earth, you hear!" declaration to Paul D; at other times, her untutored quality makes a good fit with the stoicism that is Sethe's touchstone. Winfrey is also helped by the excellent actors she's surrounded with, starting with Glover as the soul of humanity Paul D and Elise as the troubled but striving Denver. Lisa Gay Hamilton is so convincing as the young Sethe that you forget at times she's not Winfrey, and Albert Hall effectively plays the pivotal role of Stamp Paid. Most satisfying of all, perhaps, is Richards, Oscar-nominated thirty years ago for *Guess Who's Coming to Dinner*, who poignantly conveys the mystical, healing presence of Baby Suggs.

What finally pulls *Beloved* over the shoals of its initial awkwardness and uncertainty is the strength contained in its exceptional source material. By the time Paul D tells Sethe, "We got more yesterday than anybody, we need some kind of tomorrow," we have gone through enough with them to calculate the cost of survival down to the last drop of blood.

Clockers
1995

Playing under the opening credits, a series of stark images sets the mood for *Clockers*, the disturbing movie Spike Lee has made from Richard Price's best-selling novel. These careful re-creations of crime scene photos of drug-related homicides show young black men sprawled in cars, tossed face down in dumpsters, motionless on sidewalks. Though not as horrific as the real thing, the pictures are grim enough to convey the message the rest of *Clockers* underlines: Don't even think about getting comfortable while this movie is on the screen.

Clockers, Lee's eighth feature in nine years, demonstrates how accomplished a filmmaker he has become, securely in control of plot, actors and imagery. And because it is so much the film he wanted to make, *Clockers* illustrates another, less audience-friendly aspect of Lee's technique that is not always noticed: his particular combination of emotional distance and moral instruction.

Although other directors tend to make films because they want to tell stories or explore character, neither of these purposes feels paramount with Lee. He directs, or so it seems, to make points and deliver messages, and he has turned Price's novel into a cold, angry, unsettling motion picture about a cold, pitiless world.

Lee doesn't really want us to root too hard for anyone, even Strike, *Clockers'* young protagonist (effectively played by newcomer Mekhi Phifer); to his way of thinking, getting viewers to bond to any one personality is too easy an out. Lee is not after empathetic hearts who bleed for the deserving poor; he wants us to look at the larger picture and realize how deep the problem is, how much society has to change, before he allows us the luxury of getting off the hook through personal caring.

Strike, known to his mother and no one else as Ronald Dunham, is the nearly twenty-year-old head of a crew of youthful dealers who sit on the benches outside a public housing project in Brooklyn (changed from the novel's New Jersey setting) and do nothing but dispense crack cocaine.

So conscientious that he's developed stomach problems (which he sporadically treats with doses of a convenience store chocolate drink), Strike has become a particular favorite of his boss, Rodney Little (Delroy Lindo), a neighborhood Fagin who both cares about his kids and coldly exploits their willingness to sell crack, "the world's greatest product."

Quite literally losing the stomach for his work, hassled by the local police and a housing authority cop nicknamed Andre the Giant (Keith David), Strike is desperate to "get off the benches." So when Rodney talks one night about a drug rival named Darryl Adams and how grateful he would be if the guy were gone, Strike understands. After a quick stop at a neighborhood bar, where he runs into his hard-working, family-man older brother Victor (Isaiah Washington), Strike heads out, armed and dangerous.

Though we don't see it on screen, Darryl Adams is murdered that night, but to the surprise of everyone in the neighborhood, straight-arrow Victor, of all people, almost immediately confesses to the crime. He is, of course, arrested, but no one who knows anything thinks he did it, including homicide detective Larry Mazilli (John Turturro) and his especially unbelieving partner Rocco Klein (Harvey Keitel).

A cop for just about as long as Strike has been alive, Klein views the kid simply as "a known scumbag." And the longer he investigates Victor's personal history, the less likely he thinks it is that the older Dunham pulled the trigger. Convinced that the brothers are pulling some kind of scam on him, he takes Victor's confession as a deep personal affront and begins to put so much pressure on Strike that the young man's world threatens to unravel one strand at a time.

Though Lee has shifted the novel's focus from Rocco to Strike, what *Clockers* is particularly interested in is illustrating these two universes in collision, the dark spectacle of cynical, casually racist cops who joke about death battling both physically and psychologically with the kids who are inevitably the victims of violence.

What this brooding, unsettling film (written by Price and Lee) does most successfully is re-create the desperation and hopelessness of Strike's life on the benches and off it, forcefully showing how trapped he is between competing antagonists who care about no agenda but their own.

Even though Strike is allowed a few human touches, such as his love of trains and his mentoring of a younger neighborhood kid named Tyrone (PeeWee Love), the portrait of a pitiless society and the film's fierce frontal attacks on drugs ("You are selling your own people death") and shootings ("This ain't no TV violence, real guns kill") have a more lasting impact than any personal story.

Helping make these points is as strong a cast as Lee has yet worked with. As antagonists who confront each other through Strike, Keitel, and especially Lee veteran Delroy Lindo, give strong and chilling performances. Also remarkable is Tom Byrd as Errol Barnes, Rodney's heroin-addicted, AIDS-ravaged enforcer, yet another in Lee's gallery of terrifying victims of drugs. Whatever happens to Strike as not as compelling as the enduring factors that put the young man on the benches in the first place.

Contact
1997

Whatever's Out There has always fascinated people Down Here, especially movie people. But these days, instead of watching the skies (as those 1950s films encouraged everyone to do), people are listening to them. Contact tells us what one woman heard and how the world reacted.

Starring Jodie Foster in an exceptional performance as the radio astronomer who listened, and directed by Robert Zemeckis in his first outing since Forrest Gump, Contact is superior popular filmmaking, both polished and effective. But despite its success and its serious intentions, it's finally a movie where the storytelling makes more of an impact than the story.

Balanced between wanting to deal with the philosophical and scientific issues that concerned Carl Sagan, who wrote the original 1985 novel, and making sure to satisfy the cravings of a mass audience, Contact is not as profound as it would like to be, it is nevertheless more thoughtful and intelligent than skeptics may be expecting.

Expertly directed by Zemeckis, who makes this kind of prestige studio production look easier than it is, Contact never loses touch with its "who are we and why are we here" sense of wonder about the universe that is its greatest strength. Though it has a strongly sentimental side and wanders into conventional territory more often than it realizes, Contact manages an almost gyroscopic ability to right itself whenever absolutely necessary.

Much of this is due to Foster, whose skill and presence seem to increase with each of her pictures and who dominates Contact in the best possible sense. Her portrayal of astronomer Ellie Arroway, a character she knows intimately, demonstrates why no one is more persuasive at conveying intelligence and singleminded passion to the point of confrontational anger. Foster is Contact's lodestar, and when she is on the screen, the film can't help but be engrossing.

Arroway is first encountered in a prologue as an eight-year-old shortwave radio buff with a gentle father (David Morse) and an eagerness (well-conveyed by young actress Jena Malone) to hear from faraway places. Dad also ignites her interest in extraterrestrials with a folksy "if it is just us, seems like an awful waste of space" homily the film likes enough to use three times.

As an adult astronomer who has come to trust her work more than people, Arroway has turned into someone accurately characterized as "brilliant, driven, a major pain in the ass . . . obsessed with a field that's considered professional suicide." That would be her affiliation with SETI, the Search for Extraterrestrial Intelligence, a group of scientists who listen doggedly for a signal from the skies.

Arroway's superior, National Science Foundation head David Drumlin (Tom Skerritt), is markedly unsympathetic, typically greeting her with a dismissive "Still waiting for E.T. to call?" A further run-in with Drumlin leads Arroway to a reclusive billionaire, S. R. Hadden (an assured John Hurt), who lives on an airplane and knows exactly what he wants to do with all his money.

Arroway also connects with a different kind of man, Palmer Joss, played by heartthrob du jour Matthew McConaughey. A kind of self-defrocked priest, "a man of the cloth without the cloth" who "couldn't live with the whole celibacy thing," Joss is a writer who feels the modern passion for technology and science is corroding the world's moral values.

Though the science vs. religion, does-God-exist discussions he has with Arroway are some of *Contact*'s most interesting, Joss has a tendency to come off as a ruggedly handsome signboard for the film's ideas. Also, the James V. Hart and Michael Goldenberg script upgrades Joss to much more of a conventional love interest than he was in Sagan's book. It's a transition that has its bumpy aspects as Joss, a construct more than a fully fleshed-out character, pops in and out of events in a not-always-convincing way.

Clocking in at two and a half hours, *Contact* is most alive during its central section, when Arroway, sitting next to a photogenic group of dish-shaped radio telescopes near Socorro, New Mexico, and hoping as usual for a sign from the cosmos, hears what is unmistakably a signal from the beyond.

The source turns out to be Vega, a spot twenty-six light-years away, and how Arroway and her colleagues take the numerous steps necessary to decipher that message, what it says, and how Arroway fights to retain a part in its implications, are conveyed in a rush of images and sequences that are so invigorating that it's possible to overlook how skillfully it's all been put together.

For this, much credit has to go to director Zemeckis, cinematographer Don Burgess and editor Arthur Schmidt. The wizardly storytelling style they employ is seamless and involving, and all manner of elegant camera moves enhance the film. Even bravura sequences such as tracking Foster as she runs from her car through the lab to check on the signal (a scene that according to *American Cinematographer* was shot in two separate locations months apart) are so intrinsic to the narrative they never seem showy or excessive.

Contact has difficulty maintaining this momentum through its extended final segment. Partly it's that the initial section, the quest, makes the best use of the strengths of Foster's characterization, of Arroway's almost painful eagerness to make intergalactic contact. Also—and this goes to the heart of what *Contact* is lacking—the idea of the search turns out to be more involving than the knowledge that ends up being found. But what a search it is.

Courage Under Fire
1996

We know their names as well as we know our own: honesty, bravery, a sense of decency. They're the virtues we insist we honor most and they're also the most difficult to portray on screen without plunging into sentimentality, without making those who possess them look naïve or absurd or both.

Courage Under Fire avoids those traps and several others. Intelligent, involving and serious, it is as honestly emotional as Hollywood allows itself to get, a story of the search for wartime truth whose own concern for the genuine makes all the difference.

This film has the overall tidiness, the urge to dot the I's and cross the T's, that typifies projects that have attracted director Edward

Zwick (*Glory, Legends of the Fall*) and screenwriter Patrick Sheane Duncan, himself a combat veteran. But here both men have pushed past business as usual and insisted on a level of believability and evenhandedness that adroitly camouflages the story's more schematic elements.

Though publicity images hint otherwise, *Courage Under Fire*'s two stars, Denzel Washington and Meg Ryan, do not share screen time. But their joined strengths, the authenticity of their performances, gives the film's dramatization of moral and ethical dilemmas an objective edge that also touches the heart.

Washington plays Lieutenant Colonel Nathaniel Serling, a tank commander in the Gulf War. In a frenetic, confusing battle at a spot called Al Bathra (a sequence of pure chaos that makes the concept of friendly fire understandable), Serling gives an order that mistakenly results in the death of his closest friend.

Transferred back to a desk job in Washington, prevented from speaking publicly about the incident, Serling is a good man in a moral crisis. Assured that he won't be abandoned by the service he's given seventeen years to, the colonel's commitment to doing the right thing makes his mistake almost unbearably painful. He starts to develop a drinking problem and though he tells his wife, Meredith (Regina Taylor), that he's handling things, we can see that he's not.

As good as Washington has been previously—few actors have been as consistently effective—there is a sense in *Courage Under Fire* that he has raised his acting to a new plane of emotional connection. Washington's ability to convey, quietly but forcefully, intangibles such as integrity and a sense of mission help make this an inordinately moving and sophisticated performance.

The colonel's troubles, however, are only the backdrop to *Courage Under Fire*'s main drama. For that routine desk job, investigating possible candidates for the Medal of Honor, becomes anything but pro forma.

Assigned to determine whether the death in battle of Medevac helicopter pilot Captain Karen Walden (Ryan) warrants the medal, Serling finds himself under intense political pressure. For the president's men are eager for the opportunity to present the medal to the photogenic young daughter of what would be the first woman to get this preeminent combat decoration.

At first, Serling's investigation turns up the expected minor discrepancies. But the more he looks into what happened at that remote desert location, the more the incident takes on aspects of *Rashomon* in a helicopter: Each survivor remembers things with a significantly different spin. And the uncertainty the colonel feels about his own situation, his desire to believe in heroes vying with his determination to have the truth come out, seep into the investigation.

Though she's seen only in abbreviated flashbacks, the role of Walden is critical because reconstructing her character is *Courage*'s central concern. With a hard Texas twang and the determination to lead that is resented as "butch," Walden is not an easy role to play well and Meg Ryan brings to it not only skill but the critical residue of accumulated likeability that serves her well in the film's darker moments.

Courage also benefits from the strength of its supporting players. Lou Diamond Phillips gives an intense, focused performance as Monfriez, a crew member possessing an essential piece of information, and Scott Glenn adds believability to the standard sequences of a probing *Washington Post* reporter. Just as impressive is Michael Moriarty, rarely seen in features these days, who gives a convincing spin to the often pro forma role of the powerful commanding officer, General Hershberg.

Though, unlike *Rashomon*, we eventually do find out what happened on that helicopter, it is to Zwick and the script's credit that the film never tips its hand. Each of the several looks we get at Walden's actions is creditable while on the screen and it is hard to ask for more than that.

And though its re-creation of combat is not *Courage Under Fire*'s most involving aspect, the film succeeds in making the Gulf War seem more of a real event than all the footage shipped back on CNN could. And it also points out, without seeming to try, that if war has the potential to bring out the best in individuals, it does so at the most terrible price.

Erin Brockovich
2000

Underqualified, underdressed and increasingly desperate, Erin Brockovich opens the film with her name on it pleading for a skilled job she can sense is not going to be hers.

No, she says, she has no actual medical training, but she does have three kids. She's great with people, and a fast learner, too. And she's always been interested in science, to the point of once being "madly in love with geology." Doesn't all that count for anything?

Not yet it doesn't, but before *Erin Brockovich* is over those qualities will surface as major players in this irresistible, hugely satisfying feminist fairy tale that turns *Norma Rae* into the protagonist of *A Civil Action* and makes us believe it.

Based on the true story of a woman the world didn't take seriously who empowered herself by helping others gain justice, *Erin Brockovich* does more than chronicle the rebirth of a downtrodden individual. It serves as a career milestone for director Steven Soderbergh, writer Susannah Grant and, most of all, star Julia Roberts.

With films collectively hitting a worldwide gross of $2 billion, Roberts is arguably the most successful—and certainly most highly paid—of contemporary actresses. Yet there is the sense about *Erin Brockovich* that this is the part Roberts has long been looking for. It's a role that allows the actress, like her character, to use her allure for a good cause, to put her undeniable star qualities, her great gift for humor, empathy, romance and vulnerability, at the service of a character with real texture.

Make no mistake, this is very much of an old-fashioned crowd-pleasing diva part, one that allows Roberts to laugh and bawl, be sensitive and take no prisoners, but it also makes points about corporate malfeasance, self-esteem and the place of women in society that fluffier scenarios want no part of. Long determined to be taken seriously as an actress, Roberts has kissed a lot of frogs (wouldn't everyone like to forget *Mary Reilly?*) on the way to this satisfying triumph.

As to director Soderbergh, who started with the justly celebrated *sex, lies and videotape* and then went all over the place, his career has been no one-way rocket, either. But with 1998's exceptional George Clooney-Jennifer Lopez vehicle *Out of Sight*, he revealed an un-looked-for talent that's on display here as well.

What Soderbergh can do as well as anyone is bring restraint, intelligence and subtlety to mainstream material, and what a difference that makes. To infuse an essential sense of unforced reality into stories that sound formulaic is to walk quite a fine line, and Soderbergh's gift for that, combined with Roberts's stardom, should finally supply the major box-office success that eluded him with *Out of Sight*.

Writer Grant (helped by an uncredited polish from Richard La-Gravenese) has presented strong women before in *Pocahontas* and *Ever After*. But this script has more of a sense of life and it's especially adroit in placing believable and well-timed obstacles in the path of its inevitable resolution. In fact, given that the ad line ("She brought a small town to its feet and a huge company to its knees") effectively gives away the entire plot, it's amazing how much drama and pins-and-needles worry the film manages to wring from a foregone conclusion.

Helping Soderbergh realize this script's potential are top-of-the-line people on both sides of the camera, including veteran independent film cinematographer Ed Lachman, five-time Oscar-nominated editor Anne V. Coates and costume designer Jeffrey Kurland, who has had enormous fun creating clothes for a character who is not afraid of a little exposure.

For though her moral fiber couldn't be more spotless if she were played by Julie Andrews, Erin Brockovich does not dress like a saint. In fact, with her big hair, tiny miniskirts, three-inch heels and an encyclopedic knowledge of the uses of cleavage, she looks more like a hooker than the character Roberts played in *Pretty Woman*.

Erin is also in the habit of speaking truth to power, of saying whatever comes into her mind to whomever's in her line of fire. "Two things aggravate me," she claims in something of an understatement, "being ignored and being lied to." Roberts is especially adept at taking advantage of Erin's gift for devastating one-liners, none of which can be repeated in a family-friendly format.

One of the themes of *Erin Brockovich* is that appearances can be deceiving, so we know at once that Erin is a woman of sterling qualities. Yes, she's twice-divorced, is $17,000 in debt and has $74 in the bank, but Roberts's presence makes us implicitly believe it's only a matter of time until the world understands that under those skimpy clothes is a smart, hard-working, self-reliant woman just waiting to be gainfully employed.

That employment was looking chancy until Erin came into contact with the majesty of the law as personified by Los Angeles attorney Ed Masry (Albert Finney). He represents her in a personal injury lawsuit that doesn't turn out well, and because Ed's the only potential employer she knows, Erin lays siege to his office until a barely entry-level job is forthcoming.

Finney's role is largely that of Roberts's straight man, and he reacts on cue with looks of horror at her unpredictable shenanigans. Still, the importance of Finney to the film's success shouldn't be underestimated. A well-schooled veteran, he brings integrity, stature and a sense of humor to the role of audience surrogate, never too blasé to be flummoxed by what Erin is up to.

The other man in Erin's life is George (*In the Company of Men*'s effective Aaron Eckhart), a motorcycle hunk with enough skin art to necessitate a credited Tattoo Designer. George not only lives next door to Erin, he's her masculine don't-trust-your-eyes mirror image, someone who under all that leather has the temperament of a caring nanny eager to watch her children while she attempts to save the world.

Early on in her filing work at Ed Masry's office, Erin comes across some pro bono work he's doing involving residents of the Mojave Desert town of Hinkley. They're all getting sick and the mammoth PG&E corporation, the place's biggest employer, claims to have nothing to do with it. Intrigued, Erin convinces Ed to let her look into the situation, and soon enough she is using her people skills and interest in science, not to mention her world-class flirting ability, to get at the heart of the problem and convince the townsfolk to let her and the lawyers do something about their problems.

Erin Brockovich benefits, as did *Out of Sight,* from excellent acting down to its smallest roles. Finely cast by Margery Simkin, the script was strong enough to attract such talents as Cherry Jones and Marg Helgenberger to supporting but pivotal roles as townspeople and is obviously much the better for it. There are also a pair of amusing cameos, one by the real Erin Brockovich as a waitress who waits, in effect, on herself, and the other by producer Michael Shamberg, convincing as an untrustworthy corporate attorney.

Though the publicity material huffs and puffs about Erin's being a role model for the new millennium, in fact what's most exciting about this film is how old-fashioned it is at its core. It uses the standard Hollywood building blocks of big stars and a Cinderella storyline laced with laughter and tears and reminds us why they became standard in the first place. More than anything, *Erin Brockovich* reminds us how much entertainment value lies buried in traditional material, waiting for someone with the wit and skill to dig it out.

Roberts won the best actress Oscar for this role.

Hearts in Atlantis
2001

Stephen King is a writer with an eye for the grotesque, never at a loss for a strange way to make somebody die. Scott Hicks, director of *Shine* and *Snow Falling on Cedars,* is a filmmaker of noticeable, at times overwhelming, gentility. They do not seem made for each other, but *Hearts in Atlantis* shows they can be.

Assisted by a well-crafted script by the veteran William Goldman and a masterly performance by Anthony Hopkins, Hicks has turned two King short stories into a somber meditation on the dreams and frustrations of childhood and the ways the adult world makes its darker qualities known. Though the film is inevitably too pat at times, too eager to underline its message, it has in Hopkins an actor who can obliterate most objections.

The two stories from King's *Hearts in Atlantis* collection, "Low Men in Yellow Coats" and "Heavenly Shades of Night Are Falling," find the author in a mood more nostalgic than bloodthirsty. Still, Goldman has shrewdly tightened and streamlined the plot, added at least one memorable speech and, to an extent, normalized the narrative's inevitable supernatural elements.

After the briefest of prologues showing an adult Bobby Garfield (David Morse) going home for the funeral of one of his closest childhood friends, *Atlantis* shifts back in time to focus on what happened to an eleven-year-old Bobby (an engaging Anton Yelchin) in 1960.

Bobby has two tight friends, Carol (Mika Boorem) and Sully (Will Rothhaar), youngsters with whom he shares a few too many Norman Rockwell moments. But otherwise, his life is rather empty. When Bobby was five his father died, and his acerbic, distant working mother, Liz (Hope Davis, on target as always), has little time or money to spend on him, though she never loses an opportunity to blame all their problems on her departed ex.

Yet though she never seems to have money for Bobby (the flashback's opening scene shows him getting an adult library card for his birthday, not the Schwinn bicycle he's dreamed of), Liz manages to find the wherewithal for the smart clothes she says she needs for work. What Bobby needs is adult interaction as well as a substitute for his desperately missed father, which is where the enigmatic Ted Brautigan (Hopkins) enters the picture.

A nondescript, middle-aged man who arrives with his possessions in shopping bags (which does not make the best impression on Liz), Ted has rented the upstairs apartment in Bobby's house. Yet as ordinary as Ted seems, there is something strange about him, something indefinite that lurks just beyond our comprehension.

Taking the inevitable liking to the boy (who, in truth, is remarkably likable), Ted hires him for a pair of jobs. The first and most straightforward, given that the older man's eyes are failing, is to read the newspaper aloud. The second demands that Bobby keep his own eyes open for "low men" in the neighborhood, sinister strangers driving big cars. Does Ted have something they want, the boy asks. Yes, the man says, "let's leave it at that."

Though there are involving incidents with Bobby's friends and his mother, the interaction between this surrogate father and son is *Hearts in Atlantis* at its most compelling. As a man with powers that only gradually become clear, Hopkins uses his exceptional skill to make it appear that he's doing nothing at all.

His is a quiet but intense presence, and never more so than in the bravura monologue in which Ted describes for Bobby what it was like to see the pro football comeback of legendary running back Bronko Nagurski, a set piece that just about dares us to be indifferent.

As the willing protegé, young Yelchin, lively without being cloying, has the naturalness that makes holding one's own against a performer of Hopkins's caliber look easier than it is.

Not everything about *Atlantis* is as satisfying as these two, and the film, with such sentiments as "when you're a kid a day can last forever," does have a tendency to think that what it's saying is more profound than it is. But Hicks, whose style did not enhance *Snow Falling on Cedars*, proves to be a good match for this material.

Though it's almost unfashionable to be this way, Hicks is the most careful of directors, and in *Hearts in Atlantis* he's able to keep things in a satisfying balance. When the film mixes terror and the everyday, Hicks ensures that it's unnerving in a convincing but nonexploitative manner. And his natural gravity, though it can't eliminate all hokeyness and mush, keeps those qualities from getting out of hand. In this, too, Hopkins's work is essential: By grounding the proceedings in the unwavering reality of his performance, he carries out the greatest service.

House of Sand and Fog
2003

Let *House of Sand and Fog* tell you a story. A story of hopes as evanescent as the drifting fog, of dreams as unreliable as a structure carelessly built out of sand.

It's a despairing narrative about the capacity we have to destroy our own lives just when we think we're doing the opposite, a story that uses exceptional acting to wrench and twist our emotions. It sends us back to such words as "tragedy" and "catharsis" because, at its core, this film has an inescapable, unflinching fidelity to human truth. It's a story that haunts long after it's seen, not just because we're overpowered by what happens to its characters but because, if we're honest, we see how all of it, even the worst of it, could happen to us.

A film this consuming doesn't get made without a great passion, one that began with Andre Dubus III's memorable novel, a bestselling National Book Award finalist about a pair of uncomprehending strangers whose conflicting dreams put them on a terrible collision course over a nondescript Northern California house.

Successful commercial director Vadim Perelman seized on this book as his first theatrical feature with a feral intensity that can be felt everywhere, an obsessive fervor without which this kind of heartfelt but pitiless drama could never have made it to the screen with its implacable virtues intact.

Perelman persuaded Dubus to sell him the rights, cowrote the screenplay with Shawn Lawrence Otto, and oversaw the impeccable cast, which includes not only Oscar-winning stars Ben Kingsley and Jennifer Connelly in career-milestone roles, but also *Black Hawk Down*'s Ron Eldard, admired Iranian actress Shohreh Aghdashloo, beginner Jonathan Ahdout and the veteran Frances Fisher, all of whom give moving performances in crucial supporting roles.

The director also understood that to film Dubus's novel successfully he had to be guided by two conflicting notions. He had to be at home with big emotions and empathize with characters who allowed overwrought feelings to blot out all reason the way an eclipse blacks out the sun. Yet he also had to be willing to recount these people's stories with iron-willed restraint, to let everything be told with carefully chosen words, looks and gestures. For in a narrative like this, even a hint of forced or overdone acting would be fatal.

Fortunately, especially with Kingsley and Connelly, *Fog* has performers who, in their own ways, dig deeply into themselves to get to a place where this story became real to them. It's a tribute to how strong their work is that the force of their personalities does not fade even when they are not on the screen—that's how much of a disruptive presence these people are in each other's lives.

For though it never occurs to them, Colonel Massoud Amir Behrani, formerly of the Iranian air force, and impoverished housecleaner Kathy Nicolo are more alike than different, a double study in bottled-up resentment, desperation and rage. Driven, self-centered, heedless of others, both make a fetish of their grievances, and both have paid a dire price for the charades their lives have become.

Straight as a knife, impeccably dressed, his face the mask of a bird of prey, the colonel was a wealthy and significant man in the shah's Iran. We meet him, tan and fit, as the doting parent at his daughter's lavish wedding. But what, his guests wonder, does he now do for a living? No one seems to know.

A man of enormous pride and extraordinary will, the colonel, it turns out, works on a paving crew repairing highways by day and as a convenience-store clerk by night, making careful notations of even the smallest expense. Burdened by circumstance, hardened by putting up with years of disappointment and disrespect, the colonel has maintained the facade of wealth and position so that his daughter can marry well. Now he is desperate to escape his situation, to give his family, and especially his fourteen-year-old son (the soulful Ahdout), whom he fears is too soft for the world, the piece of the American dream he foolishly thought would be easily his.

The colonel's deception is toward the world, but Kathy's is toward her family. A recovered substance abuser who likely has always had difficulty coping with her life, Kathy lives in the small house her father left jointly to her and her more successful brother. Though she pretends on the phone to her mother that everything is fine, in fact her husband abandoned her months ago and she has pretty much abandoned her own life as a result, not opening her mail and often not even getting out of bed.

Those habits provoke a crisis when Kathy is abruptly evicted from her house for nonpayment of a business tax. That tax turns out to be a bureaucratic error, which, her legal aid lawyer (an effective Fisher) tells her, could have been corrected in time if Kathy had had the will to open her mail. But now there is no time, the house is put up for auction and, recognizing its value, the colonel buys it.

"Today," he says to his uncertain wife, "God has kissed our eyes." One person's kiss, however, is another's dagger to the heart. As the brutal conflict between the colonel and Kathy plays out—she heedlessly determined to reclaim her house, he just as willfully insisting it is legally his—the gravitational force of this all-consuming dispute inevitably drags other people into it. On the colonel's side, aside from his son, there is his wife, Nadi, a demure woman fated never to be at home in what will always be a strange new country to her. Aghdashloo, herself an Iranian refugee, not only persuasively conveys the graceful characteristics of a vanished culture but also quietly holds her own against the powerhouse performances of the film's stars.

The lost but stunningly beautiful Kathy could bewitch any man, but she has a special appeal for deputy sheriff Lester Burdon (Eldard), who meets her when he enforces her eviction. Unable to resist the flood tides of her emotions or her obvious need for the stability that he considers his strength, Eldard is exactly right as the decent, reasonable person increasingly radicalized by being in the orbit of these formidably rigid adversaries.

It is the particular gift of *House of Sand and Fog* to present us with antagonists who behave both badly and well, who are simultaneously right and wrong. Beautifully shot by Roger Deakins with a moody James Horner score, this film is in sympathy with people who feel so justified that they become oblivious to the cost of believing the rectification of their grievances is all that matters. It also despairs of their behavior. Its step-by-step tragedy is so ruthless in its unfolding that you may find yourself wishing it were less well done, that it left you some room to breathe. But *House of Sand and Fog* has a story to tell and it means to tell it, no matter what the cost.

The Insider
1999

Unlikely material can inspire exceptional films: witness *The Insider*. What could sound less promising than the legal fuss surrounding one man's indecision about telling what he knows about cigarettes, unless it's the internal wranglings of a television network's news division? But it is the triumph of this film, directed by Michael Mann, that those iffy scenarios result in a compelling drama, as notable for the importance of what it has to say as for the riveting skill with which it's said.

Mann's involvement, as screenwriter (with Eric Roth) as well as director, is the tip-off that something is afoot. As his credits, from *Thief* and *Heat* through television's *Miami Vice*, indicate and this film underlines, Mann practically mainlines intensity, and he uses his instinct for dramatic storytelling to fill every bit of this two-hour, thirty-eight-minute film with passion and tension.

In fact the argument could be made that Mann's career has been preparation for telling the based-on-fact parallel stories of Jeffrey Wigand, arguably the most significant antismoking source to come from the heart of Big Tobacco and one of the keys to a $246 billion settlement against the industry, and Lowell Bergman, the 60 *Minutes* producer who fought to get his story on the air. Not only is *The Insider* fiercely directed, not only does it have memorable starring performances from Al Pacino and the marvelous Russell Crowe, but it has a tale to tell that is both substantial and significant.

For as much as anything else, *The Insider* is a paradigmatic slice of twentieth-century America, a look at who we are and at what drives us as individuals and a society. It's a scathing attack on the power of serious money and the chilling effect corporate might can have on the ability to disseminate the truth.

At its core, however, *The Insider* is a story of, as someone says, "ordinary people under extraordinary pressure." It shows how difficult and torturous it can be to do the right thing on an individual level and, most important, what bravery actually means and how little the faces and personalities of heroes fit our preconceptions.

To tell this story, screenwriters Roth (an Oscar winner for *Forrest Gump*) and Mann, working from Marie Brenner's excellent *Vanity Fair* piece, have made considerable and unapologetic use of dramatic license.

Hardly a documentary (and even they manipulate), *The Insider* uses real names but does not hesitate to embellish or fictionalize situations when it suits its purposes, which include greatly enhancing Bergman's role in events to build him into more of a conventional hero. But peripheral fabrications notwithstanding, the core story the film tells, the issues it raises, remain dead-on accurate.

The Insider starts in the most unlikely place, an unidentified Middle Eastern city where a man is being blindfolded for a meeting with a leader of the terrorist Hezbollah organization. The man is Bergman (Pacino), a producer for 60 *Minutes*, and when the sheik in question asks why he should agree to an interview with "the pro-Zionist American media," Bergman unhesitatingly replies, "Because it's the highest-rated, most respected television newsmagazine in America."

That opening establishes several crucial points, not the least of which is Bergman's loyalty to and belief in 60 *Minutes* and its mainstay Mike Wallace (Christopher Plummer), whose producer and alter ego he's been for fourteen years. It also shows Bergman as the pragmatic go-to guy, the producer-as-fixer adept at convincing even the most reluctant subjects to come forward and talk.

An operative both within and against the system—a role that in some ways echoes the actor's earlier work in *Serpico*—Bergman is one of Pacino's best, most alive characterizations. It allows him to be natural and powerful, to hold the screen and convince us of someone's sincerity without resorting to mannerisms or well-worn tricks.

Able to match him stride for stride is the virtuoso Crowe. Known to art-house viewers for his award-winning roles in Australia's *Proof* and *Romper Stomper*, Crowe's ability to project internal complexity electrified a wider audience as the love of Kim Basinger's life in *L.A. Confidential*. A powerhouse actor who joins an old-fashioned masculine presence with an unnerving ability to disappear inside a role, not only has Crowe made himself look like Wigand but he even duplicates the complex personality that journalist Brenner described as "prickly, isolated and fragile" in her *VF* piece. "There's a wary quality in his face, a mysterious darkness."

When Wigand is introduced on a sunny afternoon in 1993, he and Bergman are not even aware of each other's existence. It's not a good day for the pin-striped scientist, head of research and development for Brown & Williamson, one of the biggest tobacco companies. He's just been fired, in part, we eventually learn, for objecting to measures the company wants to take to make its products more addictive.

With a comfortable lifestyle, a Southern belle wife (Diane Venora) and two children, one of whom has expensive medical problems, Wigand is not eager to jeopardize his B&W settlement or the health insurance that comes with it. Prodded by company president Thomas Sandefur (Michael Gambon), he signs a pair of confidentiality agreements; but though he doesn't necessarily show it, Wigand is a person who does not respond well to being pushed around. There is an unexpected fury in him, a rigid core that cannot be quashed or ignored, a core that Bergman will come to fear and admire.

At work on a different tobacco story, one having to do with fire safety and smoking in bed, Bergman receives an anonymous box of tobacco company documents that he needs "translated into English." A colleague gives him Wigand's name, but when Bergman calls the scientist at home for this simple task, the unexpected resistance Wigand puts up is a goad to the producer's savvy instincts.

Though he has no real idea who Wigand is, and not even a clue about what the man knows, Bergman, like a bull facing a cape, can't resist charging. And the more Wigand demurs from talking, the more Bergman increases the pressure, especially when he learns who this difficult, elusive man is and what he knows about the cigarette industry's willingness to lie about its product's effects. "He's the ultimate insider," the producer says. "He's got something to say and I want it on *60 Minutes.*"

The extended cat and mouse interplay between journalist and source is one of *The Insider*'s most involving dynamics. An elaborate ritual dance of courtship, a seduction pure and not so simple, it pits Bergman's insistence that he can be trusted ("When I talk to people in confidence, it stays that way") and Wigand's fears about his settlement and whether what he does will make any kind of a difference.

"I'm a commodity to you," he says. "Thirty million people will hear you," Bergman replies, unfazed, "and nothing will ever be the same again."

While this elaborate scenario is being played out, the tenor of Wigand's life changes in ways that up the ante on his decision. He hears intruders in his backyard, he's followed, he finds threatening messages on his computer, he finds a bullet in his mailbox. He's supposed to be scared, but instead he is angry. (Brown & Williamson, which has a history of attacking Wigand, claims the scientist manufactured his own death threats. A federal law enforcement official said the evidence either way was not conclusive.)

Alternately closed-off and furious, needy and suspicious, his marriage now in trouble, the tightly wound Wigand finds himself drawing closer to Bergman as he comes to terms with what appears to be a compulsion to come clean. If he decides to talk, finally, it will be because he cannot imagine not doing so.

Compelling as this is, *The Insider* has two more dramas to play out. One is whether or not Wigand will testify in the Mississippi-led multistate case against the tobacco industry (one of the areas where Bergman's influence has apparently been exaggerated), and the other is the crisis at CBS.

Led by an attorney (an appropriately slick Gina Gershon) worried about something called "tortious interference" and the remote possibility of a massive lawsuit, CBS corporate strong arms its news department in general, and *60 Minutes* in particular, not to air the Wigand segment. How much and when Wallace resisted this edict has become a major bone of contention between the journalist and the filmmakers, but of one thing there is no doubt: What happened at *60 Minutes* was a major debacle. (The *New York Times* calls it "one of the low points in the history of CBS News.")

Even if you know every detail of this much-reported situation, Mann and company have so effectively ratcheted up the tension of the Wigand/*60 Minutes* story, emphasizing the chaotic personal dynamics and the battle of wills that lurked behind all the headlines, that we become captured by the immediacy of what's on the screen.

Shot with exceptional crispness by Dante Spinotti (who also did *L.A. Confidential*) and energetically edited by William Goldenberg, Paul Rubell and David Rosenbloom, *The Insider* also benefits from Mann's passionate attention to detail. The strong, atmospheric score is by former Dead Can Dance mainstay Lisa Gerrard and her new writing partner Pieter Bourke (with a notable contribution by Gustavo Santaolalla on the Argentine mandolin). And Lindsay Crouse as Bergman's wife and Bruce McGill as a firebrand Mississippi attorney have impacts greater than the size of their roles.

"To get the truth out has been such an effort," Wigand said in a recent newspaper interview. "It's still an effort." More than anything else could, *The Insider* not only explains why that effort was worth making but also how hard it was to make.

The Joy Luck Club
1993

If *The Joy Luck Club* doesn't make you cry, nothing will. In an age of contrived and mechanical sentimentality, its deeply felt, straight-from-the-heart emotions and the unadorned way it presents them make quite an impact. No matter how many hankies you bring with you, it won't be enough.

Though feeble attempts have been made to pigeonhole it as a women's picture, *The Joy Luck Club* is more accurately a humane film, one that makes a point of being honest and compassionate about its characters and unashamed about their feelings. If men think this is of no interest to them, the species is in worse shape than we thought.

A story of distance and how to bridge it, of painful gaps between mothers and daughters, immigrant parents and U.S.-born children, *The Joy Luck Club* derives its strength and clarity from the best-selling novel by Amy Tan it is based on.

Working as a creative troika, Tan, coscreenwriter Ronald Bass (an Oscar winner for *Rain Man*) and director Wayne Wang (*Chan Is Missing*) have kept the quiet simplicity of style that is the core of Tan's book, honed and focused its emotional impact, and not attempted to soften the bitterness of the conflicts it portrays.

The film has also taken advantage of the powerful chord it struck in the Asian American community in general and among performers in particular. Though their names are largely unfamiliar to general audiences, the eight actresses who play the film's four pairs of mothers and daughters are not only the pick of several generations of acting talent but also women who understand these characters from the inside and know how to take advantage of the opportunities the roles present.

Hollywood conventional wisdom says that eight people's stories are too many for an audience to handle, especially if recognizable faces aren't involved, but *The Joy Luck Club* manages to preserve each tale's individuality while bringing them all together with an almost casual skill.

Though each woman's experience is involving, it is what these experiences say en masse about the drama behind the fabled golden door of immigrant dreams that is most moving. *Joy Luck* shows what happens to hope in America, how inevitable the estrangement is between parents who came here to save their children from suffering and children who, without that kind of distress, can't begin to imagine what made their difficult parents the way they are.

The film's tone is set by its opening voice-over, taken from the book's fable-like first paragraphs, where an old woman remembers a swan she once bought in Shanghai. The bird first symbolized her hopes for America, for a daughter who "would always be too full to swallow any sorrow" and finally her bafflement at ending up with an uncomprehending child who grew up "swallowing more Coca-Cola than sorrow."

The Joy Luck Club opens at a going-away party in San Francisco (Amy Tan is the first guest seen on screen) for June (Ming-Na Wen), leaving the next day for a trip to China. Together with three other Chinese women, each the mother of an American-born daughter, June's late mother Suyuan had begun the club, a weekly mah-jongg gathering of wives who considered the hope of getting lucky their only joy.

This party is the hub from which the stories of each of these eight women (including Suyuan, portrayed in flashback by Vietnam's Kieu Chinh) radiate out like spokes. A chance remark will trigger a reverie, and mothers and daughters then tell their stories in voice-over and flashback. With as many as three actresses portraying the protagonists at different ages, this may sound complex, but Wang and editor Maysie Hoy (who worked on *The Player*) bring it off with perfect naturalness and comprehension.

The mothers' stories are invariably the harsher ones, taking place as they do in the old country, a hopeless nightmare society where a woman was taught, in the words of one, "to desire nothing, to swallow other people's misery and eat her own bitterness."

Suyuan's tale involves the abandonment of children, that of Auntie Lindo (Chinese actress Tsai Chin), Suyuan's "best friend and arch-enemy," of an unfortunate arranged marriage. In their turn, Auntie Ying

Ying (*South Pacific*'s France Nuyen) and Auntie An Mei (Lisa Lu, a veteran of *One Eyed Jacks* and *The Last Emperor*) tell equally agonized tales.

Though Suyuan's daughter June and Auntie Lindo's daughter Waverly (Tamlyn Tomita) relate stories of childhood rivalry, all four daughters, including Lena (Lauren Tom) and Rose (Rosalind Chao), talk of more adult difficulties, especially problems with the feckless men in their lives, troubles that stem in one way or another from the way their mothers have formed them. "I like being tragic, Ma," one of them says bitterly. "I learned it from you."

So the mothers, who became hard to survive their pain, are surprised to find their daughters uncomprehending and resentful when that strength of will is turned on them. "Nothing I can do can ever please you," says one daughter; "My mother always does this, she has the perfect countermove," says another. The mothers, accused of turning their eager hopes into stifling expectations, likewise feel misunderstood and unappreciated by children who have not experienced the past. It is the story every wave of immigration experiences, and its truths have rarely been as beautifully delineated as they are here.

L.A. Confidential
1997

Fascinated by the spectacle of fallible men and fallen women trapped in a corrupt and heartless world that's too cold to care, filmmakers in every generation have never stopped reinventing film noir. From 1940s classics such as *Out of the Past* (1947) through the likes of *Kiss Me Deadly* (1955), *Point Blank* (1967), *Chinatown* (1974) and *Body Heat* (1981), each decade has taken its own kind of brooding look at what goes down at the dark end of the street.

L.A. Confidential, with an exceptional ensemble cast directed by Curtis Hanson from James Ellroy's densely plotted novel, looks to be the definitive noir for this particular time and place. A dark, dangerous and intoxicating tale of big trouble in paradise, smartly done with the blackest possible humor and names that include Kevin Spacey, Kim Basinger and Danny DeVito, it's conspicuously contemporary in its attitudes and in its willingness to bend the rules of the game absolutely as far as they will go.

Ostentatiously cynical, hyper-violent, dripping with attitude, L.A. Confidential holds nothing sacred. Its intricate plot is so nihilistic and cold around the heart, its nominal heroes so amoral, so willing to sell out anyone and everyone, that the film is as initially unnerving as it is finally irresistible. A cocktail of diverse elements first shaken and then stirred, it takes pride in confounding expectations and leaving us as surprised as its characters by twisting turns of events.

From top to bottom, L.A. Confidential enjoys playing around with notions of appearance and reality. It presents a fearfully corrupt police force the world thinks is a model of decorum, characters who believe in "doing what they have to do for justice" no matter how savage and even murderous their acts may seem, all operating in a city that likes to pretend it's paradise on Earth when it's really seething with pervasive corruption. Welcome to sunny Los Angeles in the year 1953.

This theme begins with the opening sequence, cheery promotional films of the Southland counterpointed by a wised-up and sarcastic narration. "Life is good in Los Angeles," sneers Sid Hudgens (DeVito). "At least that's what they tell you."

Hudgens ought to know. As the energetic editor of Hush-Hush, as in "off the record, on the qt and very hush-hush," always on the lookout for "prime sinuendo," he specializes in running scandalmonger stories, with headlines like "Ingenue Dykes in Hollywood." Hudgens's monologue not only sets the tone for L.A. Confidential, it also provides crucial background information: With the removal of major mobster Mickey Cohen, the L.A. crime scene is rudderless and up for grabs and twenty-five pounds of pure heroin have just gone missing.

Next on the scene, introduced one by one on Christmas Eve, are the three LAPD cops who are the film's protagonists. That night turns out to be crucial for each, involving them in incidents that have implications that gradually play out in bloody and unexpected ways.

Officer Bud Wilson (Russell Crowe) is first up, a relentless and unsmiling one-man wrecking crew with an inflectionless voice and an eagerness to turn psychotic to protect women in jeopardy.

On Christmas Eve, Wilson meets the beautiful but troubled Lynn Bracken (Basinger), a vision in a black hooded cape with white trim, who immediately lets him know he's got cop "practically stamped on his forehead." With chitchat like that, we know they'll be meeting again.

Sergeant Jack Vincennes (Spacey), a.k.a. "Hollywood Jack" and "the Big V," is a show-biz cop with the cushy job of technical advisor for the mock-*Dragnet* television series, *Badge of Honor*. A smoothly corrupt operator who smiles easily but not openly, Vincennes does not disappoint the superior who tells him, "I doubt you've ever drawn a stupid breath in your life. Don't start now."

Vincennes spends his Christmas Eve in one of his frequent collaborations with Hudgens, busting two young contract players for drugs in exchange for a cash payoff and prominent mention in *Hush-Hush's* next cover story, "The Movie Premiere Pot Bust." Oh, the price of fame.

Ed Exley (Guy Pearce), the son of a martyred cop and about to be made lieutenant, seems the likeliest good guy as a believer in helping people and as an enemy of corrupt policing. But the aftermath of a police riot he gets caught in on Christmas Eve shows him to be smug and priggish with an eye for human weakness, a cold-hearted and manipulative careerist who doesn't care what he has to do to get ahead.

None of these men is an obvious hero, and each has enough willingness to transgress conventional morality to have made him a villain in other times and other films. If they're knights, and they certainly don't seem to be, their armor is at best seriously tarnished. When one of them is told, "Don't start trying to do the right thing, you haven't had the practice," it's advice they could all take to heart.

With all this as backdrop, *L.A. Confidential* kicks into gear with a case big enough to involve the entire police department: the coffee shop shooting deaths of six people, including a policeman, that the press dubs "The Nite Owl Massacre."

Heading the investigation is Captain Dudley Smith (*Babe*'s James Cromwell), a shrewd veteran with a lilting way of calling everyone "Boyo." Eventually involved as well are crafty District Attorney Ellis Lowe (Ron Rifkin) and Pierce Patchett (David Strathairn), a mysterious Mr. Big that Hudgens characterizes with typical brio as "a powerful behind-the-scenes strange-o."

Diverse as they sound, all these strands and characters eventually come together as smoothly as the finish on the film's vintage automobiles. Ellroy's nearly five-hundred-page novel has so much plot, in fact, that the author thought it was his least likely book to be filmed. But screenwriters Brian Helgeland and Hanson have expertly extracted the essence of the proceedings and boiled them down to a concentrated screen story where appearances are deceptive and nobody gives any information away.

Director Hanson has already demonstrated a command of narrative drive in previous work, including *The River Wild* and *The Hand That Rocks the Cradle*, and *L.A. Confidential*'s clean, relentless storytelling sense, its ability to draw us in while always playing fair with plot details, is its quintessential asset.

Following right behind is strong ensemble acting. Spacey is the essence of corrupt charm, and Basinger provides the film's emotional center as the world-weary femme who's been around more blocks than the Thomas Guide. *L.A. Confidential*'s nerviest and most successful decision was using the unknown Australian faces of Crowe and Pearce as two of its key L.A. cops. Anyone who remembers Pearce as the youngest and most flamboyant drag queen in *The Adventures of Priscilla, Queen of the Desert* will be impressed at the transformation.

In its locations, its look and its period soundtrack, *L.A. Confidential*'s passion for authenticity has paid off. Los Angeles native Hanson and cinematographer Dante Spinotti opted to shoot in such venerable spots as the Formosa Cafe and Hollywood's Frolic Room, and production designer Jeannine Oppewall, set decorator Jay R. Hart and costume designer Ruth Myers have made sure everything else looks right.

The only potential audience drawback L.A. *Confidential* has is its reliance on unsettling bursts of violence; these include bloody shootings and intense physical beatings that give the picture a palpable air of menace. Overriding that, finally, is the film's complete command of its material. L.A. *Confidential* believes in itself because its creators got drawn into its wild story, and what an adventure that turns out to be.

L.A. Confidential *won Oscars for its screenplay and supporting actress Kim Basinger and saw to it that Russell Crowe and Guy Pearce would never be little known again.*

Liberty Heights
1999

For writer-director Barry Levinson, *Liberty Heights* is one from the heart.

The fourth film to be set in his native Baltimore (following *Diner, Tin Men* and *Avalon*), this is a mature, accomplished piece of work, both funny and deeply felt, personal cinema of the best kind. Older now, seeing more, understanding more but caring just as much, Levinson has made the memory film we always hoped he would.

Though its focus on Baltimore's Jewish community in the fall of 1954 couldn't be more specific, the issues and themes *Liberty Heights* raises, its focus on the dreams, diversions and disappointments of an increasingly multicultural America, have a universal taste of life about them.

Levinson has done this, ironically, by embracing specificity, by having characters (unlike those in *Avalon,* who never mention their Jewishness) proudly screaming out car windows as they drive from their Liberty Heights neighborhood into a Gentile area, "Get ready, folks, Jews are coming."

For Baltimore in 1954 was still a place where you could divine people's religion and ethnicity by asking where they lived. But the

Supreme Court had just desegregated the schools, barriers of all kinds were breaking down, and the reality of a more open America was beckoning everyone, even Nate and Ada Kurtzman (Joe Mantegna and Bebe Neuwirth) and their sons Van and Ben (Adrien Brody and Ben Foster).

Liberty Heights is at its funniest exposing the contours of the Kurtzmans' doomed all-Jewish world, complete with an irascible old-country grandmother (Frania Rubinek), who insists that "if it's in the Bible, it's for a reason." And what specifically might that reason be? "A good reason."

Reading from a school essay describing his still younger years, Ben recounts (and we hilariously see) his confusion at coming across Wonder bread at a friend's house. "Everything was white, there's too much white stuff," he wails to his mother, who nods and says ominously of the visited family, "They're the other kind."

Though Ben, now in high school, has already learned that "99 percent of the world is not Jewish," there's a lot he and the college-going Van don't know about what it's like to be "the other kind." For both brothers, forbidden romance will aid in the getting of wisdom, and *Liberty Heights* expertly intertwines their stories with another cross-cultural difficulty, one their father has managing his unconventional business.

The world and, more important, the IRS, think the source of Nate Kurtzman's income is a collapsing burlesque house on Baltimore's famous Block. But it actually comes from the numbers business, a gambling enterprise so beyond the pale it's never even mentioned at home. Desperate to drum up more customers, Nate and his associates come up with a bonus system, but when a small-time black drug dealer named Little Melvin (Orlando Jones) hits his number big, Nate faces a crisis that taxes even his considerable toughness and ingenuity.

Ben, meanwhile, has become fascinated with Sylvia (Rebekah Johnson), the only black student in his homeroom. The daughter of a prominent surgeon, elegant and self-possessed, Sylvia is not only a world away from Little Melvin, she is a world away from Ben as well.

Still, despite opposition from both sets of parents—her father has a rule against white boyfriends, and his mother simply says, "Just kill me now!"—Ben and Sylvia find themselves really liking each other and wanting to spend time together.

Theirs is the sweetest of friendships, even extending to a joint visit to a lovingly re-created James Brown concert, but like everything else about *Liberty Heights*, it manages to be clear-eyed and unsentimental as well as warm. Ben and his friends have accumulated considerable prejudice, old wives' tales and just plain ignorance and misinformation about blacks (not to mention about sex, but that's another story), which this relationship gracefully and often amusingly disabuses him of.

Van's romantic entanglement is just as forbidden. At a Halloween party in a Gentile neighborhood, while his friend Yussel (David Krumholtz) is getting into a bravado-induced fight for refusing to admit he's Jewish, dark and poetic-looking Van gets intoxicated with Dubbie (model Carolyn Murphy), a kind of ultimate shiksa goddess who is involved with a wealthy fellow socialite named Trey (Justin Chambers) who drinks too much and drives too fast.

Brody brings a fine poetic grace to the part of Van, and it is a tribute to Levinson's sensitive direction (and Ellen Chenoweth's adroit casting) that equally strong performances are forthcoming from the film's numerous first-time feature actors, including Foster, Johnson, Murphy, Chambers and Jones. Not even born when this film takes place, they've managed to recapture its nuances with remarkable fidelity.

But it's Levinson who's given them such rich and often comic things to say, who understands how to structure great riffs that seem to come out of nowhere. So we have Ben and his pals, faced with a sign reading "No Jews, Dogs or Colored," wondering how Jews got the first position, and Yussel's tirade about anti-Semitism: "They all pray to a Jew," he fumes. "I guess it's okay to have a dead Jew hanging over your bed but not to have one come in the front door."

Levinson's storytelling style has always been on the discursive side, and *Liberty Heights*, ebbing and flowing like a river of memory, shows that technique to its best advantage. There's almost a free-form quality to the narrative as stories weave in and out of one another, meandering a bit but never losing their novelistic grasp of feeling and atmosphere.

Aiding in the creation of that atmosphere is an eclectic soundtrack (from the Midnighters' "Annie Had a Baby" to Mandy Patinkin singing the Yiddish classic "Mein Shtetele Belz") that is a living presence in the film, as well as the fine work of the film's production talents. These include previous Levinson collaborators Stu Linder (editor) and Vincent Peranio (production designer) as well as the brilliant Hong Kong–based cinematographer Chris Doyle, a master of color and mood.

Though the film's advertising tag line ("You're Only Young Once, but You Remember Forever") sells it that way, *Liberty Heights* is hardly an exercise in simple nostalgia. Strains of darkness, pain and regret are visible through the comedy, and some of the societal and racial issues the film brings up have yet to be resolved. "A lot of images fade," Ben says at one point. "If I knew things would no longer be, I would have tried to remember better." Barry Levinson, thankfully, has remembered enough for us all.

Brody went on to win a Best Actor Oscar for his role in The Pianist.

A Little Princess
1995

"Magic has to be believed to be real," an understanding father tells his daughter in *A Little Princess*, a philosophy this enchanting fantasy has taken as its own. Unlike the creators of far too many children's films, those responsible here have taken their story's events exactly as seriously as they expect their small audience to, with appealing results.

Adapted from a novel by the venerable Frances Hodgson Burnett, who also wrote *Little Lord Fauntleroy* and *The Secret Garden*, *Princess* is dependent on its fairy-tale elements, but the filmmakers have seen to it that these are not overdone. In fact, the straightforward way the picture treats its magical and sentimental sequences enhances its tangible sense of wonder.

Sara Crewe (ten-year-old newcomer Liesel Matthews) is discovered in Simla, India, in 1914, frolicking on a riverbank and recounting tales of monsters and heroes from the Sanskrit epic the *Ramayana*. Here she first hears, from her Indian nanny, the film's philosophy that all women and girls are princesses, each in her own way.

Reality, however, soon asserts itself: Sara's father, the wealthy but first-name-deprived Captain Crewe (Liam Cunningham), has to leave India to fight the good fight in the Great War, and Sara must be taken to Miss Minchin's School for Girls in New York, the alma mater of her dear departed mother.

Though the haughty, overbearing Miss Minchin (Eleanor Bron) and her flighty, rotund sister Amelia (Rusty Schwimmer) are in awe of Sara's wealth, they are less enamored of the girl's disregard for rules, her tendency to be a freer spirit than this rigid place allows.

There is a potential pitfall in this setup, because paragons of childhood tend to be great bores with too much of the wrong kind of princess about them. Saving Sara from this trap is the innate feistiness of actress Matthews and the genuineness of her character's desire to be a friend to the friendless, especially the downtrodden servant girl Becky (well done by Vanessa Lee Chester). Soon almost the whole school is sneaking into Sara's room every night to hear her spirited versions of the tales she heard in India.

Then, once again, a reversal of fortune occurs, and this time it is a shocking one. A lawyer arrives at the school and the news he brings of Captain Crewe's disappearance in battle and the confiscation of his wealth unhinges Sara's life. Overnight she is turned from a cosseted, indulged pet into an overworked drudge, forced to scrub floors, move to the attic with Becky and exist on bitter gruel.

It is this devastating plot twist that keeps *A Little Princess* honest and lifts it above the ordinary. For one thing, Sara as a chastened orphan, her spirit crushed, plays much more effectively on our sympathies than Sara as the oblivious heiress, and Matthews's acting seems to improve as her character's situation worsens.

This change of life is especially touching because what the Richard LaGravenese and Elizabeth Chandler script does best is delineate what is essentially a father-daughter love story. Though the screenwriters have taken a number of understandable liberties with the original novel, including successfully softening and Hollywoodizing the book's ending, they have also, in such tender scenes as the Captain's goodbye to Sara at Miss Minchin's, enhanced and amplified that key emotional connection.

As always when a film more than fulfills expectations, many factors contributed to the success of *A Little Princess*, notably the acting of Eleanor Bron, expert at giving Miss Minchin just a twinge of humanity, and Errol Sitahal, who brings appropriate majesty to Ram Dass, the Asp-like Indian who happens to live next door. The soaring music by Patrick Doyle (who scored both of Kenneth Branagh's Shakespearean films) sets the emotional tone, and production designer Bo Welch has beautifully constructed Sara's fantasy India and the ominous oversized plushness of Miss Minchin's.

Finally, a great deal of credit has to go to Mexican director Alfonso Cuaron, whose only previous feature was *Love in the Time of Hysteria*. Though Cuaron has had other domestic projects fall through, this became his Hollywood debut, and it is an impressive one.

Working with *Like Water for Chocolate* cinematographer Emmanuel Lubezki, Cuaron perfectly understands how a combination of simplicity and restraint help to create a sense of wonder on the screen, how a gust of snow blowing open a window can take your breath away more than the most elaborate of machine-made special effects. Under his sure, quiet direction, *A Little Princess* casts the type of spell most family films can only dream about.

Eventually tiring of Hollywood, Cuaron and Lubezki returned to Mexico to make the quite different Y Tu Mamá También.

Malcolm X
1992

Despite his blistering anger with America, his fury over the way black people were treated by what he saw as a smug and satanic white majority, there was something quintessentially American about the character and accomplishments of Malcolm X. In a country where self-transformation is practically a religion, he was a man who reinvented himself not once but several times, changing from cynical street hustler to an ascetic apostle of racial separation to a man whose concerns for social justice were growing wider and more multicultural when he was brutally murdered at the age of thirty-nine.

It is perhaps in recognition of this that Spike Lee's somber, powerful *Malcolm X* opens with an enormous American flag filling the entire screen. Never mind that the flag burns down to a smoldering "X" and is intercut with the Rodney G. King beating footage as Malcolm's words charging "the white man with being the greatest murderer and kidnaper on Earth" are heard on the soundtrack. The thing to remember is that the last film that opened with an oversized flag was *Patton* (starring George C. Scott), a model of mainstream Hollywood biography.

For what is surprising about *Malcolm X* is not how very accomplished a piece of filmmaking it turns out to be, but exactly what Lee, who cowrote the screenplay with Arnold Perl and an uncredited James Baldwin, wanted to accomplish. The unexpected aspect of this forceful, purposeful work by a director with a reputation for being an in-your-face polemicist and provocateur is just how careful and classical a film it finally is. *Malcolm* is consciously aiming at the creation both of a hero and a mythology powerful enough to sustain those whose struggle with racism is still a reality.

With every carefully composed frame, *Malcolm X* tries with remarkable success to be a grand epic for people of color, an African American counterpart to *Gandhi* that aims to move a controversial thinker and doer who has not been much revered outside of the black community into the heart of the American mainstream. And by turning traditional filmmaking inside out, by using familiar forms to make as incendiary a thinker as Malcolm palatable, Lee may in fact be more subversive than he ever has been before.

Hewing fairly closely to *The Autobiography of Malcolm X*, this film tells the story of a brilliant, ambitious and finally abandoned man whose hard-won ability to articulate the rage and despair of the black underclass has yet to be equaled. Part of its power is that it understands that the tensions and prejudices Malcolm railed against are (witness the King footage) still with us, that his anger is still justified. And part of its fascination is that some of his solutions—his belief in family and education, even his emphasis on empowerment and pride in self— seem hardly radical at all.

Of course, the Malcolm who once preached strict racial separation because he believed all white men were devils, who famously de- clared the determination to gain human rights "by any means neces- sary," is still more than capable of arousing controversy. Yet by using Denzel Washington as Malcolm, Lee not only retained the services of a superb actor but also someone whose sympathetic persona tends to take some of the sting out of Malcolm's more biting words.

Washington's Malcolm is a heroic performance in several senses, calling for him to be on the screen in almost every scene and to make all those transformations believable, and the actor does it all with a special grace. The rest of the cast members, including Angela Bassett as Malcolm's wife, Betty Shabazz; Delroy Lindo as Harlem gangster West Indian Archie; and Albert Hall as Baines, the key to Malcolm's con- version to Islam, are excellent across the board. Lee has also shown a puckish side in some cameo casting, using progressive attorney William Kunstler as a racist judge and director John Sayles as an FBI agent.

The director himself has a role in the film's early going, playing Shorty, a zoot-suited hipster in a yellow-plaid ensemble who is young Malcolm Little's guide to the hustling life in wartime Boston. It is Shorty who gives Little's red hair its initial process, taking out the kinks with a lye solution, leading to Malcolm's pleased comment, ironic given all that was to come: "Looks white, don't it?" Ever restless, haunted by a troubled boyhood we see in flashback, Malcolm moves on to New York, where he becomes the protegé of numbers boss West Indian Archie and gets made over into a more stylish kind of hustler.

All this eventually lands Malcolm in prison, where Baines, a fellow inmate, teaches him to respect himself and believe in the Honorable Elijah Muhammad, the leader of the Nation of Islam. Malcolm has a vision, converts, changes his name to X and vows to dedicate his life "to telling the white devil the truth to his face."

The rest of Malcolm's life, from his national celebrity to his break with Elijah Muhammad and the pilgrimage to Mecca that led to a rethinking of his racial attitudes, was lived in the hot glare of publicity. Though parts of Malcolm's account have been contested by later biographers, Lee remains largely faithful to it, and, except for a kind of black power montage featuring school kids, Nelson Mandela, Magic Johnson and Michael Jordan that closes the film, does not stray from his even-handed narrative attitude.

One of the most interesting aspects of *Malcolm X* is how adroitly Lee has avoided many of the pitfalls its story presented. Though he uses the composite character of Baines as a convenient repository for all that is eventually untrustworthy about the Nation of Islam, Lee in general does not tip his hand via casting, refusing to melodramatize either side. This tactic also ensures that no component of the broad audience Lee is after will be offended by what he has put on the screen.

Even Elijah Muhammad (an eerie, restrained performance by Al Freeman Jr.) is portrayed nonjudgmentally, as is the question of whether it was his followers or the FBI, or some combination, that led to Malcolm's death. Finally, what this fascinating film leaves us with is a feeling of sadness that a man who traveled so many roads through so much difficulty should come to die so young on the floor of a Harlem ballroom, a prophet whose honor Spike Lee has taken extraordinary steps to restore.

Michael Collins
1996

Not every life is worth a movie, and of those only a few make it to the screen. Rarest of all is an epic true story, the very stuff of cinema, that has been transferred to film with matching intelligence, skill and elan. That has been the fortunate fate of *Michael Collins*.

Though his days were cut harshly short just shy of his thirty-second birthday, Collins's story, crammed with heroism and tragedy and intertwined with the fate of the modern state of Ireland, has the inevitability of myth. In life he made it possible against pitiless odds for the Irish to break free of the British Empire, and in death he symbolized the agony and unfulfilled potential of a nation divided against itself.

And though the romance, passion and excitement of the man's story stand on their own, *Michael Collins* (which won the Golden Lion at the Venice Film Festival) is more alive, more provocative as a film because the issues around that life still resonate. Collins was present at the creation of the Irish tragedy, and nothing that happens on that island today can be understood without reference to his sprawling life.

Collins is most strongly remembered as "the man they couldn't catch," the architect of the armed struggle against the British and a key theoretician of modern urban guerrilla warfare whose ideas were studied and admired by Mao Tse-tung and Yitzhak Shamir.

But, as detailed in Tim Pat Coogan's definitive work *Michael Collins: The Man Who Made Ireland*, Collins became as passionate about peace and negotiation as he'd been about warfare. And, though it sounds like a Hollywood scenario, he also found time to joust with his best friend for the love of the same woman.

Collins's story has intrigued numerous filmmakers over the years, including Kevin Costner, Michael Cimino, Robert Redford and John Huston, but Neil Jordan, who studied history at University College in Dublin, is the right choice to tell the story. The writer-director has been trying to do that since his first script on the subject in 1982, but it wasn't until Jordan had *The Crying Game* and *Interview With the Vampire* behind him that he could convince anyone to finance it.

From that first script on, Jordan always had six-foot-four Liam Neeson in mind to play the man they called "the Big Fellow," and it's more than size that makes Neeson fit the part of a leader known for his "cloudburst temperament."

An actor who does better when his characters are impetuous and larger than life (*Schindler's List*) than when they're supposed to be regular folks, Neeson, who won the best actor at Venice for his work, is perfectly suited to Collins's cocky physicality. A force of nature who never calms down, always exploding, always on the run, Neeson's Collins is confidence and indomitability itself.

The film's supporting cast is equally impressive and to the point. Aidan Quinn is effective as Harry Boland, Collins's friend and rival in love, as is Stephen Rea as intelligence operative Ned Broy. Julia Roberts is a surprise choice as Kitty Kiernan, the center of the love triangle, but she handles herself well. Taking a bit of getting used to is Alan Rickman as the ice-cold, cerebral Eamon De Valera, the calculating yin of the Irish independence movement always in opposition to Collins's passionate yang.

Though Jordan was frustrated by the years it took him to make *Michael Collins*, the additional skill he gained as a filmmaker is essential to its success. This is an extremely cinematic, beautifully made epic reminiscent of David Lean, helped by fluid and involving camera work by two-time Oscar-winning (*The Killing Fields*, *The Mission*) cinematographer Chris Menges.

Covering the turbulent last six years of Collins's life, Jordan's film is especially good at handsome and persuasive re-creations of some of the key events in modern Irish history, beginning with the doomed Easter Rising of 1916, when Britain's armed might out-and-out crushed the rebellious Irish.

Captured and incarcerated, Collins makes a vow for the future: "We won't play by their rules, we'll invent our own. We'll be an invisible army, striking and disappearing." In practice this meant using murder and terror to dismantle Britain's formidable intelligence system, with Collins recruiting a squad of hard cases nicknamed the Twelve Apostles especially for the work.

One of the strengths of *Michael Collins* is that it doesn't shirk from its protagonist's cold and ruthless streak, his facility for "bloody mayhem." Nothing is glossed over, not Irish killing nor Britain's opposing torture and murder, and as the scale of violence escalates, we get an inkling of why the passions run as deep and brutal as they do to this day.

Though the film is filled with strange-but-true events that sound like movie inventions (such as a key breaking during an attempted jailbreak), it is the overarching importance and tragedy of one man's life and fate that make this such a strong and involving piece of work. Though they're often uneasy companions, *Michael Collins* shows that history and drama make a powerful combination when the mix is right.

Million Dollar Baby
2004

What can be said about Clint Eastwood that hasn't been said before?

That he's American film's last and best classicist, a seventy-four-year-old director who's aged better than a *Sideways* Pinot Noir? That his increasingly fearless and idiosyncratic choice of material has made him more of an independent filmmaker than half the people at Sundance? That he continues to find ways to surprise audiences yet remain inescapably himself? It's all true, and never more so than in Eastwood's latest, *Million Dollar Baby*.

Perhaps the director's most touching, most elegiac work yet, *Million Dollar Baby* is a film that does both the expected and the unexpected, that has the nerve and the will to be as pitiless as it is sentimental. A tale of the power and the cost of dreams set in the unforgiving world of professional boxing, it's got some of the emotional daring of the great melodramas of Hollywood's golden age, when films considered it a badge of honor to wear their hearts on their sleeves.

Million Dollar Baby also reconfirms what *Mystic River* and its Oscars for Sean Penn and Tim Robbins made clear: that Eastwood, despite his legendary no-nonsense style, has become a gifted director of actors. It's not just the exceptional work by costars Hilary Swank and Morgan Freeman that stands out here, it's Eastwood's own performance, in some ways the most nakedly emotional of his fifty-year career.

As with *Mystic River*, Eastwood has started with commanding material, a debut collection of short stories by the late F. X. Toole called *Rope Burns*, which was published in 2000 when its author, a trainer and licensed cut man for more than twenty years, was seventy years old. A writer whose knowledge of boxing was matched by his spare skill with words, Toole, like Eastwood, was a traditionalist who saw value in the old ways.

Paul Haggis, a writer with extensive television credits, including the creation of the acclaimed *EZ Streets*, adroitly combined two of Toole's stories into the *Million Dollar* script by using the narrator of one to tell the tale of the second and fleshing it all out with touches that rarely seem extraneous to the story's main drive. Eastwood, who has perhaps the best eye in the business for the kinds of roles an aging star should be playing, is Frankie Dunn, a trainer and manager who owns a ramshackle gym in downtown Los Angeles all too appropriately named the Hit Pit.

Cantankerous as well as querulous, Frankie Dunn still manages a contender or two, but his reluctance to push his top man for a title fight speaks to a sense of pulling back, of disconnecting from life. He is painfully but apparently permanently estranged from his only child, a daughter, and he goes to church only to wind up the priest. Studying Gaelic is his sole pleasure and, with one exception, ring rust has formed on his personal relationships.

That exception is his right-hand man, Eddie "Scrap Iron" Dupris (Freeman), an imperturbable blind-in-one-eye former boxer who has run the Hit Pit day-to-day for seventeen years. It's Dupris's extensive voice-over that gives us the context for the unfolding story, garnished with home truths about boxing gleaned from Toole's stories.

Eastwood and Freeman not only share similarly laid-back styles, they've worked together before, in Eastwood's *Unforgiven*. Seeing them genially trying to out-underact each other is one of *Million Dollar Baby*'s most satisfying pleasures; a scene in which they share a conversation about, of all things, socks, is a master class in how understated acting can be used to magnificent effect.

Into this hermetic world comes Maggie Fitzgerald, a completely different type of person. A hardscrabble young woman well aware of her white trash background, Maggie has focused her entire life on a single goal: having Frankie Dunn mold her into the best fighter she can be. "Boxing is the only thing I ever felt good doing," she says, and giving up on that feeling is out of the question.

Both physically and psychologically, Swank, who put on seventeen pounds of muscle during three months of boxing training, inhabits this role as she has no other since *Boys Don't Cry*, for which she won an Oscar. Her Maggie has a feral intensity that combines with a heartbreaking eagerness and a megawatt smile to devastating effect. This is not an actress for surfacey roles; Swank's gift is bringing complete believability to the most extreme, most willful and passionate of characters.

Maggie's determination notwithstanding, Frankie Dunn, traditionalist that he is, does not believe in training women to box, calling it "the latest freak show out there." He's dismissive of her chances for success in the plainest language he can find. Of course, it's a given, especially with the looming possibility of a surrogate father-daughter relationship, that Frankie will relent and take her on, but rather than being the end of their story, that is the merest beginning.

Like many directors who work into their seventies and beyond, Eastwood has made his style even more direct and pared down, focusing on what's important, on telling the story he wants to tell in the most effective, most unadorned way. There's nothing glib or trendy about *Million Dollar Baby*; the movie is in no hurry getting started, and it even takes a leisurely detour into the story of a fighter named Danger that it could have done without. But by the time

Frankie and Maggie begin training together in earnest, we are completely invested in their story, willing to go with it no matter where it takes us.

Eastwood's belief in and loyalty to a below-the-line team that has been with him for years is a key factor in his ability to work so efficiently and so well. Cinematographer Tom Stern has collaborated with him for more than twenty years, editor Joel Cox for nearly thirty, and eighty-nine-year-old production designer Henry Bumstead has said, "I wouldn't work for anybody else at this age."

Whether Eastwood himself will want to be working that long is a fascinating question. If he were of a mind to go out on a classic high note, *Mystic River* would have been a good choice, but finding in *Million Dollar Baby* something that touched him, something he could handle beautifully, he went for it. Now, thanks to his great and ever-increasing skill, it touches us as well.

Swank did in fact go on to win her second Best Actress Oscar for her role, and the picture took three other major awards: best picture, best director and, for Morgan Freeman, best supporting actor.

Miracle
2004

The great radio monologist Jean Shepherd liked to say that the only truth to be found on television was in sports, because only in sports could the good guys end up losing. But not always. Sometimes the good guys actually win.

In the 1980 Winter Olympics, if you were an American or in fact any nationality except Russian, the good guys won big. In a victory chosen as the greatest sports moment of the century by *Sports Illustrated*, the brash and unheralded U.S. ice hockey team, average age twenty-one, defeated a four-time gold-medal-winning Soviet squad that had held a death grip on the sport for more than a dozen years.

The miracle is not that they've made a film about that legendary feat; the miracle is that it's actually a good one.

Miracle, as the story is predictably called after sportscaster Al Michaels's famous "Do you believe in miracles?" exclamation at the final buzzer, does something that's become rarer than breaking new ground or pushing the envelope.

Powered by an excellent Kurt Russell performance, *Miracle* treats old-fashioned, emotional material with an intelligence that respects both the story and the audience. This is a classically well-made studio entertainment that, like *The Rookie* of a few years back, has the knack of being moving without shamelessly overdoing a sure thing.

Director Gavin O'Connor turned out to be a good choice to take us behind the scenes of the putative miracle, to show us that, far from being an act of God, this tribute to the power of belief and how it gets created was months if not years in the making.

That *Tumbleweeds*, O'Connor's debut film and a prizewinner at Sundance, had an indie sensibility and a mainstream heart was a good sign for this venture. For what *Miracle* manages to do is combine a hockey story in which the players have all their teeth but lack the ability to swear (the reality is often the reverse) with a desire to stay as close to reality as those kinds of Disney strictures allow.

A key thing O'Connor and producers Mark Ciardi and Gordon Gray (also responsible for *The Rookie*) insisted on was as much on-ice verisimilitude as possible. That meant that almost all the actors who made up the twenty-man American squad that won the gold medal had played hockey on at least a college level.

That was critical given that 133 plays were created for *Miracle* by the film's skillful sports coordinator, Mark Ellis. Helped as well by Daniel Stoloff's cinematography and John Gilroy's crisp editing, the film smartly re-creates the sense of flow, power, speed and coordination that characterize hockey at its best.

Just as essential was the casting of Russell as coach Herb Brooks, the iconoclastic mind behind the miracle. An actor for more than forty years, Russell is turning into a true exception, a performer who is improving in a major way as he gets older and seems to relax more into his own skin.

Russell's last role, the crooked cop in *Dark Blue*, was his best ever, and his work here is quieter, less flamboyant, but just as good. With his eyes sunk deep into his face, the better to keep his players at a distance, Russell completely brings to life this complex man with a weakness for chewing gum and wearing awful clothes ("one of the worst-dressed coaches ever," one writer wrote, "in a sport that has produced a number of fashion disasters") yet with a parallel genius for diagramming plays and getting inside his players' heads.

It is one of the strengths of *Miracle* that it emphasizes a phenomenon familiar to athletes and sportswriters but often downplayed in sports movies, and that's the way successful coaches invariably turn out to be shrewd psychologists, masters of manipulative mind games. What it takes to win, what it takes to get athletes to play over their heads and sustain their crucial mental edge, is often as petty as scapegoating or as cutthroat as making them fear their jobs are at stake. Brooks used all these techniques, and more.

Because setting the scene was important to director O'Connor, *Miracle*'s opening credits use extensive newsreel footage to carefully set this story at the tail end of the 1970s, a tumultuous decade characterized by gas lines and the Iranian hostage crisis. A time, in other words, desperately in need of American heroes.

Brooks is not only an unlikely hero, his unconventional ideas made him an unlikely person to be selected to coach the U.S. team in the first place.

As he explained to the selection committee, Brooks wanted to beat the Russians at their own game, using not egotistical all-stars but young players he could personally mold into a cohesive team that would skate harder and faster for longer than any group the Soviets had ever faced.

Brooks also wanted a team whose minds he could play like the arena organ, a team whose insecurities he could personally identify with from his own history as the last player cut from the 1960 U.S. team. "I'll be your coach. I won't be your friend," he announces to the group. He becomes such a demanding taskmaster that when the team gives him a Christmas present, it turns out to be a bullwhip.

Given a protagonist who chose to be seen as the all-knowing autocrat, *Miracle* had to find ways to humanize and warm the man up. Open-faced Noah Emmerich is cast as assistant coach Craig Patrick, and, more critically, the versatile Patricia Clarkson is cast as the coach's wife, Patty. With her innate intelligence and perspicacity, Clarkson raises the level of even standard characters, and knowing that Brooks would have someone like her as a wife automatically makes him a more interesting person.

Though you can't help but wonder what would have happened to Brooks and company if his ideas had been wrong, the coach has a reason for everything he does. He wants this team to care as much as he does; he wants to infuse them forcefully with his own unbending spirit. Whether he does that with a harsh "You don't have enough talent to win on talent alone" or an inspirational "This cannot be a team of common men" doesn't matter; he just wants to get it done. "Great moments," he says, "are born from great opportunity," and no one can accuse Brooks and his players, or this film, of not taking advantage of theirs.

Mystic River
2003

Mystic River is a major American motion picture, an overpowering piece of work that involves some of the most basic human emotions: love, hate, fear, revenge, despair. Directed by Clint Eastwood with absolute confidence and remarkable control, it owes both its success and its significance to the way it seamlessly unites elements that are difficult to pull off on their own, much less together.

This film is simultaneously an intricate and gripping crime story that involves child molestation and murder and a thoughtful and disturbing emotional drama about a nightmarish past that sends destructive tentacles into the present. Instead of clashing, these elements reinforce each other every step of the way.

This is a major studio release that deals with the kind of dark and disconcerting material Hollywood usually tries to avoid. It's a star vehicle that provides memorable roles for half a dozen major players (Sean Penn, Tim Robbins, Kevin Bacon, Laurence Fishburne, Marcia Gay Harden, Laura Linney) yet doesn't neglect even the smallest speaking parts.

It's got strong source material (Dennis Lehane's persuasive bestseller) and a spare and impressive adaptation by Brian Helgeland that makes the difficult work of finding the film inside the book look simple and inevitable. And despite a respect for language that extends to the use of key dialogue from the book, *Mystic River* is faultlessly cinematic and a model of classic directorial style.

Best of all, *Mystic River* has Eastwood, a confident old master invigorated by the challenges inherent in the material. He's dealing with themes of masculinity and violence that have concerned him for decades, with emotions he understands from the inside, and he's venturing into deeper and murkier emotional currents than he's ever attempted before. What results is also Eastwood's best, most mature direction since *Unforgiven*.

Everything starts with Lehane's strong and economically written book, a breakthrough stand-alone novel coming after a series of five private-eye books. "I was living with *Mystic River* for ten years before I wrote it," the author told *Publishers Weekly*, and that undoubtedly accounts for the subtlety and intricacy of its psychology, the way it gets to more emotion than is usual for a police procedural.

Set in a hard world where "the worst things did, in fact, sometimes happen," Lehane's is a story that understands life's fatal randomness, that explores how misplaced suspicions, unresolved hatreds, missed opportunities and shattering misunderstandings can color already complex situations in which no one is really innocent and everyone lives with his or her own complicity.

Mystic River is also a story, on the page and on the screen, that has an exact sense of place. Its aura of been-there atmosphere centers on the Boston neighborhood of East Buckingham, where the film was shot, a working-class area, close by the Mystic River, also known as the Flats. "The Flats," Lehane wrote, "were nothing but a small town wrapped within a big city."

The drama begins with a critical extended flashback, set a quarter of a century in the past, a lazy late afternoon moment that finds eleven-year-olds Dave, Sean and Jimmy playing street hockey on a deserted stretch of pavement.

But, as moodily captured by cinematographer Tom Stern, even the most innocent-seeming city moments have an intangible edge of menace about them. A car pulls up, a man presenting himself as a police officer gets out and rousts the boys for a minor infraction. Dave is ordered into the car and, suddenly, things get very dark very fast. "Ever think," Jimmy is to say decades later, "how one little choice can change a person's life?" Can change, it turns out, everyone's life.

In an instant, it is twenty-five years later and the boys, still in Boston but no longer close ("now it's just hello around the neighborhood"), are adults with families and responsibilities. Dave (Robbins), inevitably, is the one the past has affected most. Still living in the area, though married to the timid Celeste (Harden) and with a son of his own, Dave Boyle has a sense of darkness and sadness around him that is so deep it seems to have swallowed the boy we saw without a trace. Of all the actors, Robbins has changed himself most for this role, taking on a strong Boston accent and transforming his usual confident body language to play a haunted interior man who's forever somewhere else in his mind.

Work, at least, has taken Sean Devine (Bacon) a little farther away. He's become a "statie," a homicide detective working for the Massachusetts State Police, but he, too, has personal problems. Six months ago, his wife left; his contact with her is limited to random telephone interludes during which she calls and stays on the line, but won't speak.

The role of Sean is the least showy of the three major characters, and it is the one most cut down from the novel, but it is essential as an anchor for the plot and for the audience to hold on to. Bacon does an expert job of getting us involved in the critical choices and decisions of, in Lehane's words, "a guy the world has always worked for."

Sean is reluctantly pulled back to the old neighborhood and his boyhood experiences when he and his partner Whitey (Fishburne) are assigned to investigate a crime in East Buckingham. It's a murder connected to the third of the boyhood pals, Jimmy Markum, a murder that will draw all three men closer together in unexpected and ultimately horrific ways.

As played by Penn, Jimmy is the inevitable center of the story. Even as a child, Lehane writes, "if he was aware there were rules—in the subway, on the streets, in a movie theater—he never showed it," and that making-your-own-law quality still defines him, though he's now the twice-married father of three daughters who owns a neighborhood convenience store called the Cottage Market.

With a look that could penetrate steel, a temper like the devil's wrath and the hawk-like presence of a predator, Penn's Jimmy sits astride his world like a god of vengeance, terrifying even in repose. When he's not in repose, you'd better just get the hell out of the way.

Probably no actor in America has access to the deep reserves of fury as well as the skill to use them as Penn, and his primordial anger and pain in this film will raise the hairs on the back of your neck. Yet it is also Penn's gift to illuminate his character's distraught, remorseful sides, and reminding us how completely human Jimmy is makes him so much the scarier.

The other above-the-line actors—Harden as the mouse-like Celeste, Fishburne as the unrelenting detective and especially Linney as Jimmy's implacable wife Annabeth—are equally impressive, as is Eli Wallach in a juicy unbilled cameo as a liquor store owner.

But *Mystic River*, exactly cast by Phyllis Huffman, is also a film in which you notice the smallest roles, people such as Emmy Rossum as Jimmy's daughter Katie; Susan Willis as an elderly key witness; and Kevin Chapman as Val Savage, one of a trio of brothers known around the neighborhood, not without reason, as "legends of psychosis."

If Eastwood had a watchword for this film, as with much of his best work, it was restraint at the service of an overpowering story. This is a director who understands that the stronger the passions, the more useful a kind of minimalism is in conveying them, who knows that paring something down can make a story more emotional, more intense than it would otherwise be.

This is also a director who knows not only just what he wants but how to achieve it and whose sureness with this material, down to knowing exactly how long he wants editor Joel Cox to stay on a given shot, seems to increase as the story progresses.

Cox, like many of Eastwood's team, has been with him for many years. Similarly, director of photography Stern, who has created a beautifully subdued, muted look that gives color the feeling tone of black and white, has been a gaffer or chief lighting technician on a number of Eastwood films, most notably those shot by Bruce Surtees, nicknamed "The Prince of Darkness" for his similar love of shadowy looks.

It's this combination of Eastwood's emphasis on keeping his crew together from project to project and his ability to make his films free of studio interference that has allowed the director the kind of artistic control we usually associate with independent films.

Mystic River's concern with violence and its aftermath, with how men behave under stress, make this very much an Eastwood film, one that is helped by the extent to which he's at home with this kind of material. The furtive recesses of the human soul neither attract nor repel him, he neither flees from nor celebrates the evil that men do. This unblinking attitude in the face of deep horror and despair gives *Mystic River* an almost elegant somberness of tone.

But Eastwood has not just summed up his career with *Mystic River*, he has gone further. He has, to an unprecedented extent, used one of his violent films to deal extensively with the pain and the anguish that can cluster around ordinary lives and such ordinary situations as marriage, divorce and family. Eastwood seems more interested in character and psychology than ever before, more compelled to investigate what can happen when malignancy festers among otherwise everyday people.

The mastery—and there really is no other word for it—Eastwood demonstrates in this, the twenty-fourth feature he's directed, was not easily won and did not come at the end of an unbroken string of triumphs. But there can be no doubt that it's here. "It's as good as I can do," the director said in a quiet moment before the film was shown at Cannes, but it's more than that. It's as good as anybody can do.

In a year otherwise dominated by Lord of the Rings, *the film won acting Oscars for Penn and Robbins.*

One True Thing
1998

What the movie business calls women's pictures get scant respect in Hollywood. The phrase signals dismissal and denigration, a casual way to brush off works that deal with emotions more than explosions, that think the complexity of personal relationships is the most compelling subject around.

But women's pictures, as *One True Thing* proves, are really human stories, accessible to anyone who is willing to feel. Based on Anna Quindlen's novel about a mother and daughter brought closer by the prospect of death, *One True Thing* demonstrates that the power of simple things, the transcendent nature of the ordinary, can make for riveting filmmaking.

It's satisfying somehow that Carl Franklin, working from a dependable script by Karen Croner, should be the director who makes this point so strongly. Though the success of his previous features, *One False Move* and *Devil in a Blue Dress,* is grounded in their psychological acuity, they're best remembered for being dark, brooding pieces where physical violence is more of a threat than the emotional kind.

It's also appropriate that Meryl Streep, without question the outstanding American actress of her generation, should be the star here. Her role as Kate Gulden—mother, suburban house frau and faculty wife—is one of the least self-consciously dramatic and showy of her career, but Streep adds a level of honesty and reality that makes it one of her most moving.

Equally fitting is that *One True Thing*, a film that illustrates the narrowness of gender and genre classification, should be about a daughter who comes to question, through the most painful experiences of her life, everything she believes about a woman whose lifestyle she can't consider without shuddering. "My mother was like dinner," novelist Quindlen has her protagonist say. "I needed her in order to live, but I did not pay much attention to what went into her."

Ellen Gulden (Renee Zellweger) grew up in suburban Langhorne, but she moved to Manhattan after graduating from Harvard. A journalist who writes for *New York Magazine*, she was proud of being someone, again in Quindlen's phrase, "who ate ambition for breakfast and anyone who got in her way for lunch."

Never close to her mother while growing up, Ellen considered herself her father's daughter. George Gulden (William Hurt) is a charismatic professor of American literature and a National Book Award winner, and Ellen, embarrassed when her mother calls her "my brilliant daughter," wants nothing more than her father's faintest word of praise.

These family dynamics are visible at a surprise birthday party Kate throws for her husband, where Ellen, scornful and vaguely contemptuous of the choices her mother has made, first mocks this thorough-going homemaker for caring which knife is the right one for cutting bread and then clumsily cuts her finger with it. When someone says, "There's no place like home," Ellen immediately responds, "Thank God."

If it wasn't for her father's insistence, Ellen would never have moved back to Langhorne when Kate is diagnosed with cancer. She's got her off-and-on boyfriend in the city and a big story she's working on for the magazine about a senator with personal problems. But when her father turns censorious and says, "You've got a Harvard education, but where is your heart?" she inevitably gives in.

It's not only Ellen who's wary about the journey back, it's Kate as well. Though Ellen mocks the Minnies, her mother's group of civic-minded housewives who do such worthwhile things as decorate the town's Christmas trees, Kate is horrified at the thought of anyone else being caring and nurturing around her house.

Much of the drama here is about a daughter who says, "The one thing I never wanted to do was live my mother's life," but who gradually and subtly realizes that she never understood this woman who is shrewd enough to nail Jane Austen on being condescending to conventional female characters. Ellen also comes to see that there are aspects to her adored father and her parents' marriage that she had no idea existed.

Summarized like this, *One True Thing* tends to sound schematic, and though the film has those elements to it, Franklin's intuitive restraint and sense of balance keep it honest. His direction brings both dignity and decency to what would have been obvious material in other hands; letting emotional situations degenerate into treacle is out of the question with him in charge.

Also benefiting from Franklin's steady, focused hand is Zellweger, an actress whose effectiveness is not a given. Zellweger's strength, which she gets to emphasize here, is how accessible and close to the surface her emotions are. As her mother's condition worsens, Ellen increasingly seethes with all kinds of resentments, and she feels free to act out what's troubling her in a way her mother never attempted.

As for Streep, this performance is the equal of her best work because she doesn't condescend to a character who is happy to be ordinary and self-effacing. Only gradually does Ellen's vision clear enough to give her and us a second sight into her mother's strength, spirit and purpose, and once that comes it makes the painful physical collapse Kate goes through that much more wrenching.

Screenwriter Kroner, most of whose work has been for television, has shrewdly put together a script that makes numerous minor departures from Quindlen's novel, including eliminating one of Ellen's brothers (the remaining one is played by Tom Everett Scott) and adding plot strands to beef up different aspects of Ellen's increasingly strained relationship with her dad.

The film's most interesting choice vis-à-vis its source is to downplay the original's melodrama. Though the film delicately frames

Ellen's story in discreet questioning by a district attorney who is investigating the possibility that her mother's death was a mercy killing, in Quindlen's novel the investigation becomes a major public event that involves jail time, newspaper headlines and large amounts of O.J.–type publicity.

It's fascinating that Franklin, whose films have tended toward storm and fury, was astute enough to see the importance of paring away even the suggestion of sensationalism the book offers. Though films similar to *One True Thing* can smother the viewer, Franklin's measured direction creates the space necessary for audiences to react fully, allowing us the freedom to step forward and embrace the emotion, making it completely our own.

The People vs. Larry Flynt
1996

In its excesses and extravagances, its fascination with sex, religion, celebrity, bad taste and making a whole lot of money, there is no more American story than that of combative pornographer and *Hustler* magazine publisher Larry Flynt. So it's poetic and appropriate that an immigrant director, Czech-born Milos Forman, has had the clarity to turn it into a provocative and engrossing motion picture.

Working from a shrewd and pointedly funny script by Scott Alexander & Larry Karaszewski, the team responsible for *Ed Wood*, Forman's contributions have enlarged *The People vs. Larry Flynt* in ways other filmmakers might not have managed.

The most obvious is having an eye for casting and a zest for mixing professionals with real people, an openness to using folks such as political consultant James Carville and Flynt himself (playing a hard-nosed judge) in cameos. And having the nerve to choose rock star Courtney Love to play opposite Woody Harrelson and being rewarded with a livewire piece of work, both kinetic and kittenish, that stands as one of the most original performances of the year.

Forman, witness films from *Loves of a Blonde* through *One Flew Over the Cuckoo's Nest* and *Valmont*, also has a willingness to tolerate ambiguity. Despite his name in the title, *The People vs. Larry Flynt* is not interested in glorifying Larry Flynt, quite the opposite. It rather delights in showing how this crass and cold-eyed hustler, a man of wildly contradictory and often offensive urges and impulses, ended up, to his own great surprise as much as anyone's, doing something significant for society.

What Flynt finally did was take a legal dispute with the Reverend Jerry Falwell about a noxious *Hustler* ad parody (showing the reverend losing his virginity to his mother in an outhouse) all the way to the Supreme Court. The top court's unanimous 1988 ruling, for the first time granting First Amendment protection to parody, is considered a free-speech landmark.

In this area, too, *The People vs. Larry Flynt* benefits from having a filmmaker who lost his parents to the Nazis and grew to adulthood under Communist censorship. Though it's hard to imagine native-born directors getting worked up about First Amendment rights they take for granted, Forman's life experiences turn those freedoms into issues he can be passionate and persuasive about.

All this is yet to come when *The People vs. Larry Flynt* opens in 1952 in a decrepit shack in the woods of East Kentucky, where ten-year-old moonshiner Larry (helped by his eight-year-old brother Jimmy) is so intent on making a buck that he doesn't hesitate to physically attack his alcoholic father for "drinking my profits."

Twenty years later, Larry (Woody Harrelson) and Jimmy (real-life brother Brett Harrelson) are still chasing the main chance, this time by running go-go dancers through a series of unimpressive Hustler Clubs in Ohio.

The men's magazine starts as a simple newsletter for the clubs, but Flynt, who enjoys getting worked up, soon turns messianic in his determination to topple Hugh Hefner by printing the most graphic shots of genitalia he can get away with. His own most satisfied customer, Flynt harangues his dubious confederates, many of whom have trouble telling even-numbered pages from odd, by holding up the rival publication and screaming, "Who is this magazine for anyway? Seven million people buy it, but nobody reads it. *Playboy* is mocking you."

About this time Larry meets too-young dancer Althea Leasure, a brazen erotic sprite whom Courtney Love, alternately vampish and vulnerable, invests with a natural blowzy sensuality. Bisexual, easily bored, invariably jealous, Love's Althea and Woody Harrelson's shrewd, promiscuous Flynt are no Hallmark card, but the actors connect beautifully and make the couple's love for each other vivid and undeniable.

Almost immediately, Flynt's off-putting magazine gets him into trouble with the authorities, introducing him to Alan Isaacman (Edward Norton), a committed civil liberties lawyer (and composite of several Flynt attorneys) who starts to educate his client (and the audience) about the overarching importance of constitutional rights.

A different kind of trouble is provided by evangelist and presidential sister Ruth Carter Stapleton (played by television anchor Donna Hanover). With her flirtatious encouragement, Flynt's life takes another unexpected turn as he becomes the unlikeliest of born-again Christians. This is much to the despair of Althea, who rightly points out that "nobody on this planet wants religion and porn together."

Everything changes yet again in 1978, when Flynt is shot leaving a Georgia courthouse, an attack that leaves him paralyzed below the waist and increasingly addicted to painkilling drugs, which become a problem for his wife as well.

Flynt and Althea relocate to Los Angeles ("We ought to move somewhere perverts are welcome" is Flynt's wry rationale), where outrageous courtroom antics such as showing up dressed in an American flag diaper and tossing oranges at a judge demonstrate Flynt's ability to turn everything into a circus and a travesty.

Though Woody Harrelson's intensity and charisma make Flynt magnetic, he is terrifying and self-destructive, not someone we admire, which is the film's point. His chaotic story mirrors *The People vs. Larry Flynt* in being without conventional boundaries, a saga that could happen only in a country where, as Flynt himself puts it, "everybody gets their shot, even a pig." His may have been the classic unexamined life, but *The People vs. Larry Flynt* does us all a favor by scrutinizing it to memorable effect.

Primary Colors
1998

If, as it's been said, the mark of a music lover is the ability to hear Rossini's *William Tell Overture* without thinking of the Lone Ranger, so the mark of a cineaste is being able to watch John Travolta and Emma Thompson in *Primary Colors* unimpeded by thoughts of Bill and Hillary Clinton. It's a test most Americans would fail without thinking twice.

Despite the expected author's note disclaimer about its characters and situations not being real, *Primary Colors* the novel is the most celebrated of modern romans à clef, a piece of informed but controversial speculation by political writer Joe Klein working under the pen name Anonymous. Not only Jack Stanton and his wife but almost all its characters are based on well-known operatives, including big state governor Orlando Ozio (read Mario Cuomo) and downhome consultant Richard Jemmons (a.k.a. James Carville).

Director Mike Nichols and screenwriter Elaine May have had the skill and the good sense to take the frisson this closeness to reality provides and run with it. Despite all the cautions and disclaimers from a legion of pundits, despite our knowledge that this is not the real thing but only a riff on the 1992 Democratic presidential campaign, *Primary Colors* is for the most part such a smart and savvy piece of work that it encourages us to feel we're eavesdropping on history. It's a sensation that can be delicious.

In the decades since he and May were the sharpest of stand-up comedy teams, Nichols has become a director known for putting a high commercial sheen on material, some of which did not reward the effort. Here, that craft (including the help of cinematographer Michael Ballhaus, production designer Bo Welch, editor Arthur Schmidt, composer Ry Cooder and costumer Ann Roth) is joined to the slightly subversive pungency of May's sharp and sarcastic script, which includes many of the book's better speeches and knows how to improve on them.

The *Primary Colors* story is told through the eyes of Henry Burton (British actor Adrian Lester), a young African American political operative, the grandson of a legend of the civil rights movement, who joins the presidential campaign of an obscure Southern governor named Jack Stanton (Travolta).

Burton was not eager to get on the team of a man he's heard described as "some cracker who hasn't done much in his own state." But as a would-be idealist whom strategist Jemmons (a low-key and effective Billy Bob Thornton) accurately diagnoses as having a case of "galloping true believerism," Burton cannot resist Stanton's color-blindness and what appears to be his genuine feeling for America's have-nots; he also admires the intellectual moxie of his wife, Susan (Thompson).

If *The War Room*, the D. A. Pennebaker-Chris Hegedus documentary on the same topic is any measure, *Primary Colors* is excellent at depicting the barely organized chaos of campaigning, following the candidate and his team from their underdog status in New Hampshire through the trials of campaigns in Florida and New York.

These peregrinations are more twisty than usual because of what a profane, take-no-prisoners Stanton loyalist named Libby Holden calls with typical brio the governor's propensity for having "poked his pecker in some sorry trash bins." After a hairdresser named Cashmere McLeod (read Gennifer Flowers) sells her tell-all story to a national tabloid, Holden is hired by the campaign to be a "dustbuster" and discredit tales of womanizing before they can harm the candidate. For Tennessee-born Kathy Bates, this gleeful, high-energy part is a lifesaver, her best performance since winning an Oscar in *Misery* and good enough to steal practically the entire picture.

Though *Primary Colors* the movie plays a bit softer than the book, partially because it eliminates a brief sexual encounter between the president's wife and the narrator, it does not avoid the questions the original raised about means and ends. How far can you allow yourself to go in cutthroat slander, deception and manipulation in order to keep a good guy's campaign alive? Is venality the price you pay to lead? Is there truth in Stanton's question, "You don't think Abraham Lincoln was a whore before he was a president?" And does Henry Burton really know what he's getting into when he says early on, "I'll take the liar over the man who doesn't care"?

Making the conundrum of compromise more than a dry, academic query are the characters of Jack and Susan Stanton as revealed through the people who play them. Though it's routinely said that adroit casting is the major part of the filmmaking battle, it's unusual to have two actors whose different approaches to their craft are not only complementary but also help illuminate their characters' relationship to each other.

Travolta, more the instinctive movie star than the highly trained technician, has chosen to model Governor Stanton, down to his silvery hair and Southern accent, on President Clinton. It's no more than a turn, an amusing and light-fingered impersonation, but like the politician he plays it's an irresistible one. The movie's Stanton is a flawed and contradictory man, baffling and hypnotic in his seamless combination of genuine caring with casual manipulation. This film's accomplishment is illustrating that contradiction, showing how such a man could captivate an intelligent, caring staff—and the American public—despite his evident shortcomings.

Essential in defining Stanton's character is his relationship with wife Susan. Thompson, the more classically trained performer, chose not to base her character on Hillary Rodham Clinton. That combination makes Susan seem twice removed from the governor, adds spice to the head and heart duality that characterizes their dynamic and makes them eerily seem like two halves of the same person.

Primary Colors also features strong performances in its minor characters. Especially worth singling out are Larry Hagman as one of the governor's political opponents; Caroline Aaron as an obstreperous friend of Susan's; and Rob Reiner as an irrepressible Miami talk-show host. Characters we see too little of, presumably because the film ran long, include Maura Tierney as Daisy, Burton's campaign partner in crime (who simply disappears at a certain point), and Diane Ladd, whose Momma Stanton is reduced to the merest cameo.

Entertaining as it mostly is, *Primary Colors* parallels the book in being least successful near its close when it tries to force more serious moral lessons than its storyline can comfortably hold. And as risqué as its speculations seemed when Klein was still anonymous, the rush of history, epitomized by the tale of Monica Lewinsky, has overtaken and surpassed what's been put on the screen.

But if parallels to reality is the hook that draws us into *Primary Colors*, it's the nature of its characters that holds us there. Governor Stanton commands our interest in somewhat the same way many a politician does: He doesn't seem to add up. If we could fully figure him out and pin down the nature of his appeal, we might be able to do the same for our political process and for ourselves. And that would be not a half-bad day's work.

Quiz Show
1994

As the subject for a major motion picture, the fuss surrounding the rigged television quiz shows of the late 1950s does not seem particularly promising. Yes, people were shocked at the time, when it turned out that programs such as *Twenty-One* and its most celebrated contestant, Charles Van Doren, were not dealing from a straight deck, but so many scandals have come and gone in the intervening years that it's hard to work up much passion about that one.

So it is an especial triumph that *Quiz Show*, directed by Robert Redford and written by Paul Attanasio, turns that footnote of television history into a thoughtful, absorbing drama about moral ambiguity and the affability of evil. Sticking moderately close to the facts and using real names whenever possible, it succeeds by pulling back and looking at the situation through an unexpectedly subtle and wide-ranging lens.

Of course, one of the focal points of any examination of the scandal has to be Van Doren, an intellectual golden boy whose downfall was classically tragic. And although he is beautifully played by Ralph Fiennes with a subtlety that is at least the equal of his Oscar-nominated performance in *Schindler's List*, *Quiz Show* succeeds as well as it does because it is structured to make Van Doren's story only part of the whole.

Doing that structuring is screenwriter Attanasio, best known for having created the television series *Homicide*. Based loosely on a memoir by Richard Goodwin, a speech writer for President John F. Kennedy who began his Washington life as a congressional investigator looking into the scandal, Attanasio's script adroitly splits its focus three interconnected ways.

Instead of providing the good versus evil face-off that might be expected, *Quiz Show* has Van Doren, Goodwin (Rob Morrow) and Herbert Stempel (John Turturro), a disgruntled former contestant who blew the whistle on the show, warily dancing around one another. And, in what is partly a tribute to Redford's clout, this is one studio picture in which even the heroes are uncomfortably complicit.

Given the number of years he's played the game in Hollywood, it shouldn't be surprising that director Redford is dead-on in depicting this atmosphere of variable morality, but it is satisfying nevertheless to see what an accomplished job of directing he does and how alive he is to the ambiguities in the situation.

Perhaps because it doesn't play out in any explicit way, the scene *Quiz Show* opens with is especially telling. The year is 1957, the place a Chrysler showroom in Washington, where the cigar-smoking Richard Goodwin, first in his class at Harvard Law but mired in a low-level bureaucratic job, is getting an almost erotic charge out of examining a stunning new Chrysler 300D.

Later on, as the investigation of Van Doren proceeds, another film might have painted Goodwin as the unalloyed force for good, and this scene shrewdly checkmates that feeling. For, as Goodwin delicately runs his hands over the smooth leather and listens to the salesman's insinuating patter, the lust for conspicuous consumption is obvious in his eyes. None of us, *Quiz Show* takes care to point out, should think we are above temptation.

After this delicate opening, the film shifts to a brisk montage detailing the hoopla surrounding *Twenty-One*, the program's showy obsession with security about its questions and the fascination all America felt for contestants who were winning five- and six-figure amounts when that was real money.

But although awkward nerd Herbert Stempel seems secure as the show's reigning champion, behind the scenes a powerful cabal is not so sure. The program's sponsor (an icily modulated cameo by director Martin Scorsese) feels Herb's Everyman qualities have worn thin and wants him gone. Although the show trumpets its inviolability, coproducer Dan Enright (David Paymer at his best) gets the message. The end is near for "the freak with the sponge memory." What is wanted to take his place is someone polished enough not only to answer questions on the show but to "get a table at '21'" as well.

Enter college English instructor Van Doren, spotted trying out for a rival show by coproducer Albert Freedman (Hank Azaria). The son of one Pulitzer Prize winner, poet Mark Van Doren (Paul Scofield), and the nephew of another, thirty-three-year-old Charles has the diffident glow that comes with being a card-carrying member of America's intellectual aristocracy. A grown-up cherub, Van Doren is also naïve enough to fall for Enright's rationalizations about why getting just the tiniest bit of help with the questions will turn him into a better role model for the youth of America.

Decent, affable, enormously likable, Van Doren is everything Stempel is not, and the first part of *Quiz Show* parallels the former's rise to national celebrity with the latter's fall to disgruntled oblivion. But once Goodwin enters the picture, motivated both by personal ambition (remember the Chrysler) and a public-spirited desire to "put television on trial," *Quiz Show*'s themes deepen as the drama gains momentum.

A Jewish outsider whose Ivy League background allows him to pass in Van Doren's world of birthday lunches with Edmund Wilson and Thomas Merton, Goodwin feels especially torn as his investigations into Stempel's charges indicate that this charming man, with good reason America's sweetheart, was tainted. Should Goodwin (whose beefy role here was apparently the biggest departure from history) expose Van Doren, protect him or just throw up his hands and flee?

The uncertain interaction between Van Doren, Goodwin and Stempel, heightened by Attanasio's trenchant dialogue, is especially good at examining the peculiarly American quality the three men unknowingly share. Each in some way feels unappreciated, on the outside of the Big Dream, open to a quick way out of the slough of despond. And each ends up realizing that getting what they want is not what they want at all.

Cast partly against expectation, *Quiz Show* is compelling enough to survive an initial feeling that both Turturro as the needy Stempel and *Northern Exposure*'s Morrow as the cocky Goodwin have a tendency to exaggerate their performances. Both roles, however, give less trouble as the film progresses, partly because the Brits they play against are so dazzling.

Paul Scofield, a celebrated stage actor, gives his best film performance since winning an Oscar for *A Man for All Seasons*, as Charles's urbane, distant father. But it is Ralph Fiennes and his poignant and ravaged portrait of the son in extremis that provides *Quiz Show* with its center of gravity. Fiennes's ability to project the pain behind a well-mannered facade, to turn intellectual and emotional agony into a real and living thing, is devastating. Impressive as the film is in all respects, *Quiz Show* would have been a very different experience without him.

Ray
2004

From the moment director Taylor Hackford starts *Ray* with a shot of Jamie Foxx's fingers hitting the piano keys and breaking into the unmistakable rhythms of "What'd I Say," it's clear that Ray Charles's unstoppable music will power this film. It's axiomatic that any picture with songs such as "I Got a Woman," "Georgia on My Mind," "Hit the Road Jack" and "I Can't Stop Loving You" is going to get cut all the slack it needs.

Ray in fact turns out to be a proudly conventional film that combines an involving true story, irresistible music and a charismatic performance in a way that makes us not only forgive but actually almost relish how standard the presentation is.

Though Charles does most of the soundtrack singing and playing, it is Foxx (a gifted pianist in real life) whose dominating performance as the blind singer is the essence of *Ray*'s success. Even those who've seen the former comic actor go from strength to strength in his earlier serious films (*Any Given Sunday, Ali, Collateral*) will be impressed by the way he emerges here as a full-blown dramatic star.

The actor spent considerable time with Charles before the singer's death in 2004 and does an uncanny job duplicating his mannerisms. But this performance goes well beyond impersonation. Foxx takes his role and runs with it, imbuing his character with all the characteristics— nerve, shrewdness, self-interest and a keen sense of humor—that the real Ray Charles needed to overcome the obstacles to his success.

One of the striking things about *Ray* is the way Foxx's performance gives the uncanny impression of watching the real Charles reliving his life on screen. The actor makes us believe that what's in front of our eyes really happened, which turns out to be more of a feat than might be imagined.

That's because so much of the script (by James L. White from a story by director Hackford and White) fits so snugly into the traditional been-there confines of movie biography. The specifics may be Charles's own, but the dialogue is so on-the-nose and the overall dramatic thrust so familiar—talented man haunted by childhood trauma, hurting his marriage by sleeping around, drawn to and finally kicking heroin—that much of what happens to Charles is completely predictable.

What paradoxically saves the situation, aside from Foxx's galvanizing performance, is that Hackford believes passionately in the value of the well-worn conventions he's recapitulating. When you combine that conviction with the reality that we're so conditioned to seeing biopics structured this way that we're more than comfortable with the approach, you get a film that is wholly entertaining despite its flaws.

It also doesn't hurt that Charles's story is a long and involving one, told with the aid of multiple flashbacks and a great number of characters. Adroitly cast by Nancy Klopper, *Ray* showcases more talented African American actors than most studios will feature in an entire year of releases.

Making perhaps the strongest impression is the film's least-known performer, a debuting Sharon Warren, who appears early and unforgettably as Charles's stick-thin firebrand of a mother, Aretha Robinson. "Always remember your promise to me," she insists to her son in an early flashback. "Don't let nobody or nothing turn you into no cripple."

Ray's narrative proper begins when the young musician takes a bus out of the South to Seattle, where he meets a young Quincy Jones (Larenz Tate) and falls under the domination of a manipulative club owner.

But Charles, whose mantra was "I might be blind but I ain't stupid," was impossible to take advantage of for long. Becoming his own man and going on the road, he refused to use either a cane or a dog. He developed a variety of strategies for coping with blindness, from insisting on being paid in singles to using his ears as his eyes. And, following other band members, he found himself drawn to the blandishments of heroin.

Gradually, Charles meets the key people in his life: his wife Della Bea (Kerry Washington) and Atlantic Records' Ahmet Ertegun (Curtis Armstrong), who wants him to develop a personal style, something Charles initially resists: "When you're blind you ain't got that many choices. What if people don't like who I am?"

They did. Charles went on to a musical career that included twelve Grammys, seventy-six singles on the bestseller charts and more than seventy-five albums. But numbers can't indicate the influence of a musician who transcended genres and created new ones, who mastered styles including jazz and country and western and is credited with combining gospel and rhythm and blues to create soul. It's hard to separate his only-in-America story from that of American popular music, hard not to be impressed by his aspirations, his abilities, his unforeseen artistic trajectory.

Always leading several lives, hiding both his heroin use and his girlfriends from his wife, Charles finds that his increasing success makes that duplicity hard to disguise. That becomes increasingly true with regard to his incendiary relationship with Margie Hendricks (a strong Regina King), the most prominent member of his backup group, the Raelettes.

Ray also gets into Charles's business dealings, from his unprecedented determination to own his recording masters to the power-behind-the-throne fights between managers Jeff Brown (Clifton Powell) and Joe Adams (Harry Lennix). In this, as in all things, *Ray* may be too by the numbers, but with Jamie Foxx out front, this is one film that knows how to make it all add up.

Ray *won a pair of Oscars, one for sound mixing and one for Jamie Foxx as best actor, cementing his transition to serious roles.*

Road to Perdition
2002

Half a century ago, James Stewart, at that point the most beloved of American leading men, decided it was time for something completely different.

In a series of bitter, disturbing, early-1950s Westerns directed by Anthony Mann—*Winchester '73, The Naked Spur* and *The Man from Laramie*—Stewart began playing ruthless loners bent on revenge, men capable of rages so terrifying that to experience them is to forget that the sentimental Stewart of *Mr. Smith Goes to Washington* and *It's a Wonderful Life* ever existed.

Stewart's chilling about-face inevitably comes to mind when watching his modern equivalent, Tom Hanks, identically reverse fields in director Sam Mendes's brooding, powerful *Road to Perdition*, playing a Depression-era gangland executioner so skilled and implacable he's known as the Angel of Death.

Hanks's Michael Sullivan is a man of few words and less inflection, capable of freezing his rivals with hard looks from impenetrable eyes as well as disconcerting his two young sons with the weight and solemnity of his presence.

It is a deadly performance, one of Hanks's best, and because it is free of mannerisms and has the feeling of coming from an unexpectedly dark and deep place, it makes Sullivan's savage pursuit of a bloody revenge particularly scary and convincing.

It is also unnerving because Hanks remains Hanks, a person we instinctively connect with no matter how bloody his trade. And so, although Sullivan's milieu is a violent one, his story is finally an emotional and personal one.

It's the story of the unavoidably difficult relationship between fathers and sons, both biological and surrogate, a touchy connection a character sums up by insisting, "It's a natural law: Sons are put on this earth to trouble their fathers."

Mendes, in only his second feature (following the Oscar-winning *American Beauty*), has told this surprisingly resonant story with the potent, unrelenting fatalism of a previously unknown Greek myth.

This is classic albeit somber filmmaking, restrained and all of a piece, by a director who believes film can tell adult stories in an adult manner, who knows the effects he wants and how to get them.

Road to Perdition started life as a 1998 graphic novel by Max Allan Collins, the art by Richard Piers Rayner. David Self, who previously wrote the focused *Thirteen Days* and the out-of-control *The Haunting*, has made some very shrewd changes to the original that increase its emotional wattage. Sullivan has a closer relationship with the crime

boss he now considers his surrogate father as well as a more unresolved, unsettled one with his twelve-year-old son.

The film opens with a spare voice-over, spoken by that son as a
grown man, that establishes an unwavering tone and sets up the plot:
"There are many stories about Michael Sullivan. Some say he was a
decent man. Some say there was no good in him at all. But I once
spent six weeks with him in the winter of 1931. This is our story."

As is fitting for a violent story, *Perdition* opens with a wake in one
of the biggest houses in Rock Island, Illinois. It belongs to John
Rooney (a faultless Paul Newman), who, at first glance, comes off as a
garrulous community leader, or maybe the indulgent grandfather to
Sullivan's two boys, the older Michael Jr. (Tyler Hoechlin) and the
younger Peter (Liam Aiken).

But in truth, Rooney is a major underworld figure, a close associate
of Al Capone's, someone of whom it is truthfully, and fearfully, said,
"You rule this town as God rules the Earth. You give and you take
away."

Sullivan is more than the top lieutenant who enforces the boss's
edicts in blood; he has been like a son to Rooney ever since he was a
young orphan taken under the powerful man's wing.

This closeness is beautifully and wordlessly conveyed in a scene at
the wake when the two men casually collaborate on a quiet piano
duet. It's a lovely thing to everyone but Rooney's natural son Connor
(British actor Daniel Craig, a long way from *Lara Croft: Tomb Raider*),
the classic Sonny Corleone–type hothead whose appetite for blood is
more apparent than his sanity.

Sullivan's two boys idolize him, although they're not really sure
what he does. They hope he's a secret agent, someone who goes on
missions like their hero, the Lone Ranger.

One night, Michael Jr. tags along hidden in a car and, in a vision
of almost primal intensity, sees his father take part in a savage blood-
bath. It's a moment that not only changes their relationship, but that
also leads inexorably to the cold-blooded murder of the boy's younger
brother and his mother (Jennifer Jason Leigh).

Sullivan is a man built for revenge, but he hadn't counted on having his son with him as he sets out on what is, of course, a drenched-in-violence journey to get it. Sullivan needs to find a way to smoke out his family's killer, to stay one step ahead of Maguire (Jude Law), the eccentric assassin sent after him, and to improve a relationship with his surviving son—whom he'd like to deposit with relatives in a town called Perdition—that is freighted with all kinds of complications neither feels equipped to handle.

Road to Perdition's excellent cast sees to it that all the ramifications of this story play out as they're supposed to. Newman, who gets nothing but better with age, is riveting as a cold-blooded man of business weighing his legacy against his feelings for a surrogate son. Law brings the right amount of strangeness to a killer whose main drive is to photograph his victims, and Stanley Tucci has an effective cameo as Capone cohort Frank Nitti. And Hoechlin, one of more than two thousand who tried out for the part of young Sullivan, effectively creates a character who gets under his father's skin.

For people who make studio films, opportunities to work on serious projects with sizable budgets are rare, and *Road to Perdition* has obtained the services of what is, in effect, an all-star team of behind-the-camera personnel, starting with graceful cinematographer Conrad Hall.

A two-time Oscar winner (including one for *American Beauty*) and a nine-time nominee, Hall has crafted, without seeming to try too hard, a series of beautifully bleak, unforgiving Midwest-in-winter vistas that use the dark colors of nightmare to recall the loneliness of Edward Hopper canvases.

Re-creating the meticulous sense of 1930s atmosphere that Richard Piers Rayner brought to the graphic novel are production designer Dennis Gassner and costume designer Albert Wolsky, a two-time Oscar winner, for *All That Jazz* and *Bugsy*. The evocative score is by Thomas Newman, and giving the film its stately pace is editor Jill Bilcock, who last did Baz Luhrmann's very different *Moulin Rouge*.

Road to Perdition has worried a great deal about the details, to the point of having fabric specially woven, aged and dyed so that costumes had the proper weight for the period, but that doesn't mean emotion has been neglected. Because it is so careful with its effects, this film's ability to create feeling sneaks up and surprises. This is a story with a will to move us and the ability to do whatever it takes to make that happen.

The Rookie
2002

It's only fitting that *The Rookie* tells the true story of an athlete who achieved improbable success, because this is a film that overcomes considerable odds itself.

Against all expectations, the *Rookie*, starring Dennis Quaid, turns out to be an unapologetically emotional film that doesn't make you gag, one that manages to be sentimental without turning into a shameless wallow.

As any sportswriter knows, the saga of pitcher Jim Morris defies plausibility. A thirty-five-year-old West Texas high school science teacher and coach whose baseball dreams had ended twelve years earlier, Morris became the oldest major league rookie in decades after being goaded to try out by his players.

The Walt Disney organization, never one to miss a marketing trick, pitched *Rookie* as being from "the studio that brought you *Remember the Titans*." This crafty sales technique (*Titans* was a considerable success) is regrettably misleading. With its old-fashioned feeling, quiet confidence and an almost unheard-of G rating, *Rookie* has more in common with *October Sky* than the shameless and simplistic *Titans*.

No one, of course, should expect an austere, somber piece of work from director John Lee Hancock and writer Mike Rich. *The Rookie* is not above providing assorted Hallmark moments about following your dream, or casting the cutest kid imaginable (Angus T. Jones) as the Morrises' eight-year-old son, Hunter. The film in general promotes the pleasant fantasy that the world is basically a decent place where events and people right themselves if given half a chance.

Yet what characterizes *The Rookie* is that this fantasy is largely honestly earned. Both debuting director Hancock, who wrote the Clint Eastwood-Kevin Costner film *A Perfect World*, and screenwriter Rich, whose feature debut was the treacly *Finding Forrester*, have managed not to push too hard here. They've given *The Rookie* a lovely, relaxed feeling that makes us happy to be in this film's company while allowing us to trust that it won't muck things up with glibness or excess.

The cast helps to keep everything in balance, starting with Dennis Quaid, a Texas native himself and able as always to project a rugged, effortless decency. The equally reliable Rachel Griffiths plays his wife, Lorri, and the protean Brian Cox, memorable in darker roles, brings the right touch of implacability to Morris's unbending father, Jim Sr.

After a brief introduction establishing Big Lake, Texas, as a place smiled on by "St. Rita, the patron saint of impossible dreams," *The Rookie* breaks its story into a trio of dovetailing sections, each of which deals with different kinds of dreams.

Up first is an extended flashback revealing Jim Morris's childhood as a navy brat forced to move frequently as a consequence of his father's job as a navy recruiter. The senior Morris is oblivious to, if not actually contemptuous of, his son's dreams of athletic glory: "There are more important things in life than baseball," he growls, "and the sooner you figure that out, the better."

The Morrises' last move takes them to Big Lake, a football-crazy town that barely knows baseball exists. There we pick up the adult Jim Morris, who is happily married and largely content with his job as a science teacher-baseball coach. Largely, but not totally.

For Morris, whose minor league career ended after four shoulder operations, still goes out late at night and throws hard at a deserted backstop. His childhood dream, we see, is still eating at him, and the look on his face as he lets the ball go—faster, it turns out, than he knows—shows how much bottling up that ambition has cost him.

When Morris chides his team after a lopsided loss, making the classic "you quit on me, and worse, you quit on yourselves" speech, and talks to them about not giving up on their dreams, the kids challenge him about giving up on his. Finally, a pact is made: If his perennially losing team gets to the state playoffs, Morris will go to a major league tryout. (Apparently, this really did happen.)

It doesn't take a soothsayer to figure out what happens from here on in, but *The Rookie* doesn't shortchange the difficulties involved for Morris, his wife, his team, even his estranged father. The pleasure of a film such as this is not in wondering where it's going to go, but in knowing its general trajectory. Getting us to pull for a foregone conclusion as if the outcome were in serious doubt is no small sleight of hand.

Schindler's List
1993

The more we know about the Holocaust, the more unknowable it seems to become. Like the mythological fruit of Tantalus, always just out of reach, its essence eludes us, too awful to fully comprehend no matter how passionately we seek to know and understand it.

One thing that does become clear, however, is that to approach the Holocaust from a dramatic point of view, detachment and self-control almost to the point of coldness are essential. The most memorable films about the period, from Alain Resnais's thirty-minute *Night and Fog* to Claude Lanzmann's nine-hour-plus *Shoah*, share this reserve with such memoirs as Primo Levi's *Survival in Auschwitz*. Only through the lens of restraint can the Holocaust be effectively seen, as Steven Spielberg persuasively demonstrates with the quietly devastating *Schindler's List*.

The Holocaust is not the usual subject matter for Spielberg, but the director, with personal and emotional ties to the world of Eastern European Jewry, clearly hungered to do something different here. And not only the subject matter but the way it is treated is a departure both for him and for the business-as-usual standards of major studio releases. Though its three-hour-fifteen-minute length is becoming familiar for prestige items, the decision to shoot it almost entirely in black and white is very much not, and neither is the absence of major stars.

And *Schindler's List*, based on Thomas Keneally's remarkable re-telling of a true story, is itself a different kind of Holocaust narrative. For if the pressure of overwhelming death and even the release of miraculous rescue have become standard fare, the dramatic, contradictory personality of Oskar Schindler has never ceased to baffle and astonish observers from his time to ours.

A gambler, war profiteer and lover of alcohol, a convivial sensualist and womanizer who, in Keneally's phrase, considered sexual shame "a concept like existentialism, very worthy but hard to grasp," Schindler the quintessential good German was not the ordinary stuff of heroes. "Though he was Jesus Christ," someone who knew him said, "a saint he wasn't. He was all-drinking, all-black-marketeering, all-screwing." He was a man whose turn to goodness probably surprised himself most of all. Yet, with a combination of nerve, money, attitude and obstinacy, he personally saved 1,100 Jews from death, and ended up being what Keneally calls probably the only Nazi Party member to be buried in Jerusalem's Mt. Zion Cemetery.

Though this film is preeminently Schindler's story, we don't meet him right away. Spielberg and thoughtful screenwriter Steven Zaillian are first concerned about setting the story in its time and place, thereby establishing the context firmly for what is to come.

Things begin in September 1939, with Germany's defeat of Poland in two brief weeks. The country's Jews are ordered to relocate to the venerable town of Krakow; the chaos that decree causes is shown through arrival scenes at the train station in which Germans are seen brandishing the first of the all-important lists that reappear throughout the film, lists that can literally separate life from death.

Schindler (Liam Neeson) is glimpsed initially as a pair of disembodied hands quietly laying out alternate coats, ties and cuff links, preparing for his own type of campaign. Off to a cabaret frequented by Krakow's Nazi elite, he enters it as an unknown, but by the evening's end, he is the most popular man in the room. Written and filmed with characteristic mastery, this scene illuminates in a few brief minutes the core of Schindler's gregarious personality and the winning effect he had on other people.

One of those men who instinctively know how to profit from the chaos of war, Schindler has come to Krakow to make his fortune. Simply indifferent to who is a Jew and who is not, he decides to take over a formerly Jewish-owned enamelware factory and hires Itzhak Stern (Ben Kingsley) to run it with cheap Jewish labor while he himself does the important work of schmoozing and bribing the military men in charge of procurement for the German army.

At first, everything about Schindler's relationship to the Jews is situational; when he rescues Stern from deportation and death, for instance, his reaction is "What if I'd gotten here five minutes later, then where would I be?" But after witnessing the Germans' brutal liquidation of the ghetto, and the relocation of those who survived to a savage labor camp run by Amon Goeth (Ralph Fiennes), a cold, unblinking sadist, Schindler's attitude is shown to change; keeping what he territorially considers "his Jews" alive at all costs becomes the focus of his activities.

The touchstone of *Schindler's List* is inevitably the way it depicts the incomprehensible brutality that took place under the Nazi heel. The danger here is to overemphasize, to yield to emotion and underline the horrors, a temptation Spielberg, who gave way to it in dealing with slavery in *The Color Purple*, has managed to resist this time around.

Using real locations whenever possible, collaborating with Polish-born director of photography Janusz Kaminski and editor Michael Kahn and making excellent use of black and white, itself a distancing element, Spielberg understands how important it is to show the casualness of the nightmare. This is a world where unimaginable humiliation was the stuff of routine, where people were murdered as an afterthought and everyone who saw it did no more than blink. Working extensively with a hand-held camera and functioning by his own admission almost as a documentarian, Spielberg has had the nerve simply to let those dreadful scenes play, and as a consequence he has created as indelible a picture of the Holocaust as fiction film allows.

In doing this, Spielberg has been helped greatly by his collaborators, most notably screenwriter Zaillian, who has pared down and focused

Keneally's text without losing anything essential. And the acting, largely by unfamiliar faces, is always strong and to the point.

Most notable are Kingsley as the self-effacing Stern; Fiennes, who understands how banal great evil can be, and, of course, Neeson. The brio of his performance knits *Schindler's List* together, and no greater compliment can be paid to it than to say its strength and assurance makes this unbelievable story believable and real.

Though it would be nice to say that Spielberg's nerve held all the way through this film, that would not quite be true. Just as there are overemphatic moments in John Williams's brooding score, so, too, there are times, especially in Schindler's closing speech, when the desire to give the audience something to hang onto gets the best of the filmmaker's more sober judgment.

But Spielberg is a popular filmmaker at his core, and it is hard to begrudge him, or his audience, these softer moments. For almost never before has he come close to this kind of filmmaking. This is a motion picture that any director, no matter what the background, would be proud to see with his or her name above the title.

Schindler's List won seven Oscars, including picture, director and adapted screenplay.

Selena
1997

Americans love success stories, particularly those with humble beginnings and unhappy endings. So when the phenomenally popular Selena Quintanilla Perez, the Grammy-winning Queen of Tejano Music, was shot to death in March 1995, scant weeks before her twenty-fourth birthday, *Selena* the movie was only a matter of time.

In the tradition of *Lady Sings the Blues*, *The Rose*, *What's Love Got to Do with It* and other sudsy tales of singers and their woes, *Selena* is in part a completely predictable Latino soap opera that should satisfy those who complain they aren't making movies the way they used to.

Selena is also reminiscent of *La Bamba*'s story of Ritchie Valens, and not just because its subject is Mexican American. Selena's father, Abraham Quintanilla, the film's executive producer, had complete script approval, and the price of family cooperation, not to mention the use of Selena's music, was the inevitable sanitizing and sentimentalization that are also Hollywood's stock in trade.

Yet, despite all this, there are chunks of *Selena* that only a stone could resist. This movie turns out to be a celebration not only of the singer but also (as *What's Love* was for Angela Bassett) of the actress who plays her, Jennifer Lopez.

Even in such forgettable films as *Money Train* and *Jack*, Lopez's presence and ability made her seem just one role away from stardom, and with *Selena* she's seized the opportunity and turned in an incandescent presentation that is especially strong during the film's numerous musical numbers.

Though Lopez lip-syncs to Selena's voice, she makes use of her background as a dancer (she was a Fly Girl on *In Living Color*) to project an irresistible joy in performance that not only does justice to Selena's appeal but also helps burn away the film's saccharine haze.

Written and directed by Gregory Nava (*Mi Familia, El Norte*), *Selena* makes full use of Lopez's charisma in its opening scene, a re-creation of the singer's triumphant appearance before the biggest Astrodome crowd ever just a few weeks before her death. From the chaos backstage through Selena's solo walk through a curtain to the rapture of her adoring fans, it's just the first of the film's string of pure Hollywood moments.

That adrenaline jolt is needed to hold attention for the next half-hour, when an extensive sequence of flashbacks goes into Selena's family history, starting with her father's attempt to start a doo-wop group called Los Dinos in Corpus Christi, Texas, in 1961.

Defeated by a combination of racism and the resistance of Mexican Americans to anything you can't dance to, Abraham Quintanilla (Edward James Olmos) puts music out of his mind until he discovers that his youngest daughter, Selena (played by ten-year-old Becky Lee Meza), has a voice like the mature Ethel Merman's.

Much to the discomfort of wife Marcela (Constance Marie), Quintanilla insists that Selena and her two siblings (once grown, played by Jacob Vargas and Jackie Guerra) form a group. He quits his job to open a restaurant so they'll have a showcase. Quintanilla even teaches his daughter to sing in Spanish, though she doesn't know the language because "you've got to be who you are, you can't change it, and you're Mexican deep inside."

Speeches like that, and a later one about the difficulties of being a Mexican American ("You've got to be twice as perfect. . . . It's exhausting") indicate that even without Quintanilla's supervision, Nava would likely have made this kind of soft film. Though the writer-director's fearlessness in the face of emotion has its charms, Nava's willingness to state everything in the most obvious terms and the film's lack of dramatic texture do become bothersome.

Most of *Selena* is taken up with the singer's gradual but inexorable rise to the top. Despite resistance of Mexican Americans to a female tejano star and the skepticism of Mexicans about a woman whose command of Spanish is less than perfect, Selena easily wins everyone over, and her willingness to accept herself as she is turns her into a key role model for Latinas.

Unlike, say, Tina Turner in *What's Love Got to Do with It*, however, the young adult Selena is presented without any life-threatening problems. Her main conflict, hardly shattering, is a budding romance with handsome, heavy metal-ish lead guitarist Chris Perez (Jon Seda) that father Abraham is determined to quash.

Overall, Selena's most persistent difficulty turns out to be dealing with her father, a man with a fierce temper and a will of iron who threw one of many fits when she first tried out her trademark bustier on stage. It's a measure of how stern a taskmaster the senior Quintanilla must have been that, despite this film's tendency to white-wash, as played by Olmos he comes off as a single-minded tyrant who loves his daughter but is determined to run her life.

Selena closes with documentary footage of the real singer, and it's a shock to realize that Lopez so much resembles her that for an instant you can't tell one from the other. And it's in fact a melding of the two, of the real story and the actress's ability to convey it, that creates emotional connections destined to outlive the doses of biopic boiler-plate that surround it.

Lopez went on to major stardom, but Selena *continues to be one of her best performances.*

Thelma & Louise
1991

Huck and Jim, meet Thelma and Louise.

Ever since canny Mark Twain sent Mr. Finn and his older, shrewder companion adrift on that raft going down the Mississippi, letting go and heading out to those wide open spaces has been the classic American way of finding out who you were and what you were about. If you had a problem, you got yourself some transportation and you went. Anywhere.

Though potentially dangerous, as the gang in *Easy Rider* discovered, this cultural rite could be undertaken at any age and from any station in life. But it has also been, in movie terms, pretty much an exclusively masculine preserve.

Thelma & Louise has changed all that. Forever. Provocative, poignant and heartbreakingly funny, this neofeminist road movie is as pointed a look at what is timidly called the war between the sexes as we have had in a while. And it manages its success almost offhandedly, with a casual grace that makes everything look as easy as, well, falling off a raft.

At first glance, *Thelma & Louise* does not seem a likely candidate to be this pleasingly subversive. Its writer never had a script produced before; its director made his reputation doing totally different kinds of movies; its stars, though more than able, are not the types who usually surprise us. If you were handicapping this film, you'd be hard-pressed to justify putting more than $2 on its chances.

But wait. In reality, writer Callie Khouri, whose last job was producing videos, has an exceptional ear and an enviable understanding of character. Her gritty, raunchy dialogue has the welcome tang of authenticity, and it is also achingly amusing as it delineates two characters so disparate they just about have to be best friends.

Thelma Dickinson and Louise Sawyer may live in the same small Arkansas town, but their minds are planets apart. Louise (Susan Sarandon) is a waitress with tidy hair under a starched white cap. When she plans a weekend trip to the country with her good buddy, she makes sure to clean every last dish and leave her place immaculate. Thelma (Geena Davis), on the other hand, is a walking nervous breakdown, submissive to the point of catatonia, whose idea of packing is casually emptying an entire drawer into a waiting suitcase.

Besides relaxing, these women have another agenda for their trip: They want to make a point to the men in their lives about being taken for granted. Louise's boyfriend, Jimmy, is a musician who travels a lot but never gets anywhere near commitment. And Thelma's husband, Darryl, is a self-absorbed porker who has a personalized license plate reading "THE1." Thelma is so fearful of his rages that she doesn't even ask him whether she can take the trip. She just gets into Louise's Thunderbird convertible and hits the road.

Determined to have some fun, even if just for this weekend, Thelma convinces Louise to stop at a raunchy roadside honky-tonk. "I've had it up to my ass with sedate," she announces after defiantly ordering some Wild Turkey. "You're always telling me to let my hair down. Look out, darlin', my hair is coming down."

Suddenly, on the proverbial dime, something happens in that honky-tonk that changes the whole nature of Thelma and Louise's trip, turning it from a jaunt into a nightmare, and one that keeps growing more and more frightening. These two women, who started out to escape their problems, suddenly find themselves in the worst trouble of their lives.

Saying this, however, is telling only a fraction of the story. Because disturbing as they are, Thelma and Louise's experiences ultimately empower them, making them stronger, more forceful, more content. And as they move through a world of for the most part thoughtless, occasionally violent men, we all gain a realization not only of the different needs of the sexes but also of how deeply society pigeonholes men and women and what it takes even to attempt to break out.

But more than this, it is the great and paradoxical pleasure of *Thelma & Louise* that, except for a regrettable incident with a Neanderthal truck driver, it makes its points while scrupulously avoiding preachyness, managing to blend political concerns with mainstream entertainment. No matter how audacious and occasionally surreal this film gets, it never loses touch with its audience or faith in its better instincts.

Though both Geena Davis and Susan Sarandon have had their share of memorable parts before, the intoxication and challenge they felt at being handed the most satisfying women's roles in memory is palpable and informs everything they do. And though it is Davis who makes the greatest impression by departing furthest from the kookie types she's previously played, both actresses run through a gamut of emotions—from agony and hysteria to tears and laughter—that is formidable in its richness.

Running this particular show is, of all people, director Ridley Scott. A man whose reputation has been built on turning out high-gloss, hardware-heavy guy films such as *Blade Runner* and *Alien*, Scott has readily admitted that he's never done anything like this before. Though his English background means that *Thelma & Louise* is a little heavier than it might be on roadside grotesqueries of the American West, Scott makes up for this by having the panache to handle the characters' action sequences and by maintaining just the right tone for their more intimate moments. He has also had the good sense to cast little-seen, understated actors such as Michael Madsen, Christopher McDonald, Brad Pitt, Timothy Carhart and Harvey Keitel as the men in Thelma and Louise's lives. Like almost everything else in this most surprising film, it works better than anyone had a right to expect.

His cameo as a sexy drifter ensured that Brad Pitt's days of being little seen were over.

The Truman Show
1998

His gifts as a comic actor are well-known, but who would have thought that Jim Carrey might simultaneously break your heart as easily as he makes you laugh?

It is only one of the accomplishments of *The Truman Show*, the nerviest feature to come out of Hollywood in recent memory, that it gives Carrey the role of his career, the opportunity to make exceptional use of his capacities in a film that is as serious as it is funny.

Adventurous, provocative, even daring, *The Truman Show* has been directed with enviable grace and restraint by Peter Weir, whose deliberate tone is essential to the film's multiple and almost contradictory successes. *The Truman Show* is emotionally involving without losing the ability to raise sharp satiric questions as well as get numerous laughs, the rare film that is disturbing despite working beautifully within standard industry norms.

If there is a key to this picture's accomplishment it is the irresistible nature of its carefully worked-out premise, shrewdly conceived by writer Andrew Niccol. *The Truman Show* is concerned with a very particular television program, one whose disconcerting qualities only gradually become completely clear.

The film starts out with a burst of information, running the delicious risk of disorienting us by providing more data than we can quite absorb. Its first shot is a tight close-up of a man in a beret who looks directly at the camera and goes to the heart of the matter: "We've become bored with watching actors giving us phony emotions. We're tired of pyrotechnics and special effects. While the world he inhabits is to some respects counterfeit, there is nothing fake about Truman. No script, no cue cards. It isn't always Shakespeare, but it's genuine. It's a life."

The speaker is Christof (Ed Harris), later described as the "televisionary" who created The Truman Show. Next comes a credit reading "Hannah Gill as Meryl" and a young woman (Laura Linney) who says, "My life is my life is 'The Truman Show.'" She's followed by "Louis Coltrane as Marlon," a hearty young man (Noah Emmerich) who insists, "It's all true, it's all real. Nothing you see on this show is fake. It's merely controlled."

After this buildup, after the card reading "Truman Burbank as himself," Carrey's familiar face fills the screen. Like Christof, Truman speaks directly to the camera, but, we slowly realize, he's under the impression he's having a completely private moment, playing out a bizarre fantasy of mountain-climbing heroics in the presumed safety of his bathroom mirror. What he can't see that we can is the small word "LIVE," in the corner of the screen. Truman is on the air, the center of a television program revolving around his life, and everyone knows about it but him.

Though this rough premise soon becomes clear, the film is savvy enough to dole out the ramifications and specifics of Truman's situation in artfully spaced doses. Only in bits and pieces do we find out the true dimensions of what has been done to Truman, how it has all been managed, and revealing more than that would spoil the fun.

In the meantime, in complicity and in the know, we become part of the audience watching television's Truman Show, just a few of the multitudes eavesdropping without shame on his so-called life in the always-sunny community of Seahaven Island, a town with a motto: "It's a Nice Place to Live."

Watching Truman trade pleasantries with Stepford wife Meryl and splitting six-packs with always available buddy Marlon is an experience both amusing and uncomfortable. We may be joining the show on day 10,909, but we've entered Truman's world at a critical juncture. Though his environment is always cheerful and sunny (courtesy of Dennis Gassner's expert production design and Peter Biziou's glistening candy-colored cinematography of the real-life Seaside, Florida), Truman is not completely happy in it. In fact, in ways neither he nor we completely understand at first, his world is threatening to come apart.

We see hints first, hints that don't immediately make sense. Why is Truman furtively calling Tahiti directory information? Why is he buying fashion magazines, ostensibly for his wife, only to clandestinely rip apart the photographs for purposes unknown. The poignancy of seeing Truman feeling trapped and desperate, hiding behind a painted-on smile but deeply unsatisfied for reasons he can't manage to put his finger on, is a splendid example of an actor's extending himself as far as he can without overreaching.

Carrey tried to push into new territory before, but *The Truman Show* is worlds apart from the unlamented misfire *The Cable Guy*. It's hard to imagine another actor as effective as this halest of well-met fellows, someone who can look completely haunted with a what-me-worry smile parked on his face. In the context of this film, Carrey's trademark high-energy mania plays like the result of the unknowing artificiality of his life, precisely the way someone might become if everyone he knew was secretly more of a costar than a friend.

In addition to being consistently moving and funny, *The Truman Show*, almost as an aside, makes accurate satiric points about conformity, commercialism, the desire to play God, and what can happen when television, or any other medium, permanently blurs the lines between what's real and what's on screen.

Yet despite these subversive underpinnings, what's perhaps most engaging about *The Truman Show* is the way it still delivers vintage

Hollywood satisfactions to its audience. With a beleaguered hero determined to live free or die, *The Truman Show* demonstrates a belief in the indomitability of the human spirit that is as four-square as anything Frank Capra put on screen.

Weir is especially critical to *Truman's* success. Benefiting from fourteen months of prep time (because Carrey had commitments to a pair of other films), Weir created and sustained the essential low-key tone for this project and carefully cast small but pivotal roles; these include Natascha McElhone as the woman who haunts Truman's dreams and Harry Shearer as an especially unctuous television interviewer.

Like any current film, this venture has precedents, everything from Rod Serling's *Twilight Zone* series to Paul Bartel's prescient 1965 *Secret Cinema*. But *The Truman Show* has been so carefully and thoughtfully worked out, it's so much its own film, that viewers will be justified in feeling that they've never seen anything quite like it. And how often can you say that in this derivative age?

The Truman Show also eerily prefigured the rage for reality television that has since taken over America.

Unforgiven
1992

The Western is back. With a vengeance. Saddle up or get out of the way.

Unforgiven is not just any Western, either. Simultaneously heroic and nihilistic, reeking of myth but modern as they come, it is a Western for those who know and cherish the form, a film that resonates with the sprit of films past while staking out a territory quite its own.

Produced and directed by and starring Clint Eastwood, *Unforgiven* is hard to imagine in anyone else's hands. No other active player has made as many Westerns, no one else has the connection with and feeling for the genre that only working in it for more than thirty years can provide. And starting as far back as Sergio Leone's A *Fistful of Dollars,* Eastwood has delighted in bending boundaries, in pushing the Western to areas outside the accepted canon.

So it's not surprising that the producer-director in Eastwood recognized the strengths of David Webb Peoples's exceptional screenplay, the unexpected turns its plot takes, the power of its idiosyncratic characters, the adroit way it mixes modern and traditional elements. More than that, Eastwood the actor was shrewd enough to hold onto the script for more than a decade until, just past his sixtieth birthday, he felt he had aged enough to do the role properly.

For *Unforgiven,* the story of a reformed killer who reconfronts his past, is very definitely an old-guy Western, as elegiac in its own way as such classics as *The Wild Bunch* and *Ride the High Country.* As *True Grit* was for John Wayne, this is also something of a last hurrah for Eastwood's "man-with-no-name" persona; but because Eastwood is who he is, it is a dark and ominous goodbye, brooding and stormy.

Unforgiven is also, and this is perhaps its most unexpected aspect, a neat piece of revisionism, a violent film that is determined to demythologize killing. Considerable emphasis is placed on how hard it is to kill even one man, on the destructive interior price that must be paid for every act of mayhem. If there are thrills to be had here, none of them come at all cheaply.

Both the time and setting of *Unforgiven*—1880 in Big Whiskey, Wyoming—emphasize this sense of mortality. The frontier West is coming to an end, both physically and spiritually, but that close is leaving considerable frustration in its wake. In the forbidding high country, a flat empty locale under cold blue skies, the West is very much an angry, hostile place, rife with fury and lawlessness.

In Big Whiskey itself, however, the law is a considerable presence. He is the town sheriff, Little Bill (Gene Hackman) by name, and in the film's opening moments he is called in to adjudicate a dispute at the local whorehouse. A cowboy from a nearby ranch has viciously cut up the face of one of the prostitutes. When the house's owner complains that "no one is going to pay good money for a cut-up whore," Little Bill decrees that the cowboy and a friend who accompanied him must pay the owner six horses as compensation.

This does not sit well with Strawberry Alice (Frances Fisher), the most outspoken of the prostitutes, who has a harsher, less mercantile punishment in mind. "Just because we let the smelly fools ride us like horses," she says angrily, giving the film a fascinating neofeminist subtext, "doesn't mean we let them brand us like horses." When Little Bill doesn't agree, Alice masterminds a sub rosa scheme to offer $1,000 cash for the death of the two cowboys, no questions asked.

None of this would normally come to the attention of William Munny (Eastwood), a destitute Kansas farmer who, having recently buried his wife, divides his time between raising their two small children and awkwardly rooting around with his recalcitrant hogs.

Munny, however, is not your ordinary farmer. Before he met his wife and went on the wagon eleven years earlier, he was a serious alcoholic and "a meaner-than-hell, cold-blooded killer" who was legendary for the heedless death he left in his path. Or so says the self-styled Schofield Kid (Canadian actor Jaimz Woolvett), a classically callow young blowhard who has heard of Munny's reputation and rides into his yard offering him half the reward if he'll join up for the hunt.

With a face looking so worn and lined it seems to have fallen off Mount Rushmore, Munny is clearly not eager for his old life. "I'm just a fella now," he tells the Kid with what sounds like conviction. "I ain't no different than anyone else."

But his impoverished condition is a goad, and Munny ends up enlisting his neighbor and former partner Ned Logan (Morgan Freeman) to join in the quest. As Munny and Logan head off for Big Whiskey, they face some troubling questions. Are they the same men, can they still kill the same way, and, more crucial, if they manage that one step back down the road to perdition, will they then be able to turn around and return to their quiet lives?

It is one of the pleasures of David Peoples's script, along with period dialogue that mixes menace with a sly and earthy sense of humor, that these kinds of questions come up at all. Peoples, whose resume includes a shared credit on *Blade Runner* and work on the exceptional documentary *The Day After Trinity*, is intent on unromanticizing the West, on portraying shootouts and gunplay, normally the stuff of heroic tales, as drunken, thuggish violence of the most craven sort.

And though he has no interest in creating out-and-out heroes, Peoples has come up with a collection of vivid, eccentric characters, from brief cameos—such as a one-armed, three-gun deputy—to the major roles, which include dime novel scribe W. W. Beauchamp (Saul Rubinek) and English Bob, a fancy-pants killer given a nice twist by Richard Harris, who never quite behave exactly as you'd expect them to.

Most memorable of all, however, is Little Bill, Big Whiskey's no-nonsense sheriff who is determined to ban firearms from his town no matter what the cost. Ruthless to the point of sadism, but possessed of both a sense of justice and a sense of humor, a homebody with a weakness but not necessarily an aptitude for carpentry, Little Bill makes up the rules as he goes along. And in playing him, Gene Hackman gives one of his most powerful and least-mannered performances, displaying an implacable strength and controlled passion that form the essential counterbalance to Eastwood's own considerable force.

For *Unforgiven* is first, last and always very much an Eastwood film. As an actor he is exactly right in a role that is as comfortable on him as an old hat; as a producer he has had the sense and nerve to cast this film for ability, not box office; and, most important, as a director he has infused it all with his sure, laconic, emotionally involving style. Eastwood has dedicated this film to the two directors who were most influential in his own career, Sergio Leone and Don Siegel, and perhaps the best thing that can finally be said about *Unforgiven* is that these two masters would doubtless both be flattered and approve.

Unforgiven swept the 1992 Oscars, taking four awards, including best picture, best director and best supporting actor for Gene Hackman.

Up Close and Personal
1996

To the casual eye, Sallyanne Atwater's first day as weather girl for Miami's WMIA Channel 9, "the News Heartbeat of the American Riviera," could not be classified as promising.

First comes throwing up in the bathroom. Then the shock of having her name changed, on air, to Tally. Thoroughly shaken up, the poor woman fumbles with props, stumbles over her lines and pretty much seems to cover herself with embarrassment.

But Warren Justice, bless his handsome, rugged heart, does not have a casual eye. One of the most respected names in broadcast journalism (if that's not a contradiction in terms) enduring self-imposed exile as WMIA's news director, Warren leans forward in his chair when Tally's spot is over, takes a breath to steady himself and says with close to awe, "She eats the lens."

Exactly. In fact, they both do.

An old-fashioned star-driven romance constructed of equal parts shrewdness and shamelessness, *Up Close and Personal* is no cinematic landmark, but if you don't care about reality and resist the impulse to take things too seriously, it's great fun to watch. Seeing this is like working through a box of seductive chocolates: Enjoying too many may feel sinful, but the experience is too satisfying to stop.

Like those chocolates, star vehicles are only as good as their ingredients, and in Michelle Pfeiffer as Tally and Robert Redford as Warren, *Up Close* has spoken up for quality. The chemistry between these two is genuine, so much so that their slyly flirtatious moments end up having more of a charge than the rather pro forma PG-13 lovemaking they eventually take part in.

Though this project began with the real-life career of television newscaster Jessica Savitch (and the film still gives a "suggested by" credit to a book on her life), Savitch's story has little to do with what's now on screen. Old movie fans will recognize this picture's true inspiration as one of the most durable of movie plots, the story of *A Star Is Born*.

Made and remade three times under its own name, most famously starring Judy Garland and James Mason, *A Star Is Born* last hit the screen twenty years ago with Barbra Streisand and Kris Kristofferson in the leads. Getting credit on that version were Joan Didion and John Gregory Dunne, who, not surprisingly, are the screenwriters here as well.

Though the scene in *Up Close* has been shifted from movies and music to a collateral branch of show business, the basic dynamic of a young female eagerly moving up, being both mentored and loved by a veteran male inescapably on the way down, has been lovingly retained.

Up Close's screenplay has smartly modernized this situation by opting to emphasize equality between the sexes in careers and romance. And it's hard not to admire the way Didion and Dunne have wholeheartedly embraced the well-worn scenario, throwing in chewy movie-movie exchanges of the "do you want to be with me/so much it hurts" variety while offering up assorted pokes at the way television news is run.

Even director Jon Avnet makes a contribution here. Keeping events moving at a fine pace and possibly unaware that he is making a highgloss soap opera, Avnet treats these sudsy doings as if he were directing *Schindler's List,* a degree of seriousness and commitment that is essential if this kind of business is going to come off successfully.

Up Close is initially as uncertain as Sallyanne on her first day on the job, but Avnet and company calm down and allow the film's ripe situations to play out as expected. Here's the renamed Tally, desperate for knowledge, falling under the tutelage of sage old Warren, who first instills humility by making her pick up his laundry and then dispenses nuggets of presumably hard-won wisdom such as "Yesterday is history, the news happens today."

It's just as much fun to see Warren and Tally falling in love, though both do resist it mightily, even after the pro forma screaming argument in a rainstorm that should have tipped them off that romance was in the air. She tells him about her hardscrabble past as a Miss Sierra Logger contestant and then conscientiously researches his glory years as a White House and war correspondent.

Naturally, *Up Close's* plot throws these two bushels of curves, including a Barbara Walters–type ex-wife (Kate Nelligan) and a big-time agent with the delicious name of Bucky Terranova (Joe Mantegna). And, of course, there are the little speed bumps: a catty coanchor (Stockard Channing), duplicitous television executives and even a bloody prison riot. Because being gorgeous and in love has never, ever, been easy.

Without the glamour of Redford and Pfeiffer, obviously, none of this succeeds, and Redford in some ways has the easier task. As an "I've been here before" kind of guy, Warren is not called upon to do much more than look dazzled by Tally's energy and effrontery. Not notably believable as a modern-day Edward R. Murrow, Redford is completely convincing only as a romantic partner for his costar, but that is the one area that counts.

As for Pfeiffer, the things she does wonderfully well are no longer news, but she does them as effectively here as she ever has. Always genuine and alive on screen, an actress who never makes a wrong move, Pfeiffer simply compels belief in her character both as waif and world-class sophisticate. This is the kind of rich performance any of the old queens of Hollywood would envy. And for a picture like *Up Close and Personal*, there can be no greater compliment.

What's Love Got to Do with It
1993

You may not respect *What's Love Got to Do with It*, but enjoying it is inescapable.

A high-energy mixture of spectacular music, vigorous acting and clichéd situations, this is a rough-and-rowdy fairy tale with a feminist subtext, and if that sounds perplexing, *Love* so pumps up the volume you won't have much time to think about it.

Though it is based on Tina Turner's autobiography, *I, Tina*, and is subtitled *The True Life Story of Tina Turner*, *What's Love* has less in common with anyone's reality than with generations of glossy show business biopics, such as *Lady Sings the Blues* and *The Doors*, in which a singer's triumphs and tragedies are written in large neon letters for the world to see and to sob over.

And Tina Turner, both during and after her tumultuous marriage to the mysterious Ike, did seem to live the kind of fast-lane soap-opera life the public expects rock stars to have, with personal tragedies jostling professional successes and an abusive, drug-using husband always lurking behind the surface glamour.

Better than that, the passionate songs Tina was singing onstage often paralleled what was happening in her life offstage, and writer Jane Lanier has cleverly structured her script around the similarities. So when Tina sings "A Fool in Love," that's just what she is; by the time she is telling audiences in "Proud Mary" that "we don't do anything nice and easy," her relationship with Ike is mired in pain.

Director Brian Gibson, best known for the television movie *The Josephine Baker Story*, was definitely a commercial choice for this audience-friendly tale of glitz and woe. He knows how to infuse the energy of the music into this often hokey story, and he is discretion itself when it comes to handling the film's drug use, judiciously focusing not on the substance but on fingers with the odd habit of wandering toward the nose.

The biggest assets *What's Love Got to Do with It* has, however, are the exceptional actors who play Tina and Ike. Angela Bassett and Laurence Fishburne worked together in *Boyz N the Hood,* and they bring to this film not only the rapport they developed there but also the ability to deepen characters in ways that are not in the script, to bring more to their roles than seems to be there.

It is Tina, appropriately enough, whom we meet first, as a little tyke named Anna Mae Bullock who scandalizes the church choir in Nutbush, Tennessee, by putting more sass into a hymn than is absolutely necessary. Returning home, Anna discovers her mother in the process of walking out, leaving her to be raised by a convenient, standard-issue kindly grandmother.

Cut to 1958, when a presumably teenaged Anna joins her mother, Zelma (Jenifer Lewis), and her sister, Alline (Phyllis Yvonne Stickney), in St. Louis. On her first night there (this movie does not waste time), she goes to a nightclub and sees local R&B star and major-league cool dude Ike Turner and his Kings of Rhythm.

As beautifully played by Fishburne, it is not difficult to see why Ike was the king of hearts. With his slow smile, polished self-confidence, impeccable hair and half-opened lounge-lizard eyes, Ike wears a pastel blue topcoat with as much aplomb as Cary Grant modeling a tuxedo. And though he relished being the center of attention, once he hears Anna's powerful voice he is smitten without a doubt.

Even though she's lip-syncing rather than singing, audiences will inevitably feel the same way about Bassett. Her Anna Mae/Tina moves gradually from an uncertain ingenue to a brassily confident performer to an in-charge woman, and Bassett is more than equal to all the changes. Whether she is strutting defiantly on stage or putting a wide smile on her mobile, emotional face, Bassett's Tina embraces life in a way that can't help but be infectious.

Because Fishburne and Bassett have this singular onscreen connection, their relationship feels more complex than it otherwise would. And at first, even though Ike changes her name and seems determined to work her into the ground, the two share a bond based on the traditional dream they both have of show-biz success.

But when that success comes, it brings, for reasons apparently drug-related but never made quite clear, a darkening of Ike's personality and physical violence toward Tina that are the emotionally strongest parts of the film. This sets up *What's Love*'s final part, where Tina, like a heroine on a quest, searches for the strength to get a room of her own and strike out toward the grail of international stardom.

Though the picture rightfully belongs to Bassett, a final word must be said about Fishburne, who never fails to make Ike seem human if not defensible. Even in defeat, he is remarkably compelling. Though *What's Love Got to Do with It* is much broader than his performance, the film and the actor do share an important characteristic: Try as you might, you won't be able to take your eyes off either one.

With the success of Ray *and* Walk the Line, *the musical biopic has proved resilient, but this remains one of the most watchable.*

William Shakespeare's Romeo + Juliet
1996

For those who have not had the experience, watching Baz Luhrmann's brash take on *William Shakespeare's Romeo + Juliet* simulates having a teenager in the house.

Like flaming youth everywhere, this film is loud, exuberant and excessive, but it has enough positive energy and dizzying high spirits to make it irresistible.

A wild-in-the-streets version of the classic romance that is desperate not to be your father's Shakespeare, this *Romeo* follows in the path of Franco Zeffirelli's 1968 film by having youthful actors, Leonardo DiCaprio and Claire Danes in this case, playing the protagonists.

But director and coscreenwriter Luhrmann, working with many of the key creative people that made his *Strictly Ballroom* debut so special, has done nothing else familiar. Juiced to the max and drenched in style, this *Romeo,* mad about its image-a-minute visual agenda, is sure to infuriate as much as it delights. But the film can't be bothered to slow down for your reaction, and it never forgets its duty to be alive on the screen.

Given this all-around bravado, squealing tires and dance-hall rhythms at no extra charge, it is especially gratifying that Luhrmann and coscreenwriter Craig Pearce have stuck to the play's original language, albeit trimmed and tailored to suit situations Shakespeare couldn't have imagined. Though memorable line readings are not the rule, the unusual staging—for instance, putting the opening "Do you bite your thumb at us, sir?" Montague-Capulet face-off at a self-service gas station—is inventive enough to send viewers back to the text to see how they did it.

And though *Romeo + Juliet* is an assault, it's a well-planned one, thought out to the smallest detail in the service of a unifying conception Luhrmann (who has mounted elaborate opera productions) calls "a created world." His mythical city of Verona Beach is unequal parts past, present and future, smartly shot by Donald M. McAlpine in and around Mexico City, an environment that has the combination of violence, passion, extremes of wealth and poverty and the omnipresence of religion that the production demanded.

Unsettling from the beginning, the film's opening image is a newscaster on a television set who is reading the play's prologue about "two households, both alike in dignity" with a "Star-Cross'd Lovers" logo behind her on the screen. The back story of the rivalry between Ted Montague (Brian Dennehy) and Fulgencio Capulet (Paul Sorvino) is shown MTV newsreel style, with bold tabloid headlines such as "Youths Brawl" tossed into the mix.

Tightly edited by Jill Bilcock and unwilling to be discreet in anything, *R+J* introduces its characters with giant letters on the screen, such as Romeo's cross-dressing friend Mercutio (Harold Perrineau) or his enemy Tybalt, "Prince of Cats" (played with a fine malevolence by John Leguizamo). And though the Capulets tend to dress in varieties of tailored black, the surfer-type "Montague boys" wear gaudy, loose-fitting Hawaiian shirts courtesy of costume designer Kym Barrett.

No visual detail in production designer Catherine Martin's hands is too insignificant to be put to use in creating a world that is both internally consistent and out of control. Good Father Laurence (Pete Postlethwaite) has a huge cross tattooed on his back, and some of the Montague boys have that name tattooed on their bald skulls. Juliet's suitor Paris becomes Dave Paris, on the cover of *Time* as "Bachelor of the Year"; and though everyone carries automatic weapons, they all have model names—Sword, Rapier and Dagger—so that a character can demand, "Give me my long sword," and not be anachronistic. There's even a delivery service called Post Haste.

The film's showiest scene is the costume ball at Capulet Mansion, a Fellini-inspired affair where Romeo and Juliet meet. We've already encountered them individually, and when they memorably catch sight of each other on opposite sides of a wall-long tropical fish tank, he in a knight's shining armor, she with an angel's wings, we know they're going to be smitten.

DiCaprio's Romeo is a sensitive scribbling boy poet, a brooding rebel favored with rock star close-ups. Better still, the performance of the film, in fact, is Danes's Juliet. Known for *My So-Called Life* as well as *Little Women*, Danes goes from strength to strength here. Her Juliet has a freshness, directness and simplicity that is just what's called for. And she makes the Elizabethan language sound more natural than the latest slang.

Though it's often too loud and refuses to forgo low comedy (especially in Miriam Margolyes's role as Juliet's nurse), director Luhrmann's film knows enough to slow down and be quiet when this dreamy couple, the only natural people in an artificial world, steal their moments alone. There's no love like young love, at least as far as the movies are concerned, and *Romeo + Juliet* is where it all began.

Without Limits
1998

Great athletes are of life and larger than it. Their personal dramas are acted out in public, their starkly outlined victories and defeats written in large, unmistakable letters. We watch their struggles with something like awe, envying, perhaps, an existence where questions of winning and losing are brutally clear-cut.

Distance runner Steve Prefontaine was one of the premier American athletes of his age. Competing for the University of Oregon, he was the only man ever to hold the U.S. records in every distance between 2,000 and 10,000 meters; and in the 1972 Munich Olympics he was a key player in perhaps the most memorable 5,000 meters ever held.

A confident, charismatic performer who rarely ran without partisan crowds chanting "Pre, Pre, Pre," Prefontaine's unusual life calls out to be filmed, and several pictures, including a documentary called *Fire on the Track,* have been made. The disappointing *Prefontaine* (starring Jared Leto) was little more than an illustrated scrapbook, but *Without Limits,* starring Billy Crudup and written and directed by Robert Towne, is the exciting, thoughtful and empathetic film the man deserves.

What makes *Without Limits* involving and unconventional is that Towne (who cowrote the script with Olympic marathoner and *Sports Illustrated* writer Kenny Moore, who knew Pre) presents a Prefontaine who, all his victories and records notwithstanding, stood apart from the typical champion.

Though it sounds heretical, Prefontaine, who died in 1975, held himself to a higher standard than simple victory. For him, races were works of art created by unbearable effort, as well as opportunities to test his own personal capacities and the limits of human endurance.

Facilitating this understanding of Pre's mindset is a man who initially did not comprehend him at all, his coach Bill Bowerman (Donald Sutherland). "From the beginning," Bowerman says in a typically lean but telling piece of voice-over, "I tried to change him. He tried not to change. That was our relationship."

Without Limits opens at a defining moment of Prefontaine's career, the Munich Olympics, where Pre faces one of the strongest fields in the Games, including the intimidating Finnish distance runner Lasse Viren. "I'd like it to come down to a pure guts race," Pre says with typical bravado in a pre-event interview. "If it does, I'm the only one who can win it."

The film then flashes back to 1969, when even as a high school competitor from Coos Bay, Oregon, Prefontaine's front-running style, his obsession with staying out by himself and far away from the crowd, was already in evidence.

Also fully developed was Pre's problematic personality. Overflowing with the unselfconscious arrogance of youth and physical ability, driven even by the standards of world-class athletes, Prefontaine was a creature of almost feral intensity.

As difficult as he could be, however, Pre often won people over, and one of the graces of the strong performance by Crudup is that he finds the irresistible boyishness and likability that coexisted with the cockiness of a high school senior who refused to consider the University of Oregon unless storied coach Bowerman, a known hater of recruiting, personally indicated he wanted the young man to attend.

Bowerman, hardly a pushover, was a master psychologist, a mind games expert who joined an iron will to withering irony and took obedience from his runners as a given. Sutherland, also a man of considerable experience, hasn't completely involved himself in all his parts, but he's done so here. The result is a commanding, almost hypnotic performance that is among the actor's best.

A shrewd and knowledgeable leader whose shoe sense led to the founding of Nike, Bowerman was initially frustrated by Prefontaine's front-running, a style he felt would lead to disaster at the international level because of the extra energy that mode of running consumes.

In a conventional sports film, this clash of Prefontaine's unstoppable force and Bowerman's immovable object would be resolved by the premium both men put on winning. Here, it's more complex—in fact almost the opposite—as Pre's insistence that victory isn't worth anything if it's not achieved by running all out all the time was a source of intense frustration to his coach. Finally, it's the truth and honesty of both men's intensity, not their specific beliefs, that forms the bond between them as the Munich Olympics approach.

Since he wrote and directed *Personal Best*, his debut film as a director in 1982, running has been something of an obsession with Towne, and his understanding of the psychology and nuances of the sport is a key asset here. Working with master cinematographer Conrad Hall, who used intricate combinations of lenses to capture the details of competition, Towne has also given *Without Limits* a vivid feel for the grinding physicality of this most primal sport.

Towne's most important contribution, aside from his gift for structure and his willingness to direct this story in a classic, straight-ahead manner, is the power of his words. Because *Without Limits* is not written in a way that calls attention to itself, because the language is not showy, it's easy to miss how much of an accomplishment it is to find beauty and poetry in spareness and to tell an often familiar story without lapsing into clichés.

Steve Prefontaine had other things on his mind besides the art of running, and *Without Limits* explores them as well. Pre spoke out against what he saw as the sham of American amateurism and helped spark a movement that eventually changed the shape of international track and field.

Given his youth and charisma, Pre was suitably attractive to women, but the key romantic relationship of his life, with fellow student Mary Marckx (Monica Potter), was, once again, different from the norm. It was a bond as much spiritual as physical and, like Prefontaine's connection with Bowerman, it had the glow of the singular that marked everything about this young man's life.

Part Four

ANIMATION

Introduction

If, even as recently as fifteen years ago, someone had said that a book such as this would not just need but demand a separate section on animation, he or she would have been quietly but firmly told to lie down until the feeling passed.

But what has happened since the release of Disney's *Beauty and the Beast* in 1991 is a great flowering of studio-distributed English language animation culminating in the 2001 creation of an animated feature Oscar category. It's a golden age all the more remarkable because hardly anyone saw it coming.

The films included here come from a variety of sources. As someone who spent pleasant childhood hours watching *Lady and the Tramp* and *Cinderella*, I find it satisfying to note that traditional Disney animation has done its share with such films as *Tarzan* and *Hercules* in addition to the landmark *Beauty*.

Aside from Disney's contribution, today's animation revival benefits from the concurrent presence of two of the art's most creative talents ever (three, if you count Japan's Hiyao Miyazaki, whose work is outside this book's scope): Nick Park of Aardman Animation and Pixar's John Lasseter.

Park, not yet fifty, but already the winner of four Academy Awards, is the reigning wizard of labor-intensive clay animation, here represented by *Chicken Run* and the Oscar-winning *Wallace & Gromit: The Curse of the Were-Rabbit*.

As for Lasseter, the five films his Pixar unit has on the list, very much including the ones he directed himself, testify not to the superiority of computer animation (Disney's hand-drawn *Lilo & Stitch* can hold its own in cleverness with anything a machine can do) but to his refusal to talk down either to the children or to the adults in his audience.

"I had a design teacher when I was at Cal Arts, Bill Moore, who said something to me in class I've never forgotten," Lasseter told me in a 1999 interview. "He said, 'Don't insult your audience.' When we got into story, I've always believed in that. I think audiences across all age groups are very, very smart and we never talk down to them. And we don't dumb it down for kids. Kids get it, you know, and sometimes kids get things quicker than adults."

Beauty and the Beast
1991

Fairy tales are not for children only. Faced with a world of painful realities and deferred dreams, what adult, given half a chance, wouldn't want to cozy up to a story that begins "Once upon a time in a faraway land" and is sure to end with everyone living happily ever after?

Beauty and the Beast, the thirtieth full-length animated feature from the trolls over at Disney and the most satisfying in decades, serves that dual audience with a practiced expertness. Smart as well as traditional, with a striking and detailed look and a strong storyline, it is sure to charm a wide audience for a long time to come.

Yet, as if underlining the reasons we crave this kind of escapism, it is difficult to watch *Beauty and the Beast* without feeling a sense of loss. For Howard Ashman, the film's brilliant lyricist, who also wrote the songs for Disney's *The Little Mermaid* and the off-Broadway sensation *Little Shop of Horrors*, died of AIDS before this project was completed.

Ashman (who worked with composer Alan Menken) was also the film's executive producer, and instrumental in conceptualizing the turning of an ancient tale that has appeared in many guises across many civilizations (including, no kidding, the tale of a girl who married not a bear or a beast but a stove) into a sprightly modern musical.

Perhaps as a reaction to criticism that that cute little mermaid was a bit of air-headed fluff, the creators of this *Beauty* (including screenwriter Linda Woolverton) have taken pains to do more than show this heroine to be a model of strong, self-reliant womanhood. They've also made the biggest obstacle to her happiness not the woebegone beast but a heroically conceived monument to male chauvinism named Gaston.

Before we meet these folks, however, a prologue, illustrated by an exquisite series of stained-glass windows, tells the back story of a spoiled, handsome prince turned into an awful beast by an avenging enchantress after he refuses her gift of a magical rose. He will remain so cursed forever, she tells him, unless he can learn to love, and be loved in return, by the time the last petal of the rose falls.

Blissfully unaware of this is the beautiful Belle (voiced by stage actress Paige O'Hara). We meet her strolling the streets of her quainter-than-quaint French village, complaining that "there must be more than this provincial life." A reader and a dreamer, she yearns for adventure, little guessing how much of it will soon be in store for her.

Belle's father, Maurice, a feckless inventor very much in the Gyro Gearloose mold, starts the plot rolling by getting himself hopelessly lost in the deep woods. He stumbles across a towering, intimidating castle, which he finds to his horror is inhabited by that foul-tempered, roaring Beast, who promptly locks him up on general principles. The feisty Belle retraces her father's steps and offers to take his place as the monster's prisoner.

According to the press notes, the reason Walt Himself had given up on an earlier Disney attempt at *Beauty* is that his team couldn't lick the problem of how to make Belle's stay at the castle less than claustrophobic. Again, it was Howard Ashman who broke the spell: He came up with the idea of enchanted bric-a-brac, such as Lumiere (Jerry Orbach), the candlestick with the personality of Maurice Chevalier, and Mrs. Potts (Angela Lansbury), a teapot with a heart of gold. In fact, one of the film's animated high spots has all these objects, as well as a brace of silverware and all kinds of crockery, go into an elaborate "Be Our Guest" production number that even Busby Berkeley would have been proud to call his own.

Also helping things in the castle is the intriguing personality of the beast. As voiced by Robby Benson (yes, that Robby Benson) and animated by Glen Keane, the Beast is a splendid creation, managing to be both intimidating and endearing, fiercer than fierce when danger threatens from a genuinely frightening pack of wild dogs, but just a big softie with a bad temper where Belle is concerned. And, yes, they do make an awfully cute couple.

Just about stealing the picture from those two lovebirds, however, is the square-jawed, fat-headed presence of Gaston (Richard White), the greatest hunter in town and Belle's wannabe lover. But though the Beast appreciates Belle for what she is, Gaston is a classic self-absorbed sexist who wants to see her barefoot and pregnant, one more trophy to add to his already sizeable collection.

Animator Andreas Deja has said he based Gaston on L.A.'s more-than-ample supply of conceited swains, and Ashman and Menken have given him the film's funniest song, a noble ode to himself in which the great man claims "no one's quick as Gaston, no one's slick as Gaston, no one's head is incred-ably thick as Gaston." Certain types of cleverness are exclusionary, but Ashman's is the opposite— effortless, effervescent and totally welcoming. We are going to miss his work. In fact, we already do.

Beauty became the first animated feature ever to be nominated for a best picture Oscar, and its success led to the creation of an animated feature category a decade later in 2001.

A Bug's Life
1998

Computer-animated movies, like computers themselves, are only as clever and funny as the people who program them. What *A Bug's Life* demonstrates is that when it comes to bugs, the most fun ones to hang out with hang exclusively with the wacky gang at Pixar. This is definitely the insect-themed computer-animated film to see if you can only manage one.

It's probably just coincidence, but *A Bug's Life* and the earlier, also insect-themed, *Antz* have several plot points in common. Both are grounded in ant colonies facing ruinous attack from outside insects;

both feature queens training their daughters in the finer points of monarchy; and both focus on a rift between conservatives who want to do things the time-honored way and a rebel with ideas of his own.

What *Bug's Life* has that the other film lacks is an unfettered imagination, a willingness to tolerate the kind of harum-scarum, anything-goes sensibility that would come up with ideas such as a wacky series of outtakes of bugs blowing their lines and calling for retakes that plays alongside the final credits.

This footloose humor comes both from the writing and the direction. Cowriter Andrew Stanton was one of the team that received an Oscar nomination for the *Toy Story* script, and his collaborators, Donald McEnery & Bob Shaw, contributed to the underappreciated *Hercules*. Directing (with Stanton getting codirection credit) is Pixar stalwart John Lasseter, who also did the honors for *Toy Story*.

Another key to *Bug's Life*'s success is that it's cast a wide net, so to speak, in terms of how many types of insects make it onto the screen. And though its voices are not always big stars (the film's story supervisor Joe Ranft did such a good job with the gemutlich caterpillar Heimlich in the first reading that he got the part), they are always at one with the material.

A Bug's Life starts with a typical example of its humor. As a line of ants carrying foodstuffs snakes its way through the grass, a leaf falls, obscuring the trail and causing consternation. "Do not panic, we are trained professionals," cries a group of leaf removers, who clear things up while commenting, "This is nothing compared to the Twig of '93."

The ants are gathering food as tribute for the annual visit of a gang of marauding grasshoppers, led by the mendacious Hopper (Kevin Spacey). Don't worry, the Queen (Phyllis Diller) tells her daughter Princess Atta (Julia Louis-Dreyfus), "it's the same year after year: They come, they eat, they leave."

No ant colony is apparently complete without its resident iconoclast, in this case a well-meaning but chronically inept young ant named Flik (Dave Foley). When Flik unintentionally causes a problem with Hopper's gang over the tribute, he decides the only way to redeem himself and save the colony is to venture off Ant Island and seek help from other insects.

Though A Bug's Life was apparently inspired by the Aesop's fable about the grasshoppers and the ants, at this point the picture cleverly turns into an entomological version of Akira Kurosawa's classic Seven Samurai, in which warriors are recruited from the big city to help embattled farmers fight off brigands.

It's not exactly warriors this time around, though. While Flik is on the road, the film allows us a peek inside the bedraggled circus of P. T. Flea (John Ratzenberger) and introduces a particularly zany and irresistible group of performing insects: cheerful Heimlich, feisty male ladybug Francis (Denis Leary), the stick-thin Slim (David Hyde Pierce), friendly black widow Rosie (Bonnie Hunt), the team of Manny the Mantis and Gypsy Moth (Jonathan Harris and Madeline Kahn), rhino beetle Dim (Brad Garrett) and the irrepressible twin Hungarian pill bugs Tuck & Roll (Michael McShane).

Visually satisfying is the film's Blade Runner vision of the Big (or is it Bug?) City, where a beggar wears a sign saying "A Kid Pulled My Wings Off." Ditto for the local bar (probably inspired by the cantina in Star Wars), where mosquitoes quaff genuine Bloody Marys and hardier insects quench their thirsts with Black Flag.

It's at the bar that Flik meets up with the newly unemployed insects from P. T. Flea's. He mistakes them for "tough bugs," and they think he's a patron of the arts when he begs them to go back to Ant Island. "These guys," one of them says, "are sure hard up for entertainment." This confusion eventually clears up, and the circus bugs try to use what skills they have against Hopper and his pesky clan. It's a sight to see.

Chicken Run
2000

As the owner and eminence grise of Tweedy's Egg Farm, the autocratic Mrs. Tweedy thinks she knows chickens. "They don't plot, they don't scheme, they are not organized," she tells her (inevitably) hen-pecked husband. "Apart from you, they are the stupidest creatures on the planet." Or so she, and the rest of us, believe.

Along with its virtues as a delightful example of clay animation, *Chicken Run* also exposes a previously hidden world of poultry behavior. Before our disbelieving eyes, a pageant of jeopardy, romance and rescue unfolds. Chickens yelling, "She's gonna blow," chickens jitterbugging to the classic "Flip Flop and Fly," chickens creating the kind of rousing action finale John Woo would relish. It's enough to make you swear off fricassee for life.

If anyone could provide this service, it would have to be Britain's foremost animator, Nick Park. The winner of three short-film Oscars ("The highest Oscar-to-output ratio," one minute-counting journalist has calculated, "in the history of motion pictures"), this is a man who knows his animals.

Park won his first Oscar for *Creature Comforts*, deadpan interviews with hyperarticulate zoo animals. Then came the Wallace and Gromit films about a dog smarter than most men. One such adventure, *The Wrong Trousers*, even has a chicken in a key role. (He's not really a chicken, as it turns out, but rather a penguin deviously pretending to be a chicken—but it's the thought that counts.)

Now Park and his Aardman Animation partner and codirector Peter Lord have put chickens front and center where they belong with this gleeful parody of prison and escape movies. No one who remembers *Stalag 17* will have to guess at the number that's on the front of the hen house, and no veteran of *The Great Escape* will fail to recognize the contours of the farm, complete with barbed wire fencing, barking dogs, and a suspicious Mr. Tweedy checking the locks and muttering about what the chickens are up to.

Hens and roosters may be unlikely heroes for an action adventure film, but Park, Lord and writer Karey Kirkpatrick have given *Chicken Run* the unmistakable hallmarks of the charming and clever style that turned Wallace and Gromit into great favorites over here as well as in Britain.

Simultaneously understated and hang-loose, the humor in *Chicken Run* is genial and playful, able to treat the wildest concepts with total seriousness. This film is also much the funnier for being site-specific: Though no one, not even the smallest child, will have any trouble following the plot, the use of such Britishisms as "you old sausage" and "give it over" add to the comic flavor.

The reason Mr. Tweedy (voiced by Tony Haygarth) is assiduously checking those locks is that one of his hens is addicted to escape attempts. That would be Ginger (Julie Sawalha of *Absolutely Fabulous*), as jaunty as the neck scarf she wears. Believing that "there's a better place out there," Ginger is determined not only to break herself out but also to free all the hens who live under the gloomy threat of death (as the pigs do in *Babe*) if they don't produce.

Ginger's accomplices include Mac (Lynn Ferguson), the mechanical genius, as well as Nick (Timothy Spall) and Fletcher (Phil Daniels), a completely funny pair of conniving black-marketeer rats, always aghast at the hens' attempt to pay them in, yes, chicken feed. Even less focused is Babs (*Little Voice*'s Jane Horrocks), who treats Ginger's confinements in solitary as the equivalent of a holiday. "It's nice," she says vacantly, "to get a bit of time by yourself."

Dropping in, literally, on this self-described "group of rather desperate chickens" is the American rooster Rocky Roads (wonderfully done by Mel Gibson), a confident Rhode Island Red who's done "that whole barnyard thing" and now considers himself something of a "Lone Free Ranger."

Much to the disgust of resident rooster Fowler (Benjamin Whitrow), a Royal Air Force veteran who mutters the classic World War II British jibe at Yanks ("overpaid, oversexed, over here"), Rocky, who claims to have had considerable experience in the area, agrees to teach the hens to fly.

Though he and Ginger don't get along (he insists on calling her "Dollface" and considers her so tough that she's "the first chick I ever met with the shell still on"), they have to cooperate because the devious Mrs. Tweedy (the letter-perfect Miranda Richardson) has come up with a scheme so evil that it makes everyone in the barn-yard quake.

Making what Park and company have accomplished here even more impressive is how labor-intensive clay animation's stop-motion technique is. The Plasticine models have to be changed frame by frame, with twenty- frames making up but a single second of on-screen time.

But though hundreds of people were employed in creating *Chicken Run,* with as many as thirty sets operating at the same time, the film never loses its priceless stamp of individuality. Reduced to its essence, this is a joke told by a person, not a corporation—and that makes all the difference.

Finding Nemo
2003

It's been suspected for some time, but *Finding Nemo* makes it official: With five successes out of five attempts, Pixar Animation Studios is now the most reliable creative force in Hollywood. Perhaps not since Preston Sturges made seven classic comedies in a row between 1940 and 1944 has one name been such a consistent indicator of audience and critical pleasure.

Finding Nemo is an engaging undersea story, written and directed by Andrew Stanton, about a fish family learning life lessons that (surprise!) humans can benefit from as well. But success here, although based on the twin factors that have always characterized Pixar productions, was not necessarily preordained. In fact, there are moments early on in *Finding Nemo* when it almost seemed as if the venture was going to lose its way.

The one Pixar factor never in doubt from the first frame is the sparkling, cutting-edge verve of *Nemo*'s visuals. A pioneer in computer animation, Pixar compulsively threw itself into the challenge of making a water world come alive.

Though *Nemo* viewers may not be interested in Pixar's five-point checklist of components needed to create a convincing undersea environment, it would be churlish not to be impressed by the rapturous undersea-world-of-our-dreams colors of the resulting re-creation of Australia's Great Barrier Reef.

Pixar films are also invariably characterized by a level of smarter-than-the-room humor noticeably wacky and sophisticated for studio family fare, a tradition that filmmaker Stanton, who codirected *A Bug's Life* and has shared writing credit on all of Pixar's previous pictures, had a big hand in creating. This is why it is surprising that *Nemo* (cowritten with Bob Peterson and David Reynolds) initially seems like the kind of cloying standard brand that Pixar has never been before.

The film starts with a happy family of colorful bright orange clown fish moving into a new home under the watchful eye of proud father Marlin (voiced by Albert Brooks). But no sooner are you thinking that no fish should be this happy then a *Bambi*-type incident leaves Marlin alone to raise his son Nemo (Alexander Gould), presumably named after the captain in *20,000 Leagues Under the Sea*.

Nemo grows up into a special-needs fish with a weak—or "lucky"—fin and an overprotective father who completely freaks out even before his son is captured alive by a diver and whisked off to who knows where.

Though setting up father and son this way allows *Nemo* to deal with the issues of overprotective parents and undertrusted offspring, the whole situation verges on being overly calculated. And Pixar's weakness for whiny characters (witness Billy Crystal's Mike in *Monsters, Inc.*) contributes to making Marlin's nonstop hysteria so initially irritating that even the gifted Brooks can't completely salvage the situation.

The first break we get is when Marlin picks up a sidekick as he swims off in a desperate search for his son. That would be Dory (Ellen DeGeneres), a regal blue tang saddled with short-term memory loss. This may sound as unpromising as Marlin's whining, but something about DeGeneres's perky voice as she calls Marlin "Mr. Grumpy Gills" makes her character successful.

The best break of all is that Pixar's traditionally untethered imagination can't be kept under wraps forever, and *Nemo* erupts with sea creatures that showcase Stanton and company's gift for character and peerless eye for skewering contemporary culture. Ladies and gentlemen, the sharks.

Chum (Bruce Spence), Anchor (Eric Bana) and most especially Bruce (*Dame Edna*'s Barry Humphries) are not ordinary sharks. They've got matey Australian accents (Humphries's is especially effective) and, conscious of their unsavory reputations, they are in a five-step program to turn them away from being "mindless eating machines." The AA-type meeting this trio attends, complete with catchphrases ("fish are friends, not food"), is a comic set piece little short of brilliant.

Nemo, who ends up in an aquarium in a dentist's office in Sydney, also runs across fishy characters as he meets his new tank mates. This gang has been behind glass so long they've become experts in dental procedure and pass the time kibitzing the dentist's treatment choices. Their leader is Gill (Willem Dafoe), a been-around Moorish idol fish who understands Nemo's passion to be free and concocts a scheme to help him out.

Meanwhile, Marlin keeps meeting the most interesting creatures on his quest to find his son. The most memorable is Crush, a giant green sea turtle wonderfully voiced by filmmaker Stanton himself as the kind of ultimate surfer who calls everyone "dude"—as in "you got serious thrill issues, dude." He lets Marlin ride on his shell after giving him a warning: "I just waxed it, so no hurling."

With characters this eccentric, *Finding Nemo*'s morals about the realities of single-parent households (not previously thought of as an undersea problem) and the importance of trust, family and friendship go down a lot easier. When a film comes up with bonuses as devilishly devious as rapacious seagulls who repeat "Mine? Mine? Mine?" in a menacing monotone, it's not difficult to cut it all the slack it needs.

Hercules
1997

Light on its feet and continually amusing, *Hercules* is a free-spirited show-biz version of Greek mythology that ranks with the best of modern Disney animation. Cleverly constructed to appeal to boys and girls, children and adults, it also has, in *City of Angels* Tony-winning lyricist David Zippel, the first person since the late Howard Ashman who's been able to write the kind of snappy musical patter these features thrive on.

The guiding spirits here, the writing, directing and producing team of John Musker & Ron Clements, worked with Ashman and *Hercules* composer Alan Menken on *Aladdin,* and this film combines much the same wisecracking aura with a dollop of romantic poignancy.

It's been done with subject matter—the Greek hero who was the strongest man on the planet while coping with a rather painful personal history—that is unlikely. But Musker and Clements (working with cowriters/stand-up comics Bob Shaw and Donald McEnery and Disney veteran Irene Mecchi) have done a brisk and successful cut-and-paste job on the original material, nervily mixing and matching elements from all over classical mythology. In comes the flying horse Pegasus to be the big guy's pal, out goes Hercules' destructive fits of madness, not to mention the time he cut the noses and ears off an unlucky group of messengers.

Kudos is also in order for how deftly the project's *A Funny Thing Happened on the Way to the Forum* comic tone has been combined with traditional Disney life lessons for little folks. Who would have guessed that Hercules was the kid who didn't fit in, the adolescent who needed to prove himself to his father and, finally, the young adult who has to discover that heroism is something measured only by strength of heart. It kind of chokes you up, it really does.

Hercules isn't slow in unveiling its comic tone. Narrator Charlton Heston gets to read no more than a handful of somber words before he's cut off with a sassy, "Will you listen to him? He's making this story sound like some Greek tragedy. Lighten up, dude."

Those words come from the Muses, cut down from the original nine to a manageable five (Lillias White, Cheryl Freeman, LaChanze, Roz Ryan, Vaneese Thomas) and transformed into a Greek chorus that is part Motown girl group and part gospel choir. Their Gospel Truth numbers introduce characters, provide back story and jump-start the film into an up-tempo gear it never abandons.

Though no one can duplicate what Robin Williams did for *Aladdin*, James Woods as Hades, the cynical, fast-talking king of the underworld, comes surprisingly close. Introduced at a party Zeus and Hera, king and queen of the gods, are giving for baby son Hercules, he enters with a Don Rickles wisecrack ("I haven't been this choked up since I got a chunk of moussaka caught in my throat") and never pauses for breath.

Hades, you should know, is not a happy god. He has a plan to replace Zeus and get the hell out of the underworld, but the Fates, who know all about the future and tell a bit ("Indoor plumbing—it's going to be big"), inform him that he won't succeed unless he's able to neutralize Hercules.

Working with comic sidekicks Pain (Bobcat Goldthwait) and Panic (Matt Frewer), Hades manages to turn Hercules human, but he still retains his godlike strength. Herc grows up to be a gawky teenager, teased as Jerkules for his clumsiness, but his life takes a better turn when he discovers that Zeus is his father and that proving himself a hero on Earth can make him a god once again.

Philoctetes, Phil for short, is a pudgy satyr who knows all about heroes. He's trained the best of them, from Achilles on down, but having "been around the block before with blockheads like you," he considers himself retired.

Naturally, Hercules changes his mind, and as played by Danny DeVito, Phil is the film's energy source when Hades isn't around. The kind of guy who calls everyone "Kid" and tells people to keep their togas on, Phil has a Borscht Belt vocabulary and a determination to make Hercules the greatest there ever was.

On the way to Thebes, the Big Olive, "a big tough town, a good place to start building a rep," Hercules runs into Megara (Susan Egan), a.k.a. Meg, a different kind of Disney heroine, the kind of been-around, good-bad girl who could have been voiced by Barbara Stanwyck. She arouses Phil's suspicion and incites Pegasus to jealousy, but the look in Hercules' eyes tells us she'll be sticking around.

Given the kind of guy he is, it's inevitable that Hercules (Tate Donovan) battles lots of strange monsters. The most impressive (and the film's only nod to Hercules' storied twelve labors) is the protean Hydra, a beast that grows new heads whenever one is cut off. A technological marvel, the Hydra is the film's most impressive computer-generated character, and no wonder: The press notes say a team of fifteen artists and technicians worked on the five-minute sequence for two years.

When our hero becomes "the greatest thing since they put the pocket in pita," a process detailed in the rousing "Zero to Hero," the film delights in satirizing Disney's well-known penchant for merchandising, including omnipresent Air-Herc sandals and the hot-selling "thirty-minute workout scroll, 'Buns of Bronze.'"

But, like any protagonist, Hercules has to discover that "being famous isn't the same thing as being a true hero," and the process of doing so involves him more intimately with Meg in a way that sentimentalists will find satisfying.

Though they're not big-star names, without the excellent work of Donovan as the adult Hercules and Egan as Meg, *Hercules* would have considerably less impact. The animation, with an assist from British illustrator Gerald Scarfe, has just enough of a different look to it to make things interesting. What remains the same is the ability of Disney feature-length cartoons to entertain like crazy. It's hard to believe that lines that move can move us so much, but they do.

The Incredibles
2004

In an unparalleled run powered by sheer inventiveness and a special kind of skill, Pixar Animation Studios has done it one more time.

The Incredibles is a worthy computer-animated successor to the two *Toy Story* movies, *A Bug's Life* and *Finding Nemo*. And it's something more as well.

For this film, written and directed by Brad Bird, aims even higher than those successes. Yes, it's got the trademark smarter-than-smart Pixar sense of humor, bursts of wild comic energy that show us how funny films can be when they have the confidence not to talk down to their audiences. But anyone who saw Bird's quietly moving first feature, *The Iron Giant*, knows that laughs are not all he's after.

Bird has dreamed the animator's big dream of doing it all, and he's made it come true. He has created the unprecedented film that is not just a grand feature-length cartoon but a grand feature, period, a piece of animation that's involving across a spectrum of comedy, action, even drama. And he's done it by working within the confines of one of the staples of cartoons and comic literature, the superhero.

In a typically wicked-clever opening, we meet Mr. Incredible (*Coach's* Craig T. Nelson), Elastigirl (Holly Hunter) and Frozone (Samuel L. Jackson) as they submit to a classic series of "is this thing on?" television interviews, revealing themselves to be as prone to irritation and frustration as the least super of their fellow citizens of Municiberg.

"Leave the saving of the world to the men?" says an incredulous Elastigirl when asked about settling down. "I don't think so." And Mr. Incredible grumbles: "No matter how many times you save the world, it always manages to get back in jeopardy again. I mean, sometimes I just want it to stay saved, you know, for a little bit."

Being a public figure is all in a day's work for the bulked-up Mr. I, as adept at saving wandering cats as capturing fleeing criminals. There's always time to trade bons mots with tart-tongued French safecracker Bomb Voyage and to shoo away ("You're not affiliated with me," he huffs) superhero wannabe Buddy Pine (Jason Lee), a pesky teenager who wants to be a sidekick in the worst way.

Then, without warning, everything starts to go terribly, terribly wrong. Superheroes get taken to court and lose, costing the government so much in damages and public ill will that they have to abandon their professions and hide out in the equivalent of witness protection programs.

That's where *The Incredibles* proper starts, fifteen years down the road, with the former Mr. Incredible now masquerading as ordinary Bob Parr, a man with thinning hair and an expanding gut. He's married to Helen (the former Elastigirl) and works under the perennially dyspeptic Gilbert Huph (Wallace Shawn) as a claims adjuster for the heartlessly corporate Insuricare.

His job title notwithstanding, Bob can't adjust to life in the normal lane. He sympathizes with the frustration his superpowered children, the blindingly fast Dash (Spencer Fox) and the invisible teen Violet (Sarah Vowell), feel at having to hide their powers in a world that wants everyone to be ordinary. Under cover of going bowling, Bob and Lucius Best, a.k.a. Frozone, sneak out and, hooded like criminals, secretly help people.

But what if, somewhere in the world, the need for an old-school superhero should arise? When Bob gets a secret communication from the sultry Mirage (Elizabeth Pena) hinting at just that, it leads him to some of the funniest, most human and most adventurous situations computer animation has yet put on the screen.

Given that his old Mr. I uniform isn't fitting the way it used to, Bob ends up paying a visit to the inimitable Edna Mode, couturier to the heroic, the ultimate fashionista who combines Louise Brooks's hair with the iron will of a samurai. Hysterically voiced by director Bird himself, this tiny terror, given to saying, "I never look back, it distracts from the now," is a gift from the gods.

While much of *The Incredibles* is blessedly funny, there is also a surprising air of poignancy about much of it. Bob's midlife passion to secretly relive his glory days puts a genuine strain on his marriage and family, something the film takes quite seriously.

It's able to do this in part because advances in computer technology have made it possible to create fake human characters in a way that, even factoring in intentional caricaturing, make Bob, Helen and the gang seem in some undefinable way more real than CGI folks ever have before.

Having realistic people as protagonists makes the astonishing actions this family of superheroes is asked to perform that much more involving. *The Incredibles'* creators help out here by doing an envelope-pushing job of conjuring up villains to confront, crises to be solved and settings for adventure worthy of Indiana Jones.

Some sixty years ago, the Walt Disney Co., Pixar's current partner, made *Pinocchio,* still considered a pinnacle of hand-drawn animation. *The Incredibles,* a pinnacle of computer art, wants to be a real story in just the same way as that celebrated puppet wanted to be a real boy. The torch between art forms and between generations couldn't be passed in a more fitting, satisfying way.

Lilo & Stitch
2002

A little girl named Lilo looks out of her window and, in traditional Disney fashion, wishes on a falling star. "I need someone to be my friend," she says. "Maybe send me an angel, the nicest angel you have."

It's a swell thought, kid, but tradition is not on the menu this time around. That star is actually a crashing spaceship, the hoped-for angel turns out to be an obnoxious genetically engineered monster, "the flawed product of a deranged mind," and *Lilo & Stitch* is definitely not the kind of animated Disney family film we've become used to.

Looser and less obviously formulaic in its fresh approach to our hearts, the brash *Lilo & Stitch* has an unleashed, subversive sense of humor that's less corporate and more uninhibited than any non-Pixar Disney film has been in time out of mind. With its hand-drawn characters and its use of watercolors for backgrounds (the first time the studio's done that since the 1940s), this is a happy throwback to the time when cartoons were cinema's most idiosyncratic form instead of one of its most predictable.

That's likely the result, at least in part, of Disney's agreeing to an unusual setup in which writer-directors Chris Sanders and Dean DeBlois, in a departure from typical animation practice, also story-boarded their script, ensuring that the anarchic spirit that infused their original concept wouldn't be diluted. For it's not only Stitch, a relentless combination of koala and chaos interested only in destroying everything he touches, who's out of the usual Disney mold. Little Lilo (voiced by Daveigh Chase) is hardly a walk in the park either.

Raised as best she can by older sister Nani (Tia Carrere), Lilo is introduced as brattiness personified, way too hostile to her sister and everyone else to be perceived as anything but a tedious troublemaker. Lilo's eccentric passion for Elvis Presley (the film makes wonderful use of six of the King's biggest hits, from "Hound Dog" to "Heartbreak Hotel") is one of her few humanizing traits.

Given that both of its title characters are scruffy, unpleasant outcasts who take considerable warming up to, *Lilo & Stitch*'s surprising ability to explain how they got that way and to motivate their inevitable transition to better behavior and genuine caring (this is a Disney film, after all) is that much more unlikely and impressive.

Lilo & Stitch begins, in a deft parody of the *Star Wars* sagas, in a meeting of the Galactic Federation on the planet Turo. Mad scientist Jumba (David Ogden Stiers) is convicted of illegal genetic experimentation, and the resulting creature, named Experiment 626, is to be exiled to a desert asteroid.

But 626, nothing if not unstoppable, manages to escape and get himself to the Hawaiian island of Kauai, where he disguises himself as a strange looking dog and is adopted by the lonely Lilo. She calls him Stitch and, happy for a friend, overlooks his wacky destructive proclivities, such as a magical ability to turn her toys into a facsimile of San Francisco only to enthusiastically stomp the city to pieces à la Godzilla. (Parents, be prepared to do a lot of explaining.)

Unknown to these fast friends, threats are forming on the horizon. *Men in Black*–inspired social worker Cobra Bubbles (Ving Rhames), given to saying such things as "You've been adrift in the sheltered harbor of my patience," is threatening to split the family. Plus the Galactic Federation, which has come to view our planet as a protected wildlife preserve for the mosquito, with humans useful only as part of that insect's food chain, dispatches creator Jumbo and deluded Earth expert Pleakley (Kevin McDonald) to capture 626 and throw away the key.

Not only is *Lilo & Stitch* set on Kauai but it features many specific references (a cart selling shaved ice and what looks like the lobby of the Hanalei Bay Resort) and uses as its theme the Hawaiian notion of "ohana," or family, meaning "nobody gets left behind or forgotten."

Lilo & Stitch makes excellent use of the best of Disney's animators. Andreas Deja, who was the supervising animator for Gaston in *Beauty and the Beast* and Jafar in *Aladdin*, takes on the recalcitrant Lilo; and Alex Kuperschmidt, responsible for the hyenas in *The Lion King*, makes the jabbering Stitch (grumbles and rumbles voiced by writer-director Sanders) remarkably expressive.

Despite the requisite happy ending, *Lilo & Stitch* is too unhinged to feel arbitrary. It's just a film that believes, as Boys Town's legendary founder Father Flanagan did, that there's no such thing as a bad boy. Or a bad girl. Or, for that matter, a bad alien.

The Nightmare Before Christmas
1993

Forget *Beetlejuice*, forget *Edward Scissorhands* and (this shouldn't be too difficult), forget *Batman Returns*. *The Nightmare Before Christmas* is the movie the decidedly quirky Tim Burton was fated to make. Part avant-garde art film, part amusing but morbid fairy tale, it is a delightfully ghoulish holiday musical that displays more inventiveness in its brief seventy-five minutes than some studios can manage in an entire year.

Though it is an animated film, *Nightmare* is not a cartoon like *Aladdin* or *Beauty and the Beast*. Rather, on the model of the original *King Kong* and the more recent Speedy Alka-Seltzer, it is a revolutionary application of stop-motion animation, a labor-intensive process that involves the frame-by-frame manipulation of three-dimensional creatures.

And though it managed to be rated PG (for some scary images), the aptly named *Nightmare* is definitely not a film for tiny tots. Although its soul is sweetness itself, its surface is disturbing and intentionally so, and its clever and satiric sense of humor is undoubtedly pitched to adult tastes.

Nightmare's first incarnation was as a hand-drawn send-up of the Clement Moore poem that Burton created more than a decade ago when he was working as a humble animator at the Walt Disney studios and dreaming of turning his idea into a television special along the lines of *How the Grinch Stole Christmas*.

In the way it details what happens when the weirdos who run Halloween decide to expand and take over Christmas as well, *Nightmare* was deemed too bizarre for public consumption, but Burton never gave up on it. His increased box-office clout, courtesy of the *Batman* films, helped persuade Disney to green-light what may be the most personal piece of animation—and one of the most personal films, period—ever to come out of that studio.

Although someone else (*The Secret Garden*'s Caroline Thompson) ended up writing the script, and the technical nature of stop-motion animation meant that an expert (Henry Selick) had to be hired to direct, *Nightmare*'s sensibility is clearly Burton's.

A live-action filmmaker with the soul of an animator, Burton has a taste for off-center, gruesome comedy—so off-putting when attached to real people, as it was in *Batman Returns*—but perfectly suited to these characters. Puppets, it should come as no surprise, make much better puppets than people ever could.

The premise of *The Nightmare Before Christmas* is the quaint one that everyone responsible for a particular holiday lives in the same self-contained enclave, cheerfully oblivious to the existence of rival festivities and other towns.

The residents of Halloweentown, for instance, are glimpsed celebrating another successful night of fright. Characters such as Big Witch, Corpse Mom and Clown With the Tear Away Face congratulate one another on a job well done while assuring us, in Danny Elfman's lightly charming lyrics, "That's our job, but we're not mean / In our town of Halloween."

Things don't look so cheery for Jack Skellington, the Pumpkin King and spiritual head of Halloween Night. Though he's the best at what he does, Jack has, sad to relate, "grown so weary of the sound of screams" and is in fact in the throes of a serious fit of existential boredom.

While wandering around in spiritual despair, Jack literally stumbles into Christmastown and is blown away by how bright and shiny everything is. "There're children throwing snowballs here instead of throwing heads," he sings exultantly in another one of Elfman's ten songs. "They're busy building toys and absolutely no one's dead."

Resentful that these clowns, so to speak, should have all the fun, Jack determines to take Christmas over from the fat round man he calls Sandy Claws and bring it all back home for the gang in Halloweentown to improve on. "This year," he declares, "Christmas will be ours."

Of course, as the intrepid Sally, the rag doll who loves Jack from afar, realizes, this won't be so easy to do. But Jack, with the evil Dr. Finklestein (Sally's crabby creator) and the malicious trio of Lock, Shock and Barrel to do his bidding, is blind to the difficulties he has in store. Until . . .

Bringing this genially demented world to life meant solving two different but interlocking problems. First off, Burton's drawings had to be turned into three-dimensional figures, and that has been done brilliantly. *Nightmare*'s crones, ghouls and grotesques—topped off by the ultimate incarnation of evil, the Oogie Boogie man (wonderfully served by Ken Page's jazzy phrasings)—are completely beyond description. And even if they weren't, it wouldn't be fair to ruin the fun of having them pop up unexpectedly in their own disturbing ways.

The other problem was making everybody move. Given that each second of onscreen action involves twenty-four different frames, and possibly twenty-four separate character movements, the amount of painstaking planning and grinding work involved in this was daunting. To ensure a variety of expressions for Jack, for instance, eight hundred different replaceable heads were made. No wonder that at maximum efficiency, the *Nightmare* crew could turn out no more than seventy seconds of finished film per week.

What they did turn out, however, is so profligate with exotic images that it overflows with a demented kind of genius, taking stop-motion to places it's never been before. Prime mover Burton has written that *Nightmare Before Christmas* is deeper in my heart than any other film," and those who are the tiniest bit twisted will find a similar place for it in theirs as well.

Shrek
2001

A gleeful piece of wisenheimer computer animation, *Shrek* doesn't have much patience for traditional once-upon-a-time fairy tales: The only time one appears, its pages end up as reading material (and then some) in the hero's outhouse.

That hero is a fierce ogre with a name that's Yiddish for fear. He made his debut in William Steig's 1990 children's book, about a cheerfully ugly monster who's "tickled to be so repulsive," that's become something of a classic.

As a more modern version of that very modern fairy tale, *Shrek*, the film, is all comic attitude, all the time. Casual, carefree, consistently amusing, it plays a lot like the earlier *Aladdin*, which Ted Elliott & Terry Rossio, lead writers and coproducers here, also wrote.

Like *Aladdin*, which did wonderful things with Robin Williams as the irrepressible genie, *Shrek* is blessed with Eddie Murphy as a motor-mouth donkey named, well, Donkey. Though his sidekick work in

Mulan seemed forced, Murphy (taking off from a script by Elliott & Rossio and Joe Stillman and Roger S. H. Schulman) is spectacular here, and he's in good company.

Mike Myers, using a Scottish accent that echoes one of his *Austin Powers* characters, brings not only sharp comic timing but also a kind of sensitivity to the role of Shrek, an ogre who's more troubled by the world's disdain than he was in the book. And Cameron Diaz is appropriately feisty as Fiona, a princess with a secret and a woman who hasn't let being trapped in a tower affect her attitude or her style.

Though Steig's book did without a classic villain, *Shrek* adds a dandy one in Lord Farquaad, a tiny Richard III type (wonderfully voiced by the tall John Lithgow) whose enormous head is packed with evil thoughts, such as how best to give the third degree to a gingerbread man who's reluctant to talk.

Farquaad is the ruler of a supersanitized place called Duloc, which he's determined to turn into the most perfect kingdom on earth. (Any resemblance between Duloc and a certain amusement park run by *Shrek* producer Jeffrey Katzenberg's former employer is probably not coincidental.)

As part of this quest for perfection, Farquaad places a bounty on such fairy-tale characters as Pinocchio and the Three Bears and forcibly exiles them. Donkey is one of them, and when he's saved by Shrek, whom he admires as "a mean, green fighting machine," he decides the two of them should be buddies. "Freaks got to stay together," he declares, adding, with perfect animated logic, "every monster needs a sidekick."

Shrek doesn't quite see it that way. He's a privacy-loving Garbo type who just wants to be left alone, which is why he keeps his property posted with "Beware of the Ogre" signs. So when all those dispossessed fairy-tale types invade his swamp, Shrek stamps off to Farquaad's castle to complain.

That miniature man is having crises of his own. His magic mirror informs him that to have the perfect kingdom, he must marry a princess. In one of *Shrek*'s many pop culture references, the mirror parodies *The Dating Game* by presenting him with a choice of three bachelorette princesses, including one, Snow White, who comes with the advisory "though she lives with seven other men, she's not easy."

Farquaad settles on Fiona, and when Shrek presents his case, he tells the ogre that he can have his swamp back if he rescues the princess from her dragon-guarded castle. So off Shrek sets on what turns out to be a most unconventional quest with the determined Donkey, "a dumb, irritating, miniature beast of burden" tagging along. "Yes, he talks," Shrek says of his annoying companion. "It's getting him to shut up that's the trick."

Shrek's pair of first-time directors, Andrew Adamson and Vicky Jenson, keep the pace brisk enough to balance flatulence jokes with an earnest theme about being comfortable with who you are. The team also makes good use of advances in computer technology that allow human creatures to look more like flesh and blood. The film's soundtrack also shrewdly utilizes pop classics, such as "Try a Little Tenderness," "You Belong to Me" and "On the Road Again," both to underline emotion and appeal to the parents of the film's intended audience.

Some of *Shrek*'s best moments, however, are when it goes off message and simply fills the screen with sharp riffs on the fairy-tale characters it keeps running across. There's fun to be had with three blind mice as well as three little hip-hop pigs, and a classic run-in with Robin Hood and his chorus line of merry men that includes a great visual reference to *Crouching Tiger, Hidden Dragon*. Not only does this fractured fairy tale know there's no substitute for clever writing but it also has the confidence to take that information straight to the bank.

The SpongeBob SquarePants Movie
2004

"There's a word for what you are," someone says to the namesake of *The SpongeBob SquarePants Movie*, but it turns out not to be a word that's immediately suggested, like "goofball" or "dork." It's "hugely popular."

All right, so that's two words, but if there's anyone who isn't going to quibble about technicalities, it's the relentlessly cheerful hero of the cartoon series that, with an estimated 60 million viewers, is being touted as "the most watched kids' show in television history."

The sponge that walks like a man, his best friend Patrick the naïve (is there any other kind?) starfish, the contrary Squidward and all the quirky residents of Bikini Bottom now have a motion picture to call their own, and that is pretty much a good thing.

Yes, SpongeBob's world is undeniably better suited to the comfy confines of a half hour at home than the more demanding environs of ninety-nine minutes on the big screen. But the experience is such a breath of playful good humor that it's difficult not to be happy it's here. Though this is hardly a film you want to force adults to watch, they might not be upset if you did.

No matter what size the screen, *SpongeBob's* popularity is due to a convergence of factors that work well together largely because they all flow from the sensibility of Stephen Hillenburg, the show's creator and the film's director.

More so than any of the wildly successful Pixar films, *SpongeBob's* hand-drawn world is aimed squarely at kids. This is an unapologetically silly universe, created with a bright and colorful visual palette, where the jokes are not ashamed to be corny and the characters honestly wonder how you make the transition from being a kid to being an adult. What older viewers like is *SpongeBob's* subversive quality, the offbeat lines (the film has six writers, including Hillenburg), such as "You can't fool me, I listen to National Public Radio," that pop up when you least expect them.

Dreamy and a bit surreal around the edges, *SpongeBob* also has a stoner-hipster appeal that is reflected in the presence of musicians such as Wilco and the Flaming Lips on the soundtrack. Though its sensibility is quite different, it occupies that corner of the culture— the one in the crucial middle position of the adult-child contin- uum—that Rocky and Bullwinkle held down in the 1960s.

In changing screen size from small to big, *SpongeBob* has done some things differently. The feature has a live-action prologue and a postcredits epilogue involving a scruffy pirate crew; *Baywatch*'s David Hasselhoff, rapidly becoming something of a counterculture icon after appearing in John Waters's *A Dirty Shame*, has a key cameo playing himself.

SpongeBob also had to come up with a longer plot than usual. It centers on Bikini Bottom's most popular fast-food restaurant, the Krusty Krab, home of the ever-popular Krabby Patty, a place so successful that a branch called Krab 2 is about to open.

Our hero SpongeBob (Tom Kenny) is so fixated on being named manager of Krab 2 that he even dreams about it. He tells pal Patrick (Bill Faberbakke) that it's a lock. After all, who else has a wall filled with 374 Employee of the Month certificates?

Plankton (Doug Lawrence), however, has other, more evil dreams. He wants, in no particular order, to make his restaurant, the Chum Bucket, as popular as the Krusty Krab and to rule the world. His nefarious plans soon come to involve our heroes as well as the ruthless lord of the sea, King Neptune (Jeffrey Tambor), and his compassionate daughter Princess Mindy (Scarlett Johansson, in her first animation role).

Trying to maintain equilibrium between its origins and its theatrical ambitions, *SpongeBob* balances the television show's voice talent (including Rodger Bumpass as Squidward) with celebrity names (Alec Baldwin plays a hit man named Dennis). If it's finally no more than an extended version of the show, so light that it almost floats away, there are worse sins. Its instinctive, unstoppable cheerfulness can be, as all those millions of viewers have found, something of a tonic if you're in the mood.

Tarzan
1999

How deep and forbidding is the jungle? How piercing is an ape-man's cry? How eager is Hollywood to cash in on something that's been previously successful? That's how many times *Tarzan of the Apes*, Edgar Rice Burroughs's 1912 tale of a man raised by gorillas, has been transferred to film.

Well, maybe not quite that many times, but historians report that *Tarzan* has been turned into nearly fifty features since Elmo Lincoln created the role in 1918, and that's not counting multipart serials, television series and Jimmy Durante's comic riff as Schnarzan in a 1934 film called *Hollywood Party*.

Yet the current Disney version is the first time Burroughs's character has been done as animation, and, in the will-wonders-never-cease department, this umpteenth *Tarzan* (directed by Kevin Lima and Chris Buck) turns out to rank with the best of the group.

Combining adroit vocal casting (based on ability not box office) with an entertaining script, an unexpectedly energetic (and non-Disney musical) soundtrack and some splendid technical breakthroughs, the animated *Tarzan* underscores why this story has captivated so many people for so long.

When we think of Tarzan, moving gracefully through the trees is close to his defining characteristic, and that's where the Disney film sets a new standard. Helped by a computer software program called Deep Canvas, which adds noticeable levels of depth and dimension to backgrounds, this Tarzan can swing through the jungle in a much more exhilarating and breathtaking way than a reality-based film can hope to match.

The ape-man's supervising animator, Glen Keane, who also did the honors for the Beast in *Beauty and the Beast*, says his son's skateboarding was one of the inspirations for Tarzan's magical fluidity. Keane has also been careful to use animation's resources to give Tarzan the kind of physically convincing musculature that makes sense for someone who's lived almost his entire life among jungle animals.

Before Tarzan can dazzle with his vine-swinging, he has to get to Africa in the first place, and the story opens with an intense and convincing fire on a ship that leaves an infant boy and his parents stranded in a jungle treehouse.

The jeopardy in this film is consistently real, and Tarzan's parents are soon terminated by a fierce leopard named Sabor. That's the same animal who recently deprived silver-back gorilla parents Kala (Glenn Close, who dubbed Andie MacDowell's voice in the Tarzan film *Greystoke: The Legend of Tarzan, Lord of the Apes*) and Kerchak (Lance Henriksen, whose live-action roles would horrify this film's intended audience) of their infant son.

After a terrifying encounter with Sabor (another example of the film's inventive visual style), Kala finds the boy and tells Kerchak she wants to raise him. "It's not our kind," Kerchak responds unenthusiastically, but though wives always win these kinds of face-offs in Disney films, Kerchak has the last word. The boy can stay, but he won't consider him his son.

With its theme of acceptance and belonging, of a son wanting to prove himself to a father figure thus set, *Tarzan* can't be accused of not fitting snugly into the tradition of well-meaning Disney animation.

But though many of the studio's cartoon features have become disappointingly pro forma, *Tarzan* puts the formula on a higher level than usual, with individual elements better conceived and executed across the board.

For one thing, the film's comic sidekicks, including gorilla galpal Terk (Rosie O'Donnell) and worrywart elephant Tantor (Wayne Knight), are actually funny. Also, though the script felt the touch of numerous hands (the studio publicity material mentions that *Gorillas in the Mist's* Tab Murphy got first crack; Bob Tzudiker & Noni White upped the family values quotient, and Dave Reynolds, who gets an "additional screenplay material" credit along with Jeffrey Stepakoff, punched up the dialogue), the result feels surprisingly of a piece.

Also effective was the decision to avoid the by-now overly familiar Broadway musical formula of having characters periodically break into song. Instead, singer-songwriter Phil Collins was retained, and he provides five original compositions that, along with Mark Mancina's score, give *Tarzan* a narrative overlay that adds coherence and energy to the proceedings.

The adult Tarzan (Tony Goldwyn), gifted with the squarest jaw since Fearless Fosdick, gets the surprise of his life when his jungle is invaded by creatures he thinks he's never seen: fellow human beings. Specifically, it's pompous guide Clayton (Brian Blessed), a professor eager to learn more about gorillas (Nigel Hawthorne) and the professor's daughter (Minnie Driver), a charming young woman whose name just happens to be Jane.

Naturally, Jane gets into trouble (with some irascible baboons) and Tarzan has to step in, leading to Jane's shocked "I'm in a tree with a man who talks to monkeys." A "me Tarzan, you Jane" sequence is all but mandatory, and how pleasantly it's presented is one of this film's many surprises.

Though they apparently never worked face to face, Goldwyn and Driver are not only excellent on their own; the push-pull of their relationship is equally satisfying. *Tarzan*'s story unfolds with dangers as well as warm humor; a jungle jam session called "Trashin' the Camp" is especially hard to resist. We may have seen it all before, but when it's done up like this, experiencing it all over again is a pleasure.

Toy Story
1995

Guilt. Envy. Nervous breakdowns and rampant neuroses. If you've ever thought that toys had an easy life, *Toy Story* will set you straight.

Although its computer-generated imagery is impressive, the major surprise of this bright foray into a new kind of animation is how much cleverness has been invested in story and dialogue. Usually when a film credits seven writers, it's not a positive sign, but *Toy Story* turns out to be smart fun on a verbal as well as visual level.

Those writers (Joss Whedon, Andrew Stanton, Joel Cohen & Alec Sokolow, from a story by Stanton, director John Lasseter, Peter Docter and Joe Ranft) have kept *Toy Story* true to what has become one of Disney's most successful formulas, visible in everything from *Aladdin* to *The Nightmare Before Christmas:* Supply onscreen pratfalls and visual dazzle to keep the kids occupied while luring the adults with feisty characterizations and clever jokes about "laser envy" and plastic corrosion awareness meetings.

What is special about *Toy Story* is that although *Tin Toy*, a short codirected by Lasseter, won an Oscar in 1988, this is the first time that computer-generated animation has been successfully stretched to feature length.

By giving its normally inanimate protagonists a magical three-dimensional quality, *Toy Story* creates the kind of enchantment that must have surrounded *Snow White* on its initial release. True, computer imagery still has trouble creating people who don't look like space aliens, but this film compensates by sensibly shoving the humans to the background and focusing on those darn toys.

Echoing a concept at least as old as Tchaikovsky's *The Nutcracker Suite*, *Toy Story* showcases toys springing to life when people aren't around. But rather than being idle playthings, these toys, the possessions of a small boy named Andy, turn out to be careworn adults, easily overwhelmed by worries and woes.

Rex, the toy dinosaur (Wallace Shawn), is in the grip of a crisis of confidence, worried that while he's "going for fearsome, it just comes off as annoying." Bo Peep (Annie Potts) fears her come-hither looks are being wasted, and gruff Mr. Potato Head (Don Rickles) alternates between grousing about mistreatment at the hands of Andy's infant sister ("ages three and up; it's on my box") to yearning for a Mrs. Potato Head to end his solitude.

Riding herd over these troubled folks is Woody (Tom Hanks), an old-fashioned floppy pull-string toy that has been Andy's favorite forever. So while the others worry that they'll turn into "next month's garage sale fodder" when new toys appear on the scene, Woody tries to calm them down with a pep talk about "being here for Andy when he needs us."

But the birthday party that opens the film turns out to be a serious shock to Woody. When Andy is given a Buzz Lightyear space ranger action figure, complete with "more gadgets than a Swiss army knife," it appears there's a new top toy in town.

Given to saying "to infinity, and beyond" at slight provocation, Buzz (Tim Allen) is one of *Toy Story*'s pleasant surprises, because, unlike the rest of Andy's possessions, he doesn't realize that he really is a toy. Self-absorbed and delusional, given to such fatuous pronouncements as "I come in peace," Buzz thinks he is a genuine space ranger, on a mission to save the universe from the menacing Emperor Zurg.

All this drives Woody crazy, as does the fact that Buzz's presence increasingly places his position as Andy's favorite toy in jeopardy. As *Toy Story* amusingly progresses, Woody and Buzz confront these unpleasant realities and face the discomforting need to cooperate with each other to save themselves from a variety of troubles.

Starting with Tom Hanks, who brings an invaluable heft and believability to Woody, *Toy Story* is one of the best voiced animated features in memory, with all the actors (as well as Randy Newman, who contributed three songs and the score) making their presences strongly felt.

Continuously inventive, *Toy Story* has a number of cheerful set pieces that keep it lively. One of the cleverest is a visit to the fast-food Pizza Planet, where Buzz and Woody end up inside a kind of gum-ball machine whose inhabitants worship the claw that conveys them to the outside world. It's a deft, wacky sequence, complete with Woody shouting, "Stop it, you zealots," at the three-eyed figures, and it typifies why *Toy Story* is a captivating first step along animation's most promising new frontier.

Toy Story was also the first step in making its production company, Pixar, an unchallenged entertainment industry powerhouse.

Toy Story 2
1999

Thirteen years have elapsed between the first Pixar film, an Oscar-nominated two-minute short about an adventurous lamp called *Luxo*

Jr., and the current *Toy Story 2*, the elaborate successor to one of the highest grossing animated features of all time. But less has changed than you might think.

For what *Luxo Jr.* (newly visible as part of a brief Pixar promo that precedes all *Toy 2* showings) and the new film have in common, aside from the gleeful guiding hand of director John Lasseter, is their pleasingly clever and fiendishly inventive sense of humor. Whether it be the first *Toy Story* or last year's *A Bug's Life*, to see a Pixar film is to know that the comedy will be as smart as the visuals are impressive. *Toy Story 2*, thankfully, is no exception to that rule.

Lively and good-humored with a great sense of fun, *Toy Story 2* picks up the story where its predecessor left off. Improvements in computer technology have made for advances such as greater use of depth of field, but the characters of frontier sheriff Woody (Tom Hanks), overmotivated spaceman Buzz Lightyear (Tim Allen) and the rest of the toys in young Andy's room are just as we remember them.

It's one of the gifts of the gang at Pixar (which includes screenwriters Andrew Stanton, Rita Hsiao, Doug Chamberlin & Chris Weber, and story folks Lasseter, Peter Docter, Ash Brannon and Stanton) that they're able to come up with convincing dilemmas for toys to contend with and us to care about, surely no simple task.

This time, the scenarios intrigue on both a psychological and an adventure level, making light and lively work of unexpected but accessible themes like the mortality of playthings and, believe it or not, the very question of what it means to be a toy. When Lee Unkrich (a codirector along with Brannon) is quoted in the press notes about "plumbing the depths of a toy's psyche," he is not really kidding.

After an amusing *Star Wars* opening focusing on a scary new Buzz Lightyear video game, *Toy 2*'s scene shifts to the familiar confines of Andy's bedroom, where Woody is preparing the gang for the few days he will be absent. He's accompanying Andy to one of the boy's favorite activities, a weekend of Cowboy Camp.

But everything changes when a tear in Woody's arm causes him to be unceremoniously left behind, bringing on a toy-sized midlife crisis accompanied by nightmares and whispered repetitions of the fatal words: "Woody's been shelved."

Still wounded, Woody is brought out of himself by the even graver dilemma of Wheezy (Joe Ranft, the German caterpillar Heimlich in *A Bug's Life*), a squeak-toy penguin who's lost his squeaker and is about to be consigned to hell on Earth for toys: the garage sale. "We're only a stitch away," he says gravely, pointing to Woody's arm and the sale table, "from here to there."

In an attempt to save Wheezy from that unkind fate, Woody comes to the attention of the rotund Al of Al's Toy Barn (Wayne Knight), an unscrupulous collector who pilfers Woody when he realizes how valuable a toy he is. A bit like the current literary star Harry Potter, Woody has never known anything about his own illustrious past.

Back at Al's apartment, he watches tapes of *Woody's Roundup*, the super-popular *Howdy Doody*–type television show he was the centerpiece of, and is exposed to so much Woody paraphernalia, from lunch boxes to record players, that it's all he can do to respond, "I'm officially freaked out here."

Helping in Woody's education are his fellow *Roundup* toys, long-lost collaborators he never knew he had, such as his horse Bullseye, irrepressible cowgirl Jessie (Joan Cusack) and the canny old prospector Stinky Pete (Kelsey Grammer), still, Jessie says in awed tones, "mint in the box."

Woody also learns that Al is planning to sell the *Roundup* gang to a posh Japanese toy museum, a situation that leads to many of *Toy 2*'s most engaging dilemmas. What does Woody owe to his *Roundup* compatriots, who will have to experience the horrors of storage if he breaks up the set? What does he owe to Buzz and the rest of his posse, who are even now moving heaven and Earth to try to rescue him? What does he owe to Andy, the owner he loves and who dearly loves him back, given the inevitability that Andy will grow up and abandon him? What the heck is a toy to do?

Even if the existential despair of toys has never previously interested you, *Toy Story 2* makes it all irresistibly comic as well as surprisingly emotional. Fast-moving and busy, piling jeopardy on top of jeopardy, but still finding time for an amusing subplot involving a Tour Guide Barbie, *Toy Story 2* may not have the most original title, but everything else about it is, well, mint in the box.

Wallace & Gromit: The Curse of the Were-Rabbit
2005

Wallace & Gromit are ready for their close-up. And do we ever need them.

Superstars of comic short films, this intrepid clay animation duo makes its much-anticipated move to features in *Wallace & Gromit: The Curse of the Were-Rabbit*, puckishly characterized by creator Nick Park as "the first vegetarian horror movie ever."

In a movie culture in which creativity is often strangled in its cradle, it is welcome and astonishing to see how successful Park's unlikely pairing of his own idiosyncratic sensibility with the most labor-intensive form of animation has become. "It was simply my own taste, the kind of film I wanted to see," the film's British cowriter and codirector said at Cannes about *Wallace & Gromit*'s origins. "It always astonishes me how universal it's become."

Park's joining more than fifteen years ago of a genially hapless inventor who's mad for cheese and his poker-faced know-it-all silent dog has led to three Oscar nominations and two statuettes for the dynamic duo. Park delayed the team's feature debut, which boasts Helena Bonham Carter and Ralph Fiennes as voice talent, until he could come up with a plot worthy of their shenanigans, and he has.

Working with a trio of cowriters (Steve Box, who also codirected, Bob Baker and Mark Burton, all previous collaborators), Park and company came up with the notion of a werewolf movie about rabbits who were ravenous for vegetables, not human flesh.

Those familiar with classics such as *Frankenstein* and *The Wolf Man* will be charmed by how well the tropes of horror lend themselves to this kind of spoofing, and viewers of all sorts will be delighted with a film that puts a smile on your face and leaves it there for the duration.

Undaunted by previous mishaps, Wallace remains the epitome of madcap inventing, coming up with wacky machines such as the Mind-O-Matic and the Bun-Vac 6000. He still loves cheese (who else has books titled *East of Edam* and *Fromage to Eternity* in his library shelves) and still gets despairing looks of polite disbelief from Gromit, the only dog whose hobby is knitting.

What is different is the pair's new business, a humane, cruelty-free way to rid gardens of invading rabbits that goes by the name of Anti-Pesto. It's an especially booming business in Wallace & Gromit's neck of the woods, a neighborhood obsessed with its Giant Vegetable Competition, in particular the impending 517th annual edition.

Then, when the moon is full, there appears on the scene a monstrous rabbit with the strength of ten, teeth the size of ax blades and ears like terrible tombstones. He lays waste to the neighborhood produce and enables the filmmakers, as Park explains, "to use typical horror movie characters like the skeptical policeman and a vicar who spouts all kinds of mumbo-jumbo about the beast within."

Especially energized by the disaster is Lady Tottington (Bonham Carter), bestower of the prized Golden Carrot, a local eco-toff who wants the beast humanely removed. Being something of a peerage groupie, Wallace (voiced as he has since the beginning by Peter Sallis) is only too eager to oblige. But standing in the way is milady's bloodthirsty suitor, Victor Quartermaine (Fiennes), who is determined to blow everything that moves to Kingdom Come.

The last thing you expect from a *Wallace & Gromit* film is surprising plot twists, but *Curse of the Were-Rabbit* boasts a few. It also has the kind of wonderful cartoon chases that were a beloved feature of the shorts as well as a riff on *King Kong* and a monster transformation sequence that is a treat.

Most of all, *Wallace & Gromit* retains the clever, one-of-a-kind sensibility that made its shorter predecessors so delightful. With every studio comedy looking for a formula for success, it's refreshing to find a heroically whimsical film that succeeds by following no formula known to dog or man.

Though *Wallace & Gromit* makes some use of computer-generated images for story elements, such as fog, its characters are still created frame by painstaking frame in the old-fashioned stop-motion way. The process is so meticulous, taking days to produce seconds of finished film, that *Curse of the Were-Rabbit* took nearly five years to finish, including an eighteen-month shooting schedule. That's a lot of work for an eighty-five-minute film, but, if you want to know the truth, it was worth every second.

Curse of the Were-Rabbit's *best animated feature Oscar was Park's fourth victory, his third for a Wallace & Gromit project.*

Part Five

SPECTACLE

Introduction

When *Sunset Boulevard*'s silent film star Norma Desmond famously said, "I am big, it's the pictures that got small," she was not referring to the films in this section.

For though they come from a variety of genres, including science fiction, historical re-creation and comic book action, these motion pictures have one thing in common: They cry out to be seen on the biggest screen possible.

Whether you're watching bugs battle humans in *Starship Troopers* or Americans take on Germans in *Saving Private Ryan*, watching the action unfold on your mobile phone is not recommended.

(In fact, there is a school of thought that says *Ryan* lost the 1998 best picture Academy Award to *Shakespeare in Love* because the latter played better on the small screen video version Oscar voters often end up watching.)

More than that, even the biggest zealots for distributing films to home screens at the same time as movie houses admit that these types of films will always enter the world first as purely theatrical releases. The scale simply demands it.

Composing for the big screen is a particular talent, so the people who are celebrated for the ability to do it well—Peter Jackson, Steven Spielberg, Ridley Scott—end up appearing on the list more than once.

Even if you have a knack for doing it well, spectacle is such a challenging genre that the best examples of it are often sequels. Listed here are *The Mummy Returns*, *Spider-Man 2*, *Terminator 3* and *X2: X-Men United*, as well as the final installment of *The Lord of the Rings*, the third time out for *War of the Worlds* and the umpteenth *Star Trek* extravaganza. Practice makes perfect, especially when the stakes are high.

Batman Begins
2005

Batman has finally come home. Not just to a story that painstakingly details his origins but to an ominous style that suits it beautifully.

Christopher Nolan's *Batman Begins* disdains the mindless camp and compulsive weirdness that mostly characterized its quartet of predecessors and unapologetically positions its hero at the dark end of the street. With Christian Bale in the title role, this is a film noir Batman, a brooding, disturbing piece of work that starts slowly but ends up crafting a world that just might haunt your dreams. In doing this, Nolan, who cowrote with comic book specialist David S. Goyer, has in effect brought the franchise back to its modern origins. That would be the appearance in 1986, three years before the first Tim Burton film, of Frank Miller's somber and ominous graphic novel *Batman: The Dark Knight Returns*, which repositioned Bob Kane's 1939 Caped Crusader as a contemporary figure of almost existential torment.

Nolan's intention with *Batman Begins*, however, is to go beyond this and create a myth grounded, as much as myth can be, in plain reality. He wants his story to be as plausible as possible, a human drama set in a believable world that resembles one we could live in but prefer not to. A film that underlines the notion that Batman is that unlikely comic-book hero who does without special powers, someone, the director has said, who "really is just a guy that does a lot of push-ups." A heck of a lot of push-ups.

Nolan was a shrewd choice to revive a franchise that has gone eight years without a film. One of the qualities shared by his exceptional but otherwise diverse trio of previous films (*Following, Memento, Insomnia*) is how skillfully they are put together on a craft level. This *Batman* is a carefully thought out and consummately well-made piece of work, a serious comic-book adaptation that is driven by story, psychology and reality, not by special effects.

In fact, with Wally Pfister (who shot Nolan's last two films) as cinematographer, *Batman Begins* tries, despite using multiple special-effects houses, to avoid computer-generated imagery when it can. The film relies instead on shooting in real locations (from the streets of Chicago to a glacier in Vatnajokull, Iceland) and extensive use of miniatures, albeit some whose height of thirty-five feet was made possible by constructing the sets in an enormous former blimp hangar with ceilings that rise to two hundred feet. Nolan also did without a second unit, preferring the tonal unity he felt would come from directing everything himself.

Though his name might not have initially been on everyone's lips, Christian Bale turns out to be an excellent fit for Nolan's conception of the Dark Knight. And though he gained back the sixty-three pounds he lost for *The Machinist* and added an extra twenty for good measure, there is a leanness, a sense of purpose about his performance.

Always a humorless, almost sullen actor, Bale uses those qualities to create a painfully earnest character driven to a life of fighting crime almost against his will. Bale even employed the physically uncomfortable Batsuit to his advantage: "I used the pain," he has said, "as fuel for the character's anger."

Though Batman's alter ego remains wealthy socialite Bruce Wayne, being the Dark Knight is not a rich man's whim. *Batman Begins* shows us in great detail how Wayne became phobic about bats as a small boy, saw that phobia contribute to his parents' untimely deaths and, driven by despair, ended up fighting the world in a prison in Bhutan.

It's there that Wayne meets the shadowy Ducard (Liam Neeson), the emissary of Ra's al Ghul and the sinister League of Shadows, a group fanatically dedicated to the stamping out of evil. They offer to make him one of their own, and, in the group's Himalayan redoubt, Wayne learns more than ninja fighting techniques and methods of psychological warfare. He learns that embracing his own fear, specifically that old phobia toward bats, will be the key to his transformation.

If this scenario sounds a bit standard, it is in fact the least involving part of the film, for *Batman Begins* does not immediately kick into its highest gear. Though the early days of a hero have an intrinsic interest, especially when they are as thought out as they are here, this backstory has a tendency to feel too pulp-fiction familiar to enthrall completely.

Also a problem, and one that recurs sporadically through the film, is that not all of *Batman's* actors have equal facility with the admittedly difficult assignment of being both comic-book archetypes and real people. Bale, who seems to feel this role in his bones, handles it with aplomb, but Neeson and Katie Holmes, who appears later as a putative romantic interest, never seem to be sure which side of the coin to favor at any given moment.

Once Wayne returns to Gotham and sets his mind on being Batman, the noir possibilities of a black-caped avenger and a city at night help things immeasurably. Not only does production designer Nathan Crowley's *Blade Runner*–influenced look suit the film, but the specifics of Batman lore—the cave, the car, the suit, the swooping late-night flights—benefit from that dark treatment as well.

The Gotham scenario also showcases the best of *Batman's* supporting cast. On the side of light, Michael Caine as Alfred Pennyworth, a Wayne family retainer, and Morgan Freeman as Lucius Fox, the film's version of James Bond's armourer, Q, make this kind of acting look easier than it is.

On the side of darkness, Cillian Murphy, memorable in Danny Boyle's *28 Days Later,* is terrifically chilling as the evil Dr. Jonathan Crane and his alter ego, the Scarecrow, who can turn a simple burlap sack into an object of total dread.

The most encouraging thing about *Batman Begins* is how individual director/cowriter Nolan has managed to make a $180-million epic. Director of photography Pfister, interviewed in *American Cinematographer* magazine, offered an explanation.

"One of the reasons Chris likes me to operate [the camera] is that it shrinks down the whole process for him," Pfister says. "We could be sitting on the set with 150 people and huge setups, but when the camera rolls, it's just Chris sitting next to me with a little monitor, and the actors right there in front of us. His entire universe is in that twelve-foot area, which brings the process down to a more personal level."

Bringing an auteur sensibility to blockbuster material may sound next door to impossible, but *Batman Begins* shows it can be done. If you're willing to do the push-ups.

Black Hawk Down
2001

Black Hawk Down is more than simply, as the opening title says, "Based on an Actual Event." As much as a movie ever has, it puts you completely inside that event, brilliantly taking you where most people, especially those who were actually there, wouldn't want to be.

For "realism" is a mild word for the way director Ridley Scott sweepingly re-creates 1993's fierce fifteen-hour battle between besieged U.S. troops and Somali fighters on the streets of Mogadishu, Somalia, in which eighteen Americans were killed and seventy-three badly injured, the biggest totals since Vietnam at that point. His is a triumph of pure filmmaking, a pitiless, unrelenting, no-excuses war movie so convincing that it's frequently difficult to believe it is a staged re-creation. *Black Hawk Down* can be tough to sit through, but the fluidity and skill involved are so impressive that it's an exhilarating experience as well.

Scott's film is based on and takes its spirit from Mark Bowden's fiendishly detailed, un-put-downable nonfiction book of the same name. Cinematic in its vividness and narrative drive, Bowden's work was embraced by military and civilian readers for its ability to penetrate the psychological states of its fighters as they struggled to survive in a locale as strange and dislocating to them as the canals of Mars.

To make this kind of a film, to re-create other worlds persuasively, has been Scott's strength as a director from his 1978 *The Duellists* debut through *Alien*, *Blade Runner* and *Gladiator*. Few directors have Scott's exceptional visual sense, his decades of experience and his ability to orchestrate large-scale action, all of which are critical to *Black*

Hawk's success. As faithfully adapted from Bowden's book by Ken Nolan, *Black Hawk* also plays to Scott's strength by keeping dialogue to a minimum. It's a cleanly told story with a noticeable absence of movie frippery, a narrative of such impeccable matter-of-factness that it respects the professionalism of the combatants while displaying unflinching honesty about mistakes made.

"It seemed to me that the film had to be an anatomy of the military process," is how the director describes things. "That's why there's no fat in the picture."

Though the result is much closer to *Battle of Algiers* than *Pearl Harbor*, this film is also an unlikely triumph for producer Jerry Bruckheimer, whose usual M.O. is so different that *Black Hawk* for the most part appears to be an anti-Bruckheimer film. Yet the producer understood what was called for here, and he put his extensive experience to use in giving the project what it needed, including cajoling the U.S. Army into providing Rangers and Black Hawk helicopters, and persuading the king of Morocco, where the film was shot, to allow these troops onto his soil.

The usual device of type on screen briefly sets up *Black Hawk*'s backstory. Famine, starvation and brutal clan warfare had combined to bring a United Nations peacekeeping mission to Somalia, but the country's top warlord, Mohammed Farah Aidid, is impervious to its blandishments. To put pressure on Aidid, the U.S. military, here personified by Major General William F. Garrison (Sam Shepard at his laconic best), decided to kidnap the people closest to him. On October 3, 1993, a raid was set to extract the warlord's top lieutenants from an area called Bakara Market. "It's an entirely hostile district," the general tells his men, and he adds, in what proves to be very much of an understatement: "Don't underestimate their capabilities."

Going in was a combination of the army's top units, the Rangers and the Delta Force, troops that turned out to be rivals. Though very much of an elite group themselves, the Rangers were younger and less experienced than the intimidating "D-boys," who wore their hair long, taped their blood types to their boots before going into combat and in general made their own rules.

It's a mark of the kind of forty-speaking-part ensemble film *Black Hawk Down* is that though there are several recognizable faces—Josh Hartnett as an idealist, Ewan McGregor as a desk jockey eager for combat, Tom Sizemore as the leader of a vehicle convoy, *Chopper's* Eric Bana and William Fichtner as Delta aces, *The Patriot* villain Jason Isaacs as a Ranger captain—no one person stands out from the excellent group. Also, though the book provided extensive back stories for many individuals, the film wisely does without them. There wouldn't be room and, in the context here, they're unnecessary.

The operation, scheduled for an hour or less, starts to unravel almost immediately. An accident leads to delays that allow the Somali fighters to organize and attack. Suddenly, the American troops are hip-deep in a nightmare in which a large, well-armed army camouflaged in street clothes materializes out of nowhere and envelops everyone in what Bowden says veterans call "the fog of war." Making things even more chaotic is the Ranger determination, stated in a creed they take seriously, never to "leave a fallen comrade to fall into the hands of the enemy."

Once the fighting begins, it's difficult to tell the soldiers apart, which is why Scott broke with actuality and mandated names on Ranger helmets. (The D-boys are identifiable by the small black helmets they wear.) But the scene and not the individual is the focus here, and as edited by *JFK* Oscar winner Pietro Scalia and shot by Slawomir Idziak, the confusion seems part of the point. Idziak, best known for working with Polish director Krzysztof Kieslowski, seems an unlikely choice here, but by using from six to eight cameras for each setup, he does a mind-bending job of counterfeiting reality.

Though it is undeniably brutal, with several unnervingly bloody sequences, the violence in *Black Hawk Down* is the opposite of exploitative. And the film also takes time at least to nod toward some more complex questions: from exploring whether we should have been in

Somalia in the first place to examining the complicated nature of what is conventionally described as heroism.

With its delineation of how well American troops did under killingly adverse conditions, *Black Hawk Down* shows why the military elements involved in the battle consider it a victory. Yet, paradoxically, the tone of this film is anything but triumphal. The sadness of so many deaths, including an estimated five hundred Somalis, that seem so pointless is strongly felt.

A line from Plato that opens the film is especially haunting by the close: "Only the dead," he wrote, "have seen the end of war."

Kingdom of Heaven
2005

Jerusalem has the power to drive men mad.

It's the paradox of this city sacred to three great religions that there are those who would kill to defend its holiness. That's as true today as it was nearly a thousand years ago, when Pope Urban II's cry of "God wills it!" sent Europe's knights to the Middle East in a series of bloody expeditions against Islam that we know as the Crusades.

Director Ridley Scott, long fascinated by knights, those heroic Boy Scouts of yore, has made a film about not the entire two-century span of those invasions but rather a brief and pointed moment between the Second and Third Crusades when the fate of Jerusalem and the region hung in the balance.

Scott, the epic director of our time (*Gladiator, Blade Runner, Black Hawk Down*), is not what you would call a political animal, but in *Kingdom of Heaven* he delivers that rare big-star blockbuster (Orlando Bloom, Liam Neeson and Jeremy Irons top the cast) that still manages to say something relevant.

Working from a strong script by William Monahan and making full use of that solid cast and his own impeccable skill with imagery,

Scott has fashioned an impressive film that resonates with lessons for an age when Crusaders, this time in American uniforms, are trying to save the Middle East from itself yet one more time.

Scott did not necessarily set out to do that. He wanted an action-adventure film that would provide satisfactions commensurate with (and able to repay) its estimated budget of $140 million. He's provided huge battles, spectacular vistas and slash-and-burn action, but given the times the film was made in, it is fortunate, and perhaps fated, that it turned into something more.

Kingdom of Heaven is not one of those cheerful combat movies that believe bloodletting is the answer to everything. It is a violent movie that laments a peace that didn't last, a downbeat but compelling epic that looks to have lost faith in the value of cinematic savagery for its own sake. If you combine this film with Scott's recent *Black Hawk Down*, you find the director in a place where he is no longer exulting in his ability simply to put violence on the screen; he wants you to feel its searing effects as well.

What Scott and screenwriter Monahan do believe in is the code of chivalry, the notion that, as one character puts it, "holiness is in right action and courage on behalf of those who cannot defend themselves." The knight who initially exemplifies these traits is Godfrey of Ibelin (a powerful Neeson), a nobleman introduced returning to France in 1184 accompanied by a member of the military order of Hospitaler (David Thewlis). Back in the East, Jerusalem has been under Crusader rule for nearly a century, but Godfrey has returned on a personal mission: He wants to find a son he's never acknowledged.

That son is humble blacksmith Balian (Bloom), who gets the news about his parentage just as he's suffered a terrible personal tragedy. Godfrey asks his son to join him in Jerusalem, "a new land at the end of the world" where "you are not who you are born but who you can make yourself to be."

There wouldn't be much of a movie if Balian didn't decide to take the trip, but he is initially more of a brooder—albeit a very masculine one—than a man of action. He worries about his faith and the state of his soul, worries that he is "outside God's grace." Truly, no one ever needed a new world more.

Once in Jerusalem, Balian follows his father's advice and aligns himself with the forces of light. They are King Baldwin IV (an especially effective Edward Norton), an intrepid ruler so eaten away by leprosy he wears a silver mask over his face at all times, and Tiberias (Irons), the man who runs the city for him.

Representing the dark side are the ambitious Guy de Lusignan (Marton Csokas) and the wily Reynald de Chatillon (Brendan Gleeson, always irresistible). Bridging the gap between good and evil is Sibylla (Eva Green of Bertolucci's *The Dreamers*), sister of the king, wife of Guy and a woman who just happens to have a weakness for brooding types newly arrived from France.

What makes the bad guys the bad guys, interestingly enough, is that they are aligned with religious zealots who are sworn enemies of a fragile truce that has existed for a precious few years under the sponsorship of Baldwin. His opposite number, the great general Saladin, is a hero who faces equal pressures from fanatics on his side of the issue to go to war for the greater glory of God.

Saladin is intensely played by the charismatic Ghassan Massoud, a major film star in his native Syria. *Kingdom*'s willingness to cast its net that far to ensure a strong performance is a sign of how scrupulously careful the film has been to be fair to both sides, not just for political reasons but to ensure good drama. It's a quest that has succeeded on all counts.

William Monahan's script for *Kingdom of Heaven* is not always convincing, but (except for liberties taken with Balian) it does a better-than-expected job of staying as close as it could to the reality of its characters' lives while tailoring them to the needs of a major motion picture. Howler lines such as "I once fought two days with an arrow through my testicles" are kept to a minimum, and the dialogue is largely intelligent and to the point.

The star of *Kingdom of Heaven* is not the script or any of the actors, it is the director's unmatched gift for the visual. Shooting in Morocco and Spain, he created a physical replica of the walls of Jerusalem by using 6,000 tons of plaster, then he masterfully tweaked the result with digital technology.

Working with editor Dody Dorn (who cut Christopher Nolan's very different *Memento*) and composer Harry Gregson-Williams, he knows just how to pace battle scenes, how to intercut aerial master shots with intimate details, and he refuses to linger on the effects of violence more than he has to.

Collaborating for not the first time with his key production crew—cinematographer John Mathieson, production designer Arthur Max and costume designer Janty Yates—Scott has accomplished the difficult feat of making his film look as real as it is exotic.

Scott and company have become so accomplished at re-creating history that the results have a welcome offhanded quality that makes them spectacular without seeming showy. No matter what we're looking at, we're thinking, "It must have looked like that." For *Kingdom of Heaven*, a better compliment would be hard to find.

The Lord of the Rings: The Fellowship of the Ring
2001

With an endeavor such as *The Lord of the Rings* trilogy, it's the numbers that catch your eye first—and how could they not? An unprecedented three feature films shot simultaneously in 274 days spread over fifteen months at a cost of nearly $300 million are enough to get anyone's attention. Not to mention 26,000 extras and a special foam-latexing oven for baking prosthetic devices—including 1,600 pairs of feet and ears—that ran twenty-four hours a day, seven days a week, including Christmas and New Year's Day.

Those figures fascinate but, as directed by Peter Jackson, *The Fellowship of the Ring* makes you forget all about them. Made with intelligence, imagination, passion and skill, propulsively paced and shot through with an aged-in-oak sense of wonder, the trilogy's first film so thrillingly catches us up in its sweeping story that nothing matters but the vivid and compelling events unfolding on the screen.

What a story it is, overflowing with invention, character and event. Here can be found hairbreadth escapes and heroism in the face of terrifying evil, violent battles and tender sentiments ("I would rather share one lifetime with you than face all the ages of mankind alone"). The basic story line—nine individuals on a desperate quest to save the world—couldn't be simpler, but the incidents surrounding it, and the very nature of that world, couldn't be more satisfyingly complex. Which is what J.R.R. Tolkien intended.

An Oxford scholar and a neo-Luddite who never owned a car, Tolkien was a procrastinator and a perfectionist, which is why it took him fourteen years to finish his masterwork of more than 1,000 pages; a publisher's edict turned it into a trilogy, a form the author apparently genially detested.

The Lord of the Rings is set in Middle-earth, a fantasy world with strong parallels to our own, where striving humans share space with numerous others races, including fierce dwarfs, potent wizards, ethereal elves, three-foot-six-inch lovers of creature comforts called "hobbits," and several types of evil creatures all owing allegiance to the dread Sauron, the Dark Lord of Mordor.

What's made Tolkien's work an overwhelming success with readers since its publication in 1954 is the extraordinary density with which he imagined this world. The *Rings* trilogy comes complete with more than one hundred pages of complex appendixes, including maps and detailed genealogies, and Tolkien, a celebrated philologist, invented several complete languages for his characters. The whole idea, the writer said, was for readers "simply to get inside this story and take it in a sense of actual history."

It is the great triumph of Jackson's work that he accomplishes this on screen with just as much verve and spirit as Tolkien did on the page—which is not to say that *Fellowship*'s script (by Fran Walsh &

Philippa Boyens & Jackson) is an exact copy of the book. Such popular characters as Tom Bombadil (described by *Wired* magazine as a "proto-hippie tree-hugger") are gone, and the few women in the story have had their roles deftly upgraded.

It's more that Jackson, a fan of the book for decades, has somehow infused his own unwavering belief into the project. Because *Fellowship* means so much to him, he has brought cast, crew and audience along and done it in a way that pleases devotees yet very much includes people who wouldn't know a hobbit from a shoe tree.

As director, coproducer and cowriter, Jackson did everything with an eye to serving the story, to enhancing the texture of its reality. That includes having characters speaking in one of the elfish languages when appropriate (with subtitles), using as many as nine individual units to shoot in the remotest and most strangely scenic corners of New Zealand (the director's home) and planting, a year before shooting was to begin, 5,000 cubic meters of appropriate vegetation in the part of the country selected to be the hobbits' home area.

The most important thing Jackson has done, however, is pay attention to character. This is not a psychological drama, as was Jackson's earlier triumph, the penetrating *Heavenly Creatures*; its protagonists are unapologetically mythic. But having someone who has an interest in, and insight into, the intricacies of human nature in charge here brings substance and authenticity to the table. It's the rarest thing to have a director with that kind of perception eager to take on an action-adventure epic with a massive budget, and it makes all the difference.

The *Fellowship* characters are not only drawn acutely, they have been cast with the same shrewdness, even if some choices seemed counterintuitive. Though it is no shock to say that the exceptional Cate Blanchett is excellent as the elf queen Galadriel, it is much more of a pleasant surprise to report that Liv Tyler does some of her best work ever as the elf princess Arwen. And as for the nine actors who do superb ensemble work as the fellowship (Elijah Wood, Ian McKellen, Viggo Mortensen, Sean Astin, John Rhys-Davies, Billy Boyd, Dominic Monaghan, Orlando Bloom and Sean Bean), nothing says more about the close bond they achieved than that they all had themselves tattooed with the number 9 in one of Tolkien's invented languages. That includes Sir Ian, the magisterial sixty-two-year-old known for his superb interpretations of Shakespeare.

As the hobbit Frodo, Wood may be the heart of the quest, Mortensen as the human Aragorn may be brooding and electric on screen, but it is McKellen as the wizard Gandalf who is the film's irreplaceable central figure. Radiating power and wisdom, tossing out piercing looks as deftly as he wields his magical staff, McKellen's exceptional presence makes the actuality of *Fellowship* unassailable. To see the man who was the fey James Whale in *Gods and Monsters* in full battle mode against the forces of evil is to understand what a great actor can accomplish.

Fellowship begins with Gandalf's visit to the hobbit Bilbo Baggins (a charming Ian Holm), an old friend who is having a birthday. Bilbo has had a magic ring in his possession for many years, and Gandalf reveals to him (and us) its terrifying history. It was a ring of power forged by the dark lord Sauron with the capacity to enslave all the free peoples of Middle-earth, hence the line: "One ring to rule them all." Although no longer in Sauron's possession, it is a ring with a mind of its own, always eager to get back to its dread creator, who is now actively searching for it as well.

Just a thin gold band, it has an almost limitless ability to corrupt. Gandalf insists that Bilbo give the ring to his nephew Frodo while he goes off to consult with another powerful wizard, Saruman the White (British horror veteran Christopher Lee). At a meeting in the land of the elf Elrond (Hugo Weaving), it is determined that for Middle-earth to survive the ring must be returned to the fires of the distant and perilous Mount Doom—where it was forged—and destroyed. Frodo is to be the ring bearer, and he's accompanied on his terrible journey not only by Gandalf and Aragorn, but also his hobbit friends Sam (Astin), Pippin (Boyd) and Merry (Monaghan), the all-too-human Boromir

(Bean), the unflappable elf Legolas (Bloom) and the fierce dwarf Gimli (Rhys-Davies). So is born the Fellowship of the Ring, whose adventures, set to Howard Shore's stirring music, we avidly follow.

The care taken with even the smallest detail by Jackson's production team makes all this seem surprisingly realistic. Conceptual artists and Tolkien illustrators Alan Lee and John Howe, cinematographer Andrew Lesnie, production designer Grant Major, editor John Gilbert, costume designer Ngila Dickson, effects wizards Richard Taylor and Jim Rygiel and others too numerous to mention all deserve to take a bow.

Interestingly enough, many of the film's special effects don't rely on computers. Expert use was made of more than sixty intricately constructed miniatures, as well as of forced perspective, a venerable way to fool the eye by means of the shrewd employment of camera angles and stand-ins of different heights. When computers were used, it was the New Zealand–based Weta Digital that employed them. Their look is a bit rougher and less polished than we're used to from domestic companies such as ILM, but it's a style that suits this rough-and-ready film.

Though *The Fellowship of the Ring* is an impressive two hours and fifty-eight minutes long, its sense of adventure never flags, with one peril leading naturally to the next. The film's only real drawback, in fact, is that it will be a full year until the next installment, *The Two Towers*, is allowed on screen. Some of us are already counting the days.

The Lord of the Rings: The Return of the King
2003

It took one ring to rule them all, and now there's one film to end it all, to bring to a close the cinematic epic of our time, the one by which all others will be judged. *The Lord of the Rings: The Return of the King* has finally arrived.

Powerfully imagined two times over, first by the matchless fantasy mind of J.R.R. Tolkien and then by the bravura filmmaking of director Peter Jackson and a cast and crew that reached 2,400 souls, *The Return of the King* is a fitting climax to a story about the quest to rescue the world from evil that has had us profoundly in its grip from the beginning.

Like anything restlessly and eagerly anticipated, *The Return of the King* will inevitably be quibbled with. At three hours and twenty minutes, it is not only formidably long but also unsure where it ought to end. The film's critical human moments include some of the strongest of the trilogy, but because *Return* by definition has to showcase battles that will literally end all battles, the brevity of those character beats at times threatens to unravel the critical human thread.

That doesn't happen, which is a tribute not only to this film but to the deep emotional connection with its numerous characters we've stored up and carry with us. In its belief that this story has meaning as well as excitement, *Return*, written by Fran Walsh & Philippa Boyens & Jackson, has made its made-up world as completely real on the psychological level as its up-to-the-moment visual effects have on the physical.

Not only have we spent hour after involving hour with these characters, but the actors who play them (and to whom they will likely be forever linked) have put in so much time with them—literally years—that they've to an unusual degree actually lived these parts.

To look at the faces of Elijah Wood as Frodo and Sean Astin as Sam, Ian McKellen as Gandalf and Viggo Mortensen as Aragorn, is to see the signs of triumphs and disappointments that only the genuine passage of time can create. As Jackson himself has said, "the moment you film a close-up of Ian McKellen, you don't want to cut to a wide shot anymore because Ian is so compelling."

It can be easier (albeit considerably expensive) to come up with a persuasive physical reality than a psychological one, but that shouldn't detract from how much success the *Rings* team, led by production designer Grant Major and cinematographer Andrew Lesnie, has had in doing so here. This film's crowning achievement is white-stoned Minas Tirith, the kingdom of Gondor's seven-hundred-foot, seven-level city of kings that, in a smooth combination of miniatures and built sets, looks like a flabbergasting cross between an Italian hill town and a Beverly Hills wedding cake.

Though viewers of the trilogy have likely seen enough bad-tempered orcs to last them a lifetime, *Return* has made the third part's new creatures as convincing (and the monstrous spider Shelob arguably too much so) as they are fantastical. Most impressive are the fell beasts, bat-like flying dragons with seventy-foot wingspans, and the mumakil, eight-stories-tall combat elephants that look as large as mountains. Most people just get out of the way.

Yet for all this, it is as characteristic of *Return* as its predecessors that some of its most memorable moments are its simplest. The presenting of a newly forged sword to a key hero, the lighting of a series of signal fires to warn the neighboring kingdom of Rohan that Gondor is under attack, are successful precisely because they bring a kind of magical directness to the proceedings.

Similarly, *Return of the King* begins with a scene of two young men fishing that is almost deceptive in its artlessness. For one of the men is Smeagol, and this flashback to how he comes to possess the ring and how that object's corrosive power gradually devolves him into the sniveling Gollum is a timely reminder of the ring's ability to bend the minds of every creature.

More than the previous films, *Return of the King* has a sinister end of days feeling about it, a doomsday sensibility as the very skies seem to darken and it becomes clear that the climactic battle between the forces of good and the Dark Lord Sauron, he of the fiery, all-seeing eye, is only a matter of time. As Gandalf, that master of the epigram, puts it, "things are now in motion that cannot be undone." The best hope of a positive outcome—the quest of the hobbits Frodo and Sam to destroy the malevolent ring in the fires of Mt. Doom—is, the wizard is forced to admit, "just a fool's hope."

Even Gandalf doesn't really know what we soon find out: Things are going badly for this duo and their treacherous guide Gollum, a creature schizophrenically divided between his desire to do good and his pathological determination to possess the ring once again. Frodo, his mind weakened by the weight of carrying the ring, is increasingly not himself and prey to Gollum's insidious, Iago-like posturings.

Thanks to the input of Andy Serkis, Gollum lives up to the director's aim that he's "probably the most actor-driven digital creature that has ever been used in a film." Aside from keeping an eye on the progress of this tormented trio, *Return* has two other plot strands to follow. The first involves Gandalf and the hobbit Pippin (Billy Boyd) as they try to rally Gondor to the fight against Sauron in the face of the opposition of its power-mad steward, Denethor (John Noble).

Also in the mix is the intrepid Aragorn, whose tasks are more complex still. He has to help rally the forces of Rohan, including the comely but powerful Eowyn (Miranda Otto), while still worrying about love-of-his-life Arwen (Liv Tyler) and coming to grips with aspects of his destiny that include a trip down the dreaded Paths of the Dead, where, not surprisingly, no one much wants to go.

One of the most satisfying aspects of *The Return of the King* is that some of the actors we've seen the most of do especially well here. McKellen capitalizes on Gandalf's moments, Mortensen increasingly becomes the epitome of heroic grace, and Astin brings the kind of dignity and quiet strength to Sam increasingly called for by the role.

With so many involving things on offer, it's understandable that though *Return* opts to do without the book's closing section detailing battles around the Shire, it still extends longer than it should. For filmmakers and viewers alike, a world this vivid is next to impossible to leave. As a model for how to bring substance, authenticity and insight to the biggest of adventure yarns, this trilogy will not soon, if ever, find its equal.

Academy Award voters agreed, giving the final part of the trilogy a remarkable ten Oscars, including best picture.

The Matrix
1999

"Imagine you're feeling a little like Alice, tumbling down the rabbit hole," someone says in the dazzling and disorienting *The Matrix*, and who has the strength to argue?

A wildly cinematic futuristic thriller that is determined to overpower the imagination, *The Matrix* combines traditional science fiction premises with spanking new visual technology in a way that almost defies description. Like it or not, this is one movie that words don't come close to approximating.

Written and directed by the Wachowski brothers, Larry and Andy, *The Matrix* is the unlikely spiritual love child of dark futurist Philip K. Dick and the snap and dazzle of Hong Kong filmmaking, with digital technology serving as the helpful midwife.

Yet because this tale has been on the minds of the Wachowskis for so long—it was written before their 1996 debut film, *Bound*—*The Matrix* never feels patched together. And its story, constructed though it is from familiar elements and pseudo-mystical musings, is nevertheless strong enough to support the film's rip-roaring visuals.

Thomas Anderson (Keanu Reeves), a software programmer in a world very much like our own who goes by his nighttime hacker moniker of Neo, has heard the Matrix whispered about all his life, but no one knows what it is. All the beautiful Trinity (Carrie-Anne Moss) can tell him is that "it's looking for you," which is certainly scary but not a great deal of help.

For that Neo has to turn to Trinity's partner, the legendary Morpheus (Laurence Fishburne), considered the most dangerous man alive by the authorities. What he says is more than frightening: What Neo thinks is the real world is no more than a computer-generated dreamscape, a virtual reality created by the artificial intelligence that really controls things to distract our human minds while our bodies are systematically plundered as an energy source to keep those nefarious machines up and running.

Sometimes those machines take human form as agents, robotic parodies of FBI men, such as the chilling Agent Smith (Hugo Weaving of *Proof* and *The Adventures of Priscilla, Queen of the Desert*), who wear security earpieces, sunglasses and white shirts with ties and are terrifyingly close to indestructible.

These Matrix men have a special interest in Neo. There's a feeling in the air, one that Morpheus and his ragtag colleagues (including *Bound* veteran Joe Pantoliano) are tempted to share, that Neo might be the One, the foretold liberator who has the power to destroy the Matrix and free the human race. But only the Oracle (a fine cameo by Gloria Foster) knows for sure, and everything she says is, well, oracular.

Obviously, there's a great deal that's familiar about *The Matrix*, including its sturdy themes of alternate realities, the deadly rivalry between men and machines, the resilient power of the human mind and the creeping dangers of conformity. And the film's fake-Zen dialogue—lines such as "Don't think you are; know you are" and "There's a difference between knowing the path and walking the path"—isn't going to win any ovations for originality.

On the other hand, the somber quality of the dialogue suits the apocalyptic quality of *The Matrix* story, and the gravity of the actors, especially the always magisterial Fishburne and the magnetically phlegmatic Reeves, makes the words more bemusing than bothersome.

Helping most of all are the riveting visuals shot by Bill Pope. The Wachowskis do have a taste for the bizarre (witness an electronic bug that turns into a body-piercing insect) but this tendency pays off in such bravura moments as the mesmerizing vista of a body farm without end (inspired by the work of comic-book artist Geof Darrow) where humans are relentlessly harvested for energy like so many replaceable Eveready batteries.

Just as exciting are *The Matrix*'s two kinds of action sequences. One strata involves John Woo–type expenditures of massive amounts of ammunition shot in super slow motion and the other uses both Hong Kong–style stunt work and a technique the press notes refer to as "bullet-time photography" that involved shooting film at the computer-aided equivalent of 12,000 frames per second.

The Matrix cast members who were involved in the film's eye-catching kung fu fight sequences also apparently committed to four months of preproduction work with Hong Kong director and stunt coordinator Yuen WoPing, someone who specializes in the technique, known as wire fighting, that gives H.K. films such as *Drunken Master, Once Upon a Time in China* and *Fist of Legend* their distinctive high-flying look.

Not everything in *The Matrix* makes even minimal sense, but the Wachowski brothers, said to be major fans of comic books and graphic novels, are sure-handed enough to pull us smoothly over the rough spots. When a film is as successful as this one is at hooking into the kinetic joy of adrenalized moviemaking, quibbling with it feels beside the point.

The Mummy Returns
2001

If you've been looking for a film like *The Mummy Returns*, *The Mummy Returns* is the film you've been looking for.

A new and much improved version of 1999's *The Mummy*, this sequel is a shrewdly conceived and efficiently executed Saturday afternoon popcorn movie. Both pleasantly old-fashioned and packed with up-to-date computer-generated special effects, the film's constant plot turns, cheeky sensibility and omnipresent action sequences have no trouble attracting our attention and holding on.

Appropriate for a story that pivots on reincarnation, writer-director Stephen Sommers has returned from *The Mummy*, as have stars Brendan Fraser and Rachel Weisz, four important costars and the original's key creative personnel, including producers James Jacks and Sean Daniel, cinematographer Adrian Biddle, production designer Allan Cameron and costume designer John Bloomfield.

Experience, as ads used to say, is a great teacher, and *The Mummy Returns* cast and crew benefited considerably from having that first film under their belts. Increasingly assured across the board, this sequel displays more action at a faster pace, which has the added benefit of less screen time for borderline inane dialogue. There are even fewer (but still some) of the yucky insect moments that have become one of the film's de facto trademarks.

Perhaps most critically for a film that showcases everything from murderous soldier mummies to bad-tempered Pygmy skeletons to an infinite army of jackal-headed warriors was the decision to rehire Industrial Light & Magic's masterful John Berton as visual effects supervisor. With press reports putting the ILM price tag alone at $20 million, *The Mummy Returns* is probably the most expensive Saturday matinee serial ever made, but the decision not to cut corners in production value was definitely a wise one.

Also back but in a bit less sophomoric form is the film's self-referential sense of humor. *The Mummy Returns* is slick enough to make good use of old-style lines that begin, "It is written . . ." and a final exasperated comeback that asks, "Where is all this stuff written anyway?"

Fraser, one of the few actors who can be convincing in both goofy and intrepid modes, is ideal to play soldier of fortune Rick O'Connell in this half-serious, half-jokey film set in Egypt and London in 1933.

Though no one looks a minute older, eight years have allegedly passed since the previous adventure, and O'Connell and Egyptologist Evelyn (Weisz) have taken that opportunity to marry and produce a young son named Alex (Freddie Boath).

That change in marital status benefits both stars. It enables them to demonstrate personal chemistry as a dashing Nick and Nora Charles–type couple with a son instead of a dog and avoid completely the tiresome "I hate you so much I must be in love" courtship ritual that dominated things the last time around.

Sommers, who seems to have evolved into a real Egyptology buff, has come up with a rather complex backstory for *The Mummy Returns*. It begins in 3067 B.C. and not a year sooner and allows for a brief wordless cameo from pro-wrestling star the Rock as a fearless warrior named the Scorpion King.

Defeated in an attempt to take over Egypt, the King sells his soul to Anubis, one of the gods of the Egyptian underworld, for enough jackal-headed warriors to help him gain the victories he thirsts for. But far too soon all those fighters turn into so many grains of sand, a magical army that, along with their king, can be awakened every 5,000 years and counted on to take over the Earth.

Hoping to piggyback on that phenomenon is Meela, the reincarnation of Anck-Su-Namun (Patricia Velasquez), the star-crossed lover of the terrifying mummy Imhotep (Arnold Vosloo), who caused so much trouble the last time around. She hopes to bring Imhotep back from the dead one last time, for if he can beat the Scorpion King two falls out of three, he can command the king's warriors and conquer the world without so much as a by your leave.

Key to this elaborate plan turns out to be an impressive piece of gold jewelry called the Bracelet of Anubis that is uncovered by the intrepid Evelyn, who has an uncanny sense of where things were in ancient times. Are these visions, hallucinations, memories of a previous life, or are they a side effect of being the only 1930s Egyptologist to run around the desert in low-cut tops?

Trying to keep the bad guys from the bracelet are two veterans of *The Mummy*, John Hannah as Evelyn's rapscallion brother Jonathan and Oded Fehr as Ardeth Bay, the leader of the Medjai, a benevolent desert brotherhood that comes off like an armed and dangerous version of the Shriners.

In telling this story, writer-director Sommers has not neglected to throw in a lot of old-fashioned elements to make us feel at home, including chests that really shouldn't be opened, birds that deliver messages and scenes reminiscent of the Biblical pageantry of *The Ten Commandments*. That's not to mention floods, fires and enough action elements to allow for cutting between four separate conflicts in the film's climactic section. It may be, as one character puts it, "the old end-of-the-world ploy," but it's fun to see it done with the energy *The Mummy Returns* brings to this twice-told tale.

The Rock went from this modest beginnings to a major action career.

Saving Private Ryan
1998

More than any of his other films, and that includes *Schindler's List*, Steven Spielberg's *Saving Private Ryan* won't leave you alone. To see it is to need to talk about it, to wrestle with the formidable impact of its unprecedented strengths and the surprising resilience of its niggling weaknesses. A powerful and impressive milestone in the realistic depiction of combat, *Saving Private Ryan* is as much an experience we live through as a film we watch on the screen.

No one needs to be told about Spielberg's ability as a popular culture tastemaker: Seven of Hollywood's twenty top-grossing films bear his mark as either director, producer or executive producer. But because his skills as a filmmaker are so great, because he can get away with working at a fraction of his capabilities, *Saving Private Ryan* is a startling reminder of exactly how spectacular a director Spielberg can be when he allows himself to be challenged by a subject (in this case World War II) that pushes against his limits.

The son of a combat veteran, Spielberg says the first movies he made as a child dealt with that war, and many critics feel that the forty minutes showing 1941 Shanghai under Japanese attack that open *Empire of the Sun* rank among the best footage he's ever shot. Spielberg is most effective when he doesn't flinch, when his respect for the material compels him to be as honest as he can, and that is largely the case here.

It's not that *Private Ryan*'s story (written by Robert Rodat) of an eight-man squad detailed to find and rescue a soldier in just-invaded

Normandy doesn't provide opportunities for conventional movie heroism. It does, and Tom Hanks as laconic squad leader Captain John Miller gives a classic performance as an elevated everyman, our ideal vision of how we all hope we'd behave under the duress of combat.

But Captain Miller is not a casually heroic John Wayne knockoff. He's despairing about his role in leading men to slaughter, troubled by the person the war has turned him into, and the periodic trembling of one of his hands reveals he's dangerously close to coming apart.

In this determination not to trivialize the nature of war and what it does to people, *Private Ryan* is often a darker and more pessimistic look at the reality of combat than we are used to from either Hollywood or Spielberg. This is a war where American soldiers mock virtue and shoot surrendering Germans, where decent and altruistic actions tend to be fatal, where death is random and stupid, and redeems hardly anything at all. Even the usually vivid American flag is, in Janusz Kaminski's remarkable cinematography, bleached out and desaturated.

More than in its attitudes, more even than in its surprising focus on the nature of cowardice, *Saving Private Ryan* reveals its determination to be accurate in the way it presents combat action. Using a trio of superlative operators (Mitch Dubin, Chris Haarhoff, Seamus Corcoran) and relying on the newsreel look of hand-held cameras, *Private Ryan* gets as close to the unimaginable horror and chaos of battle as fiction film ever has, closer in fact than some audience members may want to experience.

After a brief prelude depicting an old veteran, we're not sure exactly who, returning with his family to the American cemetery at Normandy, we flash immediately back to that beach and a shot of Captain Miller in his landing craft on D-Day, June 6, 1944. During the next twenty or so minutes, we are shown the invasion of France with a violence and an intensity that is almost beyond describing.

The slaughter starts immediately and does not let up. Men are enveloped in flames, ripped to shreds by bullets, dead as soon as they set foot on the beach or, in an agonizing mixture of horror and beauty, dying in slow-motion as they are dragged underwater. One man's leg is blown off, another loses one arm and tries awkwardly to pick it up with the other, a third lies in agony as his intestines graphically spill on the ground. Panic, pitiless fear and bloody pandemonium are everywhere; we see the raw terror on everyone's face, and for once we know exactly why it's there.

A great deal has been made about the violence level in *Saving Private Ryan*, and though it is horrific, it's a world apart from the pandering, anything-for-a-rush blood sports that characterize business-as-usual Hollywood. There's no attempt to make this violence fun and games, and special pleading is completely absent. Instead, the visual tone is the dispassionate, pitiless one of an all-seeing but uninvolved deity, inviting us to look on this awful destruction and despair.

One of the last shots of the battle focuses on the name "Ryan" stenciled on the backpack of a corpse. A scene in a military office back home produces the information that in fact three of four Ryan brothers have died in action within days of one another. When Army Chief of Staff General George C. Marshall (Harve Presnell) finds out, he focuses on the survivor, Private James Ryan, on the ground somewhere in Normandy. "We are going to send someone to find him," the general says. "And we are going to get him the hell out of there."

That someone turns out to be Captain Miller, none too happy at being assigned to what he considers "a public relations gambit" as potentially difficult and pointless as finding "a needle in a stack of needles." What is the sense, he and his men wonder as they head out, in risking all their lives to save just one? "Ryan better be worth it," the captain says. "He better go home and cure some disease or invent a new, longer-lasting light bulb."

As the squad warily picks its way through the combat zone, we get to know the men we've only caught a glimpse of during the invasion, starting with Sergeant Horvath (Tom Sizemore), the captain's level-headed right hand, and the newly added Corporal Upham (Jeremy Davis), a timid, bookish translator who's never seen action.

The rest of the guys, besides the compassionate medic Wade (Giovanni Ribisi), are all privates. The biggest talker is Reiben (Edward

Burns), who has "Brooklyn, N.Y." written on his jacket, though Caparzo (Vin Diesel) and his mouth are not far behind. Mellish (Adam Goldberg) is angrily aware of what the Nazis are doing to the Jews, and Jackson (Barry Pepper) is a religious Southern sharpshooter who prays "God grant me strength" before taking aim and firing.

Working with casting director Denise Chamian, Spielberg has adroitly cast these roles, mixing actors known mostly to followers of independent film with camouflaged veterans such as Sizemore (who does the best, most controlled work of his career), Dennis Farina and Ted Danson (who appear briefly as officers).

But even as we're admiring these performances, we can't help but be aware that this kind of multiethnic squad is one of the most venerable conventions of war movies, can't help noticing that, for instance, sharpshooter Jackson could have stepped right out of *Sergeant York*, the 1941 film about World War I starring Gary Cooper.

What nags at you about *Saving Private Ryan* is the way Rodat's script, though solid and well-structured, has not broken through convention, has not elevated itself to a higher level (or even reached the best of the old level) the way the mind-bending scenes of combat have.

As the squad moves through crises toward the elusive Private Ryan, what impacts us most are invariably scenes of action: sometimes fire fights, sometimes unexpected deaths, but never the dialogue the men trade. Just as the soldiers speculate that Captain Miller has been artfully reassembled from old body parts, so *Private Ryan's* script has been put together from familiar and shopworn material.

Because the script is only workmanlike, it highlights the hitch in Spielberg's otherwise problem-free direction, which is a tendency to be too insistent at obviously sentimental moments. The enabler here is five-time Oscar-winning composer John Williams, who has been on almost all the director's films but whose bombastic work is more and more a stranger to subtlety.

Private Ryan (handsome, open-faced Matt Damon) is inevitably located, but finding him occurs simultaneously with a brutal, cataclysmic final shootout in a ruined French village constructed with un-canny, hypnotic verisimilitude by production designer Tom Sanders that is as unforgettable as the invasion. (Given that Spielberg pre-ferred, whenever possible, not to storyboard his action ahead of time, the key player in making this and all of *Private Ryan's* action se-quences so compelling is wizardly veteran editor Michael Kahn.)

How much we begrudge *Saving Private Ryan* what flaws it has de-pends in part on how greedy we are for perfection. When he is on his game, as he is here, Spielberg is a master storyteller whose gift for nar-rative film is unsurpassed. The overdone sentiment (most noticeable in the film's shaky framing story), the occasional over-reliance on conventional elements, are simply part of the package, part of what he needs for security if he's going to push mainstream filmmaking into directions it has never gone before. As far as trade-offs go, it's a hell of a deal.

Spider-Man 2
2004

Romance and empathy are all very nice, but comic-book movies cry out for exceptional villains, and *Spider-Man 2* has come up with a memorable one.

In bringing to vivid and extravagant life Dr. Otto Octavius, the ever-menacing Doc Ock, Spider-Man's nemesis since the comic's ear-liest days, this energetic sequel has cleverly reversed the dynamic that made the first film successful.

The Green Goblin, the bad guy the last time around, is almost uni-versally conceded to have been that film's weakest element. Instead, the original prospered on the pleasure of seeing a young Spider-Man learning to use his powers as well as the onscreen chemistry between stars Tobey Maguire and Kirsten Dunst as Peter Parker, Spider-Man's alter ego, and Mary Jane Watson, the girl next door but just out of reach.

Though that relationship remains satisfying, it has been greatly overshadowed by Doc Ock. As played by Alfred Molina with both computer-generated and puppeteer assistance, Doc Ock grabs this film with his quartet of sinisterly serpentine mechanical arms and refuses to let go.

This unintentionally different focus renders *Spider-Man 2* at least equal, if not better, than the first in overall impact. There are times when it seems to be cruising, but it rewards our attention by successfully firing on more and different cylinders than the original did.

It helps that not just Maguire and Dunst are back from the first film but also Rosemary Harris as kindly Aunt May, J. K. Simmons as dyspeptic newspaper editor J. Jonah Jameson, and James Franco as Harry Osborn, Peter's best friend and Spider-Man's deadliest enemy.

Also returning is director Sam Raimi, this time assisted by a quartet of credited writers. The film's screenplay is by two-time Oscar winner Alvin Sargent, with screen story by Alfred Gough and Miles Millar, best known for television's *Smallville*, and novelist Michael Chabon, author of *The Amazing Adventures of Kavalier & Clay*.

Despite the best efforts of this group, the early parts of *Spider-Man 2* can't have the emotional impact of the first film because it is, in effect, a reprise of that initial venture. Though Maguire and Dunst are sweet together, their early interaction feels lethargic and pro forma, as if they read and believed their good notices. Also, it's just not possible to experience the glow of first love twice.

Plot-wise, Peter Parker is still pining away for M.J., whose face is all over Manhattan as the poster girl for a fancy perfume. And he is still fuming that being a responsible Spider-Man has wreaked havoc with his personal life—that is, he doesn't have one.

Though it is still a major treat to see Spider-Man take to the air, what is as hard to duplicate as first love is the first film's thrill of learning to fly. *Spider-Man 2* tries to replace it with Parker's crisis of confidence, as the young man wonders whether being Spider-Man is worth it.

Not lacking in confidence at all is that celebrated scientist Dr. Octavius, initially a heck of a nice guy albeit one focused on his forthcoming attempt to use four mechanical arms to harness a fusion reaction and create a perpetual energy source.

But something (doesn't it always) goes terribly wrong, and those thirteen-foot mechanical arms not only fuse to the doctor's body, which would be bad enough, they also take over his mind with their evil, evil thoughts. Oh, the horror of it all.

Though the original Doc Ock was conceptualized by comic artist Steve Ditko, the filmmakers have done a spectacular job of making him real on the screen. It started with vivid illustrations by conceptual artist Paul Catling (reproduced in a book on the production called *Caught in the Web*) and ended with the Doc having his own personal art director, Jeff Knipp, working with visual effects designer John Dykstra and cinematographer Bill Pope.

Computer work by Sony Pictures Imageworks and several other firms made the Doc chillingly mobile, able to climb tall buildings like a larger, more ungainly but powerfully effective spider. Best of all was the animatronic work by Edge FX puppeteers, which give those metallic arms with tentacle heads that swirl around Doc Ock's head like snakes around Medusa, very unnerving personalities.

All told, Doc Ock is such a completely realized creation, the battles he has with Spider-Man are so involving, he actually helps buck up the rest of the production. Even the romantic moments between Parker and M.J. become more poignant and moving as the menace of the Doc looms. It's not that we want the villains to actually win, but if they aren't convincing opponents, just what is the hero's victory worth?

Star Trek: First Contact
1996

This is a test. This is only a test. Can anyone outside the hardcore faithful tell the *Star Trek* movies apart? One featured whales, but was it *Star Trek IV: The Voyage Home* or *Star Trek V: The Final Frontier*?

And at this late date, who remembers just who or what it was that made Khan so angry in *Star Trek II: The Wrath of Khan?*

That blurring is not likely to happen with *Star Trek: First Contact*, the eighth movie in a series that may yet see more episodes than Andy Hardy. Blessed with clever plot devices and a villainous horde that makes the once-dread Klingons seem like a race of Barneys, *First Contact* does everything you'd want a *Star Trek* film to do, and it does it with cheerfulness and style.

Still working largely with the cast of the now-defunct *Star Trek: The Next Generation*, *First Contact* has all the paraphernalia Trekkers (apparently the name of choice) have come to expect: Lights flash, temporal vortexes get created and people say cutting things such as, "You do remember how to fire phasers?"

And, as created by a core of *Trek* veterans (including, among others, producer Rick Berman, director and costar Jonathan Frakes, writers Brannon Braga and Ronald D. Moore, and production designer Herman Zimmerman), this movie's themes place it squarely within the boundaries of Gene Roddenberry's original *Star Trek* culture of one-world idealism.

And did anyone mention those villains? Making their big-screen debut are the Borg, bad to the bone and proud of it. Part human, part synthetic (and realized with appropriate menace by costume designer Deborah Everton and makeup wizard Michael Westmore), these unstoppable high-tech zombies are not just making conversation when they tell their adversaries, "Resistance is futile."

So arrogant they take no notice of anyone not in attack mode, so flexible they adjust and overpower any weapons system, the Borg are master assimilators, determined to glom onto, absorb and destroy all life forms in the galaxy.

They're so good at it, in fact, that on the television series the Borg temporarily assimilated *Enterprise* Captain Jean-Luc Picard. *First Contact* opens with a powerful visual reference to that experience, what the *Trek* people are calling "the longest pullback in science fiction history," as Matthew Leonetti's camera goes (via 120 feet of dolly track and sharp special-effects work) from a closeup of Picard's eye to his puny place in the unimaginably large Borg Collective.

Because of that experience, when the Borg invade the Federation in the twenty-fourth century, Picard is kept away from the front lines. But he finds a way to join in and eventually discovers the Borg headed toward Earth and into the past, to mid-April 2063 to be specific. Their nefarious scheme soon becomes obvious: to change history by stopping First Contact, the great day when humans on Earth sent up a rocket at warp speed and connected with the rest of the solar system.

Naturally, Captain Picard is not amused. In fact, the commander is almost never amused, but as played by the exceptional Patrick Stewart, whose wide range includes Shakespeare and Dickens, his presence and ability to say "Get off my bridge" as if he meant it is formidable. If whoever first beamed him onto the show isn't getting profit participation from dollar one, there is no justice in the Federation.

At this point, First Contact splits in two. The softer part of the film moves to Earth, where a team is sent to find Zefram Cochrane (Babe's James Cromwell), the man who invented warp drive, and his partner Lily Sloane (Alfre Woodard), and help them get their epoch-making rocket airborne.

Picard stays back on the Enterprise, trying to fight off an attempt by the rest of the elusive Borg to take over his ship. Though they pride themselves on their collective consciousness, the Borg turn out to have a fabulously evil queen bee (a convincing Alice Krige), and her encounters with both Picard and human wannabe Lieutenant Commodore Data (Brent Spiner) are delicious and chilling.

A pageturner with the right kind of pulp sensibility, First Contact works in cultural references from Moby Dick to Steppenwolf's Magic Carpet Ride, and a way has even been found to get the Vulcans back into the picture. If the Star Trek brain trust continues turning out movies like this one, living long and prospering is not going to be a problem.

Starship Troopers
1997

Forget the Terminator, it's the Exterminator you'll be looking for after experiencing *Starship Troopers*. A film whose self-proclaimed motto is "Kill anything that has more than two legs," this picture has what it takes to premiere at a Roach Motel and be reviewed by the makers of Raid.

Based on Robert A. Heinlein's classic 1959 science fiction novel, *Starship Troopers* presents the evildoers almost no one can abide, the one kind of villain not likely to hold press conferences protesting small-minded stereotyping. It's us vs. the bugs, big time, and as one character resolutely puts it, "we're in this for the species, boys and girls."

Put together by Paul Verhoeven (*RoboCop, Basic Instinct, Showgirls*), a director for whom excess is never enough, *Troopers* does not fit any reasonable definition of a high-quality motion picture. But it certainly is a jaw-dropping experience, so rigorously one-dimensional and free from all pretense that it's hard not to be astonished, and even mesmerized, by what is on the screen.

Part of the reason is those darn bugs. Besides the hordes of gigantic Warriors, who attack in unstoppable waves like the Japanese in xenophobic World War II movies, there are flying bugs, crawling bugs, gargantuan fire-breathing Tanker bugs and even, Lord protect us, a deep-thinking Brain bug that knows lots more than we'd like it to.

Constructed out of a complex combination of model and miniature work and computer-generated imagery, *Starship Troopers*' impressive futuristic world of bugs, spaceships and total war makes you wonder about the sanity of the technicians who spent lonely hours making innumerable insects look good on camera. There must be less taxing ways to make a living.

But where *Starship Troopers* has it all over similar effects-laden efforts such as *Independence Day* and *Twister* is its complete lack of pretense. There's no mock emotion here, no nauseating pseudosensitivity.

What Ed Neumeier's script provides instead is a cheerfully loboto-
mized, always watchable experience that has the simplemindedness of
a live-action comic book; no words are spoken that wouldn't be right
at home in a funny paper dialogue balloon. Not just one comic book,
either, but an improbable and delirious combination of *Weird Science*,
Betty and Veronica and *Sgt. Rock of Easy Company*.

Also thrown into this high-energy mix, in case anyone was thinking
of getting bored, is the fascist utopianism of the original Heinlein
novel. Introduced via infomercials and news broadcasts playing on a
computer screen, *Troopers* takes us to a militaristic future where video
bulletins encourage young people to "join the Mobile Infantry and save
the world" and schools teach that "violence is the supreme authority"
and nothing solves problems with the efficacy of "naked force."

Troopers opens with its own teaser trailer, a television broadcast of
Earth's attack on bug stronghold Klendathu, in the heart of the Arach-
nid Quarantine Zone, the dread AQZ. "This is an ugly planet, a bug
planet," an onscreen reporter huffily reports before getting eviscerated
on the spot by an understandably outraged local resident.

Now that it's got our attention, *Trooper* flashes back a year and goes
into its Betty and Veronica mode, introducing its key characters as
students at a high school located for unknown reasons in Buenos
Aires. These youthful performers are by and large not familiar faces,
but they all have the shiny photogenic glow of a shampoo commercial, not to mention a sleek superficiality that makes Luke Skywalker
seem like Hamlet by comparison.

Square-jawed hero Johnny Rico (Casper Van Dien) is the captain
of the football team and in love with the beautiful Carmen Ibanez
(Denise Richards). But while Carmen is flirting with handsome Zander Barcalow (Patrick Muldoon), Johnny is oblivious to the fact that
vixenish Dizzy Flores (Dina Meyer), his attractive quarterback (the
game has changed some over the years), is carrying a major torch for
him. And brainy Carl Jenkins (Neil Patrick Harris, television's Doo-
gie Howser) is too busy perfecting his mind-reading techniques even
to have a girlfriend.

All this romantic plotting comes to a boil at graduation. Both Carmen and Zander head off to Fleet Academy to become hotshot pilots, and Johnny, under the influence of hard-nosed teacher Jean Rasczak (Michael Ironside), dismays his parents by joining the rugged Mobile Infantry in the hopes of impressing Carmen. And who should turn up in the same platoon but old pal Diz. Talk about complications.

Of course, everyone's personal life takes a back seat when those pesky bugs, who have been trouble before, launch a devastating sneak attack on Earth. Fearless, ego-less and hard to kill, the bugs are a heck of an opponent and they seem to know that after years of skirmishing this will be a battle to the death.

A very messy death it turns out to be, for *Starship Troopers* offers no shortage of all manner of carnage. The bugs are both nuked and blown away by what's been reported as the most ammunition ever used in a major motion picture, and the hapless humans are repulsively chomped up, dismembered, impaled, beheaded and completely slimed on by the enemy. "Bugs don't take prisoners," Earth's troops are warned and, for better and worse, neither does *Starship Troopers*.

Vertical Limit
2000

A man's face fills the screen. His eyes expand in terror, his mouth opens double-wide, he screams "AVALANCHE" as if the fate of nations hung on the word. You can run, you can hide, but ready or not, *Vertical Limit* is that kind of a movie.

In theory, these high-octane extravaganzas, old-fashioned in form but bristling with up-to-the-minute special-effects technology, should be business as usual for Hollywood. In reality, making a success of high-altitude heroics is something of a lost art. Which is why getting Martin Campbell to do the directing was the right idea.

After a career largely spent doing television miniseries in Britain, with the occasional feature thrown in, Campbell revealed an unusual gift for revitalizing traditional genre material, making films such as the James Bond *GoldenEye* and *The Mask of Zorro* crisper and more exciting than anyone else could have managed.

Yet Campbell's strengths are almost offset by flaws that would have hamstrung a less confident and exciting film than *Vertical Limit*. The Robert King and Terry Hayes screenplay (inspired in part by the same Mt. Everest tragedy Jon Krakauer detailed in *Into Thin Air*) is weighted down with flyweight dialogue and weak characterization, dilemmas that are not helped by problematic casting and lack of a true star performance. Still, for a film with action sequences that can wind us up the way *Vertical Limit* does when the moment is right, an awful lot of trespasses can be forgiven.

Though he's personally afraid of heights, Campbell has turned out nail-biting moments of mountaintop peril that snap, crackle and pop. Though a good deal of *Vertical Limit* is undeniably by the numbers, it has become increasingly rare to see those digits whipped into this kind of shape.

The film's thrills start with its prologue introducing the brother-and-sister climbing team of Peter and Annie Garrett (Chris O'Donnell and Robin Tunney) taking their ease on a sheer rock face high above the Utah desert. That sense of calm is illusory, however, for something happens on that godforsaken cliff that makes the next Peter and Annie meeting awkward and strained.

That would be three years later in Pakistan, at the foot of the Himalayas. Peter is now a *National Geographic* photographer (an excuse for some nice scenes of snow leopards at play) and sister Annie has progressed into a purposeful climber who's just completed a speedy ascent of the Eiger.

Peter finds himself sharing base camp space with a massive expedition put together by Elliot Vaughn (an effective Bill Paxton), a wealthy Texas entrepreneur with more money than sense who wants to tempt fate by climbing the notoriously temperamental K2 on a deadline as part of a publicity stunt for a new airline he's starting. Sister Annie turns out to be one of the climbers on Elliot's crack team.

It will surprise no one to learn that Elliot and friends get into trouble on the climb, big trouble. It's madness even to think of rescuing them, let alone actually try, but brother Peter, one of several people with unfinished business to settle on the mountain (not the best place for it), can't be dissuaded. Off he goes with a motley crew, which includes a gorgeous French Canadian medic (Izabella Scorupco) whose makeup stays fresh in gale-force conditions. And Montgomery Wick.

Just as there would be no hope for a rescue attempt without the legendary Wick, the climber's climber, so there would be much less of a film without Scott Glenn's perfectly pitched performance as the mysterious loner who knows more about K2 than any man living or dead.

Glenn not only has the ideal face for the part, as rugged and lined as a contour map of the Himalayas, but he also completely understands the demands of playing a ghost-like Rip Van Winkle who's part force of nature, part mystical seer. And his sense of the let-'er-rip spirit of the proceedings is impeccable.

Other characters are less successfully handled. The comic-relief characters of a pair of Australian stoner brothers turn out to be neither comic nor a relief. And star O'Donnell, though a capable enough actor, feels miscast. He's too puppyish and lacks the weight of personality to be as forceful as the script demands or to add the charisma that Catherine Zeta-Jones and Pierce Brosnan provided in Campbell's last two films.

Not that *Vertical Limit* lacks the resources to mount a counterattack. These include a pounding score by James Newton Howard, relentless editing by Oscar winner Thom Noble and photography by David Tattersall that makes the film's combination of effects shots and location photography (New Zealand's Mt. Cook sits in for K2) look completely real.

As crisis follows crisis on the mountain, with people falling into crevices and dangling off cliffs left and right, this is one locale whose thrills turn out to be as merciless as its weather.

Volcano
1997

Volcano glows with heat. Lava heat. The coast may be toast, but it's the lava, covering everything like a malevolent tide of melted butter, that makes this a disaster picture that's tastier than usual.

Hollywood's last volcano movie, the misbegotten *Dante's Peak*, was particularly stingy in the lava department, barely letting it flow. *Volcano* has no such qualms, and though wet-blanket scientists may question the likelihood of the scenario—raging torrents of super-heated goo, intent on swallowing Los Angeles, rising from the La Brea tar pits—the film's mightily impressive special effects will sway most doubters.

Shot on an 80 percent scale model of the Wilshire corridor constructed on seventeen-plus acres of the McDonnell Douglas plant parking lot in Torrance, *Volcano* will be particularly convincing for Los Angeles residents.

Seeing the Los Angeles County Museum of Art, the Art Deco May Co. building and surrounding sites, plus all those elegant Wilshire Boulevard palm trees, consumed by a relentless tide of lava is especially unnerving if you've spent time in the neighborhood.

As written by Jerome Armstrong and Billy Ray, *Volcano* also manages some sly moments that have special Los Angeles resonance. A subway motorman reads *Screenplays That Sell*, Metro workers are stigmatized as "the guys who collapsed Hollywood Boulevard" and a huge billboard of local icon Angelyne becomes a victim of the volcano's flames.

It's not surprising that director Mick Jackson highlights these and other funny touches; one of his credits is Steve Martin's *L.A. Story*. Jackson also has a background in documentary work, and his ability, working with cameraman Theo van de Sande and editors Michael Tronick and Don Brochu, to move things along and create a sense of continuous urgency is critical to *Volcano*'s effectiveness. Because at its core, *Volcano* is another one of those programmatic disaster movies, with dogs in jeopardy and kids wandering off at the worst possible moment. A great deal of its dialogue is of the "I know you're scared, I'm scared too" variety, and there's even room for the ever-popular "What is that?"

But a great sense of pace is a wonderful thing, and director Jackson and his crew (who made good use of hand-held and Steadicam shots and reportedly averaged an impressive thirty to forty camera setups a day) move so quickly from shot to shot and location to location that viewers have a limited time to dwell on the film's predictable implausibilities.

Volcano also benefits from crisp work from its principals, especially Tommy Lee Jones as Mike Roark, the tireless head of L.A.'s fictional Office of Emergency Management. Few actors can look as indomitable or project the kind of take-no-prisoners fierceness that's a match for any natural disaster.

When strange things start happening below the placid surface of MacArthur Park after a mild earthquake, Roark almost immediately barks, "Find me a scientist who can tell me what the hell is going on." His staff comes up with a feisty seismologist, Dr. Amy Barnes (a capable Anne Heche), who suspects a volcano. Roark smirks a sexist smirk, but it's not long before his toes are almost literally being held to the fire.

Other supporting players, including Don Cheadle as Emmit Reese, Roark's ambitious second-in-command, and Gaby Hoffmann as Roark's sullen teenaged daughter, manage to do what's necessary without overstaying their welcomes.

As that darn lava threatens to vaporize everything it touches, including Metro passengers who probably wish they'd taken their cars, Roark comes up with a wild and crazy plan to save the city. Hey, he knows it's a longshot, but that's the kind of guy he is.

In everything besides special effects, *Volcano* is allergic to breaking new ground, and viewers have to endure moments of bogus brotherhood and a chauvinist ending that pulls Dr. Barnes out of the line of fire to look for Roark's lost daughter. But it's hard to dislike a film in which a character can survey a sea of lava and say, "Better take the freeway. Wilshire looks pretty bad." After the horrendous dramatics of *Twister*, *Independence Day* and *Dante's Peak*, a disaster movie that's not a complete disaster itself can be reason enough to smile.

War of the Worlds
2005

As a boy growing up in the 1950s, Steven Spielberg was always watching the skies. He experienced meteor showers with his father, enjoyed space dramas such as *The Day the Earth Stood Still* and dreamed, he told friends, of being the Cecil B. DeMille of science fiction.

Now, half a century later, with awards and profits beyond counting behind him, Spielberg has kept faith with the boy he was. With *War of the Worlds* he has made what is arguably one of the best 1950s science fiction films ever, and that is not a backhanded compliment.

Working in the spirit of his predecessors but with the kind of uncanny special effects they could barely dream of, Spielberg has come up with an impressive production that is disturbing in the way only provocative science fiction can be. It's a traditional, even old-fashioned effort that, like its 1950s forebears, is willing to confront up-to-the-minute societal concerns more mainstream features avoid. A film that, finally, may be even more disturbing than its creator intended or we've been expecting.

Though Spielberg has said in interviews that his focus in this film is depicting an ordinary guy and his children coping with an alien onslaught, in some ways the family dynamic is the weakest link in the story. Even with Tom Cruise as what the press material delicately calls a "less-than-perfect father," the remarkable Dakota Fanning as his wise-beyond-her-years daughter, Justin Chatwin as his inevitably surly teenage son and Miranda Otto as his remarried ex-wife, what we come away with is a sense of the power of evil, not the strength of good.

This is due in large part to the potent nature of the underlying material adapted by screenwriters Josh Friedman and David Koepp: the celebrated H. G. Wells novel that has caused a sensation each of the previous three times it's been put before the public.

When *The War of the Worlds* appeared in print in Britain in 1898, one of a series of groundbreaking science fiction novels—including *The Time Machine* and *The Invisible Man*—that Wells was turning out regularly, its idea of aliens from Mars attempting a hostile takeover of the planet was startling in its newness.

When Orson Welles did a radio dramatization of the story on the night before Halloween in 1938, a genuine panic shook the nation: The *New York Times* reported that people got on the phone and said, "The world is coming to an end and I have a lot to do." And when George Pal produced a 1953 version of the tale, the film was striking enough to get a trio of Oscar nominations and to win one for special effects.

The irresistibility of the concept—at one time reportedly everyone from Alfred Hitchcock to Sergei Eisenstein considered doing adaptations—and the keenness of execution aside, the same two factors led to the success of each of those versions, factors that combine one more time to make Spielberg's rendering as potent as it is.

All these *Wars* have had the advantage of appearing at uncannily fraught moments in world history, striking a chord with a citizenry already primed to be unnerved. The original novel appeared when Britain feared an invasion from Germany, the Welles broadcast on the cusp of World War II, the Pal film during the Cold War. More than that, each version has had the additional benefit of complete plausibility, of seeming like something that could actually be happening. Wells himself was keenly aware of his story's "attempt to keep everything within the bounds of possibility . . . that from first to last there is nothing in it that is impossible."

With the specter of terrorism, the threat of nuclear weapons in the hands of North Korea, Iran and who knows who else, not to mention the invasion of Iraq (which the film takes a veiled swipe at), we certainly live in perilous times. Spielberg's *War* is a perfect fit for our paranoid, potentially apocalyptic age, a film that considers the possibility, however obliquely, that the world as we know it could end.

It's a tribute to the perspicacity of Wells that the voice-over Morgan Freeman reads to open the film comes almost word for word from the opening of the 1898 novel. "No one would have believed in the early years of the twenty-first century," Freeman reads with impeccable iciness, "that our world was being watched by intelligences greater than our own. . . . An intellect vast and cool and unsympathetic regarded our planet with envious eyes."

With this blood-chilling introduction out of the way, *War of the Worlds* (the film has lopped off the novel's initial *The* as well as all references to Mars) pulls back to introduce us to our protagonists: Cruise's parenting-challenged Ray Ferrier, Fanning as young Rachel, Chatwin as teen Robbie. A blue-collar kind of guy's guy who works on the Jersey docks, Newark resident Ray has to watch his kids for a few days while his ex (Otto) and her husband go off on a trip to which children are definitely not invited. It turns out to be one heck of a weekend.

Working, as he has on many films, with Industrial Light & Magic's senior visual effects supervisor Dennis Muren, an eight-time Oscar winner, Spielberg makes impeccable use of special effects to make the pure fantasy of an alien invasion more believable than one would think possible.

This starts with the mechanics of dread, the appearance of natural phenomena such as lightning strikes in decidedly unnatural combinations. Then the terrifying alien war machines, the two-hundred-foot-tall tripods, appear, looking so much like the book's vision they are almost identical to Edward Gorey's cover art for an edition of the novel he illustrated more than forty years ago.

Spielberg is at his best showing us the unimaginable damage these aliens do, from vaporizing people to destroying infrastructure. His effects are the opposite of showy—they aspire to be ordinary by taking place almost in the background, by being horrors we sometimes feel we are spying out of the corner of our eye. Collaborating with his veteran crew, including editor Michael Kahn, cinematographer Janusz Kaminski, composer John Williams and production designer Rick Carter, Spielberg (as he previously proved with *Saving Private Ryan*) has a way of making these indescribable nightmares both realistic and compelling.

How helpful the *War of the Worlds* protagonists are in this endeavor is more of an open question. Tom Cruise clearly knows how to hold the screen, and the film is better for that; but he's so unstoppably charismatic that we never fear for him no matter what the aliens are doing, just as we never believe that deep down he's as bad a dad as the film wants us to think.

His relationship with son Robbie is as much a trial to us as it is to the two of them, an exercise in hackneyed tedium that repeats the clichés of dysfunctional adolescence that have deadened more movies than anyone can count. It gets so bad that there are moments when it seems the aliens staged the whole invasion just to give sullen Robbie a chance to prove himself to his obdurate dad.

Dakota Fanning, who has held the screen with such heavyweights as Denzel Washington, Sean Penn and Robert De Niro, is a different story. Pound for pound, as they say in the boxing game, she is as good an actress as we have today. Fanning has a gift for naturalness and empathy that makes her the perfect audience surrogate. Her look of horror as she faces terror out the back window of a car is the film's signature image, the one shot that makes us feel the nightmare in our bones.

When the aliens finally leave their tripods late in the film, they are sinister and repulsive, but they don't drop-dead terrify us the way the shark did in *Jaws*. Spielberg is older now, less interested in juvenile jolts. Among the things that are the scariest in his current presentation are how thin the veneer of civilization is among human beings, how close to the surface panic and hysteria are in people, such as Tim Robbins's unnerved survivor, Ogilvy. We are our own worst enemy as well as our only hope.

Steven Spielberg may actually have done his job in *War of the Worlds* better than he realizes. By showing us how fragile our world is, how imperiled we might well be from without and within, he raises almost against his will a most provocative question: Is the ultimate fantasy an invasion from outer space, or is it the survival of the human race?

X2: X-Men United
2003

Brisk and involving with a streamlined forward propulsion, *X2: X-Men United* is the kind of superhero movie we want if we have to have superhero movies at all.

X2 is also an improvement over the initial *X-Men* venture, yet, paradoxically, it wouldn't be as satisfying as it is if that first one hadn't existed. Director Bryan Singer, the key members of his production team and no fewer than nine stars and the genetic mutants they portray return from the 2000 original, and all benefit from having the previous effort behind them.

If the first *X-Men* had an obstacle it never completely overcame, it was the time-consuming necessity of introducing the numerous inhabitants of its elaborate world of mutants, each with a very specific power, from the ability of Wolverine (Hugh Jackman) to fight like the devil and heal himself to the way Storm (Halle Berry) can control the weather.

Still, just having gotten it done at all seems to have put everyone involved in *X2* understandably more at ease, more confident and relaxed. Without those pressures, the film was free to, in a sense, take itself for granted, to concentrate on coming up with an involving story and telling it in the best possible way.

Though it was put together by a heaping handful of screenwriters (written by Michael Dougherty, Dan Harris and David Hayter from a story by Zak Penn, Hayter and director Singer), one of the virtues of *X2* is that its storytelling style is basically matter of fact. *X2* doesn't wink at us and doesn't get overly stylized. Its shrewd concern is to make the world its unreal characters share with ordinary humans as realistic as possible.

Even more remarkable, X2 doesn't trip over its own logistics, even though those logistics were formidable. Shot largely in Vancouver, X2 was the biggest movie ever made in Canada, complete with more than sixty miles of electrical cable running through a key soundstage and hours in makeup for returning shape-shifter Mystique (Rebecca Romijn-Stamos) and debuting teleporter Nightcrawler (Alan Cumming).

But despite this, X2 really wants to involve us in its characters' stories, to get us on its side and create belief that there is something tangible at stake in what these mutants are up to. Don't be misled, we're not talking The Hours here, but for a superhero movie, it's well above average. And this even though, at two hours and thirteen minutes, X2 goes on longer than it should.

Like Spider-Man, which also began life as a Marvel comic, X2 mines the romantic conflicts and insecurities of adolescents—and those who behave like them—for much of its emotion. Will the telepathic Jean Grey (Famke Janssen) be able to choose between bad boy Wolverine and the cleancut Cyclops (James Marsden)? How will young Rogue (Anna Paquin) resolve the fire-and-frost conflict between Pyro (Aaron Stanford) and Iceman (Shawn Ashmore)? And will any of these people be able to take a break from sorting out their raging hormones to help save the world?

X2 opens where X-Men left off, with the evil metal-controlling mutant Magneto (Ian McKellen) encased in a plastic prison and kindly Professor Charles Xavier (Patrick Stewart), the world's most powerful telepath, back running Xavier's School for Gifted Youngsters, where youthful mutants learn how to live with their gifts. Magneto and Xavier, you'll remember (or else I'll remind you), had a philosophical disagreement about the relationship mutants and humans should have on the planet that turned quite violent.

Xavier, rather like the UN's Kofi Annan, thinks everyone should get along as equals; and Magneto, borrowing a page from some in

Washington, thinks that because mutants are stronger and smarter than anyone else it makes perfect sense for them to rule the world.

This internecine conflict, however, is forced to temporarily take a backseat because of the threat to all mutants presented by Colonel Stryker, a seriously wealthy military man who wants to do to mutants what Magneto wants to do to humans.

Events conspire to give the colonel the ear of the president, and suddenly all the world's mutants face a threat the like of which they've never seen before. Really.

Though he is something like eighth-billed, X2's secret weapon and most persuasive performance comes from Brian Cox as the evil Stryker. This will not surprise anyone who's seen Cox's work as the original Hannibal Lecter in *Manhunter* or as Big John, the child molester with a heart of gold in *L.I.E.* One of the best and least appreciated of today's film actors, Cox has a powerfully convincing way with under-your-skin evil.

Actually, the acting in X2 is better than average for this kind of movie. Jackman is especially effective as the muscular, tortured Wolverine, who finds out more about his past and gets to battle the equally fierce Deathstrike (Kelly Hu) in the film's action centerpiece.

One of the unexpected aspects of X2 is the way its concerns seem to be uncannily relevant today, starting with an opening observation that "sharing the world has never been humanity's defining attribute." And the central theme of both the film and the comic—how relentlessly suspicious we are of those who are different—has equal resonance just now. X2 might not be the place you'd think to look for any kind of message, but there you are.

BEHIND THE SCENES:
CONAN THE BARBARIAN

Introduction

To read this story, published in the summer of 1979, is to enter a time machine. The magazine whose cover it graced, *New West*, no longer exists, and the film whose creation and backstory it details, *Conan the Barbarian*, was still years away from cashing in on one of the top five opening weekends of 1982. One of the film's screenwriters, Oliver Stone, now admired as a two-time Oscar-winning director, had previously directed only one forgettable item called *The Hand*. And the film's star, Arnold Schwarzenegger, now California's governor, was then no more than a charismatic bodybuilder hoping to start a movie career. The only thing that hasn't changed from then to now is the popularity of Robert E. Howard, Conan's creator and a cult figure whose durability has become legend.

That Howard remains a pop culture phenomenon (Warner Bros. recently put another Conan movie into development) is but one of the reasons it seemed appropriate to end *Now in Theaters Everywhere* with him. This behind-the-scenes story not only demonstrates how much thought and energy went into what is nominally a popular entertainment but also speaks to the primacy and durability of the written word, the aspect of intelligent studio filmmaking it is easiest to overlook. As major a worldwide phenomenon as Conan became, it is important to remember that the whole thing began with a young man in Texas willing to sit in front of a typewriter and dream.

Cross Plains is a blinking red light on Texas 279, a forgotten town on a two-lane blacktop that runs by Rising Star, Flat Rock, Cross Cut, Bangs, Thrifty and Cisco on its way through the middle of nowhere. A badly peeling billboard announces this as the home of "Miss Rodeo America, 1977," and a historical marker boasts of a visit by an obscure general, popularly known as "The Rock of Chickamauga." Yet if Cross Plains is known at all today it is not because of the lady or the general; it is because in 1936 a man named Robert Ervin Howard killed himself on its quiet, shady streets. Told that his beloved invalid mother was about to die, he took a Colt .380 automatic from the glove compartment of his car and blew his brains out. He was thirty years old.

Robert E. Howard was an elusive, contradictory man, a moody figure with paranoid tendencies, a conundrum even to his friends. He was a writer for the pulp magazines of the 1930s, but more than that he was a dreamer of fierce dreams, a man who invested his visions with such intensity that he willed an entire world into being. He called it the Hyborian Age, placed it 12,000 years in the past and made it a savage, barbarous time when magic was potent but men could act, even kill, according to their own personal codes. It was a world stocked with a sweeping variety of lands and tribes, but one man dominated them all, a man whose body was "an image of primal strength cut out of bronze," a man who liked his women full-bodied and complaisant but who spent most of his time "afire with the urge to kill, to drive his knife deep into the flesh and bone, and twist the blade in blood and entrails." A man named Conan.

Ignored and forgotten for decades by all but a handful of stubborn loyalists, Conan is on the verge of becoming the biggest popular-culture phenomenon since Superman, setting off million-dollar shock waves in New York, Los Angeles and places in between.

Though he lived and died in Cross Plains, Robert E. Howard was, by his own choosing, buried in nearby Brownwood, a medium-sized town thirty miles away that now calls itself "The Buckle of the Sun Belt." He graduated from Brownwood High in 1923, and his picture in the yearbook, one of the few known to exist, shows a sensitive-looking boy of seventeen, his haunted eyes those of someone troubled by things no one else could see.

Lorene Bishop, secretary of the Greenleaf Cemetery Association, is polite as she points out the grave Howard shares with his parents, a simple stone engraved with a somewhat chilling inscription from 2 Samuel: "They were lovely and pleasant in their lives and in their death they were not divided." Lorene Bishop did not know Howard, but she knows what people said about him.

"It was, 'Why don't you get up, Robert, and get you a job,'" she says emphatically. "He never told anybody he was writing. One year he was the only man in Cross Plains who made enough money to pay income tax, and everyone thought he was sitting around doing nothing."

Dotted around Brownwood and Cross Plains are people who did know Howard, straightforward folk who speak with fluid drawls. Yet when his name comes up, they become reluctant to talk about the wraiths of the past, unused to the attention, uncertain really why anyone wants to know.

Lindsey Tyson, Robert E. Howard's closest friend, is still so upset by how it all turned out that conversation on the subject is painful. Tyson, a quiet man who prides himself of his arrowhead collection, lives in Cross Plains in a cool house near the center of town. "Robert and I were friends ever since he moved here in 19 and 19," he says slowly, remembering. "He was kinda hard to get acquainted with; you had to know him a good while before you got to know him. He wasn't interested, like most boys, in anything that was mechanical, and he didn't care anything about hunting. He wouldn't shoot an animal. He just did what he wanted to, and he didn't care what anybody thought. He could read a great big book in thirty minutes and not forget a word. He had a great mind, but like anyone who was a genius, he was a little peculiar."

Just how peculiar comes out both in the voluminous correspondence Howard had with fellow fantasy writers such as H. P. Lovecraft, the famed "Rhode Island Recluse," and in memoirs these writers wrote about him. A sickly only child, Howard built himself up to a solid six-foot-tall, two-hundred-pound teenager: "When a scoundrel crosses me up," he explained to his country-doctor father, "I can with my bare hands tear him to pieces, double him up, and break his back with my hands alone." Though most of his neighbors regarded him as a harmless eccentric, he liked to feel the world was against him, often stopping in the middle of the street to shadow-box with imaginary opponents.

"He liked to play at violence," says Lindsey Tyson, carefully bringing out several browning photographs that show Howard sparring with gloves on, wrestling, fighting with swords, even posing bare-chested with a mock grimace on his face, a knife in one hand, a gun in the other. "That's the one what killed him," Tyson says softly, pointing to the gun. He shakes his head.

If Howard was committed to anything, it was writing. An omnivorous reader, he claimed to have raided schoolhouse libraries during summer vacations: "In my passionate quest for reading material, nothing could have halted me but a bullet through the head," he boasted. He favored Jack London and Zane Grey, had no taste for the "spineless, cringing, crawling characters" of Charles Dickens, and saw George Bernard Shaw as "a poser, an egomaniac and a jackass."

Howard began writing his own stories when he was nine or ten, creating a character called Boealf, a young Viking. "He was always interested in writing; he wasn't interested in anything else. He told me he'd write or he'd be a tramp," remembers Tyson. "He worked really day and night; he wouldn't sleep maybe for two days until he'd finished what he'd started. When he sold his first story [to the legendary pulp, *Weird Tales*, in 1924, when he was eighteen] he got down on his knees and thanked God he'd finally broken into something."

Though he wrote for pulps ranging from *Jack Dempsey's Fight Magazine* and *Western Aces* to *Thrilling Mystery* and *Argosy*, Howard sold more than sixty pieces, or a third of his output, to *Weird Tales*. And it was for *Weird Tales* that he created a veritable hoard of savage heroes. August 1928 saw the debut of Solomon Kane, a Puritan avenger given to saying such things as "Men shall die for this"; followed in succeeding years by King Kull, a barbarian ruler who hails from Atlantis; Bran

Mak Morn, the last king of the Picts; and Turlogh Dubh O'Brien, a grim highlander known for his berserk rages.

A pretty grisly bunch, all told, but they perfectly suited the philosophy Howard was developing. "To hell with the psychologists and city-bred psychoanalysts and all the other freaks spawned by our rotting civilization," is how he expressed it to a friend. Later, he had one of his characters put it this way: "Barbarism is the natural state of mankind. Civilization is unnatural. It is a whim of circumstance. And barbarism must always ultimately triumph."

This ideal of strong, noble barbarism reached its culmination sometime in 1932, when Howard became so suddenly and so totally possessed by an idea that he wondered whether he was under the influence of unnatural powers.

"I know that for months I had been absolutely barren of ideas, completely unable to work up anything sellable," he wrote about it to a friend. "Then the man Conan seemed suddenly to grow up in my mind without much labor on my part, and immediately a stream of stories flowed off my pen . . . almost without effort on my part. I did not seem to be creating but rather relating events that had occurred. . . . For weeks I did nothing but write of the adventures of Conan. The character took complete possession of my mind and crowded out everything else in the way of story-writing."

The premier Conan story, "The Phoenix on the Sword," appeared in the December 1932 *Weird Tales* and was the first of twenty-one Howard was to write before he tired of the enormously popular character two and a half years later. Though he wrote the stories in no particular order, they ended up describing with remarkable internal consistency three decades of Conan's bloodthirsty adventures, beginning when he was eighteen years old and ending when he was crowned a king.

Conan is a Cimmerian, a people Howard intended to be the ancestors of the Celts, Conan being a name well-known in Irish mythology. This particular Conan was low on the intelligence level for bona fide heroes because Howard had a weakness for thick-headed types. "They're simpler," he once told a friend. "You get them in a jam and no one expects you to rack your brains inventing clever ways for them to extricate themselves. They are too stupid to do anything but cut themselves into the clear."

It is precisely this ability to wade through life with a broadsword that is at the heart of Conan's appeal. "Conan is direct; he solves his problems the way everyone wishes he could," says Robert Weinberg, the author of an annotated guide to Howard's work. "Conan doesn't take anything from anybody; he says, 'You bother me, you're going to be in trouble.'" Adds fantasy author, Howard authority and psychiatrist Karl Edward Wagner, "He appeals to the adolescent in all of us, someone who isn't tied down by laws or rules, who does what we'd want to do and does it so well."

Yet the remarkable thing about Conan is that for all his barbarian quickness and strength, all his virtuosity with a variety of weapons, he has absolutely no superpowers. He can be menaced and he can be hurt.

Equally unusual, and equally appealing, is that Conan, big galoot though he is, has a definite philosophy of life, and one that has no small lure in an age of hedonistic self-absorption: "I seek not beyond death," Howard has him say at one point. "Let me live deep while I live; let me know the rich juices of red meat and stinging wine on my palate, the hot embrace of white arms, the mad exultation of battle when blue blades flame crimson, and I am content. Let teachers and priests and philosophers brood over questions of reality and illusion. I know this: If life is illusion, then I am no less an illusion, and being thus, the illusion is real to me. I live. I burn with life, I love, I slay, and am content." This passage points up the final reason for Conan's popularity, and that is the writing style of Robert E. Howard. It is not a style for purists or classicists, but it gets the job done. If Howard makes one wince when he has Conan saying, "I'll split your head like a ripe melon" and "It's been a hell of a night," he can also chill the blood with lines such as "Sanity went out of his face like a flame blown out in the wind" and "We kept life in him until he screamed for death as for a bride." Whether he is describing some noisome horror that Conan is about to battle or an erotic interlude laced with hints of lesbianism and flagellation, Howard believes so absolutely in what he has written, he puts so much passion into it, that he carries the reader along with him, like it or not. He is a natural storyteller, someone whose imaginary world was much more real than the one he lived in, a magnificent primitive, just like his hero.

For a man who embraced death and destruction with such avidity on the printed page, Robert E. Howard had a curious attitude toward it in real life. On one hand, death horrified and disgusted him to such a degree that when he realized his pet dog, Patch, was about to die, he packed a suitcase and left home for two or three days so he wouldn't have to face the situation. On the other hand, however, he had a romantic, almost Byronic obsession with suicide.

An only child, Howard had always been unnaturally close to his mother. "He was one of the home boys; he was never with his father, *never*," says Annie Newton Davis, a sprightly eighty-eight-year-old who knew Howard when he was a boy. "He was so close to his mother, there was nobody in the world but them two."

If most children outgrow such feelings as they get older, Howard did not. He was "a very small boy who had not yet won any understanding of life," according to E. Hoffmann Price, a fantasy writer who'd visited Howard in Cross Plains. "REH had, in a way of speaking, the five-year-old's crying need for escape and the grown man's stern resolution. He was a strange blend of the rugged, the grim and the highly emotional, the sensitive and the supersensitive."

So when Howard's mother became gravely ill in June 1936, the outcome was painfully predictable. Three times during the previous year Howard had prepared to take his life when her death appeared imminent, but she had always rallied. Yet this time, when an attending nurse told him that his mother would never recognize him again, he acted. He died eight hours after putting the pistol to his right temple; his mother died the next day without regaining consciousness. Jack Scott, the editor of the *Cross Plains Review*, rushed over to the Howard place as soon as he heard the news. "The old justice of the peace saw me and motioned me inside," Scott remembers. "He led me to a typewriter and said, 'What does this mean?'" On the typewriter were the last words Robert E. Howard ever wrote:

> All fled—all done, so lift me on the pyre;
> The feast is over and the lamps expire.

"I'm tempted to call it almost existential despair, a crumbling of the universe," says psychiatrist Wagner. "Howard wrote a story I like very much called 'The Valley of the Lost' about a cowboy who loses his way in a cave and stumbles on a secret world of monstrous creatures. He manages to escape, but the experience is so shattering, the realization that what had seemed a solid world is actually honeycombed with hidden horrors is so devastating, that he puts his six-gun to his head and kills himself. In a sense this is what happened to Howard as well. With the death of his mother his shelter collapsed, he realized this was not a steady, firm universe, and his despair was profound."

Even during Howard's brief lifetime not everyone was enamored of Conan. A young Robert Bloch, years away from his fame as the author of *Psycho* and other stories of horror, wrote to *Weird Tales* that he was "awfully tired of poor old Conan the Cluck. . . . May he be sent to Valhalla to cut out paper dolls." After the author's death, however, Conan's stock depreciated with special rapidity.

Howard's heir was his father, Dr. I. M. Howard. Devastated by the tragedy, he moved to Ranger, Texas, a town that achieved a kind of fame when it allowed derricks to drill in the local cemetery during an oil boom. There he became acquainted with a Dr. P. M. Kuykendall, who ran a small clinic.

"Dr. Howard was very old at the time, and Daddy took care of him and made him feel useful by letting him work and live at the clinic," remembers Alla Ray Morris, Dr. Kuykendall's daughter. When Dr. Howard died in 1944, he left his estate, including the rights to his son's writings, to his benefactor. "At the time it was absolutely unimportant financially," says Mrs. Morris. "Every once in a while Daddy would get a check for $12, but that was it."

The Conan revival began very timidly in 1946 when Arkham House, a small fantasy publisher, printed 3,000 copies of a collection of Howard stories called *Skull-Face and Others* with an introduction noting waspishly that any further Conan tales "would almost have to be printed on blood-colored paper." Nothing more happened until 1950, when another small house, Gnome Press, published *Conan the Conqueror*, Howard's only novel-length work, and followed it with five more Conan titles. The biggest break came in 1966 when Lancer Books, Inc., brought out the first of what was to be nine hugely popular Conan paperbacks. The wave was starting to build.

No one was more astonished by this eruption of popularity than Mrs. Morris of Ranger, who became coheir along with her mother when Dr. Kuykendall died in 1959. "It was just like finding money," she says now, still sounding stunned. "We couldn't believe it, it was so totally unexpected; we were absolutely and totally amazed. And it was all through an act of kindness, really. Whatever it is you cast upon the waters, we must have done it, because we got back pearls."

The Conan resurgence came about almost entirely because of the efforts of two individuals, Glenn Lord and L. Sprague de Camp. Each devoted decades to the Howard cause, but now that their most extravagant dreams have become a plush reality they barely speak to each other. They get along, says a source close to the situation, "kind of like Menachem Begin and Yasir Arafat."

Two men more disparate than de Camp and Lord would be difficult to imagine. The former is as erudite and loftily patrician as his name, the author of between eighty and ninety books and the winner of the Science Fiction Writers of America's Nebula Award for lifetime achievement. The latter is a modest, down-home resident of Pasadena, Texas, who works as a warehouse operator for Champion Papers.

Dr. de Camp's basic interest in Howard's stories was that of a writer who saw an opportunity to do some interesting work. Though he began by editing rediscovered Howard material, de Camp is best known for his pastiches, the nearly twenty stories, novelettes and novels he wrote, sometimes alone, sometimes with collaborators, using Howard's characters and milieu to flesh out the bare outlines left by the original stories. "I had a suspicion that if I continued to push and promote this body of work long enough, it might take hold and become a popular success," de Camp says, pointing out that he was instrumental in getting Lancer to publish its Conan books. Darrell Schweitzer, author of *Conan's World and Robert E. Howard*, notes, "It is the strength of Howard's writing and de Camp's marketing which has made possible virtually every sword and sorcery novel published in the last ten years."

Glenn Lord's interest in Howard began as "just a reader" who enjoyed the stories as they came out in those Gnome Press editions. "It kinda intrigued me. I was fascinated with this author nobody knew anything about, and one thing led to another," he says in his low-key way. Lord got so intrigued that he put together a collection of Howard's poetry called *Always Comes Evening* and paid Arkham House $836 to publish it in 1957. In 1961, he started a specialty magazine called *The Howard Collector*. And in 1965, when the man who had been handling the Howard properties and representing the Kuykendall interest died, L. Sprague de Camp suggested Lord for the job as literary agent for the Howard heirs.

Lord's function from that day on has been as keeper of the flame. He has painstakingly and tirelessly tracked down everything Robert E. Howard ever wrote, publishing his results in a "bio-bibliography" called *The Last Celt* and getting his wife "a little disgusted at times" with the extent of his mania.

A clash between these two men seemed inevitable, and though de Camp partisans feel Lord isn't a worldly enough agent and Lord partisans say de Camp is overly avaricious, the key to the conflict is those de Camp pastiches. De Camp feels that they—and he—made Conan what he is today by keeping him in the public eye, but Lord says flatly that "no one can write like somebody else; one bad pastiche does more harm than good in the long run by turning people off." Most experts in the small world of Conan seem to agree.

Many fans also feel that de Camp has perverted Conan's barbaric nature in his stories, that he is too concerned with things such as the technical accuracy of weapons used and not enamored enough of the shedding of hot blood. "Howard didn't care what was possible. If he wanted Conan to slice a guy up, he sliced him up," says one; another adds simply, "Conan is not to de Camp's temperament. He's not nearly as bloodthirsty as Howard was; he's ruined the character by making him live too much by his wits." De Camp, for his part, has heard all the criticisms and isn't particularly bothered by them.

"Some of Howard's admirers are hypercritical; they tend to look on his work as a kind of holy writ, and they feel about pastiche writing the way devoutly orthodox Christians feel about the *Book of Mormon*," he says. "But it's an ancient tradition, people have been doing it for some time, and there's no law against it."

The closest de Camp and Lord came to open rivalry was in 1973, when Lancer Books suddenly went into bankruptcy. It was not any old bankruptcy, however; it was Chapter 11, what Glenn Lord calls "the insidious kind," which meant that the Lancer people were free to dispose of their assets as they saw fit. They sold the Conan stories to a group called Playmore, Inc., that infuriated everyone by demanding a large sum of money before it would release the stories, thus complicating a lawsuit initiated by de Camp.

Lord, meanwhile, had discovered that Lancer's Conan contract was not an exclusive one. Fearful that the lawsuits would drag on for years, and never happy with the way Lancer combined pastiches and real Howard material, he sold the rights to the authentic Conan stories to Berkley Publishing Corporation. When Playmore heard about this, "they started raising Cain," in Lord's words, and quickly made a deal with Ace Books, Inc., to distribute the Lancer versions. Ace managed to beat the classier Berkley editions to the bookstores, causing Berkley to stop the series after only three of a projected six volumes were published. A spokesman for Berkley, which now has the rights to other Howard material, says, "We're not crying over spilled milk at this point." But Karl Edward Wagner, the editor of the Berkley series, is frank: "We got burned. I'm sour about it and I'm sure a lot of other people are, too. Reading the Lancer editions is like trying to study Shakespeare by reading Bowdler's version."

De Camp prefers not to discuss all this, quoting instead from *Hamlet* and saying that, if he wanted to, he "could a tale unfold whose lightest word would make thy two eyes like stars, start from their spheres, and each particular hair to stand on end, like quills upon the fretful porpentine," but he doesn't want to. He also doesn't want to go into his personal differences with anyone: "I'm a man of fairly advanced years doing very interesting work and I don't have time to waste on feuds and grudges."

Besides, de Camp points out, he and Lord are partners. In 1977, Conan Properties, Inc.—which one observer calls "an unlikely alliance of people who really don't like each other"—was formed. Members included a nonvoting lawyer, Arthur Lieberman, and three directors: de Camp, Lord, and John Troll, a patent specialist brought in to be a much-needed neutral. This surprising truce was achieved at the insistence of a nervous man who wears rose-tinted glasses and rarely speaks above a whisper. His name is Ed Pressman, and it is with his entrance that Conan's cinematic hour begins.

Cross Plains, Texas, is not the only place that has changed little in decades. The Producer's Building at the old Columbia lot in Hollywood looks as it must have in the days when Harry Cohn prowled the premises like an angry badger. Only the names on the directory are new: Robert Wise, Michael Douglas and Edward R. Pressman.

Pressman, the heir to a toy company, has produced some very intriguing projects—Terry Malick's *Badlands*, Brian De Palma's *Sisters* and *Phantom of the Paradise*—but he has not made a box-office colossus. "If my batting average was as good with movies as it was with toys," he says, smiling, "I'd be Darryl Zanuck."

In the early 1970s, Pressman was in New York in the company of Ed Summer, an aspiring filmmaker who owns a comic-book emporium called Supersnipe, and Summer's partner, director George Lucas. They were all viewing a rough cut of *Pumping Iron*, Arnold Schwarzenegger's first film, and Pressman was frankly enthralled.

"It was a whole new approach for me. Usually my films are conceived in terms of the director," he says in a voice that makes every word count. "But Arnold had a wonderful quality, and I asked Summer and Lucas what he would be right for. In unison they said, 'Conan.'"

Pressman had never heard of Conan, so Summer and Lucas immediately showed him the barbarian-inspired art of Frank Frazetta, and he became even more enthralled: "I thought, 'My God, I've been missing all this.' The phenomenon intrigued me, the idea that here was a whole gestalt that was obviously exciting to many people. And it was so naturally cinematic: The paintings showed you a movie. It seemed right, of the moment, and it hadn't been done before."

The Conan phenomenon had by this time reached spectacular proportions, influencing everything from the fantasy art of Frazetta to Conan's Pizza, Inc., of Austin, Texas, where the specialty of the house is called the Savage Barbarian.

Though Howard's stories were never published in book form during his lifetime, three major paperback houses—Bantam, Berkley and Ace—now had in print or in preparation some sixty-five books either written by Howard or using his characters, with Ace's first dozen Conan titles leading the pack with sales approaching 400,000 apiece. The total investment of the three publishers: in excess of $2 million.

For people who didn't read books, there were Marvel's series of Howard-related comics and magazines. The flagship was *Conan the Barbarian*, begun in 1970 and, with a yearly circulation of more than 4 million, one of Marvel's top sellers and godfather to a daily strip that appears in close to a hundred newspapers. Coming on strong were the racier, magazine-format *Savage Sword of Conan*, followed by *Red Sonja, She-Devil with a Sword, Kull the Destroyer* and *King Conan*, which Roy Thomas, who has written or edited all of the above, says features "the first comic-strip hero to be portrayed in his sixties, with teenage sons."

Armed with this knowledge and his fervor, Pressman convinced Schwarzenegger that he was a natural to play Conan and signed him to a five-picture deal. He then spent eighteen months dealing with the various people who had pieces of Conan, insisting that they stop squabbling or he would not make the picture. After the formation of Conan Properties, Pressman embarked on what turned out to be the most hectic project of all: finding a director.

"John Milius was interested. He was shooting *Big Wednesday*, but he said he wanted it to be his next picture," Pressman says. "At the same time, Oliver Stone had a great idea, he wanted to do *Conan* with Arnold Schwarzenegger, and he was told it was too late, someone else was doing it.

"Then I was told that John Milius had changed his mind. I immediately called Oliver and he agreed to do a screenplay. He did it full-out, he really created that world, but the thing couldn't be shot, it would have cost $70 million. We talked about Ridley Scott for a director before he did *Alien*, but the studio said he was too foreign." Smile.

"Then, on the spur of the moment I called John and he said he'd changed his mind again and now wanted to do *Conan* but he was under exclusive contract to Dino De Laurentiis, who was paying him an enormous amount of money to do another picture.

"I went to London to see Dino, expecting to have a very hard time, but I found that John had already talked to him and now Dino wanted to do it, too. In half an hour we made a deal to coproduce the film." Another smile. "It's almost mystical the way things came together without our seeking them."

There is nothing very mystical about Arnold Schwarzenegger. Five times Mr. Universe, six times Mr. Olympia, he seems as rock solid a human being as ever walked the earth, a man born for the role of Conan. Yet at the time he was approached by Ed Pressman, not only had he never heard of the barbarian, he also had never heard of Ed Pressman.

"He saw me at a restaurant on Sunset Boulevard and came over to say hello," Schwarzenegger says. "It's one of the typical things that happens to me every day. Someone comes over and says, 'Hi, I'm a producer, I want to make a movie and I want you to be the star.' I never, of course, pay any attention to this, but Pressman talked in such a low-key fashion that I took him seriously. He is a man who has a kind of weak appearance but has a very great inner strength."

Strength is something Schwarzenegger knows a lot about, and when he talks about that quality in Conan, he is clearly impressed. "I see him as an animal," he says when asked for a character analysis. "He has learned to defend himself in every kind of situation. What separates him from other people is that he doesn't think, he just acts. In his world, if you take time to think, it will be too late. No one else gives him a break; he has to do everything himself. I find him very inspirational."

Schwarzenegger also appreciates something else about Conan, and that is his vulnerability. "If somebody would have asked me to play Hercules, I would not have done it," he says very seriously. "The difference is that Hercules does things that are absolutely not believable. Anyone who can push columns apart, that is not normal. You can't sympathize with a guy like that in a fight—anyone who wipes out a temple, how can he have any trouble? But Conan is vulnerable, Conan is still a human being, and you get caught up in his fight scenes because they are really life and death. That's a very unusual quality."

To prepare for this kind of ultimate warrior role, Schwarzenegger began a complex series of exercises designed to increase his agility. He has also become proficient in kendo, the Japanese art of stick-fighting. To see a man of his bulk move fluidly around his Santa Monica office, manipulating a wooden stick like a samurai sword, is more than a little frightening.

"We are going to be shooting in Europe in the winter," the actor says, already excited. "I have been there and it's going to be very rough. They don't know how rough. You have to get the mentality that this is war, this is a battleground. You're not going to find a nice Holiday Inn or a Sheraton Plaza; you'll find a tent and you'll freeze your ass off and that's good, too. It's hard to play a primitive at 9:00 A.M. when you're taking a Jacuzzi at 6:00. It can't be done."

So excited is Schwarzenegger about playing Conan and about working with John Milius, whose *The Wind and the Lion* he's seen four times, that nothing else seems to matter. "I've never been wrong yet with my instincts, and they tell me this is going to be a really big film, a whole new phenomenon," he says with surprising fervor. "I don't care what it takes; I don't care if I have to take one year out of my life and be an animal. I know this film is going to be unbelievable for me."

John Milius met an eminent film critic recently, a woman known for her resistance to the violence in his work. They were getting along famously until she asked him what his next film was going to be. "I told her *Conan the Barbarian*," he says, "and she looked at me like she'd swallowed some bad Mexican food."

John Milius is like that; he enjoys saying things that make people start. "I am an endangered species, a ground sloth; there should be a committee to save me," he says cheerily from his office in Burbank, a green-walled room he says resembles "the inside of a British gun case." He is a man in whom charm and sharp intelligence seem to be constantly battling with suspicion, and in a town not known for plain speaking, his candor is refreshing. When you finish talking to him, you can be sure you've heard what's on his mind.

Though Hollywood appears to be ready to turn "sword and sorcery," the generic name for the kind of writing Howard popularized, into a new major trend, John Milius is not concerned. "I'm the last person to ask about trends, I have no idea what the American audience wants, and unlike many of my contemporaries, I don't attempt to figure it out," he says briskly. "I'm going to try and satisfy myself and the spirit of Robert E. Howard. Not Ed Pressman, not Dino. That's all."

Though he'd read a few of the stories and was familiar with Conan through the art of Frazetta, a sample of which is framed behind his desk, Milius never thought seriously about putting the barbarian on the screen until Pressman approached him, and didn't make up his mind to do it until he'd read Oliver Stone's script.

"It's an unbelievable script. He had armies of mutants in it, things it would have taken years to make up, but I read it and said, 'Jesus, they're gonna make a Conan movie, I've got to do it,'" Milius says. A man who believes that making the decision is the turning point in any action—"It's like the line in *Lawrence of Arabia* where Lawrence says, 'Aqaba is there, we merely have to go'"—Milius found convincing Dino De Laurentiis to go along with him no problem at all. "I showed a lot of enthusiasm," he says, smiling. "He responds to enthusiasm."

Milius has not expanded the cast past Arnold Schwarzenegger, but he has his ideas: Raquel Welch as Conan's love interest; Sean Connery as the villain; and Lou Ferrigno, television's Hulk and an old body-building rival of Schwarzenegger's, as an auxiliary bad guy. He also has a very clear notion of just the kind of film he's after. "I'm going to give people some good pagan entertainment," he says with satisfaction. "First and foremost this is going to be a romance, a classic adventure story, a movie where something big happens. The appeal will not be based on seeing a lot of neat blood, but it'll be barbaric. I'm not holding myself back. It's *Conan the Barbarian;* what do you expect? If people think it's too violent, they can see another movie."

Like Howard, Milius is fascinated with pagan history and views *Conan* as the perfect opportunity to put primitive civilizations such as the Picts and the Mongols up on the big screen. More than that, he is in complete agreement with Howard's philosophies, pounding his fist on his knee in delight as he mentions the title of a King Kull story, "By This Axe I Rule!"

"I believe in the barbarian ethic," he says. "I have a distrust of these civilizing influences that are on all of us. I favor a kind of simpler, more action-based view of things, and I'm going to give the movie a real sense of pagan morality."

Milius gets up from the sofa where he's been sitting and walks down the hall to a room filled with production sketches and drawings by Ron Cobb. They bring the world of Conan to vivid life, and Milius is stimulated by their presence. He talks of the excitement of shooting the film on the steppes of Eastern Europe in the dead of winter and his eyes dance.

"You must have this in your life; you must have adventure," he says, holding up one of the sketches. "That's why men go off to war.

It's not that they want to die; they want the sensation of throwing it all on the line."

Back in his office, Milius relaxes in a chair and remembers the time when someone asked him what he wanted to accomplish in film: Did he want to make great statements or what? "I told him I came to this business because I wanted to make B Westerns, that that was the highest dream I aspired to," he says, completely seriously. "I see Conan pretty much the same way. I'm comfortable with the material and the atmosphere. It's easy for me to live with. I'd be happy, I'd be honored, to make Conan movies for the rest of my life."

FILMS

NAMES

PublicAffairs is a publishing house founded in 1997. It is a tribute to the standards, values, and flair of three persons who have served as mentors to countless reporters, writers, editors, and book people of all kinds, including me.

I.F. STONE, proprietor of *I. F. Stone's Weekly*, combined a commitment to the First Amendment with entrepreneurial zeal and reporting skill and became one of the great independent journalists in American history. At the age of eighty, Izzy published *The Trial of Socrates*, which was a national bestseller. He wrote the book after he taught himself ancient Greek.

BENJAMIN C. BRADLEE was for nearly thirty years the charismatic editorial leader of *The Washington Post*. It was Ben who gave the *Post* the range and courage to pursue such historic issues as Watergate. He supported his reporters with a tenacity that made them fearless and it is no accident that so many became authors of influential, best-selling books.

ROBERT L. BERNSTEIN, the chief executive of Random House for more than a quarter century, guided one of the nation's premier publishing houses. Bob was personally responsible for many books of political dissent and argument that challenged tyranny around the globe. He is also the founder and longtime chair of Human Rights Watch, one of the most respected human rights organizations in the world.

For fifty years, the banner of Public Affairs Press was carried by its owner Morris B. Schnapper, who published Gandhi, Nasser, Toynbee, Truman, and about 1,500 other authors. In 1983, Schnapper was described by *The Washington Post* as "a redoubtable gadfly." His legacy will endure in the books to come.

Peter Osnos, *Founder and Editor-at-Large*